Re-membering Milton

AREOPAGITICA;

A
SPEECH
OF
Mr. JOHN MILTON

For the Liberty of Vnlicenc'd PRINTING,

To the Parlament of ENGLAND.

Τὸ λ δ̕θεον δ̕ ἐκεῖνο, εἴ τις θέλει πόλι
Χρησόν τι βέλδμ᾽ εἰς μέσον φέρειν, ἔχων·
Καὶ ταῦθ᾽ ὁ χρήζων, λαμπρὸς ἐσθ᾽, ὁ μὴ θέλων,
Σιγᾷ, τί τέτων ἐστιν ἰσαίτερον πόλι ;
Euripid. Hicetid.

This is true Liberty when free born men
Having to advise the public may speak free,
Which he who can, and will, deserv's high praise,
Who neither can nor will, may hold his peace;
What can be juster in a State then this?
Euripid. Hicetid.

LONDON,
Printed in the Yeare, 1644.

Re-membering Milton

Essays on the texts and traditions

EDITED BY
Mary Nyquist
AND
Margaret W. Ferguson

Methuen
New York and London

First published in 1987 by
Methuen, Inc.
29 West 35th Street, New York NY 10001

Published in Great Britain by
Methuen & Co. Ltd
11 New Fetter Lane, London EC4P 4EE

Printed in Great Britain by
Richard Clay Ltd, Bungay, Suffolk

Library of Congress Cataloging in Publication Data

Re-membering Milton.
Bibliography: p.
Includes index.
1. Milton, John, 1608–1674 – Criticism and
interpretation. I. Nyquist, Mary. II. Ferguson, Margaret W., 1948–
PR3588.R46   1988   821'.4   87–15383
ISBN 0–416–39730–1
ISBN 0–416–39740–9 (pbk.)

British Library Cataloguing in Publication Data

Re-membering Milton; new essays on the texts
and the traditions.
1. Milton, John, 1608–1674 – Criticism and interpretation
I. Nyquist, Mary   II. Ferguson, Margaret W.
821'.4   PR3588
ISBN 0–416–39730–1
ISBN 0–416–39740–9 Pbk.

Contents

CONTENTS

viii

Notes on contributors

ABBE BLUM is Assistant Professor of English at Swarthmore College, where she teaches Shakespeare, Renaissance literature, literary theory and feminist criticism. She is completing a book on Milton in his social contexts, 1643–5, and an article on Shakespeare's recognition scenes.

RICHARD BRADFORD is Lecturer in English, Trinity College, Dublin. He has published a number of articles on Milton, eighteenth-century poetry, and poetic form. He is currently working on a book which deals with the poetic structures and interpretative strategies of the eighteenth century.

ELEANOR COOK is Professor of English at Victoria College, University of Toronto, and the author of *Browning's Lyrics: An Exploration* (Toronto and Buffalo, 1974) and *Word-Play and Word-War: An Essay on the Poetry of Wallace Stevens* (forthcoming). She has also written on Eliot, Milton, Keats, Whitman, and a theory of allusion.

TERRY EAGLETON is Fellow and Tutor in English, Wadham College, Oxford. He is the author of *The Function of Criticism* (London, 1984); *Literary Theory: An Introduction* (Minneapolis, 1983); *William Shakespeare* (Oxford and New York, 1986); *Against the Grain* (London, 1986); and a novel, *Saints and Scholars* (London, 1987).

MARGARET W. FERGUSON is Professor of English and Comparative Literature at Columbia University. She has written *Trials of Desire: Renaissance Defences of Poetry* (New Haven, 1983) and has co-edited *Re-Writing the Renaissance: The Discourses of Sexual Difference in Early Modern Europe* (Chicago, 1986). She is currently working on a book provisionally entitled *Limited Access: Female Literacy and Literary Production, 1400–1700*.

STANLEY FISH is Arts and Sciences Distinguished Professor of English and Law at Duke University in Durham, NC. His most recently published work is "Dennis Martinez and the Uses of Theory," *Yale Law Journal*, June 1987. The essay he has contributed to *Re-membering Milton* is part of a forthcoming book entitled *Milton's Aesthetic Testimony*.

KENNETH GROSS is the author of *Spenserian Poetics: Idolatry, Iconoclasm, and Magic* (Ithaca, NY, 1985) and of various essays on the poetry of Dante, Spenser, Milton, and Marvell. He is an Associate Professor of English at the University of Rochester.

JOHN GUILLORY teaches at Yale University and is the author of *Poetic Authority: Spenser, Milton, and Literary History* (New York, 1983). He is currently working on a study of literary canon-formation.

RICHARD HALPERN is Assistant Professor of English at Yale University. He has published essays on Milton and Skelton and is writing a book on English literature and rhetorical culture during the transition to capitalism.

CAROLIVIA HERRON is Assistant Professor of Afro-American Studies and Tutor in History and Literature at Harvard University. She has been a Fulbright Fellow in Mexico where she researched Carlos Fuentes' *Terra Nostra* and Latin American epic tradition. She is completing a critical study of Afro-American epic tradition from Phyllis Wheatley to Derek Walcott.

ROBIN JARVIS teaches English Literature for the Open University. He has published articles on Wordsworth and Milton in the *Journal of English and Germanic Philology, Diacritics*, and *Studies in Romanticism*. The essay he has contributed to *Re-membering Milton* is part of a full-length study of the intertextuality of the two writers entitled *Under the Influence*.

CHRISTOPHER KENDRICK is the author of *Milton: A Study in Ideology and Form* (New York, 1986). He is currently teaching at Washington University in St Louis and working on a book about utopias.

MARY LOEFFELHOLZ is Assistant Professor of English and Women's Studies at the University of Illinois at Urbana-Champaign, where she teaches feminist literary theory and American literature. She is currently working on a book about Emily Dickinson and Romanticism.

HERBERT MARKS is Assistant Professor of Comparative Literature and English and Director of the Institute for Biblical and Literary Studies at Indiana University. His essay is part of a forthcoming book on poetic etymology.

MARY NYQUIST is Co-ordinator of the Women's Studies Programme at the University of Toronto, where she teaches in the Department of English and the Literary Studies Programme. She has published essays on Milton, Stevens, and feminist theory, and is completing a book provisionally entitled *Joyning Causes: Genesis, Gender, Discourse, Milton*.

DAVID QUINT is Associate Professor of Comparative Literature at Princeton

University. He is the translator of *The 'Stanze' of Angelo Poliziano* (Amherst, Mass., 1979) and the author of *Origin and Originality in Renaissance Literature* (New Haven, 1983).

DAVID G. RIEDE is Professor of English at The Ohio State University. He is the author of *Swinburne: A Study of Romantic Mythmaking* (Charlottesville, VA, 1978), *Dante Gabriel Rossetti and the Limits of Victorian Vision* (Ithaca, NY, 1983) and the forthcoming *Matthew Arnold and the Betrayals of Language.*

Preface

The Living Milton, a collection of essays edited by Frank Kermode, appeared in 1960, when the controversy sparked by Eliot, Leavis and other "Miltonoclasts" was still alive. In his preface, Kermode puts a certain distance between the "defence by scholarship" practised by some "Miltonolaters" of the period, and the defence subtly established by *The Living Milton*, whose contributors "have found it possible to include Milton in a characteristically modern view of literature, to treat him as a living poet."[1] Since the view is modern, the participle "living" does not announce a resurrection, nor does it promise Milton everlasting life. Instead it serves a polemical function, which is to debunk the view that Milton's oracular voice produced a dead or disembodied poetic language and that his influence on poets succeeding him could by definition be nothing but the kiss of death.

On more than one occasion in his poetry, Milton seems to identify himself uneasily with Orpheus, whose oracular powers ceased abruptly when, overwhelmed by the "rout" of frenzied women, he suffered the fate of violent dismemberment. The editors hasten to assure our readers that this volume does not intend to perform any ritual dismemberment. Nor, more than a quarter of a century later than the publication of *The Living Milton*, with "living" in all sorts of trouble, does *Re-membering Milton* simply resign itself to Milton's death or assume that the age of controversy is over. But this volume does presuppose that if Milton in some sense lives on it is owing to a process of re-articulating him limb by limb that seeks to piece together every "joynt and member" (to adapt the figure used in *Areopagitica* for the dynamics of the search for truth). It assumes, in other words, that certain forms of figurative dismemberment or dispersal have always already taken place; that the figure of Milton the author is itself the product of a certain self-construction; and that signs of motivated self-constitution can be seen even more clearly in the various critical and cultural traditions in which Milton enjoys an afterlife. Nonetheless, since Milton continues to enjoy the status of the most monumentally unified author in the canon, the process of "re-membering" cannot simply be assumed. The process must be repeatedly gestured towards and actively exposed, a project it is hoped this collection of essays will help to initiate.

Milton is of course not the only Renaissance writer to identify himself with the figure of the author or to inscribe in published works a history of his personal and authorial development. He is, however, perhaps the most impressive and notorious of self-authored authors, partly as a result of the sheer variety of the contexts in which a voice that is self-consciously or markedly "his" appears, but even more obviously because these contexts – from the *Reason of Church-Government* to the invocation in Book VII of *Paradise Lost* – are so highly charged, politically. In his essay "What is an author?" Michel Foucault discusses the various discursive operations which in different historical periods have or have not contributed to the constitution of the author, or of what he calls the "author function."[2] Foucault's comments suggest the possibility of locating the emergence of the author Milton in an historically specific conjunction of socio-economic and discursive practices, even though the exact character of that conjunction continues to be fiercely debated among historians of the Civil War period. Milton's self-authorship both participates in his political and religious radicalism and reveals features of an emerging bourgeois class-consciousness in ways that have yet to be fully explored. The distinctiveness of Milton's self-presentations, however, is complexly and problematically interrelated with the numerous representations of him to be found throughout the last three centuries. With reference to a variety of social and historical formations, several of the essays here try to address and specify some of these interrelations.

Surprisingly little work has been done on the history of the popular, broadly cultural and political, as well as scholarly, traditions which have received and recirculated "Milton." In many of these traditions the figure of the author has often functioned as a principle of legitimation, authorizing the claims both of established and of marginalized or subversive groups. An example of the latter can be found as early as the mid-1640s when Mistress Attaway, lace-maker turned preacher, justified separating from her husband on the authority of Mr Milton, author of *The Doctrine and Discipline of Divorce*. The appropriation of Milton for a radical cause frequently involves a form of active rewriting, which in recent years has been extended to Milton's life as well as his works. Christopher Hill has presented Milton as a member of the revolution's radical underground, as a militant Protestant writing and acting in solidarity with the radical sectaries. This view has been challenged most forcefully by another Marxist, Andrew Milner, in his *Milton and Revolution*. Yet Milner insists on Milton's republicanism, as well as his class interests. And the radical Milton has reappeared again in David Norbrook's historically detailed *Poetry and Politics in the English Renaissance*, where Milton is situated in the context of a long-lived, self-conscious and radical Protestant prophetic tradition. Norbrook's study has had an immediate impact, most notably in influencing the production of *The Faber Book of Political Verse*, whose editor, the radical poet Tom Paulin, refers in his introduction to "those of us who still revere Milton as the greatest English poet and the most dedicated servant of English liberty."[3]

In the influential and perhaps paradigmatic case of Blake, appropriating Milton's radicalism seems to involve saving the truly radical Milton from his false selves as well as his detractors. Related to what seems always to appear as a prior process of alienation, which has passed privilege over to the establishment or authoritarian Milton, the act of radical re-membering is fraught with necessarily unacknowledged difficulties or ambiguities. Quite often it has taken the form of liberating the characters Milton has created from his oppressive system of belief. When it is not author-centered, criticism of Milton's texts, especially, of course, *Paradise Lost*, can be interestingly and productively character-centered. For the Romantics it was Satan who was oppressed by the author's consciously held beliefs. In our time it tends to be Eve, as is witnessed by a recent article in the *New York Times*, where Hillis Miller presents a "deconstructive" reading of the lines in Book IV describing Eve's "wanton ringlets"; against what Miller calls the "apparent intention" of the poem, these lines are supposed to suggest that a certain natural excess is associated with Eve, who in good post-Romantic fashion thereby becomes associated with the poet's creative and transgressive imagination.[4] In a related but more radically revisionary gesture, Virginia Woolf subtly identifies her critical activity as a reader of the poetry of *Paradise Lost* with Eve's self-mirroring gaze at her "watry image." "The inexpressible fineness of the style, in which shade after shade is perceptible," Woolf writes, "would alone keep one gazing into it, long after the surface business in progress has been despatched. Deep down one catches still further combinations, rejections, felicities and masteries."[5] In these reflections, Woolf takes liberties with the surface, liberties that Milton's Eve is denied. And in doing so she casts an admiring but unbedazzled eye on just those features of the author's poetic practice – the "combinations, rejections, felicities and masteries" – that a post-Saussurian and post-structuralist literary criticism is perhaps in a privileged position to observe.

The tendency of commentators on Milton to fall into opposing camps, armed by Miltonoclasts and Miltonolaters, appears whether the debate is over principles that are ostensibly formal, theological, methodological, or overtly ideological. During the last decade and a half, this has nowhere been more evident than in discussions of feminist issues. Since neither the defenders of the faith nor what one defender has called the feminist "opposition" has been eager to submit the issues under consideration to historical or ideological analysis, the debate on Milton and sexual politics has been severely restricted. In using the mutually exclusive forms of praise or blame, much feminist criticism has unwittingly deployed the very rhetorical mode, the epideictic, in which the debate over "woman" was conducted throughout the Renaissance. As in the case of Milton's political alignments and interests, much yet remains to be done in the way of situating Milton's presentation of gender relations historically, including, now, in relation to the various women writers of the period who have recently been rediscovered. One of the other areas some of the essays here have only begun to explore is the history of what writers in different periods and social contexts – poets, the writers of conduct books, novelists as well as literary critics – have taken to be Milton's views on subjects such as romantic love, marriage, and gendered subjectivity, as well as the history of what interests their interpretations may have served.

Perhaps the most striking feature of the recent debate on Milton and sexual politics is that the feminist "opposition" has mounted its attack on Milton from outside the Milton establishment. To be more specific, the authors of the most controversial articles on Milton, Sandra Gilbert and Christine Froula, are associated with the Romantic and modern periods and lay claim to no specialized knowledge of seventeenth-century literature or society.[6] That Milton's apologists are identified with Milton, are, even, "Miltonists," is certainly significant. With the growth of the professionaliza- tion of academic work, the "defence by scholarship" referred to by Kermode has come to dominate Milton studies, as has an attendant but undeniable conservatism. Perhaps especially in North America, so much writing on Milton has become so narrowly professionalized that the very weight of its authority tends to crush any efforts not appearing to conform to its standards. It is also very often neo-Christian (to use William Empson's adjective), or at least neo-theological (Jackie Di Salvo's) or logocentric (Jacques Derrida's, used without reference to Milton but nevertheless applicable to much commentary on Milton's works).

As a result, the figure of Milton that is projected by the academy, if only through a process of guilt by association, is frequently the figure of a strongly individualized member of a privileged élite. The very success of the Miltonoclasts earlier in this century can be attributed to the process of institutionalization whereby Milton came, in Michael Wilding's words, "to be represented as the embodiment of the qualities of the establishment class – a classical education, a Christian theology, a cold, unapproachable demeanour."[7] That there is still a keenly felt interest in preserving this representation is evident in the biography of Milton recently published by A. N. Wilson. Written to counter the work of Christopher Hill, Wilson's biography is quite literally reactionary in its presentation of Milton as an egotistical intellectual and aesthete who manages, against great odds, to preserve his distance from the mob, the sectarian crackpots and maniacs, and the "parochialism" of his historical moment.[8] Wilson's Milton is the Milton who stands for an educated, white and phallocratic élite eager to preserve (or desperately afraid of losing) its hegemony. That this figure, or rather a close relative, can appear, unexpectedly, beyond the confines of the academy was brought home to us by an incident that occurred during the very early stages of planning this volume, when one of us ventured across the border, from Canada into the United States, in order to give a lecture on Milton. When asked by the border official what the purpose of the visit was, she answered, "to give a lecture on Milton at X university." At which the official's eyes lit up with a glow of recognition, and he said, "Oh yeah, wasn't he the guy who said all those things about women that women don't like to hear but that men do?"

The academy obviously can't be held responsible for the policing of borders. But the conservatism of much Milton scholarship has been apparent in its comparative indifference to the theoretical literature and debates which have been engaging literary critics in both Britain and North America for almost two decades. Much Milton criticism has appeared to wish to preserve its theoretical innocence, or at least to defer as long as possible its inevitable fall into the threatening Babel of theoretical tongues. The influence of psychoanalytic, Marxist, post-structuralist and new-historical literature is only now, in the last four or five years, beginning to be felt. In the past, some of the more imaginative as well as oppositional writing on Milton has often suffered from an insufficient knowledge of the historical and critical traditions into which it is inserting itself or from an inadequately developed theoretical framework. It is our hope that the essays gathered together here will help to foster the conditions needed for a more engaged, as well as more theoretically and historically informed, critical literature on Milton.

One of the things this volume has in common with *The Living Milton* is that few of its contributors are professionally concerned primarily or exclusively with Milton. Unlike *The Living Milton*, however, it has contributors who reside on both sides of the Atlantic. A heterogeneous collection of linguistic, literary-historical, historical, theoretical and ideological interests are pursued in these essays, many of which tend self-consciously to cross over the not always visible boundary separating texts signed or authored by Milton and the various texts or traditions now affiliated with his figure. As editors, we have been involved rather closely in the process of rewriting that the essays have undergone. But we should confess that our efforts to intervene have been resisted as often as not. We are hoping, now, that this collection will produce as much lively debate and desire for more new literature on Milton as the process of working with the writers included here has occasioned for us.

Mary Nyquist
Margaret W. Ferguson

PREFACE

Notes

1. Frank Kermode (ed.), *The Living Milton* (London, Routledge & Kegan Paul, 1960), ix.
2. Michel Foucault, "What is an author?", *Language, Counter-Memory, Practice*, ed. Donald F. Bouchard (Ithaca, Cornell University Press, 1977), 113–38.
3. Christopher Hill, *Milton and the English Revolution* (Harmondsworth, Penguin, 1977); Andrew Milner, *John Milton and the English Revolution* (London and Basingstoke, Macmillan, 1981); David Norbrook, *Poetry and Politics in the English Renaissance*, (London, Routledge & Kegan Paul, 1984); Tom Paulin (ed.), *The Faber Book of Political Verse* (London and Boston, Faber & Faber, 1986), 16. Milton figures prominently in the controversy sparked by Norbrook's review of Paulin's collection; see *The London Review of Books*, 5 June 1986 through October 1986.
4. J. Hillis Miller, "How deconstruction works," *New York Times*, 9 February 1986.
5. Virginia Woolf, *A Writer's Diary*, ed. Leonard Woolf (London, Hogarth, 1965), 6.
6. Sandra Gilbert, "Patriarchal poetry and women readers: reflections on Milton's bogey" (*PMLA*, 93, 1978, 368–82); Christine Froula, "When Eve reads Milton: undoing the canonical economy" (*Critical Inquiry*, 10, 1983, 321–47); Joan M. Webber, defending Milton against Gilbert's charges, refers to the feminist "opposition" in "The politics of poetry: feminism and *Paradise Lost*" (*Milton Studies*, 14, 1980, 21).
7. Michael Wilding, "Regaining the radical Milton," in *The Radical Reader*, ed. Stephen Knight and Michael Wilding (Sydney, Wild & Wooley, 1977), 120.
8. A. N. Wilson, *The Life of John Milton* (London, Oxford University Press, 1983).

Acknowledgements

This volume began when we solicited contributions to it in the *TLS* and *PMLA*. We would like to thank everyone who responded for participating in the process of creating this collection. We are grateful to Pat Parker for introducing us to one another and to our editor Janice Price for supporting this project so wholeheartedly from the beginning. Her encouragement and advice lightened our labour. Special thanks go to Angela Esterhammer, for working so efficiently on the preparation of the manuscript; to Julian Patrick, for valuable assistance in the selection and editing of essays; to Joseph Wittreich, for helpful advice; and to Jean Edmunds, Elaine Nascimento, and Doris Page for doing so much in the way of photocopying, mailing, and keeping track of expenses. Generous grants from The Social Sciences and Humanities Research Council of Canada and from the Connaught Fund of the University of Toronto have materially assisted us throughout and we want to acknowledge their importance.

I
The author function

1

RICHARD HALPERN

The Great Instauration: imaginary narratives in Milton's "Nativity Ode"

> In sapphire arenas of the hills
> I was promised an improved infancy.
> (Hart Crane, "Passages")

More than any English poet who preceded him – and, for that matter, more than any who followed him – John Milton was able to fashion a coherent poetic *career*. A strong if complex sense of poetic and spiritual vocation appears from the time of his earliest works; and the narrative which he constructs for himself comes to display an astonishing durability, absorbing immense historical and personal shocks without seeming to fragment. The redoubtable strength of Milton's literary "personality" may be said to consist mainly in his ability to revise disturbing events in accordance with a coherently narrated career, or to revise the narrative itself in such a way as to leave it seemingly unchanged. Yet the organizing power of such revision is not only retrospective; it is also strongly anticipatory. As the sonnets on his blindness (for instance) suggest, Milton tends to view himself from the projected point of a later reckoning. Almost all of the early poems insist on their place within a developing order, gesturing obscurely toward the accomplishment of some greater work or task. Milton's early dedication to an ethic of personal chastity, his insistence that "he who would not be frustrate of his hope to write hereafter in laudable things, ought himselfe to bee a true Poem, that is, a composition and patterne of the best and honourablest things,"[1] is coupled with a meticulous mastery of various literary genres as part of a self-conscious effort at poetic development. The 1645 *Poems* opens with an epigraph in which Milton declares himself a "*future* bard," and thus at a stroke converts the entire contents of that volume into elements in a scheme of self-preparation.

Milton's future development is sketched out with visionary rigor in the "Nativity Ode" by means of what I shall call "imaginary narratives." These may be defined most simply as narratives or histories which are signified or evoked by means of literary images. In the "Nativity Ode," for instance, the figure of the infant Christ is used to project a future career on which Milton can pattern his own – though this is by no means the only pattern available in the poem. Through a complex set of eidetic allusions, the "Nativity Ode" generates a plurality of imaginary narratives, some benign and some catastrophic, which together constitute a veritable grammar of possible futures.

Because the assumption of each of these futures is effected by a process of *identification* with its signifying image, such narratives are also "imaginary" in the Lacanian sense of the term. In fact, I would argue that at certain points the "Nativity Ode" seems to aim at articulating something like a poetic "ego,"[2] and that the dynamics of this process strongly resemble those of Lacan's *stade du miroir*. I would like to insist that what follows is not exactly a Lacanian "reading" of the poem – and not only because my concentration on the imaginary register conflicts with those few examples of Lacan's literary criticism which we possess.[3] Nevertheless, I think that Lacan's writings on the mirror stage are useful here on several counts. First, his insistence on the irreducible frustrations which inhere in the very structure of the ego can help illuminate that sense of perpetual crisis which attends Milton's narrative of poetic vocation. And second, his rejection of those simplified temporalities of psychic development which ego-psychology tried to foist onto the subject finds an echo in certain resistances which Milton displays toward his own ascetic schemes of poetic "growth." My use of Lacan is intended to clarify certain structures in Milton's personal mythologies and to show how Milton anticipates Lacan's distaste for normalizing, pacifying, or reductive narratives of development.

I

In his classic essay on the "mirror stage," Lacan argues that the child who is fascinated by his own image in the mirror enacts a fundamental process by which the bodily image becomes a model for the ego and hence for the subject's own relation with itself:

> This jubilant assumption of his specular image by the child at the *infans* stage, still sunk in his motor incapacity and nursling dependence, would seem to exhibit in an exemplary situation the symbolic matrix in which the *I* is precipitated in a primordial form, before it is objectified in the dialectic of identification with the other, and before language restores to it, in the universal, its function as subject.[4]

On the one hand, this identification with the image exerts what Lacan calls an "orthopaedic" function, since the "total form of the body" allows the infant to "anticipate in a mirage the maturation of his power."[5] On the other hand, it sets the subject at an irreducible distance from itself and thus fixes an alienating dehiscence at the heart of our being.

One way of understanding the mirror stage is by means of what we might call "infantile narration." A central mechanism of this stage is the conversion of spatial displacement into temporal anticipation; by transforming its specular image into a future, the infant constructs a proto-narrative out of space alone, before its accession to language.

> This development is experienced as a temporal dialectic that decisively projects the formation of the individual into history. The *mirror stage* is a drama whose internal thrust is precipitated from insufficiency to anticipation – and which manufactures for the subject, caught up in the lure of spatial identification, the succession of phantasies that extends from a fragmented body-image to a form of its totality that I shall call orthopaedic – and, lastly, to the assumption of the armour of an alienating identity, which will mark with its rigid structure the subject's entire mental development.[6]

This infantile narrative does not lack analogues among the maturer genres of fable. Heroic narrative, and particularly quest-romance, reproduces the *mythos* of an inchoate subject who travels forth through space and time to return with an ambivalent prize. Lacan himself depicts the space of the imaginary as if it were the landscape of romance:

> The formation of the *I* is symbolized in dreams by a fortress, or a stadium – its inner arena and enclosure, surrounded by marshes and rubbish-tips, dividing it into two opposed fields of contest where the subject flounders in quest of the lofty, remote inner castle.[7]

A successful quest yields its chivalric prize, the "armour of an alienating identity."

The mirror stage is also a myth of incarnation wherein an incoherent subject achieves stability by identifying with its own bodily image. The closure of both of these micronarratives offers a loop by means of which the subject can return to himself in solider form, and can convert the spatial structures of reflection into a narrative of self-mastery. Yet this project is also self-frustrating because it "situates the agency of the ego, before its social determination, *in a fictional direction*, which will always remain irreducible for the individual alone."[8]

In Milton's "Nativity Ode," the story of Christ's birth strongly parallels the micronarratives of the mirror stage, offering both a myth of incarnation and a salvational quest-romance. Moreover, the poetic treatment of Christ's infancy consistently "anticipates in a mirage the maturation of his [Christ's] power" through both spatial and temporal displacements. More interesting than this mythical content, however, is the gestural use to which Milton puts it. Milton's career is nothing if not a narrative of anticipation; there was nothing random, therefore, about his decision to open the 1645 *Poems*, his first published volume of verse, with the "Nativity Ode." By so doing he appropriates the occasion of Christ's birth to announce his own poetic nativity and to anticipate the maturation of his own powers. The infant Christ serves Milton as an orthopaedic image through which he may invest his nascent poetic subjectivity with a preliminary form. J. H. Hanford remarked in 1925 that in the "Ode," "the poet completely identifies himself with his conception and this identification calls forth all his imaginative and expressive powers" – a neat anticipation of the Lacanian thesis.[9] At the same time, this specular relation provides Milton with a narrative on which to project both his poetic development and, in general, the problems of tradition and the individual talent. Christ enables Milton to mediate his own relationship with literary history by providing a model for that history and for his place within it.

Before we turn to Milton's poem, however, it would be useful to look more closely at its mythical narrative. St Paul's description of Christ's *kenosis* – his emptying out, or humbling – presents this narrative in an elegantly concise form:

> Let this mind be with you, which was also in Jesus Christ: Who, being in the form of God, thought it not robbery to be equal with God: But made himself of no reputation, and took upon him the form of a servant, and was made in the likeness of men: And being found in fashion as a man, he humbled himself, and became obedient unto death, even the death of the cross. Wherefore God also hath highly exalted him, and given him a name which is above every name: That at the name of Jesus every knee should bow, of things in heaven, and things in earth, and things under the earth; And that every tongue should confess that Jesus Christ is Lord, to the glory of God the Father.
>
> (Phil. 2:5–11; King James version)

This sacrificial narrative is striking in its economic transparency, the "wherefore" in its midst giving it both a propositional and a contractual closure. Reformed theologians such as Calvin recoiled in horror at the notion that Christ was "earning" his reward; by translating the Greek *dio kai* as *quo facto*, Calvin tried to remove all sense that Christ was acting to his own advantage.[10] The problem here is primarily one of temporal decorum; by so foreshortening the narrative, St Paul instrumentalizes Christ's sacrifice, reducing it to a profitable ascetic investment. The temporality of this narrative is therefore extremely tricky. While its economy depends on its ultimate closure (by repayment), a premature closure renders the whole notion of sacrifice inauthentic. Any ascetic or sacrificial narrative must observe this double-bind: to be closed and yet not to seem so.

Milton takes up the problems of a sacrificial narrative beginning with Christ's *kenosis* in stanza 2 of the "Ode:"

> That glorious Form, that Light unsufferable,
> And that far-beaming blaze of Majesty,
> Wherewith he wont at Heav'n's high Council-Table,
> To sit the midst of Trinal Unity,
> He laid aside; and here with us to be,
>   Forsook the Courts of everlasting Day,
> And chose with us a darksome House of mortal Clay.[11]

Christ's redemptive mission begins with an act of cosmic largesse which willfully delimits the full power of godhead. This self-limitation is a necessary prelude to Christ's descent, for as a "Light unsufferable" he would annihilate the landscape he intends to redeem, a situation not unlike that of Melancholy in "Il Penseroso," whose "Saintly visage is too bright/ To hit the Sense of human sight;/ And therefore to our weaker view,/ O'erlaid with black, staid Wisdom's hue" ("Il Penseroso," 13–16). As it is, his advent throws much of nature into a panic. Christ's *kenosis* thus becomes necessary as an act of divine accommodation which lovingly preserves its object.

Christ's gesture directly influences Milton's poetic stance, as Michael Lieb notes:

> [Christ's] sacrificial humiliation finds its counterpart . . . in the posture that the speaker of the "Nativity Ode" assumes. In order to anticipate the coming of the "Star-led Wizards," the speaker desires to "lay" his "humble ode" "lowly at [Christ's] blessed feet". . . . That is, both through the humility of his posture and through the humble nature of his gift, he desires metaphorically to take upon himself the form of a servant. His desire, in turn, reveals his gratitude for Christ's corresponding act.[12]

Milton's parallel *kenosis*, which establishes a mirror-relation with Christ, involves a limitation of the range of poetic vision as well. For by choosing to begin his hymn with the incarnation, Milton deprives himself as well as Christ of the chance of dwelling at "Heav'n's high Council-Table," a sight which in Elegia VI he connects specifically with the epic (El. VI 55–62). In putting off epic expansiveness to dwell in the "humble ode," Milton limits his vision and genre at once, recapitulating Christ's decision to forgo heaven and lie "meanly wrapt in the rude manger." In effect he enforces on himself a poetic infancy, working on small forms in preparation for a greater future.

This Christian narrative itself finds a mirroring analogue in the Virgilian narrative of poetic development. Spenser's *Shepheardes Calender* attests to the power of Virgil's example of employing the eclogue in particular – and pastoral poetry in general – as a training ground for the aspiring epic poet.[13] Spenser, writes "E. K." in the Dedicatory Epistle, chose

> rather in Aeglogues, then other wise to write, doubting perhaps his habilitie, which he little needed, or mynding to furnish our tongue with this kinde, wherein it faulteth, or following the example of the best and most auncient Poetes, which deuised this kind of wryting, being both so base for the matter, and homely for the manner, at the first to trye theyr habilities: and as young birdes, that be newly crept out of the nest, by little first to proue theyr tender wyngs, before they make a greater flyght. . . . So flew Virgile, as not yet well feeling his winges.[14]

The language of motor incapacity, embodied in the figure of the young birds, establishes an imaginary anticipation of the whole or mature body of epic. Milton would adopt E. K.'s figure of flight in *Paradise Lost*, a work that "with no middle flight intends to soar." But meanwhile the young poet imps his poetic wings by experimenting on the eclogue form. The "Nativity Ode" is redolent of Virgil's Fourth Eclogue and Spenser's "aeglogues," specific references to which will be pursued later. For the moment it is sufficient to note the influence of the eclogue on the "Nativity Ode" considered as part of a larger career. As genre, the eclogue represents the small poetic form which must be mastered as preparation for the epic, and as vision, it represents the poetry of nature that must be mastered as prologue to the poetry of the supernatural.

These poetic considerations gain added resonance when conjoined to the story of Christ – which, as I have said, is Milton's story as well. For Christ's mission strikingly resembles that of the epic poet: his kenotic descent into a natural body parallels the epicist's within the body of the eclogue, for in both cases, imagination, whether divine or poetic, assumes the limitations of nature as part of an ascetic preparation to regain the supernatural. The eclogue is, then, Milton's poetic "form of a servant," for which he pretends to sacrifice the epic, his "form of God."

Of all the Virgilian eclogues, the fourth has the most direct influence on Milton's "Nativity Ode." A long tradition already viewed Virgil's poem as a pagan prophecy of Christ's birth and reign. But Eclogue 4 also has important things to say on the relation of poet to poetic subject, particularly in reference to Virgil's own career. Beginning "Sicelides Musae, paulo maiora canamus," Eclogue 4 strives against its generic boundaries. The poem is, indeed, largely a study of the transition from bucolic to higher poetic forms. In addressing his poem to the counsel Pollio, and in flirting with state mythologies (that the poem's "golden age" addresses the Peace of Brundisium has been questioned, but its general application to the establishment of empire is undeniable), Virgil engages the political realm of epic, which requires a higher poetic form (the Sybil's song) than is typical of the *Bucolica*.

William Berg has argued convincingly that Virgil's poetic situation in Eclogue 4 is reflected in his poetic subject, the *parvus puer* whose birth ushers in a golden age.[15] Whatever his historical identity, Berg maintains, the boy functions for Virgil as a kind of infant version of Aeneas: a figure *patriis virtutibus* (full of paternal virtues) whose coming of heroic age will catapult the poet himself to greatness. Thus it is that the poem seems to progress from a bucolic to a pseudo-georgic to an epic mode as it projects Virgil's poetical career along with the political fortunes of Rome. The *puer*'s present infancy is Virgil's comment on his own poetic immaturity and on the pastoral form in which it finds expression; yet the *puer* contains *in ovo*, as it were, the imperial mythology and history that the poet must encounter as his own poetic task and that he will in turn fully articulate. In the *kenosis* passage from Philippians, the emptied Christ is a similar emblem; hence it is interesting to note that, according to most available evidence, Philippians 2:6–11 is a *carmen christi*, a tiny Christological hymn.[16] So Virgil and Paul, two of the major influences on the "Nativity Ode," both employ figures of smallness or self-containment to figure forth the lyric as mode. Virgil and Paul, as well, both have world domination on their minds; the self-containment of their respective subjects is a prelude and counterpart to the universal expansion of their respective visions.

Virgil's "messianic" eclogue came to England as the model for Spenser's fourth "aeglogue." "Aprill"'s celebratory ode to Elizabeth does more than pay a political compliment to the Queen (who, like Virgil's *parvus puer*, was held to have established a reign of peace); it also announces Spenser's determination to make her the subject of his future epic. It is for this reason that Spenser sends the epic muse Calliope to wait on her, that he takes both of his emblems from the *Aeneid*, and that his fourth-month aeglogue, with its "Aprill shoure," invokes the *magnum opus* of Spenser's great English original. The Virgilian–Spenserian tradition offers a strong argument to see in Milton's own *parvus puer* the subject of his future epic; and this despite the fact that he later seemed to favor the idea of an Arthuriad. In any case, the "messianic" eclogue provides a literary antecedent for Milton's identification of poet and subject in the "Nativity Ode." Milton's own generic ambitiousness is prefigured by Virgil, but transformed within the context of a Christological *mythos* which welds religious and poetic asceticism and which looks forward to an apocalyptic epic. As if to confirm Milton's aspirations, the last stanza of the "Ode" offers a striking image of the infant Christ at rest, surrounded by the angels who will form the epic machinery of *Paradise Lost*:[17]

> But see! the Virgin blest,
> Hath laid her Babe to rest.
>   Time is our tedious Song should here have ending;

Heav'n's youngest-teemed Star
Hath fixt her polisht Car,
   Her sleeping Lord with Handmaid Lamp attending:
And all about the Courtly Stable,
Bright-harness'd Angels sit in order serviceable.

"In order serviceable:" that is, serviceable not only to Christ but to John Milton the poet. The two will achieve instrumental mastery together in a projected future. Nevertheless, it is worth noting the "order serviceable" that Milton has already achieved by welding Virgilian and Christian narratives of development and by inserting his own poem firmly within. The result is that a small poem becomes an infant one; it now appears as the first term in a narrative of organic growth which will issue in the full body of epic. This is what one might call the "positive" side of the imaginary, wherein specular and temporal anticipations produce the plenary satisfactions of an ideal self.

II

The workings of the imaginary are not all so smooth, however. I have already mentioned how the orthopaedic totality of the bodily image is at the same time irreducibly alienating because it constructs the subject as an other for itself. A temporal dehiscence accompanies this spatial one, moreover. Lacan insists that the projections of the mirror stage result from a "real *specific prematurity of birth* in man" which produces an "original organic disarray" and hence the need for the image of the total body. But this gap of anticipation is also in some sense irreducible and thus projects a subject which is forever trying to catch up with itself. Just as the spatial dialectic of the imaginary can fluctuate between alienation and specular capture, so its temporal dialectic is subject to mirages of foreshortening or delay. The temporal dimension proves especially critical to the "Nativity Ode" by threatening to disrupt its narrative of development. "Time is our tedious Song should here have ending:" the poem pulls itself up short in the final stanza, embarrassed by its own loquacity. More often, though, it faces the opposite problem of premature closure, which we saw exemplified in the *kenosis* passage from Philippians. In the "Nativity Ode," the infant Christ's "specific prematurity of birth" has become a kind of full-blown cosmic neoteny: "Our Babe, to show his Godhead true,/Can in his swaddling bands control the damned crew." Hence, the poem confronts "mirages" of full maturity which are no longer orthopaedic but simply delusional and even regressive. What the "Nativity Ode" must fight off is the sense that the end is already present in the announcement of nativity. The harmonies set off by Christ's birth induce a kind of anticipatory delirium:

Nature that heard such sound
Beneath the hollow round
   Of *Cynthia's* seat, the Airy region thrilling,
Now was almost won
To think her part was done,
   And that her reign had here its last fulfilling;
She knew such harmony alone
Could hold all Heav'n and Earth in happier union.

The whole middle section of the poem addresses just this threat of temporal collapse, which instead of thrusting history forward in a dialectic of anticipation may instead regress to a state of infantile plenitude:

For if such holy Song
Enwrap our fancy long,
   Time will run back, and fetch the age of gold,
And speckl'd vanity
Will sicken soon and die,
   And leprous sin will melt from earthly mold.

As one might guess, this threat also pertains to Milton's poetic development, which he has already projected onto the Christological myth. The pastoral implications of the "age of gold" suggest that the form of the eclogue, which he has borrowed for the occasion of his literary nativity, may pose unexpected problems. As we shall see, the pastoral offers images of stagnation as well as narratives of development, and Milton must confront both.

Indeed, despite its formal reliance on the eclogue, the "Nativity Ode" is an anti-pastoral. The whole line of "messianic" eclogues on which it draws is rather marginal to the genre, aspiring to the political world of epic rather than to a state of natural repose. At the very beginning of the "Nativity Ode," the infant Christ disrupts a pastoral landscape by arresting the world's natural sexuality:

It was the Winter wild,
While the Heav'n-born child,
   All meanly wrapt in the rude manger lies;
Nature in awe to him
Had doff't her gaudy trim,
   With her great Master so to sympathize:
It was no season then for her
To wanton with the Sun, her lusty Paramour.

Only with speeches fair
She woos the gentle Air

> To hide her guilty front with innocent Snow,
> And on her naked shame,
> Pollute with sinful blame,
> The Saintly Veil of Maiden white to throw,
> Confounded, that her Maker's eyes
> Should look so near upon her foul deformities.

If the image of the infant Christ offers a unifying totality, it does so by contrast with the "foul deformities" of nature. Christ's perfection of form is enhanced by his chastity, which refuses any dispersive intercourse with its surroundings; Christ simply negates the pastoral world of sexuality and nature.

To see how fully this negation is constitutive of the imagined unity of the self, we may contrast Christ's successful incarnation with an unsuccessful one, that of Milton's "Fair Infant Dying of a Cough:"

> O fairest flower no sooner blown but blasted,
> Soft silken Primrose fading timelessly,
> Summer's chief honor if thou hadst outlasted
> Bleak winter's force that made thy blossom dry;
> For he being amorous on that lovely dye
>   That did thy cheek envermeil, thought to kiss
> But kill'd alas, and then bewail'd his fatal bliss.
> ("On the Death of a Fair Infant Dying of a Cough," 1–7)

Here Milton offers another winter birth, but in this case the mortal child cannot temper nature's sexuality, which kills in kissing. The "blasted" flower, which decomposes the unifying totality of the bodily image, represents the other primary term in the vocabulary of the imaginary register. This is what Lacan has called the *corps morcelé* or "fragmented body" – and which is nothing other than an imaginary projection of the subject's original corporeal incoherence, "a primordial Discord betrayed by the signs of uneasiness and motor unco-ordination of the neo-natal months."[18] Lacan locates the origins of aggressivity in this original discord, and suggests that the "fragmented body usually manifests itself in dreams when the movement of the analysis encounters a certain level of aggressive decomposition in the individual."[19] Certainly, the killing kiss of nature which blasts the fair infant has a strongly sadistic component. Beginning with *Lycidas*, Milton's chosen image of the *corps morcelé* will be Orpheus' dismemberment, a myth which is especially suggestive for our purposes because of the way its spatial and temporal dimensions intersect. For Milton, the specular disintegration of Orpheus' body represents the cutting short of his own narrative of poetic development; it is correlative with those "abhorred shears" which "slit the new-spun life" and thus end the dialectic of anticipation. This nightmarish fantasy of premature death lurks as the not-so-hidden counterpart to the "golden age" of infantile regression, since both can short-circuit Milton's narrative of poetic development.

Nevertheless, the notion of a purely aggressive disintegration cannot fully account for the "Nativity Ode"'s chaste stance, for nature's "foul deformities" suggest that sexuality can also decompose the body. The language with which Milton describes the sexuality of nature in the first two stanzas of the hymn has an unmistakably Spenserian ring, and specifically recalls the disrobing of the "foul deformed" Duessa in the *Faerie Queene*, I.8.47–9. The woman's body represents for both Spenser and Milton a disturbing sexual excess which can "deform" and "pollute" the male, while Christ's mastery over nature is figured by his ability to repel these sexual threats and thus retain the chaste integrity of his bodily form. His "orthopaedic" quality arises in opposition to the *corps morcelé* of nature, and thus produces one of the characteristic delusions of western culture: the desexualized infant. Really, the repression of *infantile* sexuality is at stake here, not only for culturally predictable reasons but because, as Freud argued in the *Three Essays on the Theory of Sexuality*, infantile sexuality invests multiple erotogenic areas without subjecting these to the unifying rule of genital sexuality:

> The characteristics of infantile sexual life . . . [include] the facts that it is essentially auto-erotic (i.e. that it finds its objects in the infant's own body) and that its individual component instincts are upon the whole disconnected and independent of one another in their search for pleasure. The final outcome of sexual development lies in what is known as the normal sexual life of the adult, in which the pursuit of pleasure comes under the sway of the reproductive function and in which the component instincts, under the primacy of a single erotogenic zone, form a firm organization directed towards a sexual aim attached to some extraneous sexual object.[20]

For the most part, Lacan ignores the role of sexuality in "disorganizing" the infantile body.[21] But it is clear that prior to their overcoding by genital sexuality and the Oedipus complex, the erotogenic areas operate as independent "desiring machines." In its pleasures as well as its aggressive tensions, therefore, the infant's body tends to fragment.

From the perspective of the totalized or "mature" body which the "Nativity Ode" erects as its ideal, infantile sexuality poses a threat which must be mastered or repressed, as the fate of the Fair Infant illustrates. In that poem, the conjunction of nature with a deadly sexuality suggests why the genre of the pastoral might be a problematic one for Milton. In fact, the "Nativity Ode" not only aligns itself with the tradition of messianic eclogues in its search for an orthopaedic image; it specifically negates a different but related pastoral tradition which produces a fragmenting image of the self. And here too the articulation of infantile sexuality pertains to Milton's place within literary history.

Milton's image of the infant as a "blasted" flower comes from Spenser, this time from Colin Clout's complaint in the "Januarye" eclogue of the *Shepheardes Calender*:

> Thou barrein ground, whome winters wrath hath wasted,
> Art made a myrrhour, to behold my plight:
> Whilome thy fresh spring flowrd, and after hasted
> Thy sommer prowde with Daffadillies dight.
> And now is come thy wynters stormy state,
> Thy mantle mard, wherein thou maskedst late.
>
> All so my lustfull leafe is drye and sere,
> My timely buds with wayling all are wasted:
> The blossome, which my braunch of youth did beare,
> With breathed sighes is blown away, and blasted,
> And from mine eyes the drizling teares descend,
> As on your boughes the ysicles depend.
>
> ("Januarye," 19–24, 37–42)

Colin's situation reveals the other side of the mirror stage, for what the barren ground reflects is not a unifying image but a decomposing one. Instead of investing Colin with a total form, it breaks down the barriers between *Innenwelt* and *Umwelt*. Instead of anticipating the maturation of his powers, it depletes them. If what appears in the mirror is the *corps morcelé*, then the entire dialectic of anticipation breaks down.

The mirroring of Colin in Spenser's "Januarye" is itself the continuation of a pastoral tradition which runs back through Virgil's second eclogue to Polyphemus' lament in Theocritus' sixth Idyll:

> For truly I am not even ill-favored, as they say; for of late I looked into the sea, and there was a calm, and fair, as my judgement goes, showed my beard and my one eye, and it reflected the gleam of my teeth whiter than Parian marble.
>
> (Id. 6, 34–8)[22]

Clearly, Polyphemus is here a kind of low comic Narcissus who becomes enamored of his own deformity. In addition, he embodies some of the most characteristic elements of bucolic poetry in exaggerated form, and thus offers Theocritus and Spenser a way of commenting on the genre. Not only is he a shepherd, the archetypical resident of pastoral, but he is a passionate shepherd. In Idyll 11, Polyphemus cherishes the nymph Galatea with religious intensity and is even prompted to compose songs to her – but then these little flights are followed by bathetic falls in which he entreats his goddess to exchange her love for cheese. Polyphemus' loutishness represents the degeneration of pastoral simplicity, just as his beastliness represents the degeneration of "natural man." The fate of his imagination offers a limiting case for pastoral, one in which nature is no longer a setting for the mind but its upper boundary. When he describes his beloved as "whiter than curd to look on, softer than the lamb, more skittish than the calf, sleeker than the unripe grape" (Id. 11, 20–1), he reveals an imagination which cannot rise above the contemplation of its immediate environs.

Polyphemus' obtuseness constitutes a comic or parodic version of the pastoral *ethos*. By employing the Cyclops' love-sickness as an explicit analogy to his own, Theocritus suggests that, despite his urbanity, he and the Cyclops participate in the same natural order and are subject to the same passions.[23] By making the same Cyclops a poet, moreover, and a pastoral love poet at that, Theocritus declares Polyphemus a grotesque version of himself – a distorted reflection like the one Polyphemus admires in the sea. Thus Theocritus introduces into the poem a low comic *imago* of the poet, a tradition which will be transmitted as though genetically along the pastoral line through Virgil and Spenser to Milton.

Virgil adapts the Polyphemean song in his second eclogue, which rings some interesting changes on its Greek original but is important for our purposes mainly in reproducing so much of Theocritus' text. Polyphemus undergoes a physical transformation into the clownish shepherd Corydon, but his character remains almost unchanged. Virgil even takes up Theocritus' mirror image, with all its suggestions of childish narcissism:

> nec sum adeo informis: nuper me in litore vidi
> cue placidum ventis staret mare; non ego Daphnim
> iudice te metuam, si numquam fallit imago.
>
> (Ecl. 2, 25–7)[24]

[Nor am I so unsightly; on the shore the other day I looked at myself, when, by the grace of the winds, the sea was at peace and still. With you for judge, I should fear not Daphnis, if the mirror never lies.]

As Polyphemus did Theocritus, so Virgil's Corydon reflects his poetic maker, and the analogy assumes interesting implications when Corydon declares himself unwilling to leave his native woods:

> quem fugis, a! demens? habitarunt di quoque silvas
> Dardaniusque Paris. Pallas, quas condidit arces
> ipsa colat; nobis placeant ante omnia silvae.
>
> (Ecl. 2, 60–2)

[Ah, fool, whom do you flee? Even the gods have dwelt in the woods, and Dardan Paris. Let Pallas dwell by herself in the cities she has built; but let my chief delight be the woods!]

15

Clearly Corydon's intention to pursue his natural passions in the forest is also Virgil's refusal to leave, for the time being, the pastoral mode. By mentioning Pallas and Paris, Corydon projects the epic career that Virgil foresees for himself, and this in itself distinguishes his bucolic poetry from Theocritus', for unlike his predecessor, Virgil deems the pastoral a preparatory genre. Yet for the moment Virgil defends his poetic *otium* and insists on maintaining the middle flight of pastoral. In a sense, then, Eclogue 2 functions as a counter-text to the impatient Eclogue 4; its Polyphemean naturalism, which limits and constricts the imagination, stands in contrast to the Sybilline prophecies of the "messianic" eclogue, so eager to doff the poetry of nature and ascend to supernatural themes.

Spenser's "Januarye" in its turn draws heavily on Virgil's Polyphemean shepherd. Colin's love for Rosalind is patterned after Corydon's for Alexis, and in addition Spenser provides several verbal echoes of Eclogue 2, one of which is pointed out by E. K. in the notes. Like Eclogue 2, Colin's rustic love-plaint is also Spenser's commentary on pastoral and its relation to epic. Once we realize this fact, however, the differences between Virgil and Spenser become enormous, because for the later English poet, pastoral *otium* has become a crisis instead of a luxury. Much of the *Shepheardes Calender* was written in late 1579, when Spenser and the rest of Leicester's circle were smarting from the Alençon affair. It is quite likely that Rosalind represents the wayward Queen Elizabeth and that Colin's rural melancholy in part reflects Spenser's fear of alienation from the court.[25] For Spenser, the setting of pastoral could come to symbolize the possibility of permanent banishment. Hence Polyphemus invokes for him a whole constellation of fears: those of the imagination tied down by nature, of the poet dismissed from court, and of the bumpkin with aristocratic aspirations, whether toward a woman who is too high for him or toward the urbanity of courtly life.

Colin's love-plaint for Rosalind is thus Spenser's complaint for his own imagination as well. In Theocritus the muse's song is described as a remedy (*pharmakon*) for the wounds of love, but here Colin's muse fails to cure his love pangs, and in so doing she fails Spenser the poet as well:

> Wherefore my pype, albee rude *Pan* thou please,
> Yet for thou pleasest not, where most I would:
> And thou vnlucky Muse, that wontst to ease
> My musing mynd, yet canst not, when thou should:
> Both pype and Muse, shall sore the while abye.
> So broke his oaten pype, and downe dyd lye.
> ("Januarye," 67–72)

Colin's song can neither win Rosalind's approval nor raise the singer above his passion: its ineffectiveness is the archetypical one of Polyphemean song, the inability to elevate the singer. For Spenser this problem is compounded because compared to the epic the pastoral love song is a low form; the genre itself is symptomatic of imaginative mediocrity. Thus Colin's love-sickness is simultaneously Spenser's poetic disease; the sad shepherd's poetry is occasionally moving but is, on the whole, uninspired. At any rate, it gives no clue about how to rise to a higher strain, but simply collapses at the end under the weight of its own frustrated passion.

The childish regression with which "Januarye" ends offers new insights about how image produces narrative. If the *parvus puer* offers a totalizing *imago* which projects the poet's future development, Polyphemus offers a decomposing image that entails stagnation, entrapment, regression. If the *parvus puer* inserts the pastoral within a narrative that anticipates the epic, Polyphemus produces a non-narrative in which pastoral leads nowhere, having been converted from an orthopaedic form into a constraining one.

Milton's "Nativity Ode" enacts its Christological *mythos* largely in reaction to the "Januarye" Aeglogue and its Polyphemean shepherd, Colin. The influence of the *Shepheardes Calender* can be seen in Milton's choice of a celebratory ode to chastity, for which the "Aprill" Aeglogue offers a pattern, and in the assumption of a myth of heavenly origins for the imagination, to which "October" contributes. But it is against "Januarye" that the first two stanzas of the hymn most fully assert themselves.[26] Milton's revision, I believe, centers on the Spenserian trope wherein the winter landscape mirrors a non-erotic self (chaste in Christ's case, lovelorn in Colin's):

> It was the Winter wild,
> While the Heav'n-born child,
>   All meanly wrapt in the rude manger lies;
> Nature in awe to him
> Had doff't her gaudy trim,
>   With her great Master so to sympathize:
> It was no season then for her
> To wanton with the Sun, her lusty Paramour.

Milton, however, rejects the naturalistic implications inherent in the idea of the incarnation as a second creation, presenting instead a Christ whose chaste birth interrupts nature's process.[27] Ironically, he depicts the emergence of a new chaste order by borrowing a figure from the pastoral love lament. But Milton's trope reverses Spenser's by expressing strength precisely where Spenser's expressed weakness. For Christ's willed chastity sacrifices nothing, thus attesting to the power of the self against nature while Colin's attests to the power of nature against the self.

The significance of Christ's asceticism for Milton's poetic career has been suggested by Arthur Barker, who notes that the "Ode"'s rejection of wanton nature is also the poet's rejection of the kind of sensuous pastoral encountered in Elegia V.[28] What the "Ode" rejects more specifically, however, are the Polyphemean limits of Spenserian pastoral, which proves unable to break its visionary and generic limitations to move from bucolic to epic. Through the power of asceticism Milton transforms the sorrowful lay of "Januarye" into a song of joy and triumph – perhaps also of joy *in* triumph.

So far from natural entrapment are Milton and Christ that the "Nativity Ode" is threatened at the beginning by the very un-Spenserian problem of too much vision. Nature trembles at Christ's birth like a guilty thing surprised, "Confounded, that her Maker's eyes/ Should look so near upon her foul deformities." The piercing vision of godhead threatens to undo her snowy veilings with a final revelation which could end both nature and poem at once.[29] Pastoral melancholy is never a threat in the "Nativity Ode," but apocalyptic prematurity is. Not stagnation, but the imaginary transcendence of a developmental narrative is what troubles the "Ode", particularly in the image of an early millennium that occupies its middle sections. The collapse of the poem's temporality is staved off only by the intervention of a higher power:

> But wisest Fate says no,
> This must not yet be so,
>   The Babe lies yet in smiling Infancy,
> That on the bitter cross
> Must redeem our loss;
>   So both himself and us to glorify:
> Yet first to those ychain'd in sleep,
> The wakeful trump of doom must thunder through the deep.

The "no" of "wisest Fate" introduces the exigencies of the law – specifically, the Law of the Father. In this emblematic entry of what Lacan calls the symbolic order, its essential function within the poem is revealed. The symbolic supervenes to do that which the imaginary can never do for itself – stabilize the temporality of its narrative, regularize the decorum of its anticipations. The presence of the symbolic in the poem does not (indeed, cannot) assume the form of an image. Its primary manifestation is rather the degree to which the temporalities of the poem's development manage to avoid a crisis – the degree, that is, to which the poem can admit that "this must not yet be so" without thereby succumbing to the fear that it will never be.

III

In one of his seminars on Freud's metapsychological writings, Lacan considers "the internal contradiction that exists between the term *Entwicke-lung* and the term *Geschichte*" as Freud combines them in the term *Entwickelungsgeschichte*.[30] In so doing, he criticizes the narrative of

18

development promulgated by ego-psychology, which posits the subject as passing through oral, anal, and genital "stages" on its way to maturity. Lacan contrasts this with the more complex temporalities that constitute the history of the subject as analysed (and produced) by psychoanalysis. These meditations are capped by the therapeutically paradoxical insistence that in the case of the "return of the repressed," what one encounters is a return not from the past but from the *future*.[31]

The distinction between *Entwickelung* and *Geschichte* appears in their etymologies: the first is literally an evolution or unrolling, while the second is a narrative in which something *happens* (*geschiet*): anticipation, regression, trauma, fixation, and so forth. For all that, the two terms are not entirely unrelated. Lacan constructs the history of the subject by playing with narratives of development that he then subverts. The mirror "stage," for instance, is sometimes described as preceding entry into the symbolic, yet elsewhere is shown to be structured by the symbolic from the start.

It seems fair to ask, then, whether the pastoral, georgic and epic stages of the Virgilian triad do not play a role rather like those of the oral, anal, and genital "stages" of ego-psychology – if not in content, at least in reducing poetic history to poetic development. What the Christian–classical synthesis of the early sections of the "Nativity Ode" may produce after all is not a history of the poetic subject but an evolution of the poetic ego. And yet, this is clearly *not* what the poem ultimately produces, for Christ's advent is presented neither as a synthetic nor as an evolutionary event but as an historical trauma.

The disruptive force of the nativity appears most clearly in the defection of the classical gods, which occupies most of the latter portion of the "Ode:"

> The Oracles are dumb,
> No voice or hideous hum
>   Runs through the arched roof in words deceiving.
> *Apollo* from his shrine
> Can no more divine,
>   With hollow shriek the steep of *Delphos* leaving.
> No nightly trance, or breathed spell,
> Inspires the pale-ey'd Priest from the prophetic cell.

The failure of the oracles, which results from an unforeseeable event, marks a trauma for the temporality of pagan culture, an unassimilable shock that confronts it with a future not its own. The real "Infant Gods" of the poem, if we recall that *infans* means "not speaking," are now the classical oracles whose voices have been silenced or scarred, and whose distorted songs offer a plangent counterpoint to the choirs hymning the incarnation.

The temporal break which results in the defection of the oracles offers a third and final narrative of Milton's relation with literary history – this time, neither linear nor aborted but rather discontinuous and overdetermined. Apollo's emblematic displacement from his shrine repeats itself when " *Peor* and *Baalim/* Forsake their Temples dim," when Moloch flees his idol, when Osiris can no longer "be at rest/ Within his sacred chest," when "each peculiar power forgoes his wonted seat." Disenshrinement is the central action of these stanzas, represented in physical removal from an ark, chest, or temple, and in the failure of those priestly rites which figuratively enclose each deity. As poetic allegory this action is transparent: Christ's wresting of the gods from their devotional shrines is Milton's wresting of the gods from their literary shrines – that is, the texts in which they are both contextualized and worshipped, and from which they draw much of their cultural strength.

Representing a text as a shrine or monument had been a commonplace since Horace's "*monumentum aere perennius*," reinvoked in Jonson's and Milton's epitaphs on Shakespeare and in numerous other contemporary literary encomia. But commonplace or not, it is a dense image which entails its own narrative of literary history. Two related concerns emerge here: literary transmission, conceived of as immortality or fame, and literary fixity, the permanence of a text or its interpretation which assures its transmission intact. As the written utterance of a speaking subject, the monumental text allows the enshrined poet to continue speaking and to exert that influence which only confrontation with a subject can inflict. But at the same time, by insisting on the transmission of the work as verbal icon or object which remains the same no matter how often reprinted, the image of enshrinement generates the corresponding illusion of a self-contained meaning: a meaning which, like the physical text, can reproduce itself indefinitely, invulnerable somehow to the vicissitudes of individual or historical reinterpretation.

The god in his shrine thus represents the genius of a text confronted as unassailable *numen*, manifested and enclosed in the text's physical integrity and in its accretions of official scholia. Christ's disenshrinement of the pagan deities is Milton's attempt to deprive previous texts of their invulnerability as objects and force them to recognize Milton himself as subject. Literary influence thus becomes a two-way discourse which can be directed backwards as well as forwards. In the "Ode," the techniques by which Milton hopes to rewrite literary history consist largely of decontextualization and rearrangement. Milton re-enacts Christ's disenshrinement of the gods by unhousing them from their original literary contexts; then, transferring them to his poem, he watches them wither in its purer air. The result is a new song wrung from the expiration of powers which he has transfixed at the moment of their cultural supersession. Like Adam after the Fall they cry "O living death!," caught in an ironic reversal of the life-in-death they enjoyed as monuments.

The vision of literary history (*not* literary development) which the

"Nativity Ode" finally offers is rather like that described by T. S. Eliot in his essay on "Tradition and the individual talent."

> What happens when a new work of art is created is something that happens simultaneously to all the works of art which preceded it. The existing monuments form an ideal order among themselves, which is modified by the introduction of the new (the really new) work of art among them. The existing order is complete before the new work arrives; for order to persist after the supervention of novelty, the *whole* existing order must be, if ever so slightly, altered; and so the relations, proportions, values of each work of art toward the whole must be readjusted; and this is conformity between the old and the new. Whoever has approved this idea of order, of the form of European, of English literature, will not find it preposterous that the past should be altered by the present as much as the present is directed by the past.[32]

This passage might describe the Freudian temporality of the subject as well as it does the temporalities of literary history. In 1920, the same year in which Eliot's essay appeared, Freud produced its uncanny double in *Beyond the Pleasure Principle*, where he argued that traumatic dreams "are endeavoring to master the [traumatic] stimulus retrospectively, by developing the anxiety whose omission was the cause of the traumatic neurosis."[33] Both literary and psychic history assimilate the truly new through a process of *Nachträglichkeit* in which events return from the future. In the "Nativity Ode," Christ's birth is a traumatic event which rearranges the "ideal order" of the "existing monuments," but to a degree far greater than the "slight alteration" that Eliot's more conservative imagination envisioned. Christ's nativity shatters the monuments of the past and wrenches them into a wholly new pattern.

This latter section of the "Ode" restores to the genre something of its original Pindaric contentiousness. If Christ serves Milton as an orthopaedic image, he does not do so only in order to lay down a pattern of discipline. There is a certain joy as well in scrambling the earlier codes, a characteristic Miltonic aggressiveness in relation to the past. This destructive streak doesn't erase the older narratives of development, but it certainly complicates their temporality. In effect, the "Nativity Ode" reproduces the Lacanian practice of constructing an evolutionary narrative and then breaking it. It announces the birth of the subject into history by insisting that something *happens* there; and its own iconoclastic presence is the sign of that traumatic, poetic nativity.

Notes

1. *An Apology against a Pamphlet. . .* (1642), in *The Complete Prose Works of John Milton*, vol. I (New Haven, Yale University Press, 1953), 890.

2. See William Kerrigan, "The articulation of the Ego in the English Renaissance," in *The Literary Freud: Mechanisms of Defense and the Poetic Will*, ed. Joseph H. Smith, Psychiatry and the Humanities Series, vol. 4 (New Haven, Yale University Press, 1980), 261–308.

3. Besides the famous seminar on "The Purloined Letter," there is an essay on "Desire and the interpretation of desire in *Hamlet*" in *Yale French Studies* 55/56, 1977, 11–52. Since the concept of the mirror stage inhabits a largely Hegelian problematic which precedes Lacan's more radical linguistic formulations, it might be objected that my concentration on this topic results in a conservative deformation of his work. I can only concede, somewhat ruefully, that this is probably so. While Fredric Jameson has argued, conversely, that the "gradual eclipse [of the Imaginary] in Lacan's later work is not foreign to a certain overestimation of the Symbolic which may be said to be properly ideological," it may be disingenuous to invoke Jameson in defense of my admittedly ahistorical reading ("Imaginary and symbolic in Lacan: Marxism, psychoanalytic criticism, and the problem of the subject" (*Yale French Studies*, 55/56, 1977, 369).)

4. Jacques Lacan, *Ecrits: A Selection*, tr. Alan Sheridan (New York, W. W. Norton, 1977), 2.

5. ibid., 4,2.

6. ibid., 4.

7. ibid., 5.

8. ibid., 2. My emphasis.

9. J. Holly Hanford, "The youth of Milton: an interpretation of his early literary development," in *John Milton, Poet and Humanist: Essays by J. Holly Hanford* (Cleveland, Western Reserve University, 1966), 35.

10. See R. P. Martin, *Carmen Christi: Philippians ii. 5–11 in Recent Interpretation and in the Setting of Early Christian Worship* (Cambridge, Cambridge University Press, 1967), 232.

11. All quotations of Milton's poetry are taken from *John Milton: Complete Poems and Major Prose*, ed. Merritt Y. Hughes (New York, Odyssey, 1957).

12. Michael Lieb, "Milton and the Kenotic Christology: its literary bearing" (*ELH*, 37, 1970, 342–60). Quotation from 352.

13. See, for example, Richard Neuse, "Milton and Spenser: the Virgilian triad revisited" (*ELH*, 45, 1978, 606–39).

14. All Spenser quotations are taken from *The Works of Edmund Spenser: A Variorum Edition*, ed. Edwin Greenlaw, C. G. Osgood, and F. M. Padelford, 9 vols (Baltimore, Johns Hopkins University Press, 1935–49).

15. William Berg, *Early Virgil* (London, Athlone Press, 1974), 166–77.

16. Martin, op. cit., 17–41.

17. See Balachandra Rajan, "In order serviceable" (*Modern Language Review*, 63, 1968, 13–22).

18. Lacan, op. cit., 4.

19. ibid., 4.

20. Sigmund Freud, *Three Essays on the Theory of Sexuality*, tr. James Strachey (New York, Basic Books, 1962), 63.

21. But see *Le Séminaire: Livre I, Les Ecrits techniques de Freud* (Paris, Editions de Seuil, 1975), 159, 170.

22. All translations of Theocritus are taken from *Theocritus*, ed. and tr. A. S. F.

Gow, 2nd edn (Cambridge, Cambridge University Press, 1952).
23. See Edward W. Spofford, "Theocritus and Polyphemus" (*American Journal of Philology*, 90, 1969, 22–35).
24. All quotations and translations of Virgil are taken from *Virgil*, ed. and tr. H. Rushton Fairclough, 2 vols (Cambridge, Mass., Harvard University Press, 1935).
25. See Paul McLane, *Spenser's Shepheardes Calender: A Study in Elizabethan Allegory* (Notre Dame, Ind., University of Notre Dame Press, 1961), 13–46.
26. The relevance of Spenser's "Januarye" for the "Nativity Ode" is suggested by E. K.'s "Argument" to the *Shepheardes Calender*. There he examines with comic thoroughness the propriety of commencing with a poem on January, the month that begins the Christian calendar, instead of March, which begins the Roman. Whatever the value of E. K.'s erudition, it manages to elevate Spenser's revision of the classical calendar into a symbol of his revision of the classical pastoral tradition. Beginning with a January "aeglogue" becomes, in his hands, emblematic of a specifically Christian reordering of classical predecessors. E. K.'s formulation of the matter must have had its effects on Milton as he contemplated the composition of the "Nativity Ode:"

> But sauing the leaue of such lerned heads, we mayntaine a custome of coumpting the seasons from the moneth Ianuary, upon a more speciall cause, then the heathen Philosophers euer coulde conceiue, that is, for the incarnation of our mighty Sauiour and eternall redeemer the L. Christ, who as then renewing the state of the decayed world, and returning the compasse of expired yeres to theyr former date and first commencement, left to vs his heires a memoriall of his birth in the ende of the last yeere and the beginning of the next.

By composing a cold pastoral, Milton has allied himself with Spenser in the Christian pastoral tradition.
27. Milton's use of this figuration is all the more striking in that Nativity poems traditionally picture Christ's incarnation as a new spring. Herrick's "Christmas Carol" is a case in point:

> Dark and dull night, fly hence away,
> And give the honour to this day,
> That sees December turned to May.

(Quoted from J. B. Broadbent, "The Nativity Ode," in *The Living Milton*, ed. Frank Kermode (London, Routledge & Kegan Paul, 1960), 12–31). This naturalistic motif has Hebraic origins in, for example, Isaiah 35 ("The wilderness and the solitary place shall be glad for them; and the desert shall rejoice, and blossom as the rose"), and classical analogues such as (not unimportantly) Virgil's Eclogue 4:

> At tibi prima, puer, nullo munuscula cultu
> errantis hederas passim cum baccare tellus
> mixtaque ridenti colocasia fundet acantho,. . .
> ipsa tibi blandos fundet cunabula flores.
> (Ecl. 4, 18–20, 22)

[But for thee, child, shall the earth untilled pour forth, as her first pretty gifts, straggling ivy with foxglove everywhere, and the Egyptian bean blended with smiling acanthus. . . . Unasked, thy cradle shall pour forth flowers for thy delight.]

28. Arthur Barker, "The pattern of Milton's 'Nativity Ode,'" in Alan Rudrum (ed.), *Milton: Modern Judgements* (Nashville, Aurora, 1970), 57, note 6.
29. This eschatological crisis is intensified, moreover, through Milton's intertextual references. In stanza 2 of the hymn one hears direct echoes of the Book of Revelation 3:18: "buy . . . white raiment, that thou mayest be clothed, and *that* the shame of thy nakedness do not appear."
30. Lacan, *Le Séminaire*, 173. Freud's term occurs in the essay "Metapsychological supplement to the theory of dreams."
31. ibid., 181–2.
32. T. S. Eliot, "Tradition and the individual talent," in *The Sacred Wood* (London, Methuen, 1920, rpt. 1976), 49–50.
33. Sigmund Freud, *Beyond the Pleasure Principle*, in *The Standard Edition of the Complete Psychological Works of Sigmund Freud*, ed. James Strachey *et al.*, 24 vols (London, Hogarth Press, 1953–74), XVIII.32.

2

MARY LOEFFELHOLZ

Two masques of Ceres and Proserpine: *Comus* and *The Tempest*

I propose to open a feminist inquiry into Shakespeare's presence in Milton's *Comus* by considering the relation of Prospero's interrupted betrothal masque of Ceres in *The Tempest* to Milton's masque. Shakespeare's influence in *Comus* has often been discussed, most recently and at length by John Guillory, but Guillory's discussion for the most part bypasses *The Tempest* to concentrate on Milton's "interior drama" of engagement with the poetic voices of Shakespeare as represented in *A Midsummer Night's Dream*.[1] I want to make good this omission from the standpoint of a feminist auditor, one with an ear for interruptions, for in both *The Tempest*'s "external" or dramatic and *Comus*' more "internal," allusive and argumentative play of voices, interruptions are glimpses into a history, literary and otherwise, less overheard as a continuous play of echoes than envisioned, darkly and backwardly, as an abyss opening onto the question of maternal absence and the rupture (rapture?) of mother and daughter.[2] Into this abyss disappeared Proserpine as she was abducted; there she ate, even while Ceres was searching her out; and, as we know, the poetry of earth has never been the same since. Reading Shakespeare's interrupted masque of Ceres into Milton's *Comus* fills in the continuity of Milton's engagement with his literary sources but at the same time raises questions disturbing to that idea of continuity, not the least of which is, why the *Lady*? What has her gender to do with the genre of *Comus*? And what are the consequences of the gender of Milton's protagonist for Milton's revisions of the masque's "familial ethics"?[3]

There are two important interruptions in *The Tempest*, and they are intimately – familially – related. In the more conspicuous of the two, Prospero interrupts himself, in the betrothal masque anticipating Miranda and Ferdinand's wedded happiness. Dramatically, the masque is premature, as Prospero's exclamation reminds us. Caliban is still hatching plots against Prospero's rule; the families that ought to be united in the betrothal masque are still wandering separately on the island. The adequate audience to the betrothal has yet to be assembled. Thematically, however, the masque of Act IV is not premature but belated, hopelessly so. For what Prospero undertakes to do in his entertainment is not to present children to their parents (in the conventional pattern of the betrothal masque), but a parent to a child: a parent long dead, and apparently absent from the earliest memories her daughter can recall from "the dark backward and abysm of time." The masque undertakes, then, to supplement memory with myth; the last task of Miranda's education will be to recognize herself as Proserpine, daughter of the Ceres with whom Prospero presents her.

This recognition never comes, and the masque is interrupted. It is not that Miranda has no memories for the masque to supplement, for it is these very memories that prompt the first interruption in *The Tempest*, when Miranda breaks into Prospero's account of their exile from Milan:

> *Prospero:*   Canst thou remember
> A time before we came unto this cell?
> I do not think thou canst, for then thou was not
> Out three years old.
> *Miranda:*   Certainly, sir, I can.
> *Prospero:* By what? by any other house or person?
> Of any thing the image tell me, that
> Hath kept with thy remembrance.
> *Miranda:*   'Tis far off,
> And rather like a dream than an assurance
> That my remembrance warrants. Had I not
> Four or five women once that tended me?
> *Prospero:* Thou hadst, and more, Miranda.
>
> (I.ii.38–48)[4]

Miranda remembers more than her father bargains on, but not quite what he needs her to "remember" through his mediation. What "more" did Miranda have? For how long did she have a mother? Her forgetfulness may indicate that her mother died while she herself was still an infant, or may reflect child-rearing practice among the English aristocracy in Shakespeare's day, as a result of which "it was not uncommon for the child to develop an attachment towards his nurse far deeper than that for his natural mother, whom he saw but rarely."[5] The relationship of mother and child took second place to those relationships of nurse to infant and attendant to child that advertised family status. Aristocratic child-rearing practices ratified the social and political rather than the biological and "natural" order.

Miranda's mother matters in the story Prospero is about to tell of their origins only as a pattern of chastity, guarantee of legitimate succession:

> Thy mother was a piece of virtue, and
> She said thou wast my daughter; and thy father
> Was Duke of Milan; and his only heir
> And princess, no worse issued.
>
> (I.ii.56–9)

Jonathan Goldberg has noted a similar fate of the mother in other representations of Stuart families. Masques and family portraits tell the same story: guaranteeing his lineage, "the patriarch absorbs female creativity."[6] For Prospero as Stuart patriarch to answer Miranda's question "Sir, are not you my father?" in this way only emphasizes, however, the uncertainty of paternity, hinging as it does upon the fidelity of the mother now present only in Prospero's memory. As Stephen Orgel has recently noted, "The legitimacy of Prospero's heir . . . derives from her mother's word." It is not so clear, however, that Prospero is "assured," as Orgel claims, of the word that is "all that is required of [Miranda's mother] in the play."[7] Once Prospero realizes Miranda has a memory, she has to be made to "remember" the same assurance that Prospero does. Prospero's reply attempts to unify and naturalize Miranda's socially realistic memory of several women care-takers by referring them back to one true biological mother, but he inevitably exposes at the same time the most vulnerable point in the social order's reference to biological nature: the lapse in time between conception and birth, like the lapse in time between Miranda's mother's words and Prospero's here, like the gap between the hands of husband and wife in Stuart family portraiture, all iterate "the gap between nature and power that political rhetoric transforms . . . the space in which patriarchal power is constructed, the space of the mystification of power."[8]

Miranda's education on the island, before the play begins, seems to have magically elided the difficulties of using nature as a prop to social order. In the absence of mothers or other women, Prospero has managed to teach Miranda the importance of chastity on his own; if she came to the island with an idea of sexual difference, presumably he sustained it, and he coaches Miranda when her theoretical knowledge fails to rise to a new occasion, correcting her pronouns from "it" to "he" and "him" in her first encounter with Ferdinand (I.ii.415). She hasn't much room for error in any case, since as Prospero arranges matters on the island all her first extra-familial objects are male. The legitimacy of her issue, the continuity of his line, will apparently be guaranteed by her rearing in which his watchfulness has been continuous and unchallenged. Why, then, do mother goddesses preside over the betrothal masque? Why attempt to fill a lack not felt?

In his essay on *Comus* C. L. Barber argues that "preserving chastity involves keeping a relation with what is not present: the chaste person is internally related to what is to be loved, even in its absence."[9] One difficulty in *Comus*, as we shall see, lies in deciding what the Lady's "it" is, what the source of her strength, what objects – familial or otherwise – she has internalized; her relation to pleasure will be constructed for her in her absence and retrospectively, by the Spirit's epilogue. In *The Tempest*, Prospero as educator is obliged to manipulate Miranda's "it" from the outset, but the meaning of what he accomplishes emerges retrospectively, in the light the interrupted masque casts back on Miranda's first interruption and then in the light that Act V sheds on the masque. At first, Prospero is the object loved and obeyed even in his absence, but his primacy must give way, his hests be broken, if Miranda is to marry. Prospero oversees Ferdinand's usurpation of his hitherto unchallenged place; oversees, that is, Miranda's resolution of her peculiar "Oedipal" situation, peculiar in the absence of the first, maternal, object. Miranda herself feels no lack, despite her dim memories in I.ii, and is, in a famous lacuna, quite prepared to forget even those ("I do not know / One of my sex; no woman's face remember, / Save, from my glass, mine own" (III.i.48–50)) once she is in love with Ferdinand, as if she were entering belatedly upon the amnesia that latency imposes upon childhood memories of desire. On the basis of this self-description, Miranda's unique education might in Lacanian terms be said to have produced a subject without an Imaginary register, never having come to possession of her sexed ideal image in the gaze of the mother. Perhaps, as Stephen Orgel argues, such psychoanalytic terminology reveals more about our time than about Shakespeare or his play; but it does point to something that would matter to a production of the play at any time, namely, the importance of Miranda's gaze (she does not speak) and of our watching her gaze during Prospero's masque. The genre in which Prospero will offer Miranda the specular mother invites comparison, in our time, to film theory; the masque would seem to be an "Imaginary signifier" *par excellence*, an allegorization of the ego in its most idealizing identifications.[10] There is a congruence between *what* Prospero would offer Miranda – a new internal relation, to recall Barber's comment on *Comus*, to the mother – and *how* he offers it, but the Imaginary stasis of the masque is at odds with the timing of *The Tempest*'s Oedipal drama. In Prospero's offered revision of Miranda's story, the first character in the drama – the mother – enters last, after the apparent resolution of the crisis, and seems called upon to shore up or supplement the weakened paternal image to which Miranda's chastity is still tied. The figures of the betrothal masque mythologize the biological mother around whom Prospero tried to center Miranda's disorganized memories in I.ii; remembering Miranda's interruption then, Prospero seeks to restore her to a complete Imaginary family, secure from interruptions, a continuous line. A restoration, as we have already seen, both too early (not yet secured from interruption) and hopelessly too late, since Miranda has not yet realized (will never realize) the incompleteness of the Imaginary family as she has known it, and already desires elsewhere.

The mother goddesses remind the couple of their vows "that no bed-right shall be paid / Till Hymen's torch be lighted" (IV.i.96–7), but also promise what Prospero never did in his own voice: fertility afterwards.

> *Juno:* Honour, riches, marriage-blessing,
> Long continuance, and increasing,
> Hourly joys be still upon you!
> Juno sings her blessings on you.
> *Ceres:* Earth's increase, foison plenty,
> Barns and garners never empty; . . .
> Scarcity and want shall shun you;
> Ceres' blessing so is on you.
>
> (IV.i.106–17)

Ceres reunited at last with her wandering daughter: Prospero's betrothal masque presents Miranda with a version of the "family reunion" that Milton will write in *Comus* and through which, says Barber, "Milton did, astonishingly enough, convert the masque to his high purposes."[11] But Prospero offers the mother (and, consequently, the daughter) in a form that Miranda seems unequipped to recognize. Her silence during the masque leaves doubtful what she makes of Prospero's images: could she ever internalize those objects? If, to borrow Barber's terms again, "preserving chastity involves keeping a relation with what is not present," could Miranda be "internally related" to the image of fruitful Ceres as to "what is to be loved, even in its absence;" could she take up her place in the masque's relations by recognizing herself as Proserpine? The interruption of the betrothal masque would seem symbolically to answer, no. The mother cannot so belatedly materialize into the daughter's presence at the behest of the father-image, nor can the father console himself for the loss of his daughter by representing to himself the complete Imaginary family of his memories. Miranda does not hear in the masque Prospero's oblique confession that he has been, in a sense, the Pluto of the myth, her "raptor," more complicit than she knows with Caliban's desires ("this thing of darkness I / Acknowledge mine," as Prospero will famously say in Act V).[12] The myth of Ceres and Proserpine apparently will not revise Miranda's understanding of Prospero's account of their origins.

Her imaginative failure redounds on her father, or fathers. The patriarchal magician's appropriation of procreative power fails at exactly the point when the mother's presence should have been literal rather than figurative, at the end of the masque. This failure adumbrates Prospero's promise to break and bury his staff, and is not to be ameliorated, moreover, by any recognition of the "biological facts" of procreation, by any turn to the natural succession in which the literal presences of both Miranda and Ferdinand will be equally necessary to procreation. Miranda's unresponsiveness to the maternal goddesses of the betrothal masque blocks such a turn. She "lacks lack," in the paradoxical Lacanian definition of femininity; in this case, Miranda lacks the capacity or desire to add the mother to her Imaginary family. Despite, or because of, her education into what we might be supposed to recognize as mature heterosexual love, she acquires an amnesia, a forgetfulness of other women she once knew; she has no queries to make about sexual difference as she prepares to leave the island. She knows better, in her final speech, than to call all these new people "its," she now recognizes the general masculine, in "mankind," but has no curiosity about where the women are. Her betrothal has settled all her questions about how to comport herself towards ambiguous strangers. She might as well be, as the stage scene has her, the only woman in the world. Her very lack of resistance towards her assimilation into the Symbolic order of exchange, ruled by the masculine signifier, brings castration into play for her father, since she not only represents the Phallus passed from him but she has passively resisted the nostalgia, or mythic recognition, he would have had her feel for her biological origins. Prospero and his wand can produce everything except the maternal body, but this symbolic castration only consolidates patriarchal authority in the society that Prospero's abdication of magical power prepares him to re-enter.

The ambivalent success of Prospero's art is precisely that Miranda as produced and brought into circulation among men does not need the maternal body. Procreativity, by its sojourn on the island and its relay through the Symbolic, by its very obedience to patriarchal imperatives, is thus discontinuous with itself; it is an impossible but necessary, a necessarily impossible, prop to the continuity of a male lineage. The myth of Ceres and Proserpine in *The Tempest* looks back to a regime of desire and reproduction that, by Miranda's belated testimony and the evidence of the masque, never was. Mothers and children in Jacobean England there were, yet Miranda as a character in a drama doesn't need one, indeed seems to act the better floating social signifier for not recognizing a mother. Prospero's masque retrospectively illuminates the magic of ideology, in the drama of which female sexuality as tied to procreation assumes the dubious materiality of shadow-show: a poetry of earth become a poetry of the underworld.

* * * * * * * * * * * * * *

Not with so much labour, as the fables have it, is Ceres said to have sought her daughter Proserpina as it is my habit day and night to seek for this idea of the beautiful, as for a certain image of supreme beauty, through all the forms and faces of things (for many are the shapes of things divine) and to follow it as it leads me on by some sure traces which I seem to recognize.

(Milton, Epist. 7)

Meanwhile the unhappy reader is in a quandary, as if at a crossroads, uncertain which way to turn and which road to take, while all around him the missiles fly so thick that they shut out the light and involve things in deep darkness. So, at last the reader is obliged to imitate the long suffering of Ceres and go searching with a lighted torch for truth through the whole wide world, and find it nowhere; until he is brought so close to insanity as to think that he is miserably blind because there is nothing that he can see.

(Prolusion 3)

The myth of Ceres and Proserpine in the betrothal masque of *The Tempest* temporarily disrupts Prospero's powerful illusions only to reinvest the patriarchal world bravely reconstituted under his direction with a surer (if more divided and social) command over the female body. In Milton's *Comus*, the same myth, extracted as a source of dis-ease from Prospero's masque, becomes a central myth of the origins rather than the ends of poetic careers. Milton's earlier writings figure in Ceres' quest for her daughter, the quest of the poet as belated and heroically tenacious reader, negotiating the mazes of scholastic error and the multiplicity of textual traces in pursuit of truth: Ceres as reformer. In *Comus*, Milton identifies himself not with the seeking mother, but with the lost daughter, whose trials in the underworld figure the poet as resisting reader in a new way.[13] Unlike Ceres, the daughter in *Comus* has to make a virtue of passive resistance rather than of the quest after truth. She repulses a Shakespearean literary heritage that is apparently invulnerable to Ceres' searching reformation. In what might seem another gesture of resistance by *ascesis* toward the Shakespearean heritage, the *Mask Presented at Ludlow Castle* outwardly restores the order of priority that Prospero's masque reversed: wandering children are presented to their parents, instead of the other way round. In the case of the Lady, however, what is rendered to the parents in her restoration looks in another light like usurpation. Milton's revision of Ceres and Proserpine in *Comus* does not simply surrender the powers either of the mother or of Shakespeare. Rather, the masque enacts an appropriation and elision of maternal powers which is comparable to Prospero's appropriation of maternal images, but which Milton's poem qualifies to different ends and with the aid of a "higher power," a legitimating father – in Spenser.

Milton's Lady undergoes the trials and temptations of Proserpine, save that after her abduction the Lady cannot be made to eat by force or by guile. Her abstinence is not, however, enough to free her, just as Proserpine could not leave the underworld even before she had broken her abstinence. But the Attendant Spirit himself is also not enough, nor is his disenchanting haemony enough in the hands of the Lady's two brothers. Like Prospero, but without his ambivalence, the Attendant Spirit seems to need to invoke a female mythological and quasi-maternal figure to ensure the daughter's disenchantment (from Prospero himself, from his successor Comus). Sabrina finally intervenes to free the Lady, more effectively than Ceres was able to intervene on behalf of Proserpine. Sabrina is more effective because the Lady's belated chastity is more willed, "armed," proleptically conscious of danger, than that of Proserpine, but also because Sabrina is not quite the Ceres of the myth, but the product of the way in which that myth subtly revises and supplements the brief history of Sabrina's origins in *The Faerie Queene.*

The Lady's two brothers allusively inaugurate the return of Spenser into Milton's text: "they smash the enchanter's cup, repeating in that action Guyon's rough treatment of 'Genius' before the Bower of Bliss."[14] The return of Spenser will disenchant the Lady and leave Milton free to acknowledge his purer literary parentage. But it is not sufficient for Spenser to return by allusion only; Milton writes a literal appearance, a translation or exchange of the female character out of Spenser's text and into his own. Milton's retelling of Sabrina's death omits the violent death of her mother by the river, and Sabrina's own illegitimacy.[15] Spenser's Sabrina becomes a figure of Proserpine in her own right: a "guiltless damsel, flying the mad pursuit / Of her enraged stepdam *Guendolen.*" Her stepmother would seem to threaten not necessarily violence alone, but a kind of sexual violation, when Sabrina "Commend[s] her innocence" – her chastity, we cannot help thinking, in this poem – "to the flood" (829–31).[16] There she undergoes a metamorphosis like those of the nymphs Cyane and Arethusa, witnesses in Ovid to Proserpine's fate; she becomes goddess of the Severn. As such Sabrina rescues virgins in distress, becoming a figure of Ceres, mother of her own former shape; a natural sequence, as daughters do become mothers, were it not that "she retains / Her maid'n gentleness" (842–3), emerging from the river perhaps "Likest . . . to *Ceres* in her Prime, / Yet Virgin of *Proserpina* from *Jove*" (*PL* IX.394–6). Milton's Sabrina purifies her own natural – that is, illegitimate – parentage in becoming her own virgin mother, and so purifies her other allusive origins in Shakespeare's myth of Ceres and Proserpine, the masque in *The Tempest.*

In *Comus'* revision of Spenser and the Ovidian myth, the unity of mother and daughter follows violence and violation, rather than preceding it; it is a reformed unity, the consequence of Ceres' labours and Proserpine's chastity. Women enter these border-woods around the Severn always already separated from their natural parents and in danger. The resolutions or fictions of continuity that their trials yield will always be marked by dislocations from natural origins in those fiction's figures of "natural" (legitimated) sequence, and this, I would argue, makes them more rather than less important to Milton's poetics. The French theorist Luce Irigaray,

reading Freud, has noted that in a culture in which women are exchanged –
and it is arguable that all cultures known to history have exchanged women
– women are denied the means of representing their own biological origins.
Fictions of natural continuity there may be, but not for her, who assumes
"the place of the repetition of the origin, of its reproduction, of
reproduction" only when grafted onto the family tree of a male outside her
own immediate family.[17] This exchange is the material base of the process
by which, as we have seen Jonathan Goldberg describe it in discussing
images of Stuart families, female (pro)creativity is appropriated to the
construction of patriarchal continuity across the gap between nature and
culture. The woman as a floating social signifier detached from her own
biological origins (as we described Miranda earlier) is taxed at one and the
same time with conserving that all-important gap between nature and
culture and with ensuring culture's biological continuity. This double social
role gives representations of women a charged role in literary history, which
has its own local struggles for both continuity and gaps or saving divisions.
The exchange of female types or characters between and within literary
texts authored by men is one mode of the appropriation of women's
represented (pro)creativity that mediates, for Milton, his relation to nature,
to his precursors, and to politics at large, most powerfully in his contention
with his most threateningly "natural" precursor, Shakespeare.[18]

In this light we can begin to understand the Attendant Spirit's apparent
insufficiency, his need to borrow Sabrina from an earlier text, and the
persistent power of Ovidian metamorphoses in Milton's text. Comus
threatens the refusing Lady with a literary precursor:

> Nay Lady, sit; if I but wave this wand,
> Your nerves are all chain'd up in Alabaster,
> And you a statue; or as *Daphne* was,
> Root-bound, that fled *Apollo*.
>
> (659–62)

The inappropriateness of Comus' allusion lies in his using chastity's
classical defense as a threat *against* the Lady's chastity. Milton perceives, of
course, the equivocal nature of this "defense:" the maiden's change of form
may forestall violation but is itself a violation. The disruption of women's
fiction of continuity is sure in either case, whether by rapture or
transfiguration, both variations on legitimate exchanges of women. Milton
wants chastity to find better defenses in *Comus*, but so long as the chastity
defending itself is female the Ovidian metamorphosis will remain a threat,
because that chastity is an exchange value whose end is ever to be figured
and transfigured.

Sabrina's intervention quite literally incorporates the threat of metamorphosis and transforms it into a "cure," her own version of haemony
that is a less rowdy and disruptive defense of chastity than that the brothers
offer. Called by the Attendant Spirit to "Listen and save," she replies:

33

> Shepherd 'tis my office best
> To help ensnared chastity;
> Brightest Lady look on me,
> Thus I sprinkle on thy breast
> Drops that from my fountain pure
> I have kept of precious cure,
> Thrice upon thy finger's tip,
> Thrice upon thy rubied lip;
> Next this marble venom'd seat
> Smear'd with gums of glutinous heat
> I touch with chaste palms moist and cold.
> (908–18)

The "cure" is part and parcel of her fluid, metamorphosed body; Sabrina *is* "her fountain pure," her self and her origin identical and self-continuous since her immortal change. Called upon to "Listen and save," she touches and saves the Lady out of her own "fountain pure." No one else in the masque, to judge from stage directions and dialogue, is required to touch the Lady. If Comus and his rout do so in imprisoning her, we are spared the sight of it. Her touch is of course very nearly ethereal, but it is touch nevertheless, visible, real, and transformative, in contrast or supplement to the masque's prevailing summons to *listen* and save, or the Elder Brother's vision of the body's transfiguration by light (459ff.).[19] In rivalry with Shakespeare's masque, Milton ironically proclaims his ability to produce the body, on his stage, of a purified Ceres figure, here potent to bring her chaste daughter up out of the underworld. Mother and daughter in their allusive situation, not by natural procreativity, they can touch as they cannot on Prospero's "stage."

Or rather, Sabrina can touch the Lady (metonymically, via her own watery body – the "Drops" – and the Lady's chair). The Lady herself does not yet command her body and does not, in Milton's stage directions, rise out of her seat until after Sabrina has descended. Sabrina is therefore not among the masquers led out or "produced" at the end, and Milton like Shakespeare ends his drama with only one female character in view, and that female character silent. The female maternal body in Comus, once produced, can be made to disappear at Milton's will, and the Lady herself, given temporary control of her body, loses her power of speech. The Lady is "restored" to her proper allusive mode at the masque's end: the silent presence of her allusive body; restored, after "Listen and save," to a place in which she can be silent and safe, her father's house. The Attendant Spirit refers to the father directly for the first time in the masque only after Sabrina has descended and the Lady risen from Comus' chair. Only after the Spirit has demonstrated his mastery over the female body risen through the agency of a trans-natural speaking maternal body is the father's presence acknowledged openly (though the father has been there all along, in the audience to the masque). This accomplished, his leading the Lady across the boundary between stage and audience to present her to her natural parents quite patently does construct patriarchal authority across a gap between nature and culture via the exchange of women's (properly silent) bodies.

The circuit of exchange is closed in this case, unlike Milton's sources in Spenser and *The Tempest*, since Milton's Spirit pointedly renders to the Lady's father exactly what he gave up; his daughter returns "tried" but unchanged. Milton's art owes nothing to nature or culture that it cannot repay. The masque's corresponding fiction of literary borrowings would see them as a closed exchange, the next best thing to originality, or originality itself. And indeed there is a sense in which Milton does close his exchange with Spenser. Borrowing Sabrina's character bodily and under her proper name (rather than allusively), yet effacing the illegitimacy of the story of her origins in Spenser, Milton causes her to disappear from his text with the legitimacy of her literary parentage enhanced. But what of *Comus'* borrowings from Shakespeare?

In the exchange of women as organized under patriarchy, the parent who has no proprietary rights (no proper name) in the daughter, to whom nothing is owed, is of course the mother. Shakespeare, strangely enough, occupies this place in the resolution of Milton's masque. If Sabrina's departure from Milton's text is an acknowledgement, on the one hand, of a pure, legitimate, continuous and closed literary tradition as represented by Spenser, the same event on the other hand alludes to but elides the parent whose presence in Sabrina is evident on several levels but to whom nothing is owed, Shakespeare.[20] The archaic underworld of Milton's masque is thereby figured as Spenserian, not Shakespearean, and its ruler as a benevolent father (who allows Sabrina to leave the underworld in defense of virginity) rather than a raptor. The powerful contact between the Lady and Sabrina of daughter and virgin mother defends against the unruly "maternal" line of descent from Shakespeare and so prefaces the masque's return to patriarchal order, the patriarchal organization of biological origins that literally sat in audience to the historical performance of Milton's masque.

The Attendant Spirit sees to this return, handing back the children to their father and delivering an epilogue. Overseeing the restoration and exchange of women throughout the masque, he neither gives them nor receives them in his proper person. Indeed, he is among the characters in the masque who have no "proper person," since, like Comus and the anti-masquers, perhaps like Sabrina herself, he was not played by a noble person.[21] Like Prospero's Ceres, he cannot be revealed or produced, and in handing the Lady over to her father, he takes over Sabrina/Ceres' circumscribed maternal power. In Lacanian terms, he is representative of the Phallus itself, overseer of exchange, standard of value. Milton's masque, unlike *The Tempest*, separates a representation of the phallus from both the exchangeable, fetishized daughter and her biological father. The Attendant Spirit's command over female sexuality, reproduction, and time itself is thus more absolute than Prospero's, who however obliquely has to acknowledge his desire for both his wife and his daughter. His power – unlike the Lady's and Miranda's chastity which is handed over for use in the world outside the masque, unlike Prospero's power which pays the price for reconstituting a patriarchal world – symbolically stands apart from these social relations even as it makes a triumphant revisionary entrance into literary history.[22] His epilogue is relatively autonomous (or, as Angus Fletcher would put it, "transcendent") with respect to the masque's occasion and its closure upon patriarchally organized biological and political relations, as Milton's additions to the masque's published version of 1637 make clear. In the performance of 1634, the Attendant Spirit closed the masque's exchanges with political reality; the Spirit's supplemented epilogue of 1637 simultaneously opens and closes the masque's exchanges with its literary precursors.

As Guillory and others have noted,[23] Shakespeare returns in the Spirit's last lines, through echoes of and allusions to both *A Midsummer Night's Dream* and *The Tempest*:

> *Spirit*: Back Shepherds, back, enough your play,
> Till next Sun-shine holiday;
> Here be without duck or nod
> Other trippings to be trod
> Of lighter toes
>
> (958–62)

In the first echo, Milton himself, as his own precursor, defends himself against Ariel's "tripping on his toe" (*The Tempest*, IV.i.46) with "L'Allegro"'s

> Come, and trip it as ye go
> On the light fantastic toe.
> (33–4)

Like Sabrina, Milton as his own precursor in the Spirit's epilogue is both parent and child of himself, occupying a place of origin that Guillory calls "both early and *now*" – early, thanks to the acknowledged father in Spenser.[24] Milton and Sabrina inhabit two times at once; neither premature nor belated, but at once blissfully early and blessedly late, happy in both instances because in the middle is Sabrina's mother's sin and her own illegitimate birth, and Milton's questionable Elizabethan heritage, the heritage recuperated in part (with the Lady as Proserpine/Miranda released), repressed in part (with Sabrina's descent and the Lady's silence) as

Milton exploits his ability to produce and repress the female body on the masque's stage.

Extending his command of what is "both early and *now*," Milton banishes the shepherds of his own masque and the mingled dance of reapers and nymphs at the end of *The Tempest*'s masque with echoes of Ben Jonson's "Up, youths and virgins, Up and praise / The God whose nights outshine his days" (the Haddington masque), deferring with assurance these betrothal celebrations in favor of a purer dance. The casual association of Jonson and Shakespeare in the shepherds' dismissal puts the past of the Jacobean courtly masque with its ducks and nods firmly in its place, the transcended past.[25] In comparison to Milton's prospective stance in the Spirit's epilogue, Jonson's and Shakespeare's masques are not only *past* in fact but in essence. The interruption of Prospero's masque looks backward in time to reveal the inadequacy of the present with respect to the past rather than the future. The "present" of the end of Jonson's masques, their machinery and political occasion, is irrevocably past in their published form; Jonson's added comments in publication, unlike the Spirit's supplemented epilogue, only emphasize the intrinsic belatedness of the masque's "presence," both political and poetic.

The Attendant Spirit's echoes and allusions, then, evade the belatedness of their condition by looking both further back and further forward than Shakespeare or his younger brother Jonson. Their present is less fortunate than Spenser's and Milton's blissful earliness and blessed lateness. In the epilogue's second echo of *The Tempest*, Ariel's "Where the bee sucks, there suck I" (V.i.88) contends with Spenser's garden.

> *Spirit*: To the Ocean now I fly,
> And those happy climes that lie
> Where day never shuts his eye,
> Up in the broad fields of the sky:
> There I suck the liquid air
> All amidst the Gardens fair
> Of *Hesperus*
>
> (976–82)

Here, I believe, is the last contextual engagement with *The Tempest*'s betrothal masque. Although the language itself is borrowed from *A Midsummer Night's Dream*, the characters, like Iris a few lines above, enter from *The Tempest*'s stage as well:

> on the ground
> Sadly sits th'*Assyrian* Queen;
> But far above in spangled sheen
> Celestial *Cupid* her fam'd son advanc't,
> Holds his dear *Psyche* sweet entranc't

After her wand'ring labors long,
Till free consent the gods among
Make her his eternal Bride,
And from her fair unspotted side
Two blissful twins are to be born,
Youth and Joy; so *Jove* hath sworn.

(1001–11)

Venus (the "*Assyrian* Queen") and her "scandal'd" son Cupid were excluded from the company of chaste masquers in *The Tempest*, and both retired in defeat, to the relief of Ceres:

Ceres: Tell me, heavenly bow,
If Venus or her son, as thou dost know,
Do now attend the queen? Since they did plot
The means that dusky Dis my daughter got,
Her and her blind boy's scandal'd company
I have forsworn.

Iris: Of her society
Be not afraid: I met her deity
Cutting the clouds towards Paphos, and her son
Dove-drawn with her. Here thought they to have done
Some wanton charm upon this man and maid,
Whose vows are, that no bed-right shall be paid
Till Hymen's torch be lighted: but in vain;
Mars's hot minion is return'd again;
Her waspish-headed son has broke his arrows,
Swears he will shoot no more, but play with sparrows,
And be a boy right out.

(*The Tempest*, IV.i.86–101)

The united chastity of Ferdinand and Miranda is even more powerful against Cupid than that of the "imperial votaress" in *A Midsummer Night's Dream* (II.i) in that Cupid's arrows do not just glance aside "quenched," but are destroyed by their author. Milton takes Shakespeare's Jacobean revision of his Elizabethan *Dream* a step further. Venus is still withdrawn at the end of Milton's masque, but he has rehabilitated Cupid dramatically. In so doing, Milton opens a new possibility for the Lady (the better to witness to his own revisionary powers): translated to the skies, she may wander as Psyche, not as Proserpine, and in this poem may win what Ceres argues vainly in the *Metamorphoses* her own daughter deserves, a husband "by free consent the gods among." Not that she gains in freedom or voice thereby; in this final tableau of the legitimate exchange of women, the Lady/Psyche's desire, her "it," is taken as already constructed, part of a *prior* story (Milton's, Spenser's, Apuleius') as revised by the Spirit's *belated* epilogue. Wedged between what's past (temptation, metamorphosis, myth) and what's prologue (to legitimate procreation and a reformed tradition), the Lady's relation to her own sexuality, like Miranda's to her mother, has no representable present moment, only a subordinate stake in the Spirit's beginnings. The Lady's earlier power of speech *vis-à-vis* Comus, as David Norbrook among others has argued, rewrites "courtly stereotypes" of "ideal female behavior" in a feminist direction,[26] but the Spirit stands ready to reappropriate these revisions for male authority in the political as well as the literary realm.

Unlike Prospero, the Spirit has the needed "higher power" of prospectively designating the Lady's desire without ever having to be its object. This phallic power renders the Lady's silence at the end of *Comus* unproblematic as Miranda's during the masque was not; her presence is not required at this Symbolic tableau in the same way Miranda's is at Prospero's Imaginary celebration. The Spirit's internalization, in the 1637 text, of the earlier masque's tableau forestalls the need to ask whether or not the Lady's silence means she can internalize these images. She and the Spirit, unlike Miranda and Prospero, inhabit different worlds. Neither the Lady's silence nor her gaze signifies in the Spirit's epilogue; they are not parts of the masque as published in the way that Miranda's silence and her gaze must be part of any performance of *The Tempest* (even, I would argue, a performance in the study). In this fully Symbolic word-scene (or, in Fletcher's terms, this achieved "transcendental form"), the mother-daughter bond no longer needs even to be invoked as a prop to the Lady's desire or to the insertion of that desire into a patriarchal order of continuity. A mother is indeed present in the Spirit's account, to be turned from or transcended, but (as in Luce Irigaray's account of femininity) Venus is not Psyche's biological mother but her mother-in-law. Psyche turns Cupid away from his mother and so breaks *Comus'* disruptive Shakespearean mother-son line of descent. The mother-son dyad or phallic mother resolves itself into Venus mourning (rather than, as in Spenser, enjoying) her wounded young lover, while Cupid and Psyche prospectively inaugurate a newly legitimate tradition of sons.

Milton's deployment of the female body exchanged, translated, metamorphosed from and through prior texts thus ensures that his prospective stance in the epilogue is as powerful as it needs must be against his naturalized precursor, Shakespeare. The *Mask Presented at Ludlow Castle*, although formally closed as Prospero's could not be, maintains a posture of openness in the end by virtue of the very strength of its defenses against *The Tempest* and its interrupted masque, the story of which defenses can be read in brief in the epilogue's substitution of the myth of Psyche and Cupid for that of Ceres and Proserpine. To these defensive substitutions the mobility of the feminine as signifier is as important as the Lady's rigid chastity, and as much a prerequisite of Milton's selective continuity of poetic parentage. Prospero's abortive evocation of Ceres' and Proserpine's poetry of earth contributes a share to the shifting grounds of Milton's prospective power.

Notes

1. John Guillory, *Poetic Authority: Spenser, Milton, and Literary History* (New York, Columbia University Press, 1983), ch. 4.
2. For Guillory, Miltonic poems in general, and not only *Comus*, participate in an interior dialogue. "The poem as a 'succession of voices' suggests an analogy to literary history, which, if it can be said to have an intelligible structure, might be understood as poets talking and listening to one another" (Guillory, op. cit., 68). The disposition of bodies, particularly women's bodies, I will argue, sustains this play of (men's) voices in Milton's drama.
3. The phrase is William Kerrigan's. See *The Sacred Complex: On the Psychogenesis of Paradise Lost* (Cambridge, Mass., Harvard University Press, 1983), ch. 2, for an extended and very interesting psychoanalytic discussion of the relations between Milton's masque and the poet's superego. I will contend that there is a relationship between that masque of the male (understood) superego and what I will call the "Imaginary" tableau of Shakespeare's masque of mothers, watched by the Oedipal daughter.
4. Frank Kermode (ed.), *The Tempest*, Arden Shakespeare (London, Methuen, 1954, rpt. 1979), 103. All further citations from *The Tempest* are from this edition.
5. Lawrence Stone, *The Crisis of the Aristocracy* (London, Oxford University Press, 1965), 592.
6. Jonathan Goldberg, *James I and the Politics of Literature* (Baltimore, Johns Hopkins University Press, 1983), 99.
7. Stephen Orgel, "Prospero's wife" (*Representations*, 8, 1984, 1). Orgel himself later undermines this supposed initial assurance, noting Prospero's difficulty in imagining good mothers.
8. Goldberg, op. cit., 99. Mary O'Brien, in *The Politics of Reproduction* (London, Routledge & Kegan Paul, 1981), speculates on the far-reaching significance of the uncertainty and temporal alienation of paternity for male philosophy in general.
9. C. L. Barber, "*A Mask Presented at Ludlow Castle*: the masque as a masque," in *Comus and Samson Agonistes: A Casebook*, ed. Julian Lovelock (London, Macmillan, 1975), 95.
10. Christian Metz's *The Imaginary Signifier*, tr. B. Brewster (Bloomington, Indiana University Press, 1981), uses this phrase in an attempt to account for the complexity of the cinema as a mode of representation: at once an image, an object, and a signifier functioning in and with language and received by a subject in language. Prospero's masque, I would argue, shares this complexity, the more so as it is seen and heard by one audience on stage and quite a different audience offstage, which second audience is privy to some of the reactions of the first. (Admittedly I am begging an important question, that of the difference between an élite and a mass form, in comparing these two "imaginary signifiers.")
11. Barber, op. cit., 89.
12. A confession comparable to Prospero's admission in that he was negligent as a ruler, "being transported / And rapt in secret studies" (I.ii.76–7). Orgel argues in "Prospero's wife" that if Prospero can't imagine good mothers, "the other side of the assumption that all women at heart are whores" is that "all men at heart are rapists – Caliban, Ferdinand, and of course that means Prospero too" (6). While I would agree that Prospero learns to acknowledge something of this kinship, it matters to note that these male characters have at their disposal vastly

40

different powers of representing and acting on their desires; "all men" is not a class brought together by simple agglutination, but by the hierarchy Prospero structures. Prospero can represent his desire in the masque, but also, in a sense, in Caliban, who enjoys no reciprocal privilege *vis-à-vis* Prospero.

13. See Kerrigan, op. cit., 42–4 for a psychoanalytic reading of Milton's "double identification" with the Elder Brother and the Lady as, respectively, the knight and lady of quest romance. In the prose passages I have cited, Ceres is the "knight:" the more archaic (as Freud might have said) version of the quest plot? This doubling of the woman points, I think, to a less intrapsychic or even intrafamilial reading than Kerrigan's of Milton's identifications in *Comus*.

14. Guillory, op. cit., 89.

15. Angus Fletcher discusses Milton's transformation of Sabrina's sources in detail, arguing that his "alterations . . . decrease the sense that Sabrina is the victim of personal envy and increase the weight of her sacrificial innocence." *The Transcendental Masque: An Essay on Milton's Comus* (Ithaca and London, Cornell University Press, 1971), 240. See also 245–7, on Milton's suppression of "the myth of the terrible mother."

16. *John Milton: Complete Poems and Major Prose*, ed. Merritt Y. Hughes (New York, Odyssey, 1957), 109. All further Milton citations in the text will be to this edition. Guendolen recalls Pluto's part in the Greek myth, as well as the doubled raptors, Caliban and Prospero, in *The Tempest*.

17. "Elle sera le lieu de la répétition de l'origine, de sa re-production, de la reproduction. Non qu'elle répète ainsi 'son' topos originel, 'son' origine." Luce Irigaray, "La tâche aveugle d'un vieux rêve de symétrie," in *Speculum, de l'autre femme* (Paris, Editions de Minuit, 1974), 45. That all cultures, including matrilineal ones, exchange women is the conclusion of Juliet Mitchell in *Psychoanalysis and Feminism* (New York, Pantheon Books 1974, rpt 1975) and many other feminist theorists following the work of Levi-Strauss. Gayle Rubin, however, usefully insists upon the dangers of such generalization. See "The traffic in women," in *Towards an Anthropology of Women*, ed. Rayna R. Reiter (New York, Monthly Review Press, 1975), 157–210. If patriarchy, culture, and the exchange of women are not everywhere and in the same way synonymous, still this paradigm seems applicable, at any rate, to the vicissitudes of patriarchal ideology in Stuart England.

18. Milton naturalized Shakespeare as a precursor in two related senses: by denying him premeditated artfulness (Shakespeare of the "native Wood-notes wild," "L'Allegro," 134), and by associating Shakespeare with a maternal and Elizabethan line of poetic descent, motherhood being the "natural" parental relation whereas fatherhood is the construct of culture.

19. Kerrigan reads Sabrina's cure psychobiographically as the product of a reaction formation that "reproduces the defensive ethics epitomized by the anal child." "Sabrina consecrates the act of eating," he argues; "*Her ritual of undoing implies that the Lady, having figuratively drunk the potion of her tempter, is guilty*" (Kerrigan, op. cit., 46, 47, 48; his italics).

20. Fletcher stresses that Sabrina must "be rendered as royally as possible" (Fletcher, op. cit., 238). Might we compare her to the Virgin Queen, Elizabeth, whose access to power was kept at the price of her sexuality?

21. In his article "The setting of *Comus*," John Creaser argues that Sabrina's "part cannot have been taken by an aristocrat, since her name is not recorded on the title-page. The suggestion that she was played by Lady Penelope Egerton fails to do justice to Milton's originality: here decisive power is no longer wielded by social eminence" (David Lindley (ed.), *The Court Masque* (Manchester, Manchester University Press, 1984), 127). Creaser persuasively connects this to

his general argument that *Comus* is a "recuperation" or "reformation" of the masque (130). I agree that Milton's "originality" is gained against "social eminence" as well as against literary history, but wish to focus on the role of representations of women in this widened definition of originality, since the "human limitation" Creaser sees Milton inserting into the masque limits women and men differently.

22. As Fletcher eloquently puts it, "In both cases [the *Aeneid* and *Comus*] we are dealing with a deep irony in the culture bringer's passion. What he loves is never to be directly his, since to possess the loved object would be to destroy it; it can only be his if it is reflected, recreated, resonated" (Fletcher, op. cit., 187). What I would wish to emphasize is Fletcher's gendered pronouns. Male access to power in this "social system of mutual dependence, obligation, and even entrapment" is indeed fraught with ironies; it is also contingent upon the exchange of "'women and language – between men'" (Fletcher, op. cit., 235; he quotes E. M. Mendelson). Power's "transcendental forms" foster and are fostered by social relations, those of certain women and men, also those of male poets with each other.

23. Guillory, op. cit., 91–3. See also John M. Major, "*Comus* and *The Tempest*" (*Shakespeare Quarterly*, 10, 1959, 177–83), and Ethel Seaton, "*Comus* and Shakespeare" (*Essays and Studies by Members of the English Association*, 31, 1945, 68–80).

24. Guillory, op. cit., 93.

25. For an extended discussion of *Comus* as a "reformation" of the Jonsonian masque and its relations to the Caroline court, see David Norbrook, *Poetry and Politics in the English Renaissance* (London, Routledge & Kegan Paul, 1984), ch. 10: "The politics of Milton's early poetry."

26. Norbrook, op. cit., 252. Norbrook persuasively connects the Lady's voice with women's claims to prophetic authority in radical Protestantism of the day (258). While I have discussed the women of *Comus* only in relation to a literary history, I think the problem of reappropriation crosses boundaries between literary, religious, and political history.

3

CHRISTOPHER KENDRICK

Milton and sexuality: a symptomatic reading of *Comus*

When one speaks of the sexual politics of a writer's work, this usually implies that the relation between the work's political meaning and its tacit recommendations about sexuality is a relation, not simply of intimacy, but of near unity, because sexuality is quintessentially political, and vice versa. Such an assumption can easily lead, the personal being the political where sex is concerned, to an essentially ethical criticism, which examines the sexual attitudes of an author as reflected in his characters, and then, by a simple allegorical operation, reads in this stance the sign of a whole politics. In view of this tendency, it is perhaps best to begin a sexual–political reading by hypothesizing that sexuality and politics are quite different "things," and are governed by discrete orders of social determination, however concretely intertwined they may be. If one comes to Milton's work with this assumption, then one of the main problems for analysis will be how a sexual politics of Milton's poems is *possible*. And the assumption tends to dictate, already, that the solution to this problem be framed in terms of some relationship of intersection, some determination at a distance, between sexuality and politics, which might well take the form of a relation among posited contexts, or discrete levels, in the poems analyzed.

Thus this paper on Milton's *Comus* moves from a psychoanalytic reading, which operates in the essentially biographical context of what is sometimes called the young Milton's *chastity cult*; to a politico-cultural reading, set in the context of what Foucault calls the history of sexuality, in which the chastity cult appears no longer as a biographical phenomenon but as a political statement and instrument of control, as generalized sexuality; to a socio-economic reading, in which the chastity cult and generalized sexuality appear under the aspect of the reification imposed by emergent

43

capitalism, and the conditions of possibility of the confluence of sexual and political messages are clarified.

But it would be a mistake to turn to this agenda without first noting the ideological element in which the movement of the object of analysis just referred to takes place, and which stands as the initial structural precondition of any Miltonic sexual politics: I refer to religion, the continuing if crisis-ridden dominant in seventeenth-century culture. If there exists a genre of tenable universal-historical propositions, then surely the following would be among the least scandalous: first, that religion strives in its very form to be a "totalizing system," in so far as it is posited for its community as a series of rituals and an ethics as well as a metaphysic of belief; and second, that, being such a totalizing system, religion has it as one of its main duties to legislate the sex-drive, or what Freud called, in its modern incarnation, the libido. It follows from this last that any religious project of consequence is likely to possess, for us, a legible libidinal component, and to offer itself to description in terms of a libidinal politics.

Thus it is at any rate with Protestantism, and with the all-inclusive Protestant sin of *idolatry*.[1] For Protestant attacks on idolatry may without difficulty be read in a vulgar Freudian way, so that the sin of idolatry (Catholicism) becomes a disease of the unruly libido, and the Protestant virtue of faith, correspondingly, a restrained state of libidinal health. Not that Protestantism denies desire, far from it: rather it accuses Catholicism of multiplying false object-ties, of sating desire by sticking it everywhere. Against this, Protestantism minimizes object-ties, nourishing desire through repression; it insists upon the primacy of libido itself.

If such a rewriting of the Protestant program is misguided, that is not because of the equation this rewriting draws between religious and sexual "dispositions." The problem is rather that in making the translation it is all too easy to imbed the campaign against idols in some – motivating – private sphere of personal belief, and to understand it as a strictly ethical or socially irrational project. We thus forget that in a social formation in which religion is hegemonically *institutionalized* in the church, any such libidinal campaign will also involve, necessarily and immediately, a political project, and may indeed be quite specific in its institutional import.[2] The confluence of libidinal and political meanings is partly what is meant when religion is referred to as the dominant ideology, or master code, of Milton's society.

It's in this context, in relation to the dominance of religion as an ideology, that my own initial allegorical reading, in section I of what follows, is historically justified. For in so far as religion is dominant, it works in terms of a confluence of messages; it is by definition an overcoded, or *allegorical*, medium. A brief consideration of the "Nativity Ode" will give an idea of how such allegory may be grasped, and will have the additional advantage of providing a historical context in which to read *Comus*, since as we have often been told, it is in the "Nativity Ode" that Milton makes his poetic

44

entrance onto the historical stage. I need only comment here upon the significance of the ode's attack on idolatry, which takes the form of the Herculean infant Christ's metaphorical cleansing of the Augean stables, his expropriation of the "peculiar" pagan gods, in the poem's latter half. This attack conveys a clear message to the Christian reliving Christ's birth and infancy in the present (*c.* 1629–30): there was a time when idols were in their way legitimate; but that time is now past. With Christ's advent (into history, on the present Christmas day), the good Christian should begin the process of stripping the affections of all sensuous ties, of actively purging the soul of all spontaneous natural habitants. As Richard Halpern has shown, such an aggressive asceticism is required to supplement the more humble and peaceable stance evoked by Christ's imminence in the hymn's first part. By providing excess desire with a sadistic outlet, Herculean anti-idolatry rescues an otherwise psychically inadequate Christian humility.[3]

Once the libidinal message of the attack is grasped, a moment's reflection discloses within it a definite, if implicit, institutional meaning. Christ's coming leaves no question as to the possibility of following a pacific or relatively sedentary middle way within the church collective. Christmas may be the time for peace; but in this poem, peace is finally defined in terms of aggressive and continuous reformation. So much for the notion of an English church as an accomplished entity; so much for Anglicanism. Yet I would argue that the political message goes deeper, and is more historically specific than this, amounting finally to something like a Puritan call to arms. You can grasp this historical allegory if you note that the transitivistic time-structure of the poem (according to which what happens in 0 BC also happens in 1629) requires an equivalent of the Augustan Peace to be located in the present. What can this be if not the Elizabethan moment, characterized as it was by Catholicism's defeat externally, and by politico-religious compromise and cultural splendor internally? When we remember, next, that 1629 marked the point at which, with Charles I's decision to rule on his own and to aristocratize the kingdom, the Elizabethan compromise was definitively sundered, the "Nativity Ode"'s attack on the idolatry of the present acquires a yet more precise significance: the Elizabethan compromise is behind us, and idolatry accordingly outdated; the kingdom requires cleansing; full-scale reformation is again the order of the day.

Milton's enactment of his own poetic nativity coincides with the cryptic allegorical birth of a collective project, a project that may quite properly be described in libidinal–political terms. It should be evident that the fusion of poetic and collective projects, and the very existence of a sexual–political poetic of consequence, are made possible, in the "Nativity Ode" and in Milton's life, by the dominance of religion in his ideological formation. Early Protestantism, and its primary "ideologeme" of idolatry – this is the allegorical element which virtually forces libidinal and political objects to fuse. This is thus likewise the element which must automatically be submitted to analysis if the discrete orders of experience determining Milton's sexual politics are to be understood in their textual complexity.

I

Yet in *Comus*, as in the other great minor poems – "L'Allegro–Il Penseroso" and *Lycidas* – we must in a certain sense *construct* the religious element; for these works are not explicitly Christian poems, but are rather themselves more or less allegorical in relation to the master code that Christianity constitutes. The "more or less" should be taken literally: these early poetic narratives are variably distant from the religious code, and such distance is itself significant. But even where, as in "L'Allegro–Il Penseroso," the poem attempts to be opaque in relation to religious doctrine, to be anti-allegorical in the sense in which I am employing the term, still the religious system remains as an ultimate semantic horizon. And the full word of these narratives can only be fathomed through the attempt to interpret its links to that horizon.

We don't have to wait long to know what the crucial linking term will be in the case of *Comus*. The masque's protagonist provides it in her first speech. Swamped in the dark wood, troubled by Comus' doubtful after-images, the Lady counters by calling up the allegories of the Christian virtues, thereby almost dropping the classical–allegorical framework of the poem. If classical decorum is preserved, indeed, it is because chastity, and not charity, is the greatest of these. The Lady sees, we surmise, chiefly by the bodily lamp of chastity:[4]

> A thousand fantasies
> Begin to throng into my memory
> Of calling shapes, and beckning shadows dire,
> And airy tongues, that syllable mens names
> On Sands, and Shoars, and desert Wildernesses.
> These thoughts may startle well, but not astound
> The vertuous mind, that ever walks attended
> By a strong siding champion Conscience. –––––––
> O welcom pure ey'd Faith, white-handed Hope,
> Thou hovering Angel girt with golden wings,
> And thou unblemish't form of Chastity,
> I see ye visibly, and now beleeve
> That he, the Supreme good, t'whom all things ill
> Are but as slavish officers of vengeance,
> Would send a glistring Guardian if need were
> To keep my life and honour unassail'd.
>
> (pp. 84–5)

If Milton had given his masque a proper name, he might well have called it the Masque ot Chastity, for that is clearly its principal theme, the conceptual hinge of its allegorical device. As *Comus'* theme, chastity is hardly so singular as it might seem to a modern reader; and that, as Maryann McGuire has well shown, for two reasons. It is in relation to these reasons, which are really political contexts, that one can see the overt sexual politics of Milton's masque take shape.

First, chastity was a privileged theme of the court masque when *Comus* was written. One of Charles' postparliamentary renovations at court was a Platonic love cult, centered upon the figure of marital virtue he cut with the Catholic Henrietta Maria; several Caroline masques attempted to translate this ill-fated exemplary couple into a chaste ideal with affective force.[5] Even if she was played by the daughter of a court appointee, Milton's Lady exists partly in order to differentiate true chastity from this exotic idol.

Second, chastity was not unknown as a cardinal Christian virtue: the Lady's triad of faith, hope, and chastity in fact represents a specifically non-Anglican, strong Protestant canon. Charity, the social virtue of the original triad, had been made into an argument for conformity by Elizabethan Anglicanism. In this context, to substitute chastity for charity was to make charity into a stoic or self-sufficient, nonconformist virtue.[6] Thus the Lady's sexual integrity is as anti-Anglican as it is anti-Caroline.

We will have completed an initial, and quite important, stage in the decoding of the poem's allegory when we point out that in Puritan ideology both these explanatory contexts – Caroline chastity and Anglican charity – could readily be cast as versions or symptoms of the same thing, namely Catholicism or idolatry. Already at this stage we can see the way to a sexual–political reading of the masque narrative compatible with that we gave the "Nativity Ode:" Milton symbolically attacks the political love-theology of the Caroline masque and reforms it in light of the quite different libidinal politics of a left-leaning Protestantism.[7] If this reading is unacceptable as a final reading, that is not because it is wrong but because it is incomplete. It accounts well enough for the selection of the theme of chastity; but it accounts less satisfactorily for the specific form taken by the masque narrative, for the *fable* of chastity. I refer especially here to the turning-point of the masque's plot and to the questions that this perennial critical problem-spot raises about the nature of the Lady's integrity. Why is the Lady fixed in her chair? Why does she require the assistance of Sabrina? Why is she silent after being freed?

It would seem that these questions might best be answered, at least initially, in psychobiographical terms. Milton criticism has long recognized the weight of empirical evidence in favor of a psychological approach to the masque. Consider, for example, the Lady's final words of the published work:

> Shall I go on?
> Or have I said anough? To him that dares

Arm his profane tongue with Contemptuous words
Against the Sun-clad power of Chastity,
Fain would I somthing say, yet to what end?
Thou hast nor Eare, nor Soul to apprehend
The sublime notion, and high mystery
That must be utter'd to unfold the sage
And serious doctrine of Virginity,
And thou art worthy that thou shouldst not know
More happines then this thy present lot.
Enjoy your dear Wit, and gay Rhetorick
That hath so well been taught her dazling fence,
Thou art not fit to hear thy self convinc't;
Yet should I try, the uncontrouled worth
Of this pure cause would kindle my rap't spirits
To such a flame of sacred vehemence,
That dumb things would be mov'd to sympathize,
And the brute Earth would lend her nerves, and shake,
Till all thy magick structures rear'd so high,
Were shatter'd into heaps o're thy false head.

(pp. 109–10)

Lady Alice Egerton never spoke these lines: their faith in the Orphic power conferred by virginity was perhaps felt to exceed the demands of the masque's occasion. I assume that their addition in the version of the masque that was to enter the early Milton's "canon" (the 1645 poems) would have made more obvious what was probably clear enough when the masque was performed: that the Lady is a kind of Milton figure.

The Lady is in fact one of our main sources of evidence about Milton's cult of chastity. But even without *Comus*, the cult would exist as a biographical datum.[8] It constituted the practical basis, I think, of what might be called a personal myth, whose main function was evidently to "manage" the Protestant antinomy between faith and work. The myth did this by providing Milton's faith with a work (namely chastity) more adequately symptomatic of it than was his real work, which was the – slowly encompassed, potentially idolatrous – study of the classics. "If I keep my body pure" – so might the tenor of the myth read – "I will be granted major poetic power (even though my studies have not yet matured), and I will be one with, will speak for, my people (even though my studies seem to divide me from them)." The chastity cult served as a support both for Milton's major poetic aspiration and for the political desire to which that aspiration was tied.

Yet, given the religious and vocational necessity of some such support, why should it take the form of a myth of bodily purity? This is where psychobiographical explanation seems called for, and thus where one regrets the paucity of hard biographical evidence concerning Milton's domestic life. But I think that a reasonable explanation can be offered on the basis of a fact and a supposition. The "fact" is that Milton's mother, according to Milton and two of the contemporary biographies, was a wonder of virtue and modest comportment.[9] The supposition, for which there is considerable evidence, is that Milton's father represented or "brought home" to him the religious and vocational demands, mentioned above, which the study of poetry alone was hard put to silence.[10]

From this one can hypothesize that the peculiar deployment of desire known as the chastity cult reflects Milton's renegotiation of the Oedipal scenario, which may be supposed to have been "reactivated" by fatherly dissatisfaction, or in other words by a "reappearance" of the castration complex. For according to psychoanalysis it is clear what the Father's demands mean: they signify, or threaten, castration. In the ordinary course of events, in the "real" or "first" complex, the Oedipal child circumvents the castrating threat by symbolically accepting it: he gives up the mother as sexual object in *identifying* with the father; this sacrificial identification scores the ego with a mark which will serve as the support for that "differentiating grade," essential to the ego's "moral and cultural progress," known as the ego-ideal.[11] Now Milton can hardly retrace this normal path; if a temporarily insoluble conflict with the father did not exist, the castration complex would not have reappeared in the first place. Milton circumvents castration this "second" time, I would propose, not by accepting it but by avoiding it: he gives up the object-tie with the mother (and with women) only to make himself one with her; in other words, he identifies, not with the father, but with the mother, that wonder of modest deportment, whose character then overdetermines the ego-ideal. The advantages of this Oedipal fantasy, of this "secondary" identification – which is also, one should stress, a mode of sexual deployment – are readily apparent. In fantasy, Milton is not Milton, he has taken up residence in his mother's temple; he is thus no competition for his father: he has no desire but to please, so any threat must be misplaced. At the same time, and paradoxically by this same act of abdication, the power behind the father's demand, the law of his desire, is attracted and taken possession of; it is mollified and made to emanate from the pure body. On the other hand, the corresponding disadvantages or dangers of this fantasy are also fairly clear. First, the identification with the mother necessarily possesses a pre-Oedipal dimension; to circumvent the father in this way is in a certain sense to deny the law of desire itself, and thus to risk a lapse into the slovenly "self-idolatry" of primary narcissism.[12] Second, to identify with the mother is to reduce the distance between the ego-ideal and the sexual object. It is thus to risk the effects of their merger: that moral and affective anarchy and compliance, that secession of reason, which are witnessed in hypnosis and certain kinds of group-formation.[13]

Once this Oedipal fantasy or proto-narrative has been posited, our psychological–allegorical reading of *Comus* begins to come into sight. What this reading will make clear is that if the chastity cult worked as a justificatory poetic – and the minor poems attest that it did – then it worked in breaking down, so to speak: precisely by way of a display – and a *conjuring* – of its motivating fantasy's dangers. In *Comus*, this breakdown is registered in the dramatic figuration of the feminine, or of the female body.

Consider the contrary ways in which the Lady's body is represented in the debate that ends with her stasis. Comus' temptation speech makes the Lady's body a figure of copia, a metonymy for nature's swarming partial drives. It is worth emphasizing Comus' *literal* aim: sex is only the metaphorical end of this romance seduction. Comus wants the Lady to drink, to intoxicate herself – to experience her body, therefore, as a place of pleasure. Her temptation is first of all to narcissism, which he thus casts as the natural condition of the (perfect) feminine. The Lady's superstoic refusal of such femininity tips the ego's basket in the other direction; she transports her body-as-sexual-object, unified under the negative aspect of virginity, into the ego-ideal, which then becomes the seat of a power so great that it shakes Comus in his hooves ("She fables not"). The trouble is that this proclamation of virginal strength issues in a veritable seizure of power, leaving the Lady paralyzed at center stage, the seeming victim of a kind of self-hypnosis. Or to put this more correctly: the masque's conventions leave it appropriately unclear as to whether Comus' magic or the Lady's is responsible for her fix. What the masque does make clear is that the Lady's stasis is symptomatic of *something*: we will return later to the meaning of its symptomatic character, but I would argue here that the something has everything to do with the division in femininity instituted in the debate, and that this division in its starkness is motivated by Milton's secondary identification with his mother.

Thus Milton displays the dangers inherent to his Oedipal fantasy even in playing it out again in the mode of authorial identification. Yet the problems with this fantasy have not simply to do with the internal equilibrium of the ego that it is meant to preserve; they can also appear from another angle, that of the situation to which the fantasy responds. For there seems little doubt that the fantasy acted out by the Lady sins against the desires of both father and mother. And it is in fact in terms of the punishment exacted by the parents, and the reparation that must be paid for this sin, that the questions posed by the turning-point of the masque must be answered. Milton's usurpation of the feminine, the Lady's insistence on virginal power and autonomy, require that mollifying tribute of recognition be paid to the offended parental spirits. This tribute is offered in different "parts" of the masque structure. It changes hands, first, in the enclosing perspectival setting of the masque, whose significance the Lady's silence gives us time to realize, and which rewrites our previous reading of the Lady's stasis. The

Lady has not succumbed to a wave of Comus' wand, nor is she the victim of self-hypnosis. It is another magical gaze in question: in the perspectival setting, the Lady would have been fixed at a metaphorical vanishing point beneath the commanding (patrilineal) eye of her father. The father forgives the Lady, but only after the intervention of Sabrina in the resolution of the masque device. Sabrina is a virginal but *motherly* echo of the Lady; her presence lifts at least part of the fairy world from Comus' copious ambit. Since she can free the Lady, she is evidently not just a simulacrum, but the real thing; her rescue suggests that the mother must not be written out of existence by identification–usurpation but rather recognized, propitiated, and decently buried, if her generous force is to be effective. Finally, in the revels, when she dances before her real parents, the Lady speaks with her body the lessons she has learnt, symbolically accepting a more natural religion than she had preached to Comus.

What does this return of the real, this recognition of the parental spirits, signify from the point of view of authorial identification, i.e. for Milton and the chastity-cult-as-poetic? The answer to this seems fairly clear. In the *Comus* narrative, Milton both lives out (i.e. makes into story, expands upon) and edits or revises the fantasy whose expression in real life was the cult of chastity. The chastity cult is a paradoxical "justificatory poetic" because it needs to be justified or amended itself in order to lead Milton to greater things. It is this second justification that motivates the turning-point of the Miltonic plot, in which the triumphant Lady is fixed in need of aid.

We have now reached the point where we can ask about the relation of this psychoanalytic reading of the vicissitudes of chastity in *Comus* to the political–allegorical one alluded to earlier according to which chastity is anti-idolatrous (anti-Anglican and -Caroline). We can ask about the *relation*, because it is clear that these two readings are *different*, and describe at least partially discontinuous lines of force or motives. The psychoanalytic reading depends on domestic material to an extent and in a way foreign to the political–allegorical; and the ambivalence that it posits explains the crux of Milton's plot with a specificity of which the latter reading is incapable on its own terms. At the same time, one cannot reflect upon these discontinuous motives for long without realizing that, however different they may be, they relate in large part by way of condensation. For anti-idolatry is "behind," and mixed in with, Milton's youthful asceticism; it is the general enabling condition of the Oedipal fantasy that leaves its trace, in real life, in the chastity cult's myth of bodily purity. To return to my earlier expression: anti-idolatry is the *element* in which Milton's renegotiation of the Oedipus complex takes place – an element that is itself an agent in this renegotiation.

From the present vantage, then, according to which it affords representation to both political and Oedipal motives, we can discern in *Comus*' chastity theme a crucial point of intersection between a "private" and a "political" unconscious. One will in fact have earned a right to speak of a political unconscious only when she notes the correspondence between chastity's Oedipal and political allegories. It would appear that the initial moment in Milton's Oedipal fantasy of identification – or rather that identification itself – corresponds to what is most radical (most anti-Anglican and -Caroline) in his political "disposition;" while the secondary justification written into the plot of the Oedipal narrative, the editorial moment of the fantasy, involves a reciprocal political reaction, a kind of allegorical compromise with the powerful idols that be. If further evidence for the partly unconscious character of chastity's political semantics is required, it can be found in the fact that the "private" unconscious selects, or rather specifies, the terms of the masque's (and Milton's) allegorical politics. Chastity need not be so fraught, nor so vexed by the question of innate physical power(s). Our reading thus far suggests that Oedipal motives specify the political ones in fusing with them, so as to single out the fantasm of the body and the gender through which it is lived, and to make them into crucial, contradictory nodal points both in Milton's early poetics and in his politics.

II

It should now be clear how Milton's chastity cult served as a poetic at the biographical level – how it worked to ward off the demands of the father, and made it possible to keep up hope and keep writing. What is not so clear is how the chaste poetic exemplified by the Lady functioned as a *politics*. For though I have argued that the moment of Milton's usurpation of the feminine, in the masque, corresponds to what is most anti-Anglican and -Caroline in his politics, I have not yet dealt with the chastity cult as a positive political gesture in its own right. Yet the very selection, for its definitive expression, of the masque form – whose chief duty was to represent the principles of the kingdom's unity to the source of that order – tells us that Miltonic chastity should be so taken, not just as an Oedipal strategy with political ramifications, but as a political fact and recommendation. Milton's chastity is socially and politically exemplary; as an example, it stands for a new kind of socio-political regime. I will now argue that this is what Michel Foucault would call the regime of sexuality – a regime, nonterritorial by definition, whose natural ground is nonetheless the female body.

Let us rehearse what is involved in Foucaultian sexuality, before considering the temptation episode more closely. I am referring here to Foucault's late *History of Sexuality*, whose main polemical purpose, as is well-known, is to refute the so-called "repressive hypothesis:" the idea, associated with Freud, that modern (or enlightened, or middle class) society coincides with an intensification of sexual repression. Foucault argues, against this, that modern society *deploys* sex by putting it into discourse:

enlightenment entails that sex be sought out, confessed, and analyzed in speech. Whereas before (so Foucault implies), sexual desire had been one among many, it now becomes *the* sin, *the* secret, the privileged Cause and Source of Truth. Before, sex was sex, specific and distinct; now sex becomes *sexuality*, generalized and proliferate. Sex in the shape of sexuality is everywhere – in a mother's hug, a baby's cry, a characteristic gesture, a slip of the tongue. And, as sexuality, it is always at least potentially a *problem* for the individual subjects to whom its words apply: sexuality drives the subject, but it is also the weakest link in his chains, always the source of possible dysfunction. As a problem, sex in the form of sexuality requires institutional assistance – support without which, Foucault emphasizes, sexuality is in fact unthinkable. New or newly oriented institutions of enlightenment (e.g. the nuclear family, psychology, the novel, confession) undertake to regulate the sexuality that they themselves have produced in its problematical form, as an activity or a state crying out to be monitored. As the object of regulatory institutions, sexuality represents one of the nodes of a definite socio-political regime. This regime is nonterritorial in nature; its practices do not exercise sway over locales or the land. Rather they work their effects directly upon human material, and perhaps their most favored site of operation is the female body; for it is feminine sexuality which is especially subject to questioning, prompting, and manipulation. Foucault makes the figure of the Hysterical Mother one of the chief "controlling images" produced by the socio-political regime of sexuality.[14]

Here, I hope, the reader begins to gather the relevance of Foucault's anti-repressive theory to Milton's masque, whose turning-point might be read as a textbook case of anti-repression, an allegory not just of sexuality's deployment but of its emergence. Comus, for his part, is against sexuality, though he may be somewhat colored by its pervading temper. As noted before, Comus seduces the Lady with *pleasures*, among which sex is only a salient one; his glass is a synecdoche for pleasure's soul, which Comus locates in a natural way of life, an opulent temperance, and in which sex is thus included as one pleasure among many. But the Lady's closing words turn the glass into a metaphor for sex. After rebutting Comus' temperance with a panegyric upon stoic moderation, she refuses sex by blazoning the sage and serious doctrine of *virginity*, thus revising her initial, chaste response; for this "magical" substitution converts sex itself into a disposition, and suffuses all previous ethics with the abstract power of sexuality. The Lady, as Virginity, is an allegory of sexuality. At the heart of Milton's masque, the regime of sexuality – a regime predicated upon institutions of counsel – begins to be counselled.

We can begin to specify the formal consequences of this counsel if we deliberate on exactly *how* the "reduction" of chastity to virginity, and the concomitant hypertrophy of sex into sexuality, is *affirmed*. This is a simple matter at first. The Lady's turn to sexuality is affirmed by the event, by the story itself. Preaching virginity's merits, she claims that she *could* make like Orpheus and call nature to her support; but the story gives a real foretaste of this magical power: Comus staggers back. The Lady begins to exert in a new mode the natural magic that she had only echoed in her previous song. She is empowered, in the event, by virginity–sexuality. But *only* in the event. The paradox of the Lady's assertion of power is that it ends there. The Lady is allowed to preach sexuality, and in a certain limited sense to practice it, but not to discourse upon, to urge, its sustained practical effects. Just when she might begin to moralize, to *counsel* sexuality, she is forced to *keep* her counsel. So the moral of sexuality is affirmed, not by the Lady, nor by any person precisely, as we shall see, but only in and by the event.

Such a paradoxical affirmation is perfectly in keeping with what Foucault calls the *principle of latency* that is fundamental to sexuality, and which makes it a problem for regulation.[15] Though the subject of sexuality (e.g. the hysterical woman) is the source of a new social power, it is not for her to say what her power is or means; the desire that makes up her disposition must be interpreted and controlled from a space outside itself. And it is this space of interpretation, implied by the latency intrinsic to sexuality, which is then occupied, in Foucault, by a whole host of counselor and manager-figures. The Lady, then, doesn't only institute sexuality in her preaching; she installs it as well by her silence, by leaving the question of her truth, of her real desires, hanging. This completes my case that sexuality does "appear" in Milton's masque. To show how sexuality is indeed finally counselled requires further analysis of the formal effects of its latency principle, as manifest in its affirmation by the event.

I have already argued in the Freudian part of this paper that the Lady's insistence upon the power of her virginity represents the climax of the Oedipal fantasy in which Milton identifies with the mother, and actually occupies her body. I would now like to "forget" this interpretation, in order to cast attention on the form of the narrative that made it possible (or at least encouraged it), and upon the *meaning* of this form, as it were, in itself. For in interpreting it in terms of Milton's domestic and vocational problems, I was treating the Lady's virginal poetic as a *symptom*: as, that is, a kind of expressive excrescence, an argumentative quirk, which can't be accounted for in terms of the masque's own discursive decorum. What can be remarked now is that it is particularly the Lady's *magical* effusion that makes her discursive one seem so symptomatic: even if we knew nothing of Milton's biography, we would still be left asking why the Lady's rhetorical power spills over into the "action" of the masque; we would still feel that this virginity was a symptom of *something*, of some – latent – motive on Milton's part, some inexpressible contradiction. Which is to say that our interpretation was conditioned and solicited by Milton's narrative itself, that a discrepancy between apparent and real events, decorous and latent motives, was already implicit before we specified it. The symptomatic character of the masque hinge is not simply felt, but actually thickens the plot, or casts a shadow upon its spectacular progression, by imposing, in the form of a retroactive effect, a discordant image from classical myth upon the Lady's silent figure. The Lady represents herself, under the aspect of her virginity, as a new Orpheus: her song will inspire the consent of "dumb things" and "the brute Earth" in her overthrow of Comus' regime. But the action represents her, surely, as a somewhat more sinister figure, "setting her off" from Comus by the stony gaze that threatens to harden his copious temperance into its image as well as by her rhetoric. The action that affirms virginity also imports a Medusa image into the text of the masque's spectacle.[16]

The Lady-as-Medusa is obviously possessed of an extreme ambivalence. The point here, however, is not to explore this ambivalence, but to note that the appearance of such a symptomatic or *textual* image transgresses against the *visibility* of masque conventions. Orgel has well emphasized the primacy of spectacle in these conventions:[17] even in the Jonsonian masque, the masque's action was ordinarily coded in terms of a visual contrast between masque and antimasque, order and disorder, good and evil. Though a tension was manifest from the genre's origins between speech and spectacle, doctrine and allegory, it was only that – a tension – and tended to be mooted as a question of emphasis; Jonson, true, was obstreperous on behalf of the morality of speech, but I think it could be shown that he was so chiefly in his capacity as poet–moralist: he may have balked at the hegemony of the spectacle's condign allegory, but he did not attempt to subvert it by making it seem symptomatic.[18] It was left for Milton, writing on behalf of a new historical content, to "textualize" the spectacle in this way. He thus makes the hinge of the masque, which was ordinarily marked by an epiphanic contrast, into a problem, a crux, which cannot be solved by a presentation of truth but must rather be worked out in something like dramatic terms.

It is largely for this reason – because of the dramatic character of its action – that *Comus* solicits comparison with Shakespeare's romances more than with any of Jonson's masques. Yet to set *Comus* against *The Tempest* – the play it most resembles in setting and characterology – is to feel how straitened the later work's drama is. We can best grasp the principle responsible for this straitening, I think, if we focus on the way in which these two works figure the springs of their own action.

In *The Tempest*, the question concerning narrative springs clearly has to do with Prospero's magic, which controls the main plot. At the same time it involves the issue of power, specifically political power. For Prospero is a *Machiavellian* magus: on the one hand, his ultimate aim is to recover the dukedom of Milan – an aim whose undoubted justice seems to sanction whatever means are necessary to accomplish it; on the other hand, his magical role on the island is presented as a dubiously benevolent despotism.

So all the questions about Machiavellian power (what is its real purpose? where does it tend? when can it be laid aside?) are posed within the magical context of romance, and given a singularly "metaphysical" inflection. The drama "answers" these questions by drawing forth from this peculiar narrative apparatus a moral that may best be put, I think, as a topographical paradox: that power emerges with an opposition between center and periphery; or again, that power, while it strives to occupy the center, is by nature peripheral, an effect of peripherality. This topographical axiomatic is illustrated by the staging of the drama, in which Prospero either exerts power upon the center of the stage from its periphery (as he does in the log-bearing scene between Ferdinand and Miranda),[19] or converts the center that he occupies into a periphery in relation to the "real action," which, for all that he is directing it, lies elsewhere.[20] The literal peripherality of power is never so evident, however, nor his identity as a Machiavellian subject so clearly apparent, as in those climactic moments when Prospero truly does occupy the center of the stage, which he can only do by dropping his magic act, and appearing as mere man. Consider, for example, the play's masque scene and its denouement. Prospero offers the masque in order to commemorate the betrothal of Ferdinand and Miranda, and to conjure the possibility of premarital "intemperance" on Ferdinand's part by showing the generous effects of waiting for Hymen. He refers to this display of his power as no more than an idle show; yet, when the conclusion of the masque is interrupted by his sudden memory of Caliban's drunken insurrection against him, its illusion is revealed to be more compelling than Prospero allowed: it unleashes in him a fit of rhetorical intemperance, the expression of an epochal skepticism in which all human things, now, take on the quality of illusion, become the stuff of dreams.[21]

What has happened is that Prospero has momentarily forgotten himself "to the center," responding to the creatures of his magic as if they were real representations. When he is recalled, by that part of the plot (Caliban) over which he has least control, to his position as magus, he recoils against his painful consciousness of peripherality by generalizing *from* it, i.e. as if from outside it: Prospero, holding forth not as magus but as man, seems to speak for the ultimate source or locus of the play's action, which is figured as the sea, or the mysterious island that is the sea's essence.[22] It is largely because Prospero's power is so clearly peripheral in *The Tempest*, so phenomenal in relation to the magical forces of the island, that the play's thematic is so rich, and the effect of dramatic freedom so impressive.

The Tempest's topographical axiomatic constitutes an implicit critique of the masque form. This is clearest in the scene just discussed. Prospero's "identification" with his masque creation, his imaginative movement toward the center of the scene, mimes the real movement of the king, the eclipsing of the border between stage and audience, fiction and truth, in the decorous conclusion to the Jacobean masque. But whereas the expansion of the stage, in the Jacobean masque, marks the moment of the symbolic triumph of regal power, and of the order whose center it commands, in *The Tempest*'s masque scene it underscores the limits of princely power, and sets the Machiavellian problematic of power off against the romance's copious and transformative, but unfathomable, order of things. To put this in more general terms: the topographics of the masque puts (kingly) power both at the periphery and the center; it involves a symbolic equation between the power of the king and the condign appeal of the spectacle; it makes the king's power central to a representation of ultimate order, and thus celebrates that power in the form of virtue. But the topographics of Shakespeare's play cuts a trench between kingly power and the center; it makes Prospero's power into an inherently contradictory right of *jurisdiction* – contradictory, because overweening in relation to the true locus of the natural order, and of the social narrative.

It would seem plausible that *The Tempest*'s treatment of the masque is in good part responsible for its special relationship to *Comus*: one imagines that Milton had reservations about the conventional politics of the masque, and that he would have been receptive to Shakespeare's point as to how power doesn't work the way the masque has it work. But *Comus* does not simply duplicate *The Tempest*'s critique: it hardly could, of course, if only because – like a good masque – it replaces what was more or less explicitly a thematic of political power, in *The Tempest*, with one that evidently concerns virtue and its unmediated efficacy. The Attendant Spirit, who might be taken to represent the very spirit of the Masque, does more than anyone else to keep Machiavelli's spectre from encroaching. From his perspective the Brothers, for example, are too nearly "political," too legalistic; intent on re-establishing their own proper relationship with their sister, they smash Comus' cup, the obvious instrument of his power, but omit to sever him from his power's source, his wand. Thyrsis makes amends for their rashness by bringing the action back to earth and making it into a battle of spirit, which he translates, in his epilogue, as a matter of virtue. This ministry of the Attendant Spirit is but the primary and as it were visible token in the plot of a larger narrative transformation, which might be described in terms of a general displacement and diffusion of the power thematic. The semiotic elements of Shakespeare's character-system are reshuffled in such a way that Prospero's magic is siphoned off into several of Milton's characters: the Attendant Spirit is like Ariel in his "lightness," but also has Prospero's magical power; Comus has some of Caliban's "beastly" associations, but his occupation of the abundance topos, of a more traditional kind of temperance than the Lady advocated, aligns him with Prospero; the Lady combines Miranda's innocence with Prospero's peremptory and overweening righteousness; Sabrina obviously has her own magical force, and the Brothers have potential. In assuming a more virtuous

57

form, Prospero's magical power is dispersed across the stage. *Comus* is full of magical epicenters.

Yet the Lady is a special magus, and we cannot see how *Comus* "innovates" upon *The Tempest*'s critique of power unless we think upon the effect of her peculiarly insistent claims in the new context, now, in which magic figures as an array of discrete forces. The Lady's Orphic speech superimposes, upon the focal opposition between good and evil, a second, "superior" opposition, or rather tension, between two "good" forces or sites. When the Lady's silence removes her to the vanishing point, the father comes into view on the periphery of the masque's perspectival setting, as the true absent center of its action, the real power-figure. At the same time, retroactively, the father claims as his own a piece of the chill effluence that we had initially read as the Lady's symptom. The effect of this shift is to make the power of virtue, of which the effluence is the sign, seem the result of the tension between father and daughter, and to throw virtue–power *outside* the peripheral center that each in turn occupies. Power become virtue is thus quite literally displaced, and given a freedom it does not know in *The Tempest*; it is no longer merely peripheral, nor does it appear limited and paltry in the face of a jurisdiction that it infringes. The most salient power in *Comus* – the Lady's power – is extra-peripheral: it does not inhabit a site, but rather results from a relationship between magical "centers," and so is more abstract, more strictly functional, than was Prospero's power. Though the Lady's effusion coincides with her transgression against the father's jurisdiction, her power is not so dramatically limited, in relation to that jurisdiction's source, as was the case in *The Tempest*; instead, we now see that the Lady pulls her father into her circuit, so to speak, and makes his jurisdiction the source of a spell it was not in its power to cast before, inasmuch as the father is drawn into the role of the inter-preter which her symptom in its very form presupposes and requires: the father no longer simply prohibits, as we had it before; he is also given a more positive role to play, though this is a role that he cannot act with his person but must serve as a function.

Once we grasp the functional role attributed to the father by the crux of Milton's masque, we are in a position fully to appreciate its polemical formal relation to the masque tradition. Milton's power-figure does not represent in his person a virtuous natural and social order. He is, more crucially, an administrator, functional in an order that cannot even be summed in his place, much less his person. The spectacle is overdetermined – and undermined – by the text of the action once again, as its power-figure is decentered and stripped of transparency.

One might object that this decentering is only appropriate to *Comus'* occasion, since the earl is not the king, but in his employ. To argue thus, I think, is to forget the absolutist character of the masque form, and to mistake a decorous cover, an empirical fact, for the thing itself. The power-figure in such an ambitious masque as *Comus* must, at one level, be a king-figure. Surely Milton, by making the earl functional, is denying the king's power its just representational weight. I would add, however, that the empirical location of the masque, away from court and on the Welsh border, is not only to be considered as a kind of alibi for the absolutist censor, but should at another level be read as the literal referent of a more specific political message. Milton, like most Puritans, would have been in favor of subjecting England's "dark corners," as much as possible, to the center; but for different reasons than the Crown had – for the sake, that is, of their "enlightenment," more than of their fealty.[23] How to express this difference and avoid betraying Puritan to monarchic values? The institution of sexuality symbolically equips the earl with the right ruling principles when it removes his power from his seat and casts it in a relationship on stage, disposing it in a more dramatic, less ceremonial fashion than the masque precedented.

More dramatic: yet, as I noted before, *Comus'* drama is remarkably straitened by comparison with its dramatic precedents. And with the specification of its drama as the solution to the political problem its provincial occasion posed, we can see one reason for the suspension of the dramatic element. To carry the drama further, to implicate the power-figure any more clearly in the Lady's virginal power, would be not just to transgress against, but actually to leave behind, the masque's fundamental ceremonial purpose. The earl must remain a political *fact*, as his place in the spectacle permits him to do; he cannot become a political *actor*. But our comparison with *The Tempest* should have made it possible to grasp a more strictly formal reason for the suspension of *Comus'* drama. The drama of *The Tempest*, though it centers on Prospero, is notably extensive with regard to its locus of reference – never more so than when Prospero is stopped at center stage by the masque's interruption; he acts against a mysterious backdrop of which we are made acutely aware, the source of his masque's illusory power and of his jurisdiction alike. It is the existence of this backdrop that permits Prospero to work out his fate, to resolve the problem of his power in relation to the charmed figures, such as Caliban, that the island affords him. By contrast, the drama of *Comus*, which centers on the Lady, is remarkably intensive. By making the power-figure extra-peripheral, it suffuses the stage with (virtue-) power, and shuts the backdrop that is the source of jurisdiction out of the central action. When the backdrop "returns," and provides a mediating agent in the figure of Sabrina, this gesture seems somehow incommensurate with what has preceded. Sabrina may be symbolically necessary, we feel, but she exists in a lyric mode. If the action were to be forwarded in dramatic terms, it would seem natural for it to take place in a dialogue; but this would not be so "dramatic" as Shakespeare's action. Power has been given a greater freedom, but to the detriment of dramatic capaciousness.

So it is that the institution of sexuality, while it works to dramatize the masque, also accounts for the straitening of its drama. We might go on, remembering that the Lady's silence is in keeping with sexuality's latency principle, and argue that sexuality actually suspends the drama. But this, I think, would be to go too far. It forgets that sexuality, which is by Foucault's definition generalized and proliferate, proliferates especially in discourse. The principle of latency's privileged medium is speech, whose every syllable and intonation it strikes with a pregnant silence. Were speech to become transparent communication, sex would no longer be a problem, and the regime of sexuality would be overthrown. The drama of sexuality, once it is set in motion, ought to be interminable: the problem that sexuality must pose to remain itself can be worked upon, transformed, modified, but never removed. This means that a dramatic resolution such as *The Tempest* finally attains, in which Prospero *cedes* his power, and thus overcomes the ambition and desire that constituted his problem, is out of the question in *Comus'* emergent drama of sexuality, since the Lady's power is not so easily or readily sited as to be cede-able; yet the continuation of the drama, in which some new disposition of power would be arrived at, is *not* out of the question, and is in fact called for by sexuality's own canons, according to which one must speak if one is to play the game. So the Lady's initial silence is in keeping with sexuality, but her continued silence comes to be something of a problem. In so far, then, as the Lady's silence is one with the continued suspension of the drama, it marks the point at which the masque threatens to go beyond sexuality's purview, and invites an explanation "from outside;" it makes us suspect that the institution of sexuality itself needs to be grasped in terms other than the ones Foucault provides in his description.

Our argument as to how sexuality not only appears but is actually affirmed, silently counseled by its formal effects within the masque, ends then with a question. Before pursuing the question, however, we should take stock of the implications of sexuality's counsel with respect to the biographical or Freudian reading that has preceded it. This accounting will lead us from the level of the masque form to the level of content, and to brief genealogical observations regarding the ideological and institutional matrices of chastity.

Since Foucault exhibits considerable hostility to Freudianism, to the point of making the psychoanalytic situation into a sort of paradigm of "enlightened" political control and oppression,[24] it might be thought that my argument about sexuality in *Comus* must be incompatible with the discovery of an Oedipal fantasy at the heart of the masque. In response to this objection, I am tempted to suggest that Foucault's hostility toward the Freudians resembles the treatment given the bourgeoisie by Marx, who at one point in *Capital* explains that, while the bourgeoisie and its apologists are not painted in rosy colors in his book, yet in the strictest sense they too are the victims of the capitalist system. Foucault's attack on Freud is politically, rather than theoretically, justified, and does not involve direct disagreement or incompatibility so much as it indicates a shift in the *level* of analysis from the individual to the social–political terrain; so if there exist real differences, a real incompatibility, between Foucault and psychoanalysis, then this should be taken to mark out a place of disjunction within the "total object" of analysis, a dislocation in the social substance itself. It is one of the chief virtues of *The History of Sexuality* to have shown how the experiences – of speech, of the body, of individuality – which psychoanalysis takes for granted, and upon whose basis it founds itself as an institution, may themselves be understood as effects, in his terms, of power, or as institutional products. From Foucault's point of view, a hypothesis such as that of the Oedipus complex is to be considered practically an institution in its own right, by virtue of the power relations it presupposes and implies both in its object of analysis (the patriarchal, nuclear family) and in its application (the analytical situation). His problem with the hypothesis would not be that it is wrong, but rather that it does not understand the institutional conditions of its accuracy, or what one might call its socio-political form; nor, by that very reason, does it understand the political function or effects or *meaning* of its accuracy.

If we now reconsider the progress of our reading thus far, it is not surprising to find that completing the argument about sexuality's appearance required an analysis of the *formal* rearrangements compelled by the incursion of the Oedipal fantasy into the masque, and that this analysis helped to give a much stronger sense than had been given before of the Oedipus complex itself as a – historically novel – social form, at the same time as it fixed a new political meaning in Milton's Oedipal drama. Nor is it unexpected that the one obvious point of incompatibility between these readings should concern the political significance of the masque's crux, in which the father is called into sight by the Lady's fixed silence (from the Freudian point of view, the weight of the father's gaze marked the moment of political compromise, in which the radical fantasy was edited; while from the point of view of sexuality, it symbolically dethrones the king). This incompatibility ought not to be erased or harmonized, but left to speak of the dislocation in the social substance attendant upon sexuality's emergence.

Once we have considered the masque as an institution, or have grasped what might be called the ideology of *Comus'* form, then we are in a much better position to trace the genealogy of chastity; then we will be able to describe the form of its ideology, which a certain kind of scholarly criticism has done much to distort. The commonplace of this criticism is that *Comus* cannot be appreciated by the modern audience until it is realized that chastity, in the Renaissance and for Milton, does not signify mere sexual repression, which is how we moderns spontaneously read it, but rather a disciplined mode of conduct that is part and parcel of a whole, truly noble, way of life. Spenserian chastity is often cited to support this point, as a gloss on what Milton really meant by chastity.[25]

Now the reader of Book III of the *Faerie Queene* might well wonder whether chastity, for Spenser, is as disciplined and orderly as all that. For it can hardly be an accident that the book of chastity is the one in which the narrative order of the poem "comes apart." Despite Britomart's heroic stature in the book, she does not move through a "career" in the way that Red-Cross and Guyon have; her book is organized less in terms of a character-line than in terms of chaste exempla (Florimel, Amoret, Belphoebe, and herself). It might be argued that the point of this new narrative order is not to make chastity seem a comparatively disorderly virtue, but to underscore that chastity is a *state* more than a story. This seems true enough; it ought not, however, to be taken to imply that chastity is a peculiarly *stable* state: on the contrary, chastity designates a remarkably charged and unstable quantity.[26] The "stuff" of chastity, the instincts proper to the virtue, represent an archaic or primary, preindividual energy (hence the absence of an informing career): chastely virtuous acts seem to spring from a spontaneous self-regard (witness, for example, Britomart's rejection of Malecasta, in canto ii), and thus emit a curiously amoral effect; even chastity's paragons display an affinity with its natural enemies, the twin dangers of fixation and formlessness. Chaos, then, is the indelible stuff of Spenser's chastity. Yet this very fact – which chastity's scholarly advocates rarely appreciate – makes chastity into an especially exemplary virtue, and so justifies the scholarly argument that chastity signifies not repression but a noble and disciplined life. Chastity's unstable or archaic character patently requires support from more developed or comprehensive virtues: thus, in the *Faerie Queene*, Book III runs into and is completed by Book IV, the book of friendship; and thus Book III comes into existence *after* Book II, chastity emerges *in the context of* temperance, in a way that Book II had not followed on Book I. Because chastity is so archaic and asocial, it needs help from the other virtues; because it is in special need of help, it figures the *series* of virtues, the way of life implied by the just society; because of its very insufficiency, it becomes a comprehensive figure of virtue.

So the scholarly commonplace about chastity, that it is really a more *positive* thing than we are likely to appreciate today, and represents a whole way of life, turns out paradoxically to hold for Spenser. But if, as I think we might, we take Spenser's chastity as exemplary for his period, then much of the historical interest of Milton's masque comes to reside in his innovation upon this ideological theme. For the commonplace, as should already be clear, misses its mark when used to apologize for Milton. Milton's chastity retains the basic characteristics of Spenser's: it is archaic in essence, and peculiarly threatened by its own intense flow, by formlessness and fixation. But Milton's masque explodes chastity's paradox by eclipsing its synecdochic status in relation to the other virtues. The movement through which Comus' temperance becomes (i.e. is combatted by, put on the same level with) the Lady's chastity, only to devolve into the "sage and serious doctrine of virginity" – this movement makes the stuff of chastity into the very form of virtue. From being one of many, chastity becomes the thing itself; and no matter how the final episode is taken, no matter what modifying message is read in Sabrina's "forgiveness," it continues to be closely identified with virtue: the series is not restored. If it is now objected that Milton's "innovation" is only the illusory consequence of his putting chastity in a masque, which precluded any contextualization of chastity comparable to Spenser's, our best recourse is to point to the formal modifications that we have already described, for it is precisely the effect of Milton's peculiar dramatization of the masque to decontextualize chastity – to "individualize" its archaic power in a way that Spenser does not, and as a more conventional masque need not have done, thus to fix virtue in chastity's form.

So does virtue begin to be a function of sexuality. But perhaps the most interesting consequence of this historical change concerns the status and nature of chastity's gender. Chastity is decidedly a feminine virtue in Spenser: Britomart and all the exempla are women; and Arthur, the hero of the whole poem, plays only an incidental role, and fares badly, in Book III. But the fact that chastity is an archaic virtue, and requires support, makes its femininity less strictly female. The virtuous soul, it is implied, will be the product of different kinds and levels of virtue, most of them dominantly masculine, but some feminine. Gender traits are interdependent in relation to each other, and partial in relation to character or the soul.

In *Comus*, chastity is also feminine, as the Lady testifies. But the Lady's femininity, like her chastity, is both less modest and more exclusive than that associated with Britomart. The reduction of chastity to virginity – which as we have seen accompanies its dramatization and individualization – goes far toward making chastity absolutely feminine, and femininity absolute. Not that only a woman can be chaste or feminine; what tends to be implied, instead, is that a chaste man is feminine, or *identifies with* the feminine in so far as he is chaste. This "absolutization" of femininity represents a highly significant ideological shift. I can only suggest two of its implications here: 1) It installs a neutral or paradigmatic dimension in femininity (and in masculinity as well). If I do not include feminine components, but identify with its powers, then the feminine becomes a repository defining the limits of my otherness; it becomes an image, a mirror, of abstract human potential. Thus there is a sense in which the Lady, in declaring her virginal power, is no longer feminine, but simply marks the limit of individual virtue. 2) This shift selects the questions concerning the source and end of archaic passion that characterize Spenser's chastity, and attaches them securely to the feminine, re-posing them as questions of desire. We know what Britomart wants, in Spenser; she wants Arthegall.

But what does the Lady want? What is the true source of her virginity, her denial of desire? That the crux poses these questions as it empowers and subjects the Lady is thoroughly in keeping with psychoanalytic propositions about female sexuality, according to which the question as to the true nature of woman's desire constitutes her place in the "system of desire."[27] From Foucault's point of view, on the other hand, this means that *Comus* enacts a new deployment of the feminine. For him, the regime of sexuality subjects and controls women by provoking the question of their desire – by giving them too much sexuality, one might say, and too little desire.

Having noted some of the ramifications of the deployment of sexuality both at the level of the masque's form and of its content, we are now led to ask a further question. If the expression of femininity in an "occasional" cultural artifact such as *Comus* implies power relationships, then we ought to look for the corollary of this expression in the material institutions that govern "everyday life." Is there a basic institutional shift that corresponds to the integral status, the "absolutization," of the Lady's femininity? This corollary is not far to seek, and is of course spoken of in many other places, in many other discourses, than Milton's masque: I refer to the tendential separation of the household from the workplace, and concomitant "domestication" of femininity, that took place throughout the seventeenth century.[28] When women are cut off from the workplace, when they work in the house alone, then they must and can be controlled by their desires. The deployment of sexuality correlates to an ulterior domestication of femininity, and to a redrawing of the battle-lines between the sexes.

III

Thus far, though we have described Foucault's sexuality hypothesis and shown how it can make sense of the politics of Milton's masque, we have not touched on the question of how and why the deployment of sexuality occurs. Nor have we described the whole masque in terms of sexuality, but only a part of it; we have not dealt with the "contradictions" of the masque's form (for example, with the outstanding question of the Lady's continued silence). This is because Foucault makes the deployment of sexuality its own reason.

The problem with this solution becomes apparent if we ask about the corollary institutional conditions of the separation of the household from the workplace, which can hardly have happened in a vacuum. The accumulation and concentration of capital taking place in the late sixteenth and seventeenth centuries in England, which required a reorganization of (for example) much industry and many crafts in accordance with the needs of manufacture, is clearly one principal such corollary. Equally clearly – since such "events" as the expropriation of the English peasantry and the currency inflation of the sixteenth century, two of the chief sources of capital accumulation, are hardly to be understood as responding primarily to some movement within the English family[29] — the concentration of capital stands as the *reason* for the separation of the household, in a way that the latter does not for the former. To put it more precisely: the logic of capital enjoys a determinative primacy in relation to the separation of the household. Now Foucault is not averse to ranking causes. But he will undertake this in a purely *descriptive* way: his ontology of power-discourse commits him to an endless articulation of institutions, and rules out in advance the discovery of any molar social logic traversing and structuring the plural realm of power-discourse itself (which roughly corresponds to, and conflates, what are traditionally termed the political, ideological, and cultural levels). More particularly, Foucault's genealogy is premised on a repression of the economic as a level with its own — contradictory — dynamic, whose determinative primacy stands forth especially clearly in the case at hand. Foucault cannot think what in Marxism is called *determination in the last instance* — which, as Althusser has argued,[30] never happens purely, but still happens all the time. The sexuality hypothesis, then, is the product of a new kind of (political) positivism, a positivism that institutionalizes power.[31] That it can teach us much about political relations and the domination of women is not surprising, from Marxism's point of view, since the logic of capital determines the (relative but real) autonomization of the political level and is sex-blind (i.e. does not directly determine the domination of women).[32] But it cannot really think the conditions of these relations, their historical basis or their total dynamic. The theoretical assumption to be argued in this brief section is that Marx stands to Foucault in something like the same relation that Foucault stands to Freud — with the significant difference that Marxism's "coordinating ability" is far greater than that of Foucault's philosophy.

For Marxism, there are two separate but related ways of explaining the deployment of sexuality. First, it can be understood in terms of the agency of a social class (or classes). Though Foucault adds novel analyses and nuances to the existing description, it can hardly be denied that the *History* amounts to a powerful rewriting of what is commonly understood to be bourgeois sexuality. If it is objected that sexuality in Foucault's sense is the effect of a whole series of institutions, and is too generalized to be the property of a single class, the proper response would be that these cavils provide the very definition of a hegemonic or ruling ideology.[33]

But let us return to *Comus*, in which the fundamental class character of the Lady's chastity would seem patent. We can indeed observe a nuanced class allegory — or rather an allegory of class ideals — shadowing the movement of the central dialogue. To Comus' voluptuous, neo-aristocratic argument for temperance, the Lady first responds by citing the social effects of a stern moderation; such chastity would produce a disciplined society where everyone has enough and the poor do not go to the wall. If this vision seems archaic, that is not so much because it calls up stoic values as because it harks back to the early humanists whose secret ideal, in terms of which they construed those values, was a world of small-scale production and commerce.[34] But the pre-Elizabethan humanist ideal is not enough, or is no longer viable – that is the ambiguous inference to be drawn when the Lady goes on to preach virginity. At this point, the class allegory fades in "explicitness:" virginity is not made to allude to an ideal society, being altogether too fierce for that; it simply puts the Lady in collision with Comus' neo-aristocracy, and gives her Nature as a second at need. Yet the previous class associations ask us to infer a new one here, even though it is textually absent. What class does the intact self of the Lady speak of and for if not the bourgeoisie, which has by now emerged in England from the broken ranks of the small-holding class? Whose social triumph could she desire other than that of the class which distinguishes itself, and justifies its right to rule, not by its blood nor by its preponderance, but by the power and the reason of its *deportment*?

One suspects, at this juncture, that the stridency of the Lady's final speech must have something to do with the situation of the bourgeoisie in English society, or with the nature of its agency. But this matter does not become clear until we move to Marxism's second explanatory level, that of the economic, or alternately of the modes of production.[35] This is the level at which the full explanatory value of the crucial concepts of contradiction and uneven development (or, in its Althusserian formulation, *overdetermination*) can come into play: for while contradiction and overdetermination may affect and afflict classes, they *inhabit* modes of production and regulate their various dynamics, defining in their articulation the structural conditions of existence or limiting principles by which given classes at given moments must abide, and to which they must respond. These principles manifest themselves, for example, as general tendencies, particular countertendencies, secular crises, and sudden disjunctions, and they cannot be securely *known* in lived experience – so the axiom goes – but only *recognized*; they cannot be thoroughly controlled, in class societies at least, but only responded to. So it is that the Lady's stridency and her continued silence may best be accounted for in their ambiguity – not as simple allegories or expressive figures, but as *symptoms* of contradiction and overdetermination.

Of *contradiction*: for on the one hand, these problematical details respond to an eternal condition of the bourgeoisie; or rather, to one of the essential, properly contradictory, features of bourgeois existence at least from the moment of capitalism's emergence – namely that this class knows its solidarity precisely in the isolation imposed by competition, or in other words as universal individuality.[36] This "eternal condition" particularly illuminates the fading of the class allegory that occurs when the Lady steps forth as a bourgeois; her declaration of individual integrity and power may indeed be taken to herald the eventual demise of traditional or uncontrived political allegory. Here, too, what was left implicit at the level of the class allegory can be explicitly stated: namely that the appearance of sexuality is, in part, an expression of the bourgeois' contradictory isolation. More precisely, sexuality represents an overdetermined displacement of this isolation's chief structural support: the commodity of labor power, or of abstract human energy, which emerges as a controlling category with the generalization of commodity relations, and which determines for all members of capitalist society a certain definite "take" on nature and on their bodily forces even as it provides the bourgeoisie with its fundamental distinction as a class – that its labor power is its own, that it does not have to sell. When this distinction becomes a social one, when labor-power "migrates" to the political and cultural fields, it there interacts with the received sexual institution, redisposing its elements while undergoing a modification into libidinal energy, and this institution is thus assigned a new – relatively autonomous – function, as an "atomized" form of social control and solidarity. The Lady's femininity, then, may be taken in part as a metaphor for labor-power, and its unwonted stridency read as a displaced trace of labor-power's eternally contradictory character.

Of *overdetermination*: on the other hand, the Lady's stridency and silence testify to the peculiar historical situation of English capitalism in Milton's time. Throughout the general period, the English capitalist class, though emergent (i.e. economically established), was still largely dependent for its accumulation on various sorts of political expropriation, several of which were enabled, contradictorily enough, by the feudal form of the state. But at the time of *Comus'* writing, this class's position – subjected as it was to Charles' depredations, stripped of political representation, and groping towards new oppositional institutions – was exceptionally fraught. It only becomes evident in this more historical context, I think, why the bourgeois interests that Milton's chastity allegorizes should be fixed in the anticipatory form of virginal energy. Since capitalism is emergent but not politically consolidated – because it does not even know whether it wants or can afford to rule – it cannot sustain a discourse of sexuality yet, but only make a momentous gesture in the direction of what will prove to be an appropriate form of social power. The Lady's continued silence may also best be grasped in this context, as the insinuation of an impasse. Given the obligations imposed by the overdetermination just sketched, what statement on the Lady's part would not seem "merely" symptomatic, and out of keeping with the masque's ceremonial purpose? Silence is one of the least forceful symptoms; yet it can still mark outstanding interests. The Lady's stridency and silence, then, symptomatically figure the contradictory and uneven development of English capitalism within late feudal society; and it is only at this level, when the masque's salient features appear as socially over-determined effects, as strategic but unequal responses to capitalism's historical dilemma, that all traces of positivism are removed from our reading.

But it is particularly the concluding movement of the masque that requires to be understood symptomatically, at the level of the problematic of modes of production. For the formal unevenness almost programmatically introduced by this episode poses the chief problem for interpretation to address. The masque deliberately *regresses* to a more popular or traditional mode, invoking it in the spirit of Spenser.[37] Yet in so regressing, the masque returns to the present of the masque tradition: its lighter cadences are those of the more lyrical, purely celebratory Caroline masque.[38] The episode distinguishes itself from the masque of the moment, I think, primarily in two features. First, by the prominence of its popular (or "Elizabethan") element: it is especially striking that the Lady's predicament is rudely diagnosed; the role of Echo, whom she had called on before for assistance, turns out to be filled by a healer of virgin's disease.[39] And second, by the exceptional lightness of the invocatory verses: these would make excellent exhibits in a demonstration of the purely signifying property of poetic language, the excess of poetic code over message.

We might take this last feature as a request, on the part of the masque itself, to be read as form. If we are to oblige, we must recognize that the masque's poetic code fully signifies only as a figure for historical overdetermination. Its qualified regression/return to the contemporary Caroline form reveals itself as a complex symbolic act only if the final form of the masque is taken as a mute symptom, an overdetermined gesture desperately trying to address and negotiate with the uneven exigencies of the emergent bourgeoisie's political situation. As long as we remember that the return to form is really symptomatic, there is no danger in expressing its relation to the real as a homology, thus: The unevenness in the masque's form corresponds to the unevenness of the situation of English capitalism. Or alternately: the return to form constitutes a response to the chief political dilemma of the English capitalist class (which is both ahead of and behind itself in aspiration, wanting both to leave absolutism behind and to return to Elizabeth's more popular times).

We might stand back now and note a general correspondence that appears between the problem-points of the masque and the structural and conjunctural difficulties of the capitalist mode: the Lady's fixation and silence jarringly discover capitalism's "permanent" contradiction; while the formal break represented by the Sabrina episode registers its historical situation, the uneven development of its emergence. Yet the Caroline conclusion, in temporizing with its moment, also attempts subtly to "keep up" the contradiction, and indirectly to defuse the scandal of its content. It does this in two ways, which I can only touch upon here. The first of these has to do with the lightness, the poetic emptiness, of the verse. In (uneven) context, this lightness breeds a peculiar irony, to be distinguished sharply from the "avuncular" irony informing the dialogue between the Brothers. This irony is neither conscious nor risible, and stems from the sensible knowledge that Milton is deliberately holding back, practicing a "mere" lyrical skill *instead* of piling on the sense. In context, the irony must be read as the formal aftereffect of the Lady's virginal repression, which thus appears to resurface, after its own chastening, in a much modulated, less fearsome guise. So does sexuality come positively to figure itself in poetic tact, and to inhere in the *capacity* that this tact both connotes and, for the sake of the common enjoyment, replaces. So, by extension – and by elaborate mediation – is the isolating effect of labor-power overcome by a sheerly formal solution.

The second tentative solution to the scandal of capitalist content is more "thematic," having to do with the nymph Sabrina's precise nature as a border-spirit. Traditionally Sabrina was a Welsh figure of justice;[40] but Milton does not perpetuate her Welsh or justicial associations. Sabrina's justice is attenuated into a merciful disposition toward young virgins; her Welshness is subtracted to leave only an abstract territorial association, and supplemented by a sympathetic knowledge of the soil. In light of the Lady's aggressive summons of a universal nature, the thematic logic of these "changes" assumes shape. The Lady need not be judged, nor invigorated with her (new) region's blood. Her virtue is rather put in contact with a more concrete nature than her universal one; it is abstractly reterritorialized. This abstract regrounding probably bespeaks an immediate political wish, that the rift between country and city bourgeoisie be nullified. But it also gropes, I think, toward a new form of collective solidarity, one which might redress the isolation etched in the Lady's stony profile and imposed, finally, by capitalist productive relations. Is not the utopian category alluded to here the abstract territory of the capitalist nation – which, once in place, will prove to be at least as invidious, in its effects, as sexuality?

Meanwhile, I ought not to conclude without referring once again to the *element* in which this symbolic action takes place. It was necessary to refer to the religious code in order to grasp the enabling social conditions of Milton's chastity as biographically posited by the first stage of our reading, which has thus been political at each of its levels. But it is only at the ultimate "symptomatic" level of modal overdetermination that the real function and site of religious ideology is revealed, as the conditioning overdetermination of the masque's formal message. Religion's continued dominance constitutes yet another of emergent capitalism's uneven developments – a particularly crucial one. This dominance receives eloquent witness in such a necessarily "secular" work as *Comus*, where a religious paradigm clearly controls the action in spite of its own enforced absence, as if from afar. To see an allegory of grace in the masque is perfectly compatible with a symptomatic analysis.[41] It is a simple story. The Lady fights the temptation of sin (Comus); sins while at it, committing idolatry of the will or of her own intactness; but is then accorded grace. One should note that the unevenness of the masque form already described contributes to the expression and management of a principal theological aporia, the Protestant antinomy between free will and predestination, such that the Lady is granted her strength and freedom, while the grace she receives is imparted a predestinary quality. *Comus'* form figures its political messages through the elementary narrative matrix provided by religion even when "absent" – which matrix we must assume to be amenable to such use because, religion remaining dominant, it is already comprehensively engaged, is already the site of fundamental political thought and struggle. This leads to a final point, more crucial both from a Marxist and an aesthetic vantage than any mere coincidence between religious and political antinomies or problems. It is that the dominance or controlling character of religious ideology, and the relative simplicity of its paradigms – in other words, the continued presence of religion as an allegorical medium – conditions the masque's weight and complexity as a symptomatic or symbolic act, making it possible for Milton to get so much so coherently into so compact a space. The situation of emergent capitalism can be responded to with such figurative consequence because Milton has the grace to use it so.

Notes

1. For an authoritative discussion of reformation anti-idolatry, see Keith Thomas, *Religion and the Decline of Magic* (New York, Scribner's, 1971), esp. 51–77.
2. Be it noted that the word *hegemonically* in this sentence refers, first, to the dominance of religion in relation to other ideologies (i.e. as the repository of the most basic and controlling problematic, or series of assumptions concerning social, and therefore natural, life), and second, to the dominance of ideology itself, in the paradigmatic form of religion, as an instance or level of the social formation (i.e. as that level that is most crucial in securing the relations of production, or reigning form of exploitation). I am assuming throughout this essay that both kinds of dominance obtain, and contribute to religion's allegorical character, in Milton's time. It should hardly be necessary to add that an ideology dominant in the first sense need not be dominant in the second: in modern capitalist societies for example, liberal individualism remains, I think, the dominant ideology; but it is surely *not* the dominant instance. See Louis Althusser's "Contradiction and overdetermination," in *For Marx*, tr. Ben Brewster (London, New Left Books, 1977), 87–128, for a clear explanation of the notion of a dominant instance. For an attempt to rebut the notion that Christianity was ever, in either of the senses above, a dominant ideology, see Nicholas Abercrombie, Stephen Hill, and Bryan S. Turner, *The Dominant Ideology Thesis* (London, Allen & Unwin, 1980), 59–94. I find this discussion interesting in many respects, but vitiated by sociological positivism. To cite but one example: the authors take the fact that most late-medieval peasant rebellions were heretical in orientation as evidence that Christianity was not dominant where the lower classes were concerned!
3. See Richard Halpern's essay in this volume.
4. I quote, here and throughout, from the Scholar Press Facsimile of Milton's 1645 poems: *John Milton: English Poems, Comus, 1645* (Menston, 1968).
5. See Maryann Cale McGuire, *Milton's Puritan Masque* (Athens, Ga., University of Georgia Press, 1983), 130–8.

6. ibid., 139–41.
7. In the illuminating pages cited above, McGuire tends to detract from the *militance* of this symbolic gesture by arguing that Milton *replaces* chastity from a political (Caroline) into a theological (Puritan) context. She thus in practice underestimates what I have designated the allegorical character of ideology (it could be shown that the Caroline love cult was hardly "untheological:" in so far as it elevated the chaste lady and made her soul the object of worship, the cult provided both an "alibi" and a feminized model for the Arminian relation between priest and believer, on the one hand, and the "divine right" relation between king and subject, on the other).
8. See William Kerrigan, *The Sacred Complex* (Cambridge, Mass., Harvard University Press, 1983), esp. 42–56 for other evidence, and for an extended and subtle psychoanalytic interpretation of the cult as it informs *Comus*. My own reading closely parallels Kerrigan's at several points (e.g. on the subject of Milton's mother), though with substantial differences in formulation and to a quite different end. I should probably add that when this section of the paper was first sketched, for an MLA talk in 1982, I had not read Kerrigan's manuscript.
9. See *The Complete Prose Works of John Milton*, ed. Don M. Wolfe *et al.*, 8 vols (New Haven, Yale University Press, 1953–82), vol. IV, 612, and *The Early Lives of Milton*, ed. Helen Darbishire (London, Constable, 1971), 36, 55.
10. Milton writes in his *Second Defense* that "my father destined me in early childhood for the study of literature," but it seems the elder Milton wanted other things for his son as well. In "Ad Patrem," Milton counsels his father to give over his professed scorn for verse. And Milton the elder is said to have remarked caustically on having "kept" the poet until he was past thirty. See Christopher Hill, *Milton and the English Revolution* (New York, Penguin, 1977), 39.
11. See, e.g., Freud's exposition of the Oedipal complex, and his brief remarks on the ego-ideal, in *A General Introduction to Psychoanalysis*, tr. Joan Riviere (New York, Washington Square Press, 1963), 333–46, 434–5.
12. See Freud, *Group Psychology and the Analysis of the Ego*, tr. and ed. James Strachey (New York, W. W. Norton, 1959), 38–9.
13. See ibid., 43–8.
14. Michel Foucault, *The History of Sexuality, Vol. I: An Introduction*, tr. Robert Hurley (New York, Vintage Books, 1980).
15. ibid., 66.
16. In "Puritanism and Maenadism in *A Mask*," Richard Halpern holds that the Lady as Virginity resembles a Dionysian maenad, and that this resemblance indicates Milton's (patriarchal, Puritan) unease at the thought of independent feminine sexuality. See *Rewriting the Renaissance*, ed. Margaret W. Ferguson, Maureen Quilligan, and Nancy J. Vickers (Chicago, University of Chicago Press, 1986), 88–105. I think the Lady looks more like Medusa, once her claim to power is accredited by Comus; but in any case it is not far from maenad to Medusa, and I don't think Halpern's reading incompatible with mine.
17. Stephen Orgel, *The Jonsonian Masque* (New York, Columbia University Press, 1981). One of Orgel's main themes is that Jonson *enriches* the spectacular setting by "organically" building upon it, thus making it "literature." See, e.g., 189.
18. I don't mean to deny that there is a satiric element in several of Jonson's masques; nor would I hold that the satiric criticism is absent from the spectacle (for a discussion of Jonson's politic thrusts at James, see Jonathan Goldberg, *James I and the Politics of Literature* (Baltimore, MD, The Johns Hopkins

University Press, 1983), 123–31). What I would suggest rather is that Jonson's criticisms of the court and complaints against the primacy of spectacle were not so fundamental as to lead him to subvert the masque's formal presuppositions.

19. *The Riverside Shakespeare*, ed. G. Blakemore Evans *et al.* (Boston, Houghton Mifflin, 1974), 1624–5.

20. Cf., e.g., IV.i.170ff. (op. cit., 1630–1), and V.i.7–32 (op. cit., 1632).

21. IV.i.145–58 (op. cit., 1630).

22. See Reuben Brower, "The mirror of analogy: *The Tempest*," in his *Fields of Light* (London, Oxford University Press, 1951).

23. See Christopher Hill, "Puritans and the 'Dark Corners of the Land,'" in *Change and Continuity in Seventeenth Century England* (Cambridge, Mass., Harvard University Press, 1975).

24. Note, though, that Foucault's position on psychoanalysis is nuanced. The psychoanalytic moment proper coincides with the moment when all of society is saturated with sexuality, and when it thus becomes important for the middle class to attribute its own sexuality with superior qualifications. See Foucault, op. cit., 118–19, 130.

25. C. S. Lewis is not far from my thought (see, e.g., the letter to Charles Williams that prefaces *A Preface to Paradise Lost* (London, Oxford University Press, 1971)), but I am referring here more to a certain climate of opinion than to a distinct group of texts.

26. See Harry Berger, "'Faerie Queene' Book III: a general description" (*Criticism*, 11, Summer 1969, 234–61), to which these remarks are indebted.

27. See *Feminine Sexuality: Jacques Lacan and the Ecole Freudienne*, ed. Juliet Mitchell and Jacqueline Rose (New York, W. W. Norton, 1982), esp. 118–21.

28. See Alice Clark, *Working Life of Women in the Seventeenth Century* (London, Cass, 1968), which was originally published in 1919, for the classic study of this separation; and for an excellent Marxist feminist discussion, see Michele Barrett, *Women's Oppression Today* (London, New Left Books, 1980), 152–87.

29. For the accumulation of capital, see Maurice Dobb, *Studies in the Development of Capitalism* (London, Routledge, 1946), *passim*; for expropriation and currency inflation, see 41–70, 182–3. This is the place to register Michele Barrett's very important point that the separation of the workplace from the household need not have resulted in the domestication of women: this was its "natural" effect only because the pre-existing sexual division of labor assigned to women, and familial ideologies designated as feminine, tasks that became strictly domestic after the separation. See Barrett, op. cit., 181ff.

30. Althusser, op. cit.

31. Limited space and the practical nature of this essay dictate the cursory nature of these critical remarks, which I hope will not appear too unjust. For an extended Marxist critique of Foucault's institutionalism, more particularly as it affects his theory of the subject, see Peter Dews, "Power and subjectivity in Foucault" (*New Left Review*, 144, March–April 1984, 72–95).

32. See Barrett, op. cit.

33. As noted before, Foucault does not hesitate to call sexuality bourgeois, and even speaks at times of the bourgeoisie contributing or "administering" its sexuality to the working class in the latter part of the nineteenth century. See Foucault, op. cit., 130.

34. In "More's *Utopia* and uneven development" (*boundary 2*, 13, 2/3, Winter/Spring 1985, 233–66), I make the case that More's utopia was predicated upon "petty" (i.e. small-scale) independent ideals.

35. For a stimulating exposition of the crucial value of the problematic of modes of production to historical and cultural studies, see Fredric Jameson, "Marxism and historicism" (*New Literary History*, 11, Autumn 1979, 41–73).
36. See Louis Althusser, "Rousseau: *The Social Contract*," in *Politics and History*, tr. Ben Brewster (London, New Left Books, 1972), 153.
37. See John Guillory's – more or less Bloomian – reading of the poem in *Poetic Authority: Spenser, Milton, and Literary History* (New York, Columbia University Press, 1983), 68–93, for a quite different explanation of the masque's turn to Spenser than I am about to give.
38. See David Norbrook, *Poetry and Politics in the English Renaissance* (London, Routledge & Kegan Paul, 1984), 263–5.
39. Sabrina, the Attendant Spirit says, "can unlock/ The clasping charm, and thaw the numming spell,/ If she be right invok't in warbled Song,/ For maid'nhood she loves" (112).
40. See Leah Sinanoglou Marcus, "The milieu of Milton's *Comus*: judicial reform at Ludlow and the problem of sexual assault" (*Criticism*, 25, Fall 1983, 320).
41. The most influential theological interpretation of the masque, which explains away all idiosyncracies, is to be found in A. S. P. Woodhouse, *The Heavenly Muse: A Preface to Milton* (Toronto, University of Toronto Press, 1972).

4

ABBE BLUM

The author's authority: *Areopagitica* and the labour of licensing

Milton's work as licenser or censor under Cromwell has posed serious problems for critics who represent Milton as a champion of intellectual liberty, and it has also provided ammunition for those who stress his conservatism.[1] Both sides tend to frame the debate in terms of Milton's earlier tract on unlicensed printing. "That the author of the *Areopagitica* should be found in such a capacity is certainly a surprise," writes David Masson, who goes on to explain how these later activities do not mean that the "defender of free speech" has reversed himself.[2] Those who view *Areopagitica* as advancing a narrow, conditional freedom are, on the other hand, unsurprised by his activities as licenser; Frederick Siebert cautions that one should not read "into *Areopagitica* a broader statement on the freedom of the press than is to be found in the words themselves."[3] Both positions assume a connection between the tract of 1644 and the licensing activities of 1649, though for divergent ends. But both implicitly posit a coherent political philosophy and an autonomous authorial presence. They consequently make it difficult to notice the fundamental contradictions that mark Milton's texts and actions of both periods.

That there are such contradictions is the thesis of this essay, in which I argue, further, that these contradictions testify to Milton's desire both to repudiate and to embrace a discourse of power associated with a principle of authorial autonomy. The problem inherent in this principle of autonomy appears when in *Areopagitica* we see Milton defining an ideal of authorial independence that seems inseparable from the perception of threats to that ideal. In arguing for the author's right not to be touched, initially, by the state or any individual, Milton in fact indicates the extent to which such intervention is inevitable, is indeed a precondition of the subject's desire for

74

discursive power. Examples of what might be called "contaminated" autonomy occur in *Areopagitica*'s theoretical defense against and dependence upon the idea of prescriptive authority; in a different but related manner, such contamination is also an effect of Milton's activities as licenser or censor under Cromwell. Centrally concerned with prescription, *Areopagitica* presents for analysis various images of an author who would reform authority but who inevitably ends up partially reconstituted by it. Both in *Areopagitica* and in his work as licenser and censor, Milton deploys strategies for redefining prohibitive regulations that are at once rhetorical and political, and that require interpretation within a specific historical context.

Milton's wielding of proper names (including his own), his studied relation to the activity of printing, and his implied interest in some rudimentary form of copyright all assume significance in the context of the unsettled conditions of the publishing industry in seventeenth-century England. His framing of his own name stages Milton as a unique presence who simultaneously identifies with and dissociates himself from other polemicists writing during the upheaval of the 1640s. Adopting authorial roles unusual even for this unsettled period, Milton transgresses against the regulations which circumscribed polemic's relation to prescriptive authority. His work is thus of interest to students of history and discourse because it encodes much that is symptomatic of what was occurring in England at this tumultuous time; it also allows some inquiry into the general question of where and how new modes of discourse arise, and how the realms of "public" and "private" are historically defined.

Milton and the printing controversy

A brief discussion of the authorial practices and regulations in the early stages of the Civil War is necessary in order to see how Milton is and is not a typical author of the time. He published *Areopagitica* in November of 1644, after a three-year period from 1641 to 1643 when Parliament's lack of a system for control of printing effectively sanctioned unlimited publishing. Members of Parliament still believed in the enforcement of strict printing regulations but had not had time to replace those of the Star Chamber, which Parliament had dismantled along with the Star Chamber in 1641. When in June of 1643 Parliament finally enacted a printing ordinance, this document testified to an essential continuity with the crown's philosophy of regulation even as it strove to undo the crown as the source of regulation.[4] Three years of comparative freedom for authors and printers were not easily relinquished, however, and it is against the Licensing Order of 1643 that Milton specifically writes in his advancement of the author's control over his work. Milton also necessarily takes on the designated enforcers of that order: the licensers (Parliamentarians and Divines divided up according to expertise) and the Stationers Company – the monitors of "ancient custom" (as they are termed in the 1643 Ordinance), comprised of booksellers, printers, and others whose monopoly on the book trade had also suffered from the lack of regulation during 1641–3.[5]

It is impossible that Milton was unaware of Parliament's ultimate intentions; each of its orders, up to the June 14, 1643 one against which Milton wrote, increased the stringency of regulation. To the end of enhancing the power of the author, Milton proposes as sufficient not the 1643 edict but rather a small part of an earlier, clearly temporary Parliamentary measure of 1642.[6] He emphasizes the importance of this earlier measure by discussing it near the end of *Areopagitica*'s peroration and misrepresenting it as an all-inclusive order. From this 1642 edict Milton singles out the stipulation that a book must have "the Printers and the Authors name, or at least the Printers" in order to be registered.[7]

Milton's mystification here consists of presenting the author as the centerpiece of publishing regulations (and he is able to suppose this centrality even with the stipulations about the printer, since a work could, presumably, be traced back to its author through that agency); he obscures Parliament's undiminished stake in having ultimate control over the production of any printed work. He also ignores Parliament's direct command, in that same pre-1643 order, to the Stationers Company that they control maverick printers through search and seizure of presses. He thus neglects to mention how the enforcement of the order is clearly to the Company's economic advantage.[8] *Areopagitica*, moreover, would not even meet the stipulations of the 1642 edict since it had been published without the printer's name, thereby creating a fiction of the writer's autonomy, as we shall see.

The actual 1643 order which Milton fails to mention in *Areopagitica*'s peroration in fact rendered the 1642 provisional edict obsolete and undercuts Milton's argument for autonomy. Rather than stressing authorial permission, the 1643 edict states that no book can be lawfully licensed and entered with the Stationers Company "without the license and consent of the owner or owners thereof."[9] It is significant that an owner is frequently not the author. Until as late as the Licensing Act's repeal in 1694, authors sold their books as they would any other property; when a book was entered in the Stationers Register perpetual copyright was granted to a member of the Company who was not likely to have been the author as well.[10]

Although the tract's selective presentation and omission of licensing ordinances thus seems to argue that an author is centrally responsible for a work, other statements in *Areopagitica* make the extent of authorial control a much more ambiguous matter. Milton does not wish to tolerate "Popery, and open superstition, which as it extirpats all religious and civil supremacies, so it self should be extirpat" (565). He calls for "a vigilant eye [as to] how Bookes demeane themselves, as well as men;" it is necessary "to confine, imprison, and do sharpest justice on them as malefactors" (492). Milton further suggests in the peroration that mischievous or libellous books which "otherwise come forth" be given to the "fire and the executioner" (569). How are we to read a tract which encodes much greater initial freedom and recognition for an author (aside from a Catholic) and at the same time grants the state's right to exercise corporal punishment on the offending author's product?[11] And Milton's call for not violating Christian liberty in "things indifferent" can be taken either as obfuscatory, or as greatly extending what may be published and who may do so, depending on how indifference is defined.[12] The ambiguity of Milton's attitudes towards toleration, however, should not cause us to neglect the ways in which Milton throws the author very vigorously into the fray, with the paradoxical effect of advancing and rendering problematic the author's autonomy.

As might be anticipated, current scholarship offers contradictory explanations for what appears to be contradictory in the tract. Milton is variously seen as a canny tactician who moderates his stance on toleration in order to convey the appearance of solidarity with those who could repeal the 1643 Licensing Act (especially Parliamentary groups and members of the Westminster Assembly – the latter then meeting to decide religious matters);[13] a brilliant moral instructor who employs irony to move ethically upright, intellectually superior readers (who as kindred liberal Christians will affirm his rhetorical prowess);[14] a conservative party-line Protestant spokesman for intolerance who constructs a conditional restricted freedom of expression tailored only for the elect.[15] Most recently *Areopagitica*'s seeming contradictions have been interpreted as Milton's "manifesto for indeterminacy," a conversion of various factions' disagreements into a nonoppositional celebration of intellectual energy,[16] and finally and quite differently, as the product of a self-validating, monistic ethos which registers the tensions deriving from a bourgeois problematic.[17] Instead of looking once more at the twists in the official argument, I want to examine those aspects of both *Areopagitica* and Milton's tenure as licenser which most stubbornly resist explanation according to a totalizing system. My point is this: the discussions in which Milton presupposes the author's indispensable societal functions are not innocent; rather they betray the author's ambiguous state. Nor do Milton's attempts at situating the author seem precise. The very lack of precision, however, allows for an examination of shifts in the definition of public and private discourse. In redefining what constitutes published and unpublished texts, authors and political and social authority, Milton challenges and momentarily disrupts a traditional if partially threatened alignment of power and property. He makes it seem possible that he can participate in the reconstitution of authority that would occur if his recommendations were followed. At the same time, his reworking of authors' "rights" suggests the unsettled, unequal power arrangements which embroiled author, government, licenser, printer, and bookseller at this historical moment.

Behind Milton's polemic is the larger, more shadowy struggle among those then striving for control of publishing in England: Parliament and its Committees (who wished to take the place of the Star Chamber and its commission as administrators of the printing industry); the Westminster Assembly; licensers who were themselves often Parliamentarians or in the Westminster Assembly; and the Stationers Company. The tremendous increase in the number of unlicensed pamphlets even after the appearance of the 1643 ordinance, in particular between 1640 and the year of *Areopagitica*, 1644,[18] suggests the magnitude of the struggle. Upheaval over ownership of books and presses coincided with debates about who had the right to dispute in public, preach as laymen or women, and address Parliament in print.

The short-term chaos of the printing industry which fed these controversies testifies to a much broader and ongoing cultural process of change. "[F]rom the late Middle Ages and the early Renaissance on," writes Norbert Elias, "there was a particularly strong shift in individual self-control – above all, in self-control acting independently of external agents as a self-activating automatism, revealingly said today to be 'internalized.'"[19] Milton publishes as a private individual precisely for the reason Elias details: Milton calls for books to be printed independently of the initial censoring process of the licensers, though he also stresses the necessity of public debate once the book is published. *Areopagitica* reflects in subtle but pronounced ways the increasing concern with personal control and individual self-consciousness which characterized the early modern age.[20] Milton reinforces an artificial construct of individual identity when he presents himself as one whose acts arise solely from a private integrity which does not initially recognize regulations of the state. His representation of private, individual identity depends, however, upon its dissemination in a published (hence public) and potentially volatile forum.

Milton was by no means alone in his concern with public and private authority; as William Haller has noted, a number of tracts precede *Areopagitica* in calling for the removal of licensing. More generally, Milton's work appears in the midst of a printed debate that ran from January 1644 through and after November, the month in which *Areopagitica* was published, on the subject of toleration both religious and political.[21] Earlier tracts' implicit or explicit positions on liberty of conscience, and more especially the effect of printing regulations on their publication, help us to determine what is typical or atypical about Milton's authorial practice. The formal presentations of such tracts, particularly the ways in which they initially mark themselves as public documents, reveal a range of possible choices on the parts of the author, the printer, and sometimes the stationer.

The decision to publish or withhold the author's name, to obtain the imprimatur of the licenser, to display the printer's mark and the place and date of printing, to register with or avoid the Stationers Company, orchestrate the text in relation to authority. In some cases the lack of permission to print a duly licensed work also shaped the circumstances of its appearance.

The tract which fires the opening salvo in the debate over conscience, *An Apologeticall Narration* (January, 1644), was not very radical in calling only for some further freedoms for ministers and their congregations while opposing the Presbyterian consolidation of religious policy. What is significant for our purposes is its public stance toward religious and state authority: the tract named its five authors (all Independents and members of the Westminster Assembly), was registered with the Stationers Company, and was, according to the title page, "humbly submitted to the honourable houses of Parliament."[22] By thus orchestrating a variety of published, public "marks," these men obtain the sanction of secular authority in moving religious debate outside of the Westminster Assembly (where they were convinced they would not prevail); they also undermine the exclusive-seeming nature of their religious authority by addressing Parliament and a wider reading public. They do so, moreover, using their names and prestige as respected religious leaders in order to win an enlargement of power.[23]

Conservative Presbyterian replies to *An Apologeticall Narration* such as Westminster Assembly member Adam Steuart's *Some Observations and Annotations Upon the Apologeticall Narration* (February, 1644) try to contain this bid for authority by arguing that printing arguments best confined to debate in the Assembly might undermine the state's control over publishing. Pamphlets such as Steuart's which were in line with the status quo could emerge in the public eye licensed, printed according to order, and strengthened by ministerial power and an Assembly signature comparable to that of their opponents. Authors who opposed the Assembly could publish their names if they were able to use their ministerial status to obtain license and press for their works, as in the case of the nonconformist pastor John Goodwin's θεομαχια (October, 1644), a tract which called for a free pulpit and congregation. Other tracts relied on notoriety rather than formal religious authority to publish their authors' names: William Prynne's attack on separatists, *Twelve Considerable Serious Questions Touching Church Government* (September, 1644), aggressively underscored its author's high visibility and flaunted its unlicensed, unregistered status. It is in this pamphlet that Prynne alludes to Milton's *The Doctrine and Discipline of Divorce* as encouraging "divorce at pleasure."

Being outside the religious establishment and only recently notorious in some circles for his divorce tracts, Milton could not be considered famous, nor did he use the press in order to stage a hyperbolic and visibly orchestrated personal drama – of Prynne's kind, at any rate. In fact,

Milton's position is closer to that of a number of anonymous and unlicensed tracts such as *Queries of highest consideration, proposed to the five Holland Ministers* (February, 1644) which, in the course of arguing for religious toleration, also point out the role of the press in freeing England from the bishops.[24] Nor were authors always successful in publishing through official channels: Henry Robinson's *John the Baptist* (September, 1644), which argued for individual freedom in religious decisions, was "licensed but not permitted to be printed according to order," and thus appeared anonymously and without reference to printer or publisher.[25]

One anonymous tract attributed to William Walwyn, *The Compassionate Samaritan* (1644),[26] anticipates *Areopagitica* in arguing for freedom of printed expression but also reveals how Milton departs from usual practice in his public positioning. Bearing no printer's mark, author's name, imprimatur or sign of registration with the Stationers Company, this pamphlet attacked the clergy's monopoly on published opinion, a monopoly furthered by their use of the 1643 Licensing Ordinance to become masters of the press. Walwyn's anonymity results, he argues, from the clergy's tyranny:

> notheing may come to the Worlds view but what they please, unlesse men will runne the hazard of imprisonment, (as I now doe), so that in publike they may speake what they will, write what they will.[27]

Unlike Walwyn, Milton deliberately publishes his name and runs "the hazard of imprisonment." He goes far beyond Walwyn's protest against the clergy in urging his own authority as sufficient grounds for writing what he will "in publike." The violation of printing regulations, Milton's deliberately transgressive posture, is in fact crucial to an understanding of how he delineates authority in *Areopagitica*.[28] I argue that the tract presents an author whose public presence threatens and is in turn threatened by regulations in a drama which only partly conceals the interdependence of author and authority.

Transgressive signature in *Areopagitica*

Before *Areopagitica* properly begins, prior even to its first sentence, something happens which might be called an event of the signature or drama of the title page (see frontispiece). In the pamphlet as originally printed, the letters of *SPEECH* are blacker and larger than the rest, and they focus attention on the printed form in which the oration is represented. The speech, however, is "of" Mr John Milton, and appears to be dominated and even possessed by the author's name. And while the letters of that name are of the same size as those which print the tract's title, they are spaced so that they stretch very nearly from border to border; the N of *MILTON* expands with a flourish nearly to the edge of the inner margin. They seem to claim possession of the horizontal space of all the title page above the first black bar. The printed name MR. JOHN MILTON physically divides SPEECH from the announcement of the speech's purpose, For the Liberty of UNLICENC'D PRINTING, and intended audience, To the PARLAMENT OF ENGLAND, and so becomes something like a fulcrum of this space.

We cannot conclusively prove that Milton rather than the printer was responsible for the ultimate look of the title page; I strongly suspect, however, that Milton at least had something to do with its ordering. According to Phoebe Sheavyn, the author "was expected to attend personally to supervise during the actual printing."[29] An author's involvement could go well beyond mere superintendence and correction, at least since the time of Ben Jonson. Jonson's obsession with his 1616 Workes as printed, autonomous text; his self-conscious ordering of his pieces; and even his general, "'textual' certification of his name (Jonson, not Johnson)"[30] make him a striking precursor for Milton. Milton's practical attention to his works can certainly be demonstrated. He carefully arranged the order of the poems within and the general appearance of the 1645 Poems which came out the year after Areopagitica;[31] this volume, like Areopagitica but unlike any of the other tracts of domestic liberty (the divorce pamphlets and Of Education) is advertised as the product "of Mr. John Milton." Both works function as exercises in self-documentation.

The typography signals only part of the signature event, though it does indicate spatially the issues of control and authority so central to Areopagitica's argument. The print as arranged on the page is the first, most dramatic gesture toward self-authorization, by which Milton advances the writer as the literal publisher of his work. By producing his proper name in an "improper" transgressive political context, Milton directly challenges the power structure (which is of course the point). He prints an unlicensed book for the liberty of unlicensed printing. But how does this act define the discourse of power? When in Areopagitica Milton "presume[s] upon the meek demeanour of [Parliament's] civill and gentle greatnesse . . . as what your publisht Order hath directly said, that to gainsay, [he] might defend [him] selfe with ease" (489), he specifically positions himself against the Parliamentary licensing order of 14 June 1643 while at the same time asking for Parliament's recognition. According to the order no book was to be produced or sold unless

> first approved of and licensed under the hands of such person or persons or both, or either of the said Houses shall appoint for the licensing of the same, and entred in the Register Book of the Company of Stationers, according to Ancient custom, and the Printer thereof to put his name thereto.[32]

The title page of Milton's tract has no licenser's name or imprimatur, no bookseller's title, printer's name or identifying devices. The absences have the effect of rendering the name of Mr. John Milton more immediately present. He represents himself as author there and so appears to take sole responsibility for the entire enterprise; conversely, the totality projects authority upon the author, and perhaps also upon his name, causing it to linger. Just as that N reaches to touch and cross the margin of the page, MR. JOHN MILTON and the author John Milton toy with the boundary function of the name reproduced on the page – calling attention to the singular, bordered, framed, signed, (and in this case) dated aspect which separates the title page from the text.

Areopagitica early on thus highlights the complicated and shifting status of Milton's name in particular and the author's name in general. By not registering the tract with the Stationers Company, Milton strikes at both it and Parliament, erasing the already obscure and shifting lines of power that Parliament was attempting to redraw. Just as important, Milton's silence on the title page as to the printer of his tract superficially protects his printer and that printer's press. It also, however, presents the author as autonomous agent in the process. The act of "signing" any text further complicates matters by evincing the separation of text and author;[33] the presence of the name is by necessity a sign of the absence of the author. Milton's drama of the author–signature–proper–improper–name takes this idea as its departure point: because attention is directed to the author at the breach or title page event of Areopagitica, the small part of the text that is the signature appears to redraw and reappropriate the boundaries of the discourse so that the rest of the text is made into a small part of the signature.[34] A fictionalization thus occurs at the margin of the discourse, for the author's name (or that name as signature) is put on stage and becomes a kind of character with speaking part.

Yet this stage for authorial inscription doubles as the site of authority's implicit or explicit naming, an historically specific coupling. As Foucault puts it, "Speeches and books were assigned real authors, other than mythical or important religious figures only when the author became subject to punishment and to the extent that his discourse was considered transgressive."[35] Milton qualified for "real authorship" in that his earliest divorce tract had repeatedly drawn official censure. Deriving from a variety of quarters, attacks upon Milton illustrate how authority was then being reconstituted by a constellation of moral and political forces. First, in a move which suggests that Milton's violation was perceived as much as a usurpation of the traditional religious authority as the publishing of "immoral" opinions, the conservative Presbyterian divine and member of the Westminster Assembly, Herbert Palmer, publicly deemed Milton's second edition of The Doctrine and Discipline of Divorce transgressive. The form of this attack is as important as its vehemence, for it comprises part of a sermon against religious toleration preached before Parliament (four months before Areopagitica on 13 August 1644) and later published.

Palmer declared, "a wicked booke is abroad and uncensured, though deserving to be burnt." Just as offensive to Palmer and significant for Foucault's notion is the fact that the book's "Author hath been so impudent as to set his Name to it, and dedicate it to your selves;"[36] a further sting to Milton here results from Palmer's dwelling on the offense of a published name without ever mentioning Milton specifically. Palmer thus conjures and effaces Milton's singularity in one stroke. Next, the Stationers Company invoked the Licensing Order of 1643 and registered a complaint against the divorce tract's unlicensed condition; two days later Parliament's Committee on Printing was instructed to move against the author of the divorce tract. Although nothing appears to have happened to Milton as a result of these formal proceedings, they show how the apparatus of authority partially defines the territory of the author.

Tokens of manly prowess: erasure, naming, and the monumentalizing of the author

Milton's presentation of orators who are his precursors in *Areopagitica* reveals an author's dependence upon various pre-existing power relations. His strategy of "monumentalizing" the text – by which term I mean his creation of a fiction of permanence and singularity through the threat of erasure – can be illustrated by a passage toward the end of the exordium. Milton there defends himself from the charge of being "new or insolent" when in fact he is most open to the charge of transgression. He identifies with Dion Prusaeus, the first private authority ("privat" is Milton's adjective) named in the tract, paradoxically in a casual way:

> And out of those ages, to whose polite wisdom and letters we ow that we are not yet *Gothes* and *Jutlanders*, I could name him who from his private house wrote that discourse to the Parlament of *Athens*, that perswades them to change the forme of *Democraty* which was then established. Such honour was done in those dayes to men who profest the study of wisdome and eloquence, not only in their own Country, but in other Lands, that Cities and Siniories heard them gladly, and with great respect, if they had ought in publick to admonish the State. Thus did *Dion Prusaeus* a stranger and a privat Orator counsell the *Rhodians* about a former Edict: and I abound with other like examples, which to set heer would be superflous.
>
> (489–90)

Two Greek models, the elaborately unnamed, tantalizing one of Isocrates and his sketched-in discourse, and the named "stranger and privat orator" Prusaeus with his unspecified Rhodian counsel, position Milton as private person and public advisor to his Parliamentarian audience. The rhetoric of the passage directs much more attention to Isocrates and his *Areopagiticus*, a major namesake for Milton's tract, than to Prusaeus (also known as Dio Chrysostom, d? *c.* 117 BC).[37] Wedged between allusions to Isocrates and Milton in Milton's only reference to him,[38] Prusaeus flows into the oblivion of Milton's self-consciously superfluous refusal to supply any superfluous examples.

Yet it is precisely Prusaeus' status as marginal support, along with the even more supplemental, unexplained subject matter of the Rhodian discourse that should interest us here. The enigmatic reference to Prusaeus, like Milton's signature on the title page, serves to half publish and half conceal a problem with the conception of authority. Indeed, if we pursue the clue Milton gives us, we can see that Prusaeus' situation resembles Milton's in significant ways.

Prusaeus' speech to the Rhodians argues against their low-budget practice of recycling statues by erasing the old inscription and chiseling in new names:

> For the pillar, the inscription and being set up in bronze are regarded as a high honour by noble men, and they deem it a reward worthy of their virtue not to have their name destroyed along with their body and to be brought level with those who have never lived at all, but rather to leave an imprint and a token, so to speak, of their manly prowess.[39]

Prusaeus' speech is pertinent because both he and Milton are concerned with the power of civil authorities to erase or replace names. In unfixing the seemingly permanent relation between identity and artifact, the analogy between statue and text problematizes individual identity. In both cases, sustaining the name's integrity depends upon the negative witness of those who see and threaten to reinscribe differently the "proper" relation between signifier and signified. In *Areopagitica* the licenser's ability to blot out or alter the author's name occasions the monumentalizing of the name and text. Put another way: Milton inscribes Prusaeus' name but effaces the "body" of Prusaeus' text; in portraying Prusaeus Milton both defends against and comes to be dependent upon the half-told story of effacement that *Areopagitica* continually strives to transmute into the narrative of the author's autonomy.

The monumental aspects of those books threatened by the licenser can be discerned especially clearly when Milton discusses the products of dead authors (an obvious trope for Milton's concern with his own authorial afterlife). Implicitly identifying books as the epitaphs of their authors, Milton emphasizes that while licensing "disesteem[s]" knowing persons, it is "most injurious to the writt'n labours and monuments of the dead, . . . an undervaluing and vilifying of the whole Nation" (535). And in the section of *Areopagitica* which sets out the history of licensing, Milton describes how the Council of Trent and the Spanish Inquisition engendring together brought forth, or perfeted those Catalogues, and expurging Indexes that rake through the entralls of many an old good Author, with a violation wors then any could be offer'd to his tomb.

$$(502-3)^{40}$$

While Milton's charnelhouse imagery vividly stresses the violation against these authors' works, it also attempts to describe what is suppressed, mutilated, vulnerable to violation because seemingly undefended. But description results in indistinguishability; it is difficult if not impossible while reading this passage to separate out the "person" of the book, the text itself, from *either* the author or his violator.

The dynamics of reading such a passage hint at the general power configuration of author–text–reader–censor–authority to which *Areopagitica* is a response. By insisting on the helplessness of the text, Milton can create a correspondingly powerful, threatening enemy who in turn prompts the appearance of an even stronger author-defender able to rescue his predecessors. Yet the uncertain status of the text – its effect, its ability to convey perpetual fame upon its author, even its ability to do harm – is suggested by the essential circularity of this epic story. If the texts are "orphaned remainders" (534), then their producers must eventually cease their parental function and thus lose their singularity. The monumentalizing of a work is thus occasioned by the need for a testament to permanent power. The testament, however, betrays the ties that bind author, text, and authority.

We have also seen a slightly different version of the monumentalizing strategy on *Areopagitica*'s title page, where Milton tried to conjure authority by means of aggressive opposition. And the controversy over *The Doctrine and Discipline of Divorce* evidently empowered him to write aggressively against those who judged him to have transgressed. Yet Milton is dependent on the judgments of prescriptive authorities. Freud's notion that unattackable authority is internalized by the child by means of the psychic defense of identification is pertinent here. The seemingly autonomous author narrates the story of victimized books and argues to save them; but in doing so he assumes the role of father as well as the role of the son who protests against the father. External agency is simultaneously distanced and internalized by means of a story of independent, authorial self-control.[41]

Milton's unsettled attitudes toward authority also appear in his depiction of the author's victimization at the oppressive "hands" of external force. His discussions of the licenser's stamp or *imprimatur* (L. "let it be printed"), the term which actually appears on the title page of many licensed and registered books, suggest that the text's physical alteration at the hands of the licenser is one version of the way the author may perceive himself a victim of intellectual violation. The force suggested by Latin *imprimere* (in + press) illustrates the extent of op-press-ion by prescriptive authority. In one case the English people themselves are figured as printed texts: the threat to "things indifferent" causes Milton to "fear yet this iron yoke of outward conformity hath left a slavish print upon our necks" (563–4). The "manual stamp" (563), the pressure of another hand, marks, signs and annuls the force or impression of the author, defacing him in the process. Subject to a younger licenser or one inferior in judgment, the author is "pressed" as victim into print "like a Punie with his guardian;" the "censor's hand" on the title page must be his "bayl and surety, that he is not an idiot or seducer" (532). The hand/signature of the licenser not only erases and thus undoes the singularity represented by the author's signature-hand, but also places the author in a symbolic position of disgrace, dependence, debt and immaturity.

Printed works, not just ideas, are vulnerable.[42] Like the imprimatur, licensing, in Milton's eyes, belongs to the "persecution we raise against the living labours of publick men" (493). Books are subject to "a kind of homocide" or even "martyrdome:"

> and if it extend to the whole impression, a kinde of massacre, whereof the execution ends not in the slaying of an elementall life, but strikes at the ethereall and fift essence, the breath of reason it selfe, slaies an immortality rather then a life.
>
> (493)

The massacre of an immortality involves two definitions of "the whole impression:" a full or impressive force attacks books, and the whole of the "issue," the aggregate copies of the printed book, is destroyed. The physicality of books as printed, impressed matter is not so much transcended as supremely (if subliminally) valorized; the violence against the books results in the conflation of their physical and ethereal essence.[43] As his description of textual massacre demonstrates, Milton attempts to control a variety of threats to the author by means of narration. What we are given are further events of the signature, in this case a recurrent sleight of hand which betrays the author's vulnerability to cultural and political prohibitions and is perversely animated by them. Figuration is here and at other places actually generated by the blockage which stems from repressive authority.[44]

The author as licenser

We have seen that Milton arose as publicly marked author by means of the perverse recognition afforded by transgression. Is his authority as author confirmed or undermined when he adjudges the transgression of others? As Latin Secretary for the Commonwealth from 1649 to 1652, the power and name of licenser were his, and Milton seems sometimes to have exercised them in violation of *Areopagitica*'s (admittedly qualified) defense of private thought. His activities in service of the Commonwealth thus supply the "authorized" half, as it were, of the argument for the inescapable interdependence of author and authority. Milton becomes an agent of restriction, part of the state authority which defines individual self-control by determining what constitutes violation of the public domain.

Upon official order, Milton performed acts which reveal the potentially prescriptive aspect of interpretation. During 1650 Milton was most probably involved in sifting through the private papers of at least six men and women who were accused of treasonous activity, and he also searched William Prynne's rooms.[45]

Milton's relation to one of the accused, Clement Walker, who had been placed in the Tower on charges of high treason, blurs the line between public and private, published and unpublished states of discourse. On 24 October 1650, the day Walker was imprisoned, Milton and the Parliamentary Council's sergeant at arms were ordered to examine the books and papers of this Presbyterian and former Parliamentarian (expelled during Pride's Purge of 1648). Walker's challenge to Parliament – and to Milton – as author of the 1649 *Anarchia Anglicana: or, The History of Independency* (written under a pseudonym but widely known as his work) clearly prepared the way for this showdown. In the course of defending Levellers and suggesting that by his own criteria, Cromwell could be executed on the same grounds as Charles, Walker had attacked Milton's divorce pamphlets and referred to him as a "Libertine that thinketh his Wife a Manacle, and his very Garters to be shackles and fetters to him:"

> one that (after the Independent Fashion) will be tied by no obligation to God or Man wherein he undertaketh to Prove, "That it is lawful for any that have power to call to account, Depose, and put to Death wicked Kings and Tyrants (after due conviction) if the ordinary Magistrate neglect it."[46]

Walker identifies what he sees as Milton's personal and voiced power as anarchic and lewd, qualities which reinforce each other. The boundary between the authority of the author and that of the licenser blurs when we consider the unvoiced, unpublished aspect of the language of prescription with which Milton "speaks" or replies in his role as searcher of papers. The subtexts of this "speech" include both Milton's and Walker's earlier books. Milton's review of Walker's papers helps justify Parliament's reprisal, but it was not necessary that Milton's conclusions become public; the silence of that review, its adjunct status, happens, however, to make Milton's action look indistinguishable from revenge on this occasion.

Did Milton use his duties as licenser to subvert licensing and free up the publication of books? Yes and no. The representation of Milton by his biographer Parker as a largely autonomous agent who managed to get around the prescriptive side of his duties is not helpful; Parker depicts freedom as the victory of the individual will, and Milton appears as the lone defender in an ongoing, epic, moral, and intellectual battle. A brief examination of Milton's relation to the Licensing Order of 1649 (enacted during his tenure as Latin Secretary) demonstrates that Milton joined himself to prescriptive power even when, paradoxically, he most tried to enlarge certain freedoms.

A word about the Parliamentary document, the Licensing Order (or Bradshaw Press Act) of 20 September 1649. It is often seen as containing loopholes that argue, as Masson writes, for the "partial adoption, though in . . . a merely tacit way, of the principle of the *Areopagitica*," with the result that stringent publishing controls are *implicitly* relaxed. Masson concludes:

> though this Act recognises and continues [the system set in motion by the Printing Ordinance of 1643] in a general way, it is clear from the whole tenor . . . that it contemplated the rigid application of the Licensing System thenceforth only to one class of publications, viz. Newspapers and Political Pamphlets, leaving the licensing of books at large much more a matter of option.[47]

The Order, however, explicitly states that *any printed matter* requires license, "according to ancient custom."[48] According to Siebert, rather than creating unambiguous freedom for an interpreter clever enough to note the Act's ambiguous tenor or phrasing, the Bradshaw Press Act attempted to enforce control over newsbooks as well as to continue the practice of licensing books.[49]

Not surprisingly, Milton himself provides an extreme interpretation of the Order, one which implies that authors have full control of and responsibility for their work. His interpretation eventually lands him in hot water. He writes in a letter to Samuel Hartlib, "There are no licensers appointed by this last Act, so that everybody may enter in his book without licence, provided the printer's or author's name be entered, that they may be forthcoming if required."[50] Yet there was no need to appoint licensers in this latest Act, since they were *already* appointed by the 1643 Ordinance and continued to carry out their duties.[51]

Clearly, both the author's and the printer's judgments as to the printed material's nature had to occur even before publication, just as certainly as other judgments occurred afterwards. It is not especially helpful to explain, as Parker does, that continued licensing practices were merely the fruit of obtuseness on the part of "some of Milton's contemporaries."[52] Rather, the ambiguity of the regulation points to two things: first, the desire for authorial control was being expressed and even acted upon, as Milton himself indicates. Second, what is new is that the prescriptive methods have been made less visible. There seems to be more freedom in that the agents through which the Act is to be enforced are not acknowledged; but this enlarged room to manoeuvre conceals yet again the unvoiced language of prescription. Nor is it immediately apparent who actually benefits from such concealment, Milton's letter to Hartlib in which he attributes freedom to authors notwithstanding.

Milton himself exposes the contradictory impulses at the heart of the Bradshaw Press Act, though he does so only by being exposed in the act of secretly exercising the power of the licenser in just the way that he had suggested to Hartlib the Act had made unnecessary. The occasion is the furor over the publishing "by authority" of the Socinian work known as the *Racovian Catechism*, a tract denying the Trinity, Original Sin, and Christ's divinity. The tract's printer, William Dugard (also the recent printer of Milton's *A Defense of the English People*) apparently told the Parliamentary Council that Milton had licensed the *Racovian Catechism*, for both Milton and Dugard were subsequently examined by a Parliamentary committee of forty.[53] Milton had used the power of the licenser to let the book come forth, but he did so without making the stamp public, and most important, without affixing his name to the title page, even though publishing the licenser's name seems to be most common with regard to controversial material. Authority is perversely displayed by the withholding of its display, with a resulting fiction of free publication. Milton twice obfuscates matters: once when he writes to Hartlib that anyone may enter a book without license, and once when he tells the Parliamentary committee that he had simply *approved* the book (we might add "as if untouch't by the licenser" – to recall the phrase from *Areopagitica*). By licensing the *Racovian Catechism* he used the licenser's office to interpret both the book and the licensing Act; licensing in that case was not the same as simply "refraining from forbidding books," as a Dutch diplomat reports Milton had said.[54] Milton's power resides in his ability to interpret a law and to act on it as if the interpretation is the law. In such a case interpretation substitutes for the author function. Such power can be exercised only at the margins of discourse where it is not readily visible, and indeed can be viable only to the extent that it remains invisible.

Milton was not disciplined for transgressing against this order, even though he was an employee of the Council of State. We may surmise that he remained invisible here because of the usefulness to the Commonwealth of his concurrent visibility as author of the officially licensed *Defensio pro Populo Anglicano* (*A Defense of the English People*). "By 2 April 1652," Parker observes, "Milton was the internationally known defender of the English Republic, a figure much admired by foreigners. Parliament, we may well believe, neglected to punish so embarrassing an offender."[55] Milton's *Defensio* replied to the *Defensio Regia Pro Carolo I* by the famous European scholar Claudius Salmasius (ironically, this tract was considered so dangerous that Parliament banned its importation to England); Milton's tract defended the legitimacy of the new English Commonwealth against the charge of tyranny and chaos, and it did so in part by besting Salmasius as a scholar and thus giving some effect to *Areopagitica*'s earlier images of intellectual potency. Milton's justification of the Commonwealth which that Commonwealth had commissioned him to perform allowed him to gain his own authority, reciprocally. Unlike *Eikonoklastes*, which came out earlier in Milton's secretaryship and whose title page announced that the reply to *Eikon Basilike* was "PUBLISHED BY AUTHORITY," bore only Milton's initials, and was described by him as a work assigned rather than "chosen and affected," the *Defensio* named Milton in uppercase letters just as *Areopagitica* had done; now, however, the authority derived not from the pose of autonomy and staged transgression but from the arms of the Commonwealth which accompanied the name on the title page. Milton's voice and name appeared synonymous with the governing power of England. It was Salmasius who had published the *Defensio Regia* anonymously with the understanding that his fame signed the tract for him. In signing the *Defensio* Milton poses as one who is bolder than Salmasius; at the same time, the production of his full name gives the impression of his independent voice and control, as if he is indeed his own licenser – an author witnessed by the supportive "stamp" of England's coat of arms.

Yet a combination of licensing and authorial activities was responsible for earning Milton English and foreign prominence at this time. During work on the *Defensio* and even after its publication, Milton was the official licenser of *Mercurius Politicus*, a weekly, semi-official newsbook of the Commonwealth, a post he evidently held even when he was not named explicitly. Milton's name does, however, appear with increasing frequency at one point: "By order of Master Milton" and his signature are registered in all but one or two issues in which the newsbook's continental correspondent reported the reception of Milton's *Defensio*.[56] In a move of staggering circularity, Milton licensed the publication of periodicals that increasingly published his fame and conferred legitimacy upon him.

The newspages of *Mercurius Politicus* portray the reception of Milton's tract in heroic colors. The Leyden correspondent writes that he greedily expects an answer to Salmasius who, "Goliah-like," despises all adversaries "as so many Pigmies;" in another issue, burning Milton's book in France "will make it a Martyr . . . and the Cause and Book be more inquisitively desired;" Salmasius leaves Sweden "because Milton's book having laid him open so notoriously, he became thereby very much neglected."[57] These and other such passages recall *Areopagitica*'s images of the burned, martyred book in which the life and prestige of the author fused with the author's product. Now, however, Milton wears many different and official hats at once. We also circle back to the anticipatory description of Dion Prusaeus which Milton *did* include in *Areopagitica*. Recall that Prusaeus was one of those wise, eloquent men who had honor done to them "in other lands" (489); Milton gained authority by going outside the boundaries of his land at a time when those boundaries were not recognized as legitimate by "foreigners." By externalizing the threat to the book as an action taken in foreign lands against a "proper," home product, *Mercurius Politicus* masks the inevitable "foreignness" or otherness at the heart of Milton's already monumental effort to retain control over his writing. And the story of the *Defensio*'s heroic, single effort also masks the complicated interdependence of reader, writer, printer, and licenser.

The publishing history of *Mercurius Politicus* adds the final complicated strand to the interweaving of prohibition and transgression in the discourse of power. The publisher of this newsbook was Marchamont Needham, another of those like Clement Walker whose papers Milton had been ordered to examine in 1650. Needham's frequent changes in loyalty both before and after his writing for *Mercurius Politicus* make it extremely unlikely that he was, in Parker's words, "a real convert to republican theory."[58] In fact, Needham fills the newsbook with materials critical of republicanism at a time when Milton can be presumed its official licenser. In his editorials for issues nos. 27–34, Needham employed unattributed quotations of the government's enemies, Salmasius and Hobbes, which he lifted from the appendix to the second edition of his own book *The Case of the Common-wealth*. These passages had been correctly attributed and debated in that earlier work; ironically, that book had previously convinced Parliament of Needham's solid devotion to the Parliamentary cause and resulted in his being awarded £50 plus the salaried editorship of *Mercurius Politicus*. Thus, as J. Milton French has indignantly shown, "While Milton was losing his eyesight forever from the strain of answering Salmasius the Great, his own paper was feeding Salmasian doctrine to his own public."[59]

What are we to make of the infiltration of such material into the paper at the same time that it was licensed by Milton and publishing accounts of his epic struggle with Salmasius? French decides that Milton reacted in one of three ways: he was in the "greatness of his genius" horrified by "such fly-by-night tactics;" "shrugged his shoulders" at a necessary evil "on the theory that all is fair in war, and left the ethics to the consciences of the Council;" or last, and most likely, according to French, Milton licensed the newsbook in a perfunctory fashion: "In comparison with a Latin tome which should make all Europe ring from one end to the other, the vulgar little weekly Mercuries were petty things not worth a serious thought."[60] Adopting any of French's versions tends to perpetuate a public, published "story" of Milton as autonomous, heroic, true champion of the English people; the story stalls recognition of the movements at the margins of the discourse of power even as it incorporates events at those margins. Does the nearly blind Milton not read what he licenses, or does he note, ignore, compromise? It is impossible to decide. That very impossibility argues that the silent language of prescription attends upon any attempts to speak the discourse of power and infiltrates a printed work just as surely as the language of opposition. In the midst of Milton's authorized, named, and declared bid for authority come unnamed voices which cut across his official power even as they were sanctioned by the licenser. Transgression occurs as what is prohibited turns, crosses against and thus defines authority. This time, however, Milton does not take up Needham's challenge. To do so would, perhaps, expose to view the extent to which Milton's authority is nourished by his desire to restrict and be restricted, to embrace and repudiate the language of powerful, prohibitive authority.

Notes

1. Milton was first appointed Latin Secretary on 13 March 1649. His first licensing act was the 16 December 1649 registration of *Histoire entière & véritable du Procez de Charles Stuart* (London, 1650), which appeared on or before 3 March 1650. See William Riley Parker, *Milton: A Biography*, 2 vols (Oxford, Clarendon Press, 1968), II.960.
2. David Masson, *Life of Milton*, 7 vols (Cambridge and London, Macmillan, 1859–94), vol. IV (1649–54), 324. Masson then launches into an incisive if overly ingenious interpretation of the Bradshaw Press Act in order to posit Milton's surreptitious hand in its wording (324–5).
3. Frederick Siebert, *Freedom of the Press in England 1476–1776* (Urbana, University of Illinois Press, 1965), 197. In fact, most debate centers on the more (seemingly) easily defended or attacked *Areopagitica*. See John Illo, "The misreading of Milton," for an argument that *Areopagitica* uses a rationale of revolutionary censorship, militant exclusion of the majority of English and European intellectuals: "The restriction of a conditional, not absolute, freedom of expression for the elect is the main proposition of the *Areopagitica*." In *Radical Perspectives in the Arts*, ed. Lee Baxandall (Harmondsworth, Penguin, 1972), 182; 178–92. I find Milton's relation both to restriction and to the authority which carries it out much more complicated and riddled with contradiction than does Illo.
4. Siebert, op. cit., 187. I am heavily indebted to Siebert's account for the summary of printing regulations. Compare Harry Ransom's less detailed account in *The First Copyright Statute: An Essay on an Act for the Encouragement of the Press* (Austin, University of Texas Press, 1956), 66–75, and Lyman Ray Patterson, *Copyright in Historical Perspective* (Nashville, Vanderbilt University Press, 1968), 28–142.
5. Licensers presided over fields such as divinity (twelve licensers, the most of any category), law, physick and surgery, heraldry, and philosophy, among others; even these classifications derived from the Star Chamber. See Siebert, op. cit., 187–8.
6. Ernest Sirluck notes that the entry in the Commons Journal for 29 January 1642 indicates that this order was never meant to stand alone. See *The Complete Prose Works of John Milton*, ed. Don M. Wolfe *et al.*, 8 vols (New Haven, Yale University Press, 1953–82), II.160–1. Hereafter abbreviated "YP."
7. YP II.569. Hereafter page numbers will be noted in the text.
8. The 29 January 1642 order stated that a printer who printed without the consent and name of the author "shall be proceeded against, as both Printer and Author thereof." Parliament here attempted to control the whole industry, for the order is addressed in particular to "the Master and Wardens of the Company of Stationers." Reprinted in YP II.160.
9. Reprinted in YP Appendix, II.798.

10. Marjorie Plant, *The English Book Trade* (London, George Allen & Unwin, 1939; 3rd edn 1974), 177–8. Compare Edwin Miller's account in *The Professional Writer in Elizabethan England* (Cambridge, Mass., Harvard University Press, 1959), 137–70.

11. See *The First Copyright Statute* for the specific argument that Milton was participating in the separation of points of justice in property right from points of policy in press control; Ransom thus makes a case for Milton's self-conscious endorsement of actual copyright (see esp. 71–4). I find Milton's stance more problematic than does Ransom, given the ambiguity of Milton's position on the author's relation to state regulation.

12. Ernest Sirluck provides an excellent discussion of the various factions that Milton considered in constructing *Areopagitica*'s argument. See YP II.164–81; 68–9. He concludes that Milton "enormously enlarges the scope of indifference" (170) to compensate for concessions on toleration. For a general discussion of the principles of Christian liberty see Arthur Barker, *Milton and the Puritan Dilemma* (Toronto, University of Toronto Press, 1942), 52–9.

13. This is Sirluck's position. Compare Barker, op. cit., 80–97. See esp. Barker's attempt to wrestle with the inconsistencies of Milton's treatment of licensing ordinances, note 92, 361. For the most insistent argument that Milton is being practical (unlike the "totally unrealistic" and politically naïve tolerationists), see Christopher Hill, *Milton and the English Revolution* (New York, Penguin, 1977), 149–60, esp. 156.

14. See Joseph Anthony Wittreich, "Milton's *Areopagitica*: its Isocratic and ironic contexts" (*Milton Studies*, 4, 1976, 101–15). This line of criticism has produced some views of the tract as a textbook for reader-response dynamics. See Henry S. Limouze, "'The surest suppressing': writer and censor in Milton's *Areopagitica*" (*The Centennial Review*, 24, 1980, 103–17). Limouze finds Milton deliberately unspecific, so that readers, the subject of the tract, can supply their own meaning. He finds that critics merely project their own conclusions onto the text.

15. See Illo, op. cit., esp. 182–4. Compare Willmore Kendall, "How to read *Areopagitica*" (*The Journal of Politics*, 22, 1960, 439–73). It is against Illo's position that Hill emphasizes Milton's tactical concessions: "it is not quite fair to sneer at [Milton] as if he were a twentieth-century fellow traveller who had learnt nothing from the career of Joseph Stalin" (Hill, op. cit., 158).

16. Annabel Patterson, *Censorship and Interpretation* (Madison, University of Wisconsin Press, 1984), 112; 112–17.

17. Christopher Kendrick, "Ethics and the orator in *Areopagitica*" (*ELH*, 50, 4, Winter 1983, 658–72). Kendrick's elaborate tracing of how and why *Areopagitica*'s figurative network is antidiscursive is consistently illuminating.

18. Siebert (op. cit., 191, note 71) notes that twenty-two pamphlets were published in 1640, and one thousand each year for the next four years.

19. Norbert Elias, *The Civilizing Process*, tr. Edmund Jephcott (New York, Urizen Books, 1979), 257.

20. Francis Barker argues that it is possible to detect in Milton's tract the separation of what he terms the civil realm of the private citizen from the "public arena of the state apparatus." *The Tremulous Private Body* (London, Methuen, 1984), 46. Barker's very suggestive work on *Areopagitica* came out when this article was already in draft form, and in many ways parallels my project. See also note 28.

21. William Haller, "Before *Areopagitica*" (*PMLA*, 22, 1927, 875–900). My summary of this debate closely follows Haller.

22. See William Haller, *Tracts on Liberty in the Puritan Revolution*, 3 vols (New

York, Columbia University Press, 1934), I.47–9. Hereafter abbreviated as *Tracts*.

23. For detailed accounts of the debate see A. Barker, op. cit., 80–120, and William Haller, *Liberty and Reformation in the Puritan Revolution* (New York, Columbia University Press, 1955), 100–42.
24. The debate over religious control developed out of the original discussion of Church government into more general issues about individual freedoms – just what the conservative ministers of the Assembly feared would come to pass.
25. See *Tracts*, I.67–8, esp. note 58.
26. Haller notes that the bookseller Thomason knew or at least guessed the identity of the author (*Tracts*, I, Appendix A, 124). More work needs to be done on the unofficial network of identification which seems to have existed around booksellers and others in the trade.
27. Reprinted in Haller, *Tracts*, III.84. See also Sirluck's discussion of *The Compassionate Samaritan* as primarily a secular-oriented, anticlerical-biased tract, YP II.84–7.
28. Compare Francis Barker: "The subject, now emerging as a private citizen although not legally named as such . . . may do as it pleases up to the point of transgression where its activity will be arrested by the agents of the apparatus who patrol the frontier between the two spaces" (Barker, op. cit., 46). My point is rather that the citizen is constituted in part by his forays into and between the public and private spaces; the policing which results from transgressions seems too monolithic a way to describe what happens to Milton's authority *vis-à-vis* his publishing endeavors during the Civil War.
29. Phoebe Sheavyn, *The Literary Profession in the Elizabethan Age* (Manchester, Manchester University Press, 1909), 82.
30. Richard C. Newton, "Jonson and the (re-)invention of the book," in *Classic and Cavalier*, ed. Claude J. Summers and Ted-Larry Pebworth (Pittsburgh, University of Pittsburgh Press, 1982), 37. The list of Jonson's practices is Newton's.
31. On the subjects of Milton's arrangement of the *Poems* and the unity of the volume, see Louis Martz, "The rising poet," in *Poet of Exile* (New Haven, Yale University Press, 1980), 31–59. Compare Newton, op. cit., 46–7.
32. Reprinted in Appendix B of YP II.797–8.
33. See Jacques Derrida, *Signsponge*, tr. Richard Rand (New York, Columbia University Press, 1984), 18–28.
34. ibid., 122. For a quite different treatment of the title page, consider Annabel Patterson's analysis, op. cit., 115–17. Patterson especially concentrates on Milton's epigraph from *The Suppliants* to conclude that he combines "the plainest intentionality with the finest allusiveness" (115). I do not agree that Milton so easily can be seen as defending multivocality; to take *Areopagitica* as a "powerful manifesto for indeterminacy" (112) is to beg some of the messier questions of his relation to various forms of authority.
35. Michel Foucault, "What is an author?" in *Language, Counter-Memory, Practice*, tr. Donald Bouchard (Ithaca, Cornell University Press, 1977), 124. Foucault, however, locates the emergence of the "real" author at a later time, "when a system of ownership and strict copyright rules were established (toward the end of the eighteenth and beginning of the nineteenth century)" (124–5). The English Civil War, however, provides evidence of much earlier instances than those Foucault cites; surely interest in the assignment of authorship does not have to wait for a fully developed copyright system.
36. Quoted in Sirluck's summary of the immediate occasions for the divorce tracts and *Areopagitica*, YP II.142.

37. The note on *Areopagitica*'s title YP II, 486, sets out the variety of allusions. See Wittreich, op. cit., for a treatment of Milton's particular use of Isocrates.
38. See "Milton's marginalia," in *Milton Encyclopedia*, vol. 5, ed. William B. Hunter (Lewisburg, Bucknell University Press, 1979), 73–4. In 1636 Milton had purchased a 1604 Paris edition of the *Orations* in Greek.
39. *Dio Chrysostom: Works*, tr. J. W. Cohoon and H. Lamar Crosby, 5 vols (Cambridge, Mass., Harvard University Press, 1940), III, ll.20–5.
40. Compare Prusaeus: "this plea of ignorance and of antiquity is about the same as if a person should say that those who rifle the very old tombs do no wrong, on the ground that no one of the dead is related to them and we do not even know who they are," *Dio Chrysostom: Works*, III, ll.94–9.
41. *Civilization and Its Discontents*, in *The Standard Edition of the Complete Psychological Works of Sigmund Freud*, ed. James Strachey *et al.*, 24 vols (London, Hogarth Press, 1953–74), XXI.129–30. I am indebted to Margaret Ferguson's discussion of this concept in *Trials of Desire* (New Haven, Yale University Press, 1983), 122–4. References to actual fatherhood in *Areopagitica* veer back and forth in being associated with permissive or restrictive authority. A man cannot be a "Doctor in his book" if "under the correction of his patriarchal licenser" (532–3; "patriarchal" alluding to the contemporary idea that Archbishop Laud wished to be the first Patriarch of a Roman Catholic England – see Sirluck's note, 533); Parliament would, in essence, reinforce "an abrogated and mercilesse law, that fathers may dispatch at will their own children" (559) if it retained its licensing policy.
42. Contrast Limouze who finds that Milton's concern is not the mutilation of a book but the "inward state of its author" (110). It seems rather that the materiality of the author's project helps to define the complex realm of public discourse.
43. Compare Christopher Kendrick on this passage, op. cit., 658–72. Kendrick's suggestive discussion of the "uncentered ethical orientation" of the literary subject (688) is crucial for thinking about the problem of the subject in this tract.
44. The threat to the author results in comic figuration when Milton portrays the "authors" of the licensing "invention" as several "glutton friars" who produce "5 Imprimaturs . . . together dialoguewise in the Piatza of one Title page, complementing and ducking each to other with their shaven references, whether the Author, who stands by in perplexity at the foot of his Epistle, shall to the Presse or the sponge" (503–4). Literally pressed down by his interchangeable keepers, the author is oppressed by emptily repetitive action; he is also suspended in a benignly static condition. Also, the author is the one who both must alter his text by going to the sponge and is himself text on the verge of expungement. The seeming disarmament provided by the comic actually causes the "arresting" transgression of the author, his coming into being by means of violation.
45. See Parker, *Biography*, I.355; II.958–9, 971, 972, and Masson, *Life*, IV.88, 89, 121, 146, 147, 149, 150.
46. Reproduced in Parker, *Milton's Contemporary Reputation* (Columbus, Ohio State University Press, 1940), 82.
47. Masson, *Life*, IV.118.
48. Part of the document attempts to prevent "false, imperfect, and impertinent" descriptions of Parliamentary proceedings and other news by ordering that "no person whatsoever shall compose, write, print, publish, sell or utter, or cause to be made, written, printed, or uttered, any Book or Pamphlet, Treatise, Sheet or Sheets of news whatsoever, unless licensed as is hereafter mentioned, upon the like penalty."

The order later states that any printed matter cannot be readied for publication and sale unless first approved and "licensed under the hand of the Clerk of the Parliament, or of such person as shall be authorized by the Council of State for the time being . . . the same to be entered in their several Registers . . . and also in the Register-Book of the Company of Stationers, according to ancient custom." Printers seem to be the nodal point for the enforcement of this order, since they are required to enter a £300 bond which would be forfeited if they printed anything "seditious, scandalous, or treasonable" "not licensed as aforesaid." They also are required to place "the Author's name, with his quality and place of residence, or at least the Licensers' names where licenses are required" in addition to their own names and addresses on the title page (see Masson, *Life*, IV.117–18). The order moved most severely against any kind of newsbook: all were prohibited from publication, and earlier licenses were revoked; obviously Parliament wanted more control over the dissemination of new material.

49. See Siebert, op. cit., 222–3, for his conclusion that the 1649 order applied just as rigidly to books as to other forms of printed material.
50. Quoted in Parker, *Biography*, I.35.
51. Masson, *Life*, IV.118.
52. Parker, *Biography*, II.955.
53. Dugard had been called to appear before the Parliamentary Council on 21 January 1652. The *Racovian Catechism* had been published in March 1651 but only registered eight months later in November; it seems likely that Dugard was feeling the heat and needed to link up his action to the official licensing (especially since printers could forfeit £300 for irregular practice). Dugard subsequently had the entire entry cancelled out at his request on 29 January 1652.
54. Report by Dutch diplomat Leo Aitzema, 5 November 1652. Quoted in J. Milton French, *The Life Records of John Milton*, 5 vols (New Brunswick, Rutgers University Press, 1954), III.206. See also Parker, *Biography*, II.994.
55. Parker, *Biography*, II.993–4.
56. Issues nos. 44–6 appeared by permission of authority; nos. 47–50 had Milton as explicit licenser, while nos. 51–85 showed Milton the weekly licenser (Parker, *Biography*, II.993). See also J. Milton French's brilliant piece of detective work, "Milton, Needham, and *Mercurius Politicus*" (*Studies in Philology*, 33, 1936, 238–41). *Defensio*'s progress on the continent is featured in *Mercurius Politicus* issues nos. 45, 48, 56, 57, 58, 66, 82, 84, among others. I follow Parker and French on the spelling of "Needham."
57. Quoted in Parker, *Milton's Contemporary Reputation*, 86–8.
58. Parker, *Biography*, I.394. Needham had been writing lively and seditious prose for the royalist newsbook, *Mercurius Pragmaticus*, before his arrest, escape, and rearrest by Parliament. Before *Pragmaticus*, he had written for the Parliamentary organ, *Mercurius Britanicus*, but his early support for Parliament ended when that body castigated him for some critical remarks and Needham retaliated by going down on his knees before Charles I to obtain his pardon. Needham also changed his mind a few times under the governments which followed the Commonwealth. For Needham's biography see *The Dictionary of National Biography*, 22 vols (London, Oxford University Press), XIV.159–64.
59. French, op. cit., 242.
60. ibid., 246.

II
Texts in their contemporary contexts

5

MARY NYQUIST

The genesis of gendered subjectivity in the divorce tracts and in *Paradise Lost*

It appears that one can now speak of "third-wave feminism" as well as "post-feminist feminism." Like other labels generated by the historical moment to which they refer, these await a lengthy period of interrogation. But if they should stick, their significance will be associated with the variety of attacks mounted against Western bourgeois or liberal feminism over the past decade and a half. Now, as never before, what has to be contended with – precisely because it has been exposed in the process of contestation and critique – is the historically determinate and class-inflected nature of the discourse of "equal rights." The questions, equal with whom, and to what end? have been raised in ways that have begun to expose how, ever since the early modern period, bourgeois man has proved the measure. They have also shown how the formal or legal status of this elusive "equality" tends by its very nature to protect the status quo.

Because much academic criticism on *Paradise Lost*, especially that produced in North America, has been written within a liberal–humanist tradition that wants Milton to be, among other things, the patron saint of the companionate marriage, it has frequently made use of a notion of equality that is both mystified and mystifying. The undeniable emphasis on mutuality to be found in *Paradise Lost* – the mutual dependency of Eve and Adam on one another, their shared responsibility for the Fall – is for this reason often treated as if it somehow entailed a significant form of equality. Differences that in *Paradise Lost* are ordered hierarchically and ideologically tend to be neutralized by a critical discourse interested in formal balance

99

and harmonious pairing. To take just one, not especially contentious, example, Milton is said to go out of his way to offset the superiority associated with Adam in his naming of the animals by inventing an equivalent task for Eve: her naming of the flowers. In this reading, Milton, a kind of proto-feminist, generously gives the power of naming to both woman and man.[1] The rhetorical effectiveness of this point obviously depends in important ways upon the suppression of features suggestive of asymmetry. Left unquestioned must be the differences between Adam's authoritative naming of the creatures – an activity associated with the rational superiority and dominion of "Man" when it is presented by Adam, who in Book VIII relates to Raphael this episode of the creation story in the second chapter of Genesis – and Eve's naming of the flowers, which is revealed only incidentally in her response to the penalty of exile delivered in Book XI. In a speech that has the form of a lament for the garden she has just been told they are to leave, Eve's naming in Book XI appears in such a way that it seems never to have had the precise status of an event. It is, instead, inseparably a feature of her apostrophic address to the flowers themselves: "O flow'rs / . . . which I bred up with tender hand / From the first op'ning bud, and gave ye Names" (XI.273–7).[2] Here Eve's "naming" becomes associated not with rational insight and dominion but rather with the act of lyrical utterance, and therefore with the affective responsibilities of the domestic sphere into which her subjectivity has always already fallen.

In recent years, a remarkably similar critical current, intent on neutralizing oppositions, has been at work in feminist biblical commentaries on Genesis. Within the Judeo-Christian tradition, claims for the spiritual equality of the sexes have very often had recourse to Genesis 1.27, "So God created man [*hā'ādām*, ostensibly a generic term] in his own image, in the image of God created he him; male and female created he them."[3] This verse, which is part of what is now considered the Priestly or "P"creation account (Genesis 1–2.4a), has always co-existed somewhat uneasily with the more primitive and more obviously masculinist Yahwist or "J"creation account in chapter 2, where the creator makes man from the dust of the ground (thereby making *hā'ādām* punningly relate to *hā'ādāmâ*, the word for ground or earth) and woman from this man's rib. Within a specifically Christian context, the relationship between the two accounts has been – at least potentially – problematical, since 1 Timothy 2:11–14 uses the Yahwist account to bolster the prohibition against women taking positions of authority within the Church: "Let the woman learn in silence with all subjection. But I suffer not a woman to teach, nor to usurp authority over the man, but to be in silence. For Adam was first formed, then Eve. And Adam was not deceived, but the woman being deceived was in the transgression." Recently, in an effort to reconcile feminism and Christianity, Phyllis Trible has tried to harmonize the differences between the Priestly and the Yahwist creation accounts. Trible holds that the exegetical tradition alone is responsible for the sexist meanings usually attributed to the Yahwist creation story, which she renarrates using methods that are basically formalist.

More specifically, Trible argues that the second chapter of Genesis tells the story not of the creation of a patriarchal Adam, from whom a secondary Eve is derived, but the story of the creation of a generic and androgynous earth creature or "man" to whom the sexually distinct woman and man are related as full equals. Throughout, Trible's retelling is strongly motivated by the desire to neutralize the discrepancy between the "P" and the "J" accounts by assimilating "J" to "P," which is assumed to recognize the equality of the sexes and therefore to provide the meaning of the two creation accounts taken together as one. Because "P" suggests the possibility of a symmetrical, non-hierarchical relationship between male and female, "J" is said by Trible to tell the story of the creation of a sexually undifferentiated creature who becomes "sexed" only with the creation of woman. The simultaneous emergence of woman and man as equals is signalled, she argues, when Yahweh brings the newly fashioned partner to the previously undifferentiated *hā'ādām* or "man," who responds with the lyrically erotic utterance: "This is now bone of my bones, and flesh of my flesh: she shall be called Woman, because she was taken out of Man" (Genesis 2:23) (in Trible's reading "taken out of" means "differentiated from").[4]

Trible's revisionary and profoundly ahistorical reading is significant in large part because it has been so widely influential. Among feminist theologians it would seem to have established a new orthodoxy. And it has recently been ingeniously elaborated for a secular readership by Mieke Bal, who assumes with Trible that the commentator can, by an effort of will, position herself outside the traditions of masculinist interpretation; and that Genesis bears no lasting traces of the patriarchal society which produced it.[5] Yet it is far too easy to adopt the opposing or rather complementary view that Genesis is a text inaugurating a transhistorically homogeneous patriarchal culture. This is, unfortunately, a view that is frequently expressed in connection with *Paradise Lost*. For in spite of the existence of scholarly studies of Genesis in its various exegetical traditions, the view that the relationship of *Paradise Lost* to Genesis is basically direct or at least unproblematically mediated continues to flourish. And so, as a result, does an entire network of misogynistic or idealizing commonplaces and free-floating sexual stereotypes, relating, indifferently, to Genesis and to this institutionally privileged text by Milton, English literature's paradigmatic patriarch.

The notion of a timeless and ideologically uninflected "patriarchy" is of course vulnerable on many counts, not least of which is its capacity to neutralize the experience of oppression. I would therefore like to attempt to situate historically Milton's own appropriation of the Genesis creation accounts. In the process, I hope also to draw a preliminary sketch, in outline, of the genealogy of that seductive but odd couple, mutuality and equality. It is certainly not difficult to recognize the reading given Genesis by Trible and Bal as a product of its time. Especially in North America, the notion of an originary androgyny has had tremendous appeal to mainstream or liberal feminism. Taken to represent an ideal yet attainable equality of the sexes, androgyny is often associated metaphorically with an ideal and egalitarian form of marriage. A passionate interest in this very institution makes itself felt throughout Milton's divorce tracts, in which his interpretation of the two creation accounts first appears. Milton's exegesis, too, is the product of an ideologically overdetermined desire to unify the two different creation accounts in Genesis. Not surprisingly, at the same time it is representative of the kind of masculinist "mis"-reading that Trible and Bal seek to overturn. By emphasizing its historical specificity, however, I hope to show that it is so for reasons that cannot be universalized.

II

Milton appropriates these two texts, first in the divorce tracts and then in *Paradise Lost*, by adopting the radically uni-levelled or this-worldly Reformed method of reconciling them. For leading commentators such as Calvin and Pareus, the two accounts do not correspond to two stages in the creation of humankind, the intelligible and the sensible, as they do in an earlier, Greco-Christian tradition. Indeed there are not in their view two accounts in this sense at all but instead one story told in two different ways, once, in the first chapter of Genesis, in epitome, and then, in the second chapter, in a more elaborated form. Simplifying matters considerably, and using terms introduced into the analysis of narrative by Gérard Genette, one could say that in the view articulated especially cogently by Calvin and then elaborated, aggressively, by Milton, the *story* consists of the creation in the image of God of a single being supposed to be representative of humankind, Adam, and then the creation of Eve; the *narrative discourse* distributes this story by presenting it first in a kind of abstract and then in a more detailed or amplified narrative fashion. More specifically, the first two statements of Genesis 1:27, "So God created man in his own image, in the image of God created he him," are thought to refer to the creation of the representative Adam, told in a more leisurely and graphic fashion as a creation involving the use of the dust of the ground in the second chapter; while the concluding "male and female created he them" is taken to refer to the creation from this Adam of his meet help, Eve.

Echoing similar statements by Pareus, Milton writes of the second chapter's narrative of Eve's creation for Adam: "This second chapter is granted to be a commentary on the first, and these verses granted to be an exposition of that former verse, 'Male and female created he them.'"[6] Yet the second chapter can have the status of a commentary in part because of the gaps, ambiguities, or troublesome suggestions to be found in the first. Commenting on the blessing of fertility in Genesis 1:28, for example, Calvin says that it is actually given to the human couple after they have been joined in "wedlocke," even though this event is not narrated until the following chapter.[7] As this indicates, for Protestant commentators, in so far as the rhetorically amplified second version is capable of interpreting and completing the account that comes before it in this way, it is the last creation account that tends to take precedence over the first.

If the Protestant exegetes Milton cites in his divorce tracts find the meaning of "male and female created he them" in the narrative of the creation of a help meet for Adam, they do so by reading that narrative ideologically, as proving that marriage, far from being what in their view the Roman Church would have it, a remedy prescribed for the spiritually weak, is divinely instituted, indeed recommended. That woman was created solely or even primarily for the purposes of procreation is the low-minded or "crabbed" (Milton's adjective) opinion the Protestant doctrine of marriage sees itself called to overturn.[8] Emphasizing, eloquently, the psychological needs sanctioned by the deity's words instituting marriage ("It is not good that the man should be alone," Genesis 2:18), the Reformers enable an emerging bourgeois culture to produce what has the appearance at least of an egalitarian view of the marital relation. The very phrase "meet for him" is said by Calvin to suggest in the Hebrew *kĕneged*, the quality of being "like or answerable unto" (*quia illi respondeat*) the man and to indicate vividly that psychological rather than physical likeness founds marriage as an institution.[9] Milton endorses this view when he takes the untranslatably expressive Hebrew "originall" to signify *"another self, a second self, a very self itself"* (T 600), and also when he has the divine interlocutor promise Adam, "Thy likeness, thy fit help, thy other self, / Thy wish, exactly to thy heart's desire" (*PL* VIII.450–1).

As has often been pointed out, in the divorce tracts Milton raises to unprecedented and undreamt of heights this early modern tendency to idealize the marriage bond. The extent to which he relies upon an implicit privileging of "J" over "P" (indeed, over the other texts he treats, as well) in order to do so has, however, not been commented upon. Milton's advocacy of a more liberalized interpretation of the grounds for divorce proceeds by countering the mean-spirited misinterpretations of scripture promulgated by scholastics and canonists.[10] On its more constructive front, it seeks to harmonize different and radically conflicting scriptural texts. The most taxing exegetical feat Milton has to perform is the reconciliation of Matthew 19:3–11, which suggests that remarriage after divorce is forbidden on grounds other than "fornication," and Deuteronomy 24:1–2, which Milton reads as sanctioning divorce for reasons of what we would now call incompatibility. *Tetrachordon*, the tract in which Milton's skills as exegete are most on display, announces in its very title his determination to establish unity and sameness in the place of seeming difference and contradiction. Meaning "four-stringed," and thus referring to the four-toned Greek scale, *Tetrachordon* attempts to harmonize what on the title page are referred to as the "foure chief places in Scripture, which treat of Mariage, or nullities in Mariage." The first text given on the title page is "Gen. 1.27.28 compar'd and *explain'd by* Gen. 2.18.23.24" (*T* 577; my emphasis).[11]

The explaining of Genesis 1 *by* Genesis 2 is of multi-fronted strategic importance to Milton's polemical attack on existing English divorce laws, which don't properly recognize the spiritual nature of marriage. First and foremost, it permits Milton to exploit rhetorically the sexual connotations of "male and female," essential to the divorce tracts' central, most tirelessly worded argument, which is that neither sexual union in and of itself nor procreation is the primary end of marriage as originally constituted. Commenting directly on "Male and female created he them" in *Tetrachordon*, Milton states it has reference to "the right, and lawfulness of the mariage bed." When relating this text to its immediate context, he claims that sexual union is an "inferior" end to that implied by the earlier "So God created man in his own image, in the image of God created he him" (Milton's detailed exegesis of which I'll be coming back to later on) (*T* 592). As this suggests, a bi-polar and hierarchical ordering of the spiritual and physical dimensions of experience structures many of the exegetical moves in these tracts. The following commentary on "male and female" is fairly representative, and illustrates, in addition, the important role played by "J:"

> He that said *Male and female created he them*, immediately before that said also in the same verse, *In the Image of God created he him*, and redoubl'd it, that our thoughts might not be so full of dregs as to urge this poor consideration of *male and female*, without remembring the noblenes of that former repetition; lest when God sends a wise eye to examin our triviall glosses, they be found extremly to creep upon the ground: especially since they confesse that what here concerns mariage is but a brief touch, only preparative to the institution which follows more expressely in the next Chapter. . . .
>
> (*T* 592)

The divorce tracts seek to persuade the mind that doesn't want to creep upon the ground that it should be duly impressed with the fact that in Genesis 2:18 God himself speaks, revealing in no uncertain terms what the end of marriage is: "And the Lord God said, It is not good that the man should be alone; I will make him an help meet for him." Expounding the true meaning of the earlier verse, "Male and female created he them," this verse declares "by the explicite words of God himselfe" that male and female is none other "than a fit help, and meet society" (*T* 594). Milton is willing to put this even more strongly. It's not just that we have here the words of God himself, expounding the meaning of an earlier text. God here actually explains *himself*: "For God does not heer precisely say, I make a female to this male, as he did briefly before, but expounding himselfe heer on purpos, he saith, because it is not good for man to be alone, I make him therefore a meet help" (*T* 595).

In Milton's exegetical practice, then, "J"'s narrative makes possible a spiritualized interpretation of the more lowly and bodily "male and female." Indeed, "J"'s narrative, understood as instituting a relationship primarily psychological, provides the very basis for the passages emphasizing mutuality to be found throughout the divorce tracts. The above citations don't begin to convey the eloquence with which Milton can celebrate the pleasures of a heterosexual union that is ideally – that is, on the spiritual plane intended by its divine institution – fitting or meet. And there are numerous other moments in these works where without rhetorical flourish mutuality is clearly asserted or implied. The woman and man of the marriage relation can, for example, be referred to as "helps meete for each other."[12] On a more practical level, and of direct relevance to the legal reforms he is proposing, is the statement Milton offers of his position when opening the first chapter of *The Doctrine and Discipline of Divorce*: "*That indisposition, unfitnes, or contrariety of mind, arising from a cause in nature unchangable, hindring and ever likely to hinder the main benefits of conjugall society, which are solace and peace, is a greater reason of divorce then naturall frigidity, especially if there be no children, and that there be mutuall consent*" (*DDD* 242). The explicit reference to "mutuall consent" here is matched or perhaps even deliberately introduced by the opening words of the subtitle appearing in both the first and second editions of this work: "Restor'd to the Good of Both Sexes, From the bondage of Canon Law, and other mistakes. . . ."

Yet much as the dominant discourse of the academy might like to celebrate this praiseworthy attention to mutuality, there are very few passages of any length in the divorce tracts that can be dressed up for the occasion. For over and over again, this laudable mutuality loses its balance, teetering precariously on the brink of pure abstraction. And the reason it does so is that it stands on the ground (to recall the play on *hā'ādāmâ*) of a lonely Adam who is not in any sense either ungendered or generic. It becomes clear, finally, that the concluding phrase of Milton's position-statement – "and that there be mutuall consent" – is not expected to stand up in a court of law. In the penultimate chapter of the second edition of *The Doctrine and Discipline of Divorce*, Milton states his view "that the absolute and final hindring of divorce cannot belong to any civil or earthly power, against the will and consent of both parties, *or of the husband alone*" (*DDD* 344; my emphasis). Even if this could, improbably, be attributed to a moment's forgetfulness on the part of an author busy revising and enlarging his original, it still wouldn't be able to pass itself off as an instance of simple self-contradiction. For as I hope to show, this particular assertion is also the self-consistent outcome of the deeply masculinist assumptions at work in Milton's articulation of a radically bourgeois view of marriage.

Time and again, the language of the tracts passes through the use of plural forms potentially inclusive of both sexes only to come to rest with a non-generically masculine "he." As the discussion up to this point has indicated, in so far as the story of Eve's creation from Adam's rib is thought to articulate the Protestant doctrine of marriage, it is not her creation *after* Adam *per se* that is so significant but her creation *for* him, to remedy his loneliness. The egalitarian sentiments expressed, sporadically, throughout the divorce tracts therefore cannot finally obscure Eve's secondary status as a "gift" from one patriarch to another. Created for Adam, Eve is, as Adam puts it in *Paradise Lost*, "Heav'n's last best gift" (V.19). Yet Eve is also, of course, created *from* Adam, as well as *for* him. And in Milton's view, as Adam's "likeness" Eve does not even have the status – to use Satan's description of "man" in *Paradise Lost* – of the Father's "latest," meaning most recent, "image" (IV.567). For by unifying the two creation stories in the way Reformed principles permit him to, Milton's exegesis makes possible the production of two ideologically charged and historically specific readings, contradictorily related: on the one hand an interpretation of "male and female" that psychologizes heterosexual union and dignifies marriage, and on the other an explication of "created man in his image" that tends to restrict the meaning of "man" to an individual Adam, from whom and for whom the female is then made.

It is important to put this exactly, for of course biblical commentators always claim that woman is also in some sense made in the image of God. Calvin, like Milton, however, locates the generic sense of "man" directly in the first and gendered man's representative status. Commenting on Genesis 2:18, "I will make him an help meet for him," Calvin responds to the question, why isn't the plural form "Let us make" used here, as it was in the creation of "man"?:

> Some think, that by this speach, the difference which is betweene both sexes is noted, and that so it is shewed, how much more excellent the man is, then the woman. But I like better of another interpretation, which differeth somewhat, though it be not altogether contrarie: namely, that when in the person of man, mankinde was created, the common worthinesse of the whole nature, was with one title generally adorned, where it is said, *Let us make man*: and that it was not needful to be repeated in the creating of the woman, which was nothing else but the addition and furniture of the man [quae nihil aliud est quam viri accessio]. It cannot be denied, but the woman also was created after the image of God, though in the seconde degree. Whereupon it followeth,

that the same which was spoken in the creation of the man, perteineth to womankind.[13]

Milton's stridently masculinist, "Hee for God only, shee for God in him" in *Paradise Lost* obviously goes much further than Calvin in drawing out the masculinist implications of this hermeneutical practice, which forges an identity between the generic and the gendered "man." In *Tetrachordon*, too, Milton pursues the logic of this exegesis with a maddening and motivated precision. In his commentary on "in the image of God created he him," the intermediate statement of Genesis 1:27, he states that "the woman is not primarily and immediately the image of God, but in reference to the man," on the grounds that though the "Image of God" is common to them both, "had the Image of God been equally common to them both, it had no doubt bin said, In the image of God created he them" (*T* 589).

So it continues to matter that Adam was formed first, then Eve. As a further means of taking the measure of Milton's interest in this priority, I would now like to discuss three seventeenth-century texts more favourably disposed towards an egalitarian interpretation of Genesis. Although research in this area is still underway, it is safe to say that Milton could not but have known that questions of priority figure prominently in the Renaissance debate over "woman" we now know as the "Querelle des Femmes." In *A Mouzell for Melastomus, the cynicall bayter of, and foule mouthed barker against Evahs sex*, for example, one of the feminist responses to Joseph Swetnam's *The Araignment of lewd, idle, forward and unconstant women*, Rachel Speght appeals several times to the privilege assumed to be a property of firstness. Speght mentions that although it is true that woman was the first to sin, it is also woman who receives the "first promise" that God makes in Paradise; she argues that the dignity of marriage is proved by Jesus honouring a wedding ceremony with "the first miracle that he wrought;" and that the spiritual equality of the sexes is shown when after his Resurrection Christ "appeared unto a woman first of all other."[14]

In the restricted intellectual economy of the "Querelle," orthodox views of male superiority are frequently countered by paradoxical assertions of female superiority. Lastness is therefore placed in the service of overturning firstness, as in Joan Sharpe's poetic defense of women against Swetnam's *Araignment*, where it is claimed: "Women were the last worke, and therefore the best, / For what was the end, excelleth the rest."[15] Speght, however, deliberately avoids the use of this kind of paradox. Like other Renaissance and Reformed commentators, preachers and courtesy-book writers, Speght places a strong emphasis on marriage as involving the "mutuall participation of each others burden." And this emphasis is sustained rhetorically throughout the tract. For example, while accepting the conventional view that woman is "the weaker vessel," Speght supplies a subtly polemical reference to man as "the stronger vessel."[16] In deploying a linguistic stress on balance and mutuality to neutralize hierarchical oppositions, this young, early seventeenth-century Protestant may very well be the most important unsung foremother of modern liberal feminist commentators on Genesis and on *Paradise Lost*.

Speght does not offer any programmatic statements on the relation of "P" to "J," nor does she attempt systematically to assimilate one to the other. But like all feminist participants in the "Querelle des Femmes," she assumes that Genesis 1:26 and 27 provide a clear statement of the spiritual equality of the sexes. The passage in which she briefly explicates Genesis 1:27 is distinctive, however, in its provisional but decidedly revisionary reconciliation of the two creation accounts: "in the Image of God were they both created; yea and to be brief, all the parts of their bodies, both externall and internall, were correspondent and meete each for other."[17] By referring to both woman and man, and in relation to one another, the terms "correspondent and meete" ("correspondent" being, as modern commentators point out, a good translation of the Hebrew *kĕneged*) deftly unite the "male and female created he them" of the "P" account with the account in "J" of Eve's creation for Adam, which here, momentarily, loses its narrative identity. Speght's brief exegesis carefully preserves an emphasis on bodily fitness, while pointedly ignoring questions of chronology that might threaten the egalitarian statement.

At one point Speght refers to marriage as "a merri-age, and this worlds Paradise, where there is mutuall love."[18] The same celebratory word-play ("the very name whereof should portend unto thee merry-age") appears in a work published just two years before Swetnam's provocative tract, Alexander Niccholes' *A Discourse, of Marriage and Wiving*. Interesting for, among other things, its citation of lines from the Player Queen's speech in *Hamlet*, Niccholes' *Discourse* eulogizes the special pleasures of marital friendship in one of the very phrases used in *Tetrachordon*: the wife is "such a friend, which is to us a second selfe."[19] Niccholes' brief commentary on the two creation accounts differs significantly from Milton's, however. Appearing in the first chapter, "Of the First Institution and Author of Marriage," Niccholes' exegetical remarks follow the citation of Genesis 2:18 ("It is not good for the man to bee alone"):

> so the creation of the woman was to be a helper to the man, not a hinderer, a companion for his comfort, not a vexation to his sorrow, for *consortium est solatium*, Company is comfortable though never so small, and Adam tooke no little joy in this his single companion, being thereby freed from that solitude and silence which his lonenesse would else have bene subject unto, had there beene no other end nor use in her more, then this her bare presence and society alone: But besides all this, the earth is large and must be peopled, and therefore they are now the Crowne of his

Workemanship, the last and best and perfectest peece of his handiworke divided into Genders, as the rest of His creatures are, Male and Female, fit and enabled *Procreare sibi similem* to bring forth their like, to accomplish his will, who thus blessed their fruitfulnesse in the Bud: Increase and multiply, and replenish the earth.[20]

In this passage, as in the divorce tracts, the two different creation accounts, presented in their "real" order of occurrence, are discussed as if each revealed a different end or benefit of the first institution. And "J"'s narrative of the creation of a meet help for Adam, given a strictly psychological and social interpretation, is given priority over "P"'s. But Niccholes significantly omits any discussion of the creation of "man" in God's image. This absence permits the plural "they" easily to take over, so that it is the (now happily united) first man and woman alike who are "the last and best and perfectest peece of his handiworke." Although Niccholes mentions that woman was made both "for" and "out of" man, he maintains his emphasis on mutuality by erasing any explicit or evaluative commentary on her having been made *after* man, as well.

The commentary I would like to examine next is one produced during the same period as the divorce tracts, that is, at the very time when egalitarian issues of all kinds were being hotly contested, and when women in the sectaries not only laid claim to their spiritual equality with men on the basis of Genesis 1:27 and other texts, but publicly proclaimed the extra-textual significance of this equality by preaching and prophesying.[21] Unlike Speght's and Niccholes', the text I turn to now belongs, officially, to the commentary genre. Issued in association with the Westminster Assembly and published in 1645, the annotations on Genesis in *Annotations Upon All the Books of the Old and New Testaments* have not, to my knowledge, ever been studied.[22] Yet they shed an extraordinarily clear, not to say glaringly bright, light on the distinctive and motivated features of Milton's exegesis.

An annotation on 1:26 takes up directly the question of the meaning of the signifier "man" or "Adam." With reference to the phrase "let them" (in "And let them have dominion over the fish of the sea," etc.), the annotation states: "The word *man*, or the Hebrew, *Adam*, taken not personally or individually for one single person, but collectively in this verse, comprehendeth both male and female of mankind: and so it may well be said, not *let him*, but *let them* have dominion." Here the generic sense of *hā'ādām* is made completely to override the gender-specific sense. To this end, the use of the plural pronoun in the latter section of Genesis 1:26 is privileged over the singular pronoun, used with reference to the image ("in the image of God created he him"). This annotation alone therefore reveals a process of interpretation diametrically opposed to that at work in *Tetrachordon*, where, as we have seen, Milton seizes upon the difference between singular and plural forms in Genesis 1:26 and 27 to argue that only the gender-specific Adam is made immediately in the image of God.

What makes comparison of the *Annotations* with *Tetrachordon* possible and of crucial importance is that both accept the Reformed view of the relationship between the two creation accounts. Adam and Eve are said to be formed on the same, that is, the sixth, day, but their creations are presented first in chapter 1, where "their creation in the generall was noted with other creatures," and then again in chapter 2, where "in regard of the excellencie of mankind above them all, God is pleased to make a more particular relation of the manner of their making, first of the man, vers. 7. and here [vers. 22] of the woman." Yet as these words suggest, the *story* assumed by the *Annotations* is slightly different from Milton's, which starts unabashedly with a "man" taken personally or individually. The difference is fine, but extremely significant. Like Milton and other Protestant commentators, the *Annotations* rejects the view that male and female were created simultaneously, together with the view that both sexes were originally embodied, hermaphrodite-like, in a single being. "J"'s narrative ordering is respected, which means that woman was indeed created after man. But this is how the gloss on verse 27's "male and female" puts it:

> Not at once, or in one person, but severally; that is, though he united them in participation of his image, he distinguished them into two sexes, male and female, for the increase of their kinde: their conformitie in participation of Gods Image is clearly manifest by many particulars, for in most of the respects fore-mentioned, Annotation in ver. 26, the image of God is equally communicated to them both, and Eve was so like to Adam (except the difference of sexe which is no part of the divine image) in the particulars fore-mentioned, that in them, as she was made after the image of Adam, she was also made after the image of God: as if one measure be made according to the standard, an hundred made according to that, agree with the standard as well as it.

By associating differences between the sexes solely with reproduction, this comment seems to hearken back to a Platonically inflected division between the spiritual and the physical. The concluding analogy, however, shows this truly remarkable text grappling with hierarchically ordered notions of secondariness. Working with reference to the production of things in the form of commodities, the analogy attempts to take on the difficulties resulting from the view that man and woman were made "severally." And it tries to effect, on its own, an egalitarian synthesis of "P" and "J." That man was first made in the image of God is implicitly conceded. But that woman was made "after" man becomes a statement referring not so much to an order of temporality as to an order of materiality. Woman is made "after" the image of Adam in the sense of being made "according to the standard" of the image of Adam. The analogy argues, by ellipsis, that since Adam was himself really created "after" the image of God, which is the original "standard," being created "after" Adam's image, Eve is equally created "after" the image of God. Thanks to this highly ingenious and polemically motivated analogy, Eve's being created "after" Adam loses its usual sense of secondariness.

Read in the context of other learned Protestant biblical commentaries, this analogy has a jarring effect since, in exceeding by ninety-nine the requirements of logic, it seems to testify to the contemporary phenomenon of the growth of mercantile capital. For the sake of an egalitarian synthesis between "P" and "J," this workmanly analogy tries to undermine not only a hierarchically inflected logic of temporality but also the generally Platonic logic whereby original is privileged over copy. It is true that man is still, quite literally, the "measure." And to give the analogy its force, woman is placed in the position of being not the first commodity made "after" this measure but rather the "hundred" that can be produced on its basis. The logic deployed by the analogy from production insists, however, that it is not really possible to measure any residual differences between the image of God, man, and woman. Of the great variety of attempts made in the Renaissance and seventeenth century to come to Eve's defense, this must be the least chivalrous in content, the most lacking in conventional grace or charm. But it definitely does the job. And it certainly establishes, dramatically, the possibilities open to Milton, which he rejected.

In rejecting a position like that of the *Annotations*, Milton implicitly takes what would seem, from another perspective, though, to be a "progressive" stance, namely that the difference between woman and man is not a simple matter of biology; that it is not a difference of sex *per se*. In both *Tetrachordon* and *Colasterion* Milton rejects the view that Adam would have been given a male not a female partner had companionship been the end of marriage. The following passage from *Tetrachordon*, which comments on the all-important "*It is not good for man to be alone,*" suggests why Milton would not want to imagine Eve's being created according to the same "standard" as Adam:

> And heer *alone* is meant alone without woman, otherwise *Adam* had the company of God himself, and Angels to convers with; all creatures to delight him seriously, or to make him sport. God could have created him out of the same mould a thousand friends and brother *Adams* to have bin his consorts, yet for all this till *Eve* was giv'n him, God reckn'd him to be alone.

> (*T* 595)

By specifying a desire that only "woman" can satisfy, and by associating that desire with a transcendence of sexual difference as vulgarly understood, the divorce tracts seem almost to open up a space for the category of "gender." Yet that this space is in no sense neutral can be seen in the language with which friendship between men gets differentiated from the marital relation. In *Colasterion* Milton opposes "one society of grave freindship" to "another amiable and attractive society of conjugal love."[23] Elsewhere Milton can associate the marriage relationship with the need man has for "sometime slackning the cords of intense thought and labour" (*T* 596); or he can refer to the seeking of "solace in that free and lightsome conversation which God & man intends in mariage" (*DDD* 273). It should go without saying that man can have this need for companionship remedied, can intend to enjoy "lightsome conversation" as opposed to "grave freindship," only if woman is constituted as less grave, more attractive, more lightsome and more amiable than her male counterpart; and if both she and marriage itself are associated with a world apart.

III

As has already been suggested, the priority bestowed upon Adam in Milton's divorce tracts is not associated directly with the order of creation. It tends, instead, to be inscribed in the divine words instituting marriage, "It is not good that the man should be alone; I will make him an help meet for him" (Gen. 2:18). These words, which Milton frequently refers to simply as "the institution," are in turn often taken to gesture towards a prior loneliness or "rational burning" experienced by the first man, Adam. I have already argued that the priority Milton gives "J" over "P" is inscribed indelibly in every one of his major rhetorical and logical moves. In concluding this discussion of the divorce tracts, I would like to show how consistently or systematically this priority is associated with the deity's instituting words and thus, by implication, with Adam's needs.

It has not yet been mentioned that Matthew 5:31, 32 and Matthew 19:3–11, which together constitute one of the four texts treated in *Tetrachordon*, and which appear unequivocally to forbid divorce except for fornication, are susceptible to Milton's polemical appropriation of them precisely because in chapter 19 Jesus is represented as quoting from Genesis. The relevant verses, cited by Milton, are the following, verses 3–6:

> The Pharisees also came unto [Jesus], tempting him, and saying unto him, Is it lawful for a man to put away his wife for every cause? And he answered and said unto them, Have ye not read, that he which made them at the beginning made them male and female, And said, For this cause shall a man leave father and mother, and shall cleave to his wife: and they twain shall be one flesh? Wherefore they are no more twain, but one flesh. What therefore God hath joined together, let not man put asunder.

The two texts cited here are the now-familiar "male and female created he them" in Genesis 1:27 and "Therefore shall a man leave his father and his mother, and shall cleave unto his wife: and they shall be one flesh" (Gen.

2:24). Milton's strategy in commenting on the verses from Matthew is to subvert their literal and accepted meaning by referring the citations back to the divine words of institution, which, he points out, are *not*, significantly, quoted. Although the tempting Pharisees, his immediate interlocutors, aren't worthy of receiving this instruction, Jesus's intention, Milton argues, is to refer us back to the uncited words of institution in chapter 2, "which all Divines confesse is a commentary to what [Jesus] cites out of the first, the *making of them Male and Female*" (*T* 649). The instituting words are thus made to govern the manner in which those cited by Jesus from chapter 1 are to be interpreted.

Also cited is Genesis 2:24, which Milton regards as spoken by Adam. Yet Milton's exegesis has already determined that Adam's speech too has meaning only with reference to the words of divine institution. In the first part of Adam's speech ("This is now bone of my bones, and flesh of my flesh: she shall be called Woman, because she was taken out of Man," Gen. 2:23), Milton finds Adam referring to and expounding his maker's instituting words, regarded as constituting a promise now fulfilled (*T* 602). By establishing a dialogic relation between Adam's words and those of his maker, Milton can argue that anyone who thinks Adam is in these words formulating the doctrine of the indissolubility of marriage "in the meer flesh" is not only sadly mistaken but guilty of using "the mouth of our generall parent, the first time it opens, to an arrogant opposition, and correcting of Gods wiser ordinance" (*T* 603). It is the next part of Adam's speech, however, verse 24, which is commonly thought to be "the great knot tier," as Milton correctly points out: "Therefore shall a man leave his father and his mother, and shall cleave unto his wife: and they shall be one flesh." In Milton's view, *by* opening with "therefore," this verse clearly indicates that Adam confines the implications of his utterance only to "what God spake concerning the inward essence of Mariage in his institution" (*T* 603). With reference to both parts of Adam's speech, Milton's position thus is that the deity's words are the "soul" of Adam's and must be taken into Adam's utterance if it is properly to be understood.

This is not, interestingly, the reading given these verses by Calvin, who assigns verse 23 to Adam, but draws attention to the interpretative choices open with regard to 2:24, for which three different speakers are eligible: Adam, God, and Moses. After a brief discussion Calvin opts for Moses, suggesting that, having reported what had historically been done, Moses in this passage sets forth the end of God's ordinance, which is the permanence or virtual indissolvability of the marriage bond.[24] For reasons that are obvious, Milton would want to reject this reading. By making Adam the speaker of this passage, Milton weakens its authority as a text enjoining the indissolubility of marriage. Since this is the very text cited by Jesus in Matthew, such an assault on its status as injunction is a decisive defensive move. But it is also more than that. For by assuming Adam to be its speaker,

Milton also strengthens the contractual view of the first institution his exegetical practice implicitly but unmistakably develops.

That Milton's understanding of the first institution is implicitly both contractual and masculinist can perhaps be seen if his exegetical practice is compared with that of Rachel Speght. Towards the beginning of *A Mouzell for Melastomus*, Speght argues that Eve's goodness is proved by the manner of her creation:

> Thus the resplendent love of God toward man appeared, in taking care to provide him an helper before hee saw his owne want, and in providing him such an helper as should bee meete for him. Soveraignety had hee over all creatures, and they were all serviceable unto him; but yet afore woman was formed, there was not a meete helpe found for *Adam*. Mans worthinesse not meriting this great favour at Gods hands, but his mercie onely moving him thereunto: . . . that for mans sake, that hee might not be an unit, when all other creatures were for procreation duall, hee created woman to bee a solace unto him, to participate of his sorrowes, partake of his pleasures, and as a good yokefellow beare part of his burthen. Of the excellencies of this Structure, I meane of Women, whose foundation and original of creation, was Gods love, do I intend to dilate.[25]

Were Milton to have read Speght's tract, I suspect that midway through the first sentence here he would have discovered himself a resisting reader. The notion that God acted on Adam's behalf "before hee saw his own want" would have seemed highly provocative, if not downright offensive. Speght draws strategically on orthodox Protestantism's doctrinal emphasis on divine grace as radically transcendent, as an active principle utterly unconnected with human deserts. In the process, Adam becomes a passive recipient of a gift, meetness abounding, while Eve is subtly positioned in relation with her true "original," divine love.

By contrast, in the divorce tracts and, as we shall see, in *Paradise Lost* as well, Milton foregrounds an Adam whose innocent or legitimate desires pre-exist the creation of the object that will satisfy them. But this is to put it too abstractly. In Milton's exegesis, the significance of the gift – woman – passed from maker to man is determined by two speeches, first the maker's and then Adam's, precisely because these speeches are construed as a verbal exchange that is basically contractual. In Genesis 2:18 Adam's maker promises him that he will assuage his loneliness and provide him with a meet help; in 2:23 and 24, Adam accepts this gift by acknowledging it is exactly what was promised him, and then promises to honour it on these very grounds. Eve's status as a divinely bestowed gift is exploited polemically by both Speght and Milton. But unlike Speght's transcendent lord of love, Milton's veiled but systematic insistence on the contractual form of the first institution is produced by a Protestantism pressed into the service of an historically specific form of individualism, an individualism paradigmatically masculine, autonomous, articulate, and preternaturally awake to the implications of entering into relations with others.[26]

IV

One of the questions concerning *Paradise Lost* that this discussion of the divorce tracts has, I hope, made it possible to address is: why does Milton's Eve tell the story of her earliest experiences first, in Book IV? Why, if Adam was formed first, then Eve, does Adam tell *his* story to Raphael *last*, in Book VIII? An adequate response to this question would require a full-scale analysis of the ways in which *Paradise Lost* articulates a putative sequential order of events or story with the narrative discourse that distributes this story. As a genre, epic is of course expected to develop complicated relations between a presumed chronological and a narrative ordering of events. But *Paradise Lost* would seem to use both retrospective and prospective narratives in a more systematic and motivated manner than does any of its predecessors, in part because it is so highly conscious of the problematical process of its consumption. I would like to argue here that *Paradise Lost*'s narrative distribution of Adam and Eve's first experiences is not just complexly but ideologically motivated, and that the import of this motivation can best be grasped by an analysis aware of the historically specific features of Milton's exegetical practice in the divorce tracts.

This practice is crucially important to *Paradise Lost*'s own use of the Genesis creation texts. In the case of the passage it most obviously informs, Raphael's account of the creation of "man" on the sixth day of creation in Book VII, certain features are intelligible only in the light of this historically specific context. If commenting on this passage at all, critics have tended to suggest that Raphael gives something like a heavenly, as compared with Adam's later more earthly, account of creation.[27] This doesn't, however, even begin to do justice to the intricately plotted relations of the "P" and "J" accounts in the following:

> Let us make now Man in our image, Man
> In our similitude, and let them rule
> Over the Fish and Fowl of Sea and Air,
> Beast of the Field, and over all the Earth,
> And every creeping thing that creeps the ground.
> This said, he form'd thee, *Adam*, thee O Man
> Dust of the ground, and in thy nostrils breath'd
> The breath of Life; in his own Image hee
> Created thee, in the Image of God
> Express, and thou becam'st a living Soul.
> Male he created thee, but thy consort

Female for Race; then bless'd Mankind, and said,
Be fruitful, multiply, and fill the Earth,
Subdue it, and throughout Dominion hold
Over Fish of the Sea, and Fowl of the Air,
And every living thing that moves on the Earth.
Wherever thus created, for no place
Is yet distinct by name, thence, as thou know'st
He brought thee into this delicious Grove,
This Garden, planted with the Trees of God,
Delectable both to behold and taste;
And freely all thir pleasant fruit for food
Gave thee, all sorts are here that all th' Earth yields,
Variety without end; but of the Tree
Which tasted works knowledge of Good and Evil,
Thou may'st not; in the day thou eat'st, thou di'st;
Death is the penalty impos'd, beware,
And govern well thy appetite, lest sin
Surprise thee, and her black attendant Death.
Here finish'd hee.

(VII.519–48)

Genesis 1:26–8 is here given in what is virtually its entirety. But the principal acts of Genesis 2:7–17 are also related: Yahweh's making of "Man" from the dust of the ground (2:7), his taking of this man into the garden of Eden (2:15), and his giving of the prohibition (2:16,17). One could argue that even Milton's "artistry" here hasn't received its proper due, since this splicing economically makes from two heterogeneous accounts a single one that is both intellectually and aesthetically coherent.

Yet it does more, far more, than this. For Raphael's account removes any trace of ambiguity – the residual generic dust, as it were – from the Priestly account of the creation of hā'ādām or "man" in the image of God. This it does by a set of speech-acts unambiguously identifying this "man" with Raphael's interlocutor, Adam. The direct address in "he form'd thee, *Adam*, thee O Man / Dust of the ground" has what amounts to a deictic function, joining the representative "Man" to Raphael's gendered and embodied listener, who is specifically and repeatedly addressed here, while Eve (though still an auditor) very pointedly is not. It is clearly significant that these very lines effect the joining of the Priestly and Yahwistic accounts. By placing "thee O Man / Dust of the ground" in apposition to the named "Adam," it is suggested that this individualized "Adam" actually *is* hā'ādām or representative man and the punning hā'ādāmâ "ground," an identity that only the joining of the two accounts reveals.

The impression this joining creates is that the two accounts have always already been one in narrating the creation of Adam. The same cannot be said of Raphael's account of the creation of Eve, however. For in contrast (I would like to say something like "in striking contrast," yet it has not really been noticed) to the ingenious joining that takes place for the sake of Adam, Raphael refers to Eve's creation only in the statement immediately following, which is again, significantly, addressed to Adam: "Male he created thee, but thy consort / Female for Race" (529–30).[28] Outside of this meagre "but thy consort / Female for Race," Raphael's account does not otherwise even allude to the creation of Eve, although, as we have seen, other details of the narrative in the second chapter are included in it. Indeed, if we examine the matter more closely, it appears that the Yahwist account is made use of only up to and including Genesis 2:17 (the giving of the prohibition) precisely because Genesis 2:18 inaugurates the story of the creation of a help meet for Adam.

But of course the story of Eve's creation is not excised from *Paradise Lost* altogether, which is, presumably, why readers have not protested its absence here. It is told later, by another narrator, Adam. One of the effects of this narrative distribution is that in Milton's epic Adam's story comes to have exactly the same relation to Raphael's as in the divorce tracts and in Protestant commentaries the second chapter of Genesis has to the first: it is an exposition or commentary upon it, revealing its true import.[29] Yet the second telling can have this status only because it is Adam's. As my discussion indicates, Milton's argument in the divorce tracts rests on a radical privileging of "J" over "P" in the specific form of a privileging of the words of divine institution in Genesis 2:18. Had Milton interpolated the story of Eve's creation into Raphael's creation account, he would have had to record these words in the form of indirect speech (as he does the words of prohibition in lines 542–7) or else to have reproduced both the creator's speech and Adam's. In either case, the instituting words would have been displaced from their centres of authority. By transferring the entire narrative to Adam and by interpolating a dramatic colloquy into this narrative, *Paradise Lost* ensures the coincidence of narrator and auditor of the instituting words, of narrator and of the first man's instituting response. By dramatizing this commentary, this necessary supplement to Raphael's account, in the form of a colloquy narrated by Adam, *Paradise Lost* makes sure that the doctrine of marriage is both produced and understood by the person for whom it is ordained, just as in the divorce tracts it is the privileged male voice, Milton's, which expounds the true doctrine of divorce.

As the divorce tracts never tire of insisting, the true doctrine of marriage relates only to the satisfaction of that which the wanting soul needfully seeks. In *Paradise Lost* this doctrine is co-authored by Adam and the "Presence Divine," who work it out together. It is also communicated, formally, by the extraordinary emphasis placed on Adam's subjectivity, on his actual experience of desire. As Milton has masterminded the exchange, the divine instituting words come *after* Adam has been got to express his longing for a fitting companion (VIII.444–51), so that this longing has the kind of priority that befits the first man. Yet the longing is also clearly a rational burning. With its strong filiations to the disputation, the very form of the colloquy establishes that this desire is rational, and that merely reproductive ends are certainly not what Adam has in mind. Although procreation is referred to, it is presented as a kind of necessary consequence of the conjunction of male and female, but for that very reason as a subordinate end. Adam's language cleverly associates it with a prior lack, a prior and psychological defect inherent in his being the first and only man (VIII.415–25). The way Milton's Adam responds to the deity's formal presentation to him of his bride, Eve, is just as motivated. The Genesis 2:23–4 speech is cited, but only after it has been introduced in a way that joins it explicitly to the causes implicit in the deity's instituting words:

> This turn hath made amends; thou hast fulfill'd
> Thy words, Creator bounteous and benign,
> Giver of all things fair, but fairest this
> Of all thy gifts, nor enviest. I now see
> Bone of my Bone, Flesh of my Flesh, my Self
> Before me; Woman is her Name, of Man
> Extracted; for this cause he shall forgo
> Father and Mother, and to his Wife adhere;
> And they shall be one Flesh, one Heart, one Soul.
> (VIII.491–9)

This speech is presented as a species of spontaneous lyrical utterance ("I overjoy'd could not forbear aloud" (490)) and according to Adam is "heard" by Eve. Yet it is obviously addressed *not* to her but to her maker, who is thanked for the gift itself, but not until he has been praised for having kept his word. Before letting Adam commit himself to the project of becoming one flesh with Eve, Milton has to make it clear that Adam does so believing that the "Heav'nly Maker" has done what he has promised, that is, created a truly fit help.

Not only the placement of Adam's narrative after Raphael's but also its most salient formal features can thus be seen to be motivated ideologically, and to illustrate the causes joining the divorce tracts and *Paradise Lost*. Before turning to Eve, I would like to summarize the discussion so far by emphasizing that these causes are joined, and to man's advantage, both when "P" and "J" are united and when they aren't. By joining "P" and "J" as it does, Raphael's account specifies the gendered Adam of *Paradise Lost* as the "man" who is made in the divine image. By disjoining them, Raphael's account lets Adam himself tell the story of the creature made to satisfy his desire for an other self.

We can now, more directly, take up the question, why does heaven's last best gift tell her story first? One way of approach might be to suggest that had Eve's narrative of her earliest experiences appeared where "naturally," in the order of creation, it should have, that is *after* Adam's, *Paradise Lost* might have risked allowing her to appear as the necessary and hence in a certain sense superior creature suggested by what Jacques Derrida has called the logic of the supplement, undeniably set in motion by Adam's self-confessed "single imperfection." *Paradise Lost*'s narrative discourse would seem to want to subvert this logic by presenting Eve's narrative first. And it seems to want to subvert it further by placing immediately *after* Adam's narrative a confession in which Eve's completeness and superiority is made to seem an illusion to which Adam is, unaccountably, susceptible. In this part of Adam's dialogue with Raphael, the language of supplementarity as artificial exteriority seems curiously insistent: Eve has been given "Too much of Ornament" (VIII.538); she is "Made so adorn for thy delight the more" (VIII.576) and so on.

Yet a displaced form of the logic of supplementarity may nevertheless be at work in the place of priority given Eve's narrative. For if Eve is created to satisfy the psychological needs of a lonely Adam, then it is necessary that *Paradise Lost*'s readers experience her from the first as expressing an intimately subjective sense of self. From the start she must be associated in a distinctive manner with the very interiority that Adam's need for an other self articulates. Or to put this another way, Eve's subjectivity must be made available to the reader so that it can ground, as it were, the lonely Adam's articulated desire for another self. Appearing as it does in Book IV, Eve's narrative lacks any immediately discernible connection with the Genesis creation accounts on which the narratives of both Raphael and Adam draw. Its distance from Scripture as publicly acknowledged authority is matched by Eve the narrator's use of markedly lyrical, as opposed to disputational, forms. Set in juxtaposition to the rather barrenly disputational speech of Adam's which immediately precedes it in Book IV, Eve's narrative creates a space that is strongly if only implicitly gendered, a space that is dilatory, erotic, and significantly, almost quintessentially, "private."

In a recent essay, Christine Froula reads Eve's first speech thematically and semi-allegorically, as telling the story of Eve's (or woman's) submission of her own personal experience and autonomy to the voices (the deity's, then Adam's) of patriarchal authority. As the very title of her essay – "When Eve Reads Milton" – indicates, Froula wants to find in Milton's Eve if not a proto-feminist then a potential ally in contemporary academic feminism's struggle to interrogate the academic canon together with the cultural and political authority it represents. Milton's Eve can play the part of such an ally, however, only because for Froula the privacy of Eve's earliest experiences and the autonomy she thereby initially seems to possess are equivalent to a potentially empowering freedom from patriarchal rule.[30] Given the liberal assumptions of the feminism it espouses, Froula's argument obviously does not want to submit the category of personal experience to ideological analysis.

In attempting to give it such an analysis, I would like to suggest that Eve's speech plays a pivotal role, historically and culturally, in the construction of the kind of female subjectivity required by a new economy's progressive sentimentalization of the private sphere.[31] It is possible to suggest this in part because the subjective experiences Eve relates are represented as having taken place before any knowledge of or commitment to Adam. That is, they are represented as taking place in a sphere that has the defining features of the "private" in an emerging capitalist economy: a sphere that appears to be autonomous and self-sustaining even though not "productive" and in so appearing is the very home of the subject. In Book VIII Adam recalls having virtually thought his creator into existence and having come up with the idea of Eve in a dialogue with his fellow patriarch. By contrast, Eve recalls inhabiting a space she believed to be uninhabited, autonomous, hers – but for the "Shape within the wat'ry gleam." It is, however, precisely because this belief is evidently *false* that it is possible to see this space as analogous to the "private" sphere, which is of course constituted by and interconnected with the "public" world outside it. Illusory as this autonomy is, inhabiting a world appearing to be her own would nevertheless seem to be the condition of the subjectivity Eve here reveals.

It has long been a commonplace of commentaries on *Paradise Lost* that a network of contrasts is articulated between Eve's narration of her earliest experiences and Adam's, the contrasts all illustrating the hierarchically ordered nature of their differences. Yet it has not been recognized clearly enough that while shadowing forth these bi-polar oppositions, Eve's narrative is supposed to rationalize the mutuality or intersubjective basis of their love. For by means of the Narcissus myth, *Paradise Lost* is able to represent her experiencing a desire equivalent or complementary to the lonely Adam's desire for an "other self." It is not hard to see that Adam's own desire for an other self has a strong "narcissistic" component. Yet Adam's retrospective narrative shows this narcissism being sparked, sanctioned and then satisfied by his creator. By contrast, though in Book IV Eve recalls experiencing a desire for an other self, this desire is clearly and unambiguously constituted by illusion, both in the sense of specular illusion and in the sense of error. Neo-Platonic readings of the Narcissus myth find in it a reflection of the "fall" of spirit into matter. Milton transforms this tragic tale into one with a comic resolution by instructing Eve in the superiority of spirit or, more exactly, in the superiority of "manly grace and wisdom" over her "beauty." But because this happily ending little *Bildungsroman* also involves a movement from illusion to reality, Eve is made to come to prefer not only "manly grace and wisdom" as attributes of Adam but also, and much more importantly, Adam as embodiment of the reality principle itself: he whose image she really is, as opposed to the specular image in which her desire originated.

To become available for the mutuality the doctrine of wedded love requires, Eve's desire therefore must in effect lose its identity, while yet somehow offering itself up for correction and reorientation. As has often been noted, Eve's fate diverges from that of Narcissus at the moment when the divine voice intervenes to call her away from her delightful play with her reflection in the "waters." We have seen that in Book VIII Adam's desire for an other self is sanctioned by the divine presence's rendering of "It is not good that the man should be alone; I will make him an help meet for him." When the divine voice speaks to Eve, it is to ask that she redirect the desire she too experiences for an other self:

> What thou seest,
> What there thou seest fair Creature is thyself,
> With thee it came and goes: but follow me,
> And I will bring thee where no shadow stays
> Thy coming, and thy soft imbraces, hee
> Whose image thou art, him thou shalt enjoy
> Inseparably thine.

(IV.467–73)

Unlike the instituting words spoken to Adam in Book VIII, these have no basis in the Yahwist creation account. Yet they are clearly invented to accompany the only part of that account which Milton has to work with here, the brief "and brought her unto the man" (Gen. 2:22), which in Genesis immediately precedes Adam's words of recognition. Marked inescapably by literary invention and uttered by a presence that is invisible to Eve, the voice's words have a curiously secondary or derivative status, at least compared with those spoken to Adam. They seem indeed, fittingly, to be a kind of echo of the divine voice.

In so far as it effects a separation of Eve from her physical image, this word in a way echoes what Milton calls the creator's originary "divorcing command" by which "the world first rose out of Chaos" (DDD 273). But the separation of Eve from her image is not the only divorce effected here. Before this intervention the "Smooth Lake" into which Eve peers seems to her "another Sky," as if the waters on the face of the earth and the heavens were for her indistinguishable or continuous. The divine voice could therefore much more precisely be said to recapitulate or echo the paternal Word's original division of the waters from the waters in Genesis 1:6–7. Before describing her watery mirror and her other self, Eve mentions "a murmuring sound / Of waters issu'd from a Cave" – murmurs, waters and cave all being associated symbolically with maternality, as critics have pointed out. When the paternal Word intervenes, Eve's specular auto-eroticism seems to become, paradoxically, even more her own, in part because it no longer simply reflects that of Ovid's Narcissus. And when Eve responds to the verbal intervention by rejecting not only his advice but also Adam, "hee / Whose image" she is, preferring the "smooth wat'ry image," an analogical relationship gets established between female auto-eroticism and the mother–daughter dyad. But – and the difference is of crucial importance – this implicit and mere analogy is based on specular reflection and error alone. Grounded in illusion, Eve's desire for an other self is therefore throughout appropriated by a patriarchal order, with the result that in *Paradise Lost*'s recasting of Ovid's tale of Narcissus, Eve's illusion is not only permitted but destined to pass away. In its very choice of subject, Milton's epic seems to testify to the progressive privatization and sentimentalization of the domestic sphere. That this privatization and sentimentalization make possible the construction of a novel female subjectivity is nowhere clearer than in Eve's first speech, in which the divine voice echoes the words originally dividing the waters from the waters, words which in their derived context separate Eve from the self which is only falsely, illusorily either mother or other.

This takes us to the very last feature of Eve's story-telling to be considered here. As has been suggested, Protestant exegetes consider Adam's declaration in Genesis 2:24, "This is now bone of my bones, and flesh of my flesh," to be part of the first wedding ceremony. A version of this ceremonial utterance appears in Adam's narrative and (highly abridged) in Eve's. In Genesis, this declaration follows "and brought her unto the man," a verse which is translated into action in both of *Paradise Lost*'s accounts. Calvin, when commenting on this phrase, views the action from Adam's point of view, as involving the exchange of a gift: "For seeing Adam took not a wife to him selfe at his owne will: but tooke her whome the Lord offered and appointed unto him: hereof the holinesse of matrimonie doeth the better appeare, because we know that God is the author thereof."[32] Yet Milton is not alone in seeing this moment from Eve's point of view as well as from Adam's, for Diodati, commenting on "And brought her unto him," says: "As a mediator, to cause her voluntarily to espouse her self to Adam and to confirm and sanctify that conjunction."[33] In *Paradise Lost*, the story Eve tells stresses with remarkable persistence both the difficulty and the importance of Eve's "voluntarily" espousing herself to Adam. Many years ago Cleanth Brooks mentioned that Eve's speech in Book IV seemed to anticipate Freud's observations on the comparative difficulty the female has in the transition to adult heterosexuality.[34] But if it does so, it is in a context that constitutes female desire so as to situate the process of transition within competing representational media, within what is almost a kind of hall of voices and mirrors.

This entire discussion of the relation between *Paradise Lost*'s retrospective creation narratives and the divorce tracts can therefore be put in the following, summary terms. If in Book VIII's recollected colloquy Adam is revealed articulating the doctrine of marriage, in Book IV's recollected self-mirroring Eve is portrayed enacting its discipline. Or to formulate this somewhat differently, by associating Eve with the vicissitudes of courtship and marriage, and by emphasizing her voluntary submission both to the paternal voice and to her "author" and bridegroom, Adam, *Paradise Lost* can *first* present the practice for which Adam *then*, at the epic's leisure, supplies the theory. In doing so, *Paradise Lost* manages to establish a paradigm for the heroines of the genre Milton's epic is said to usher in. In the Yahwist's creation account, Adam may have been formed first, then Eve. But Milton's Eve tells her story first because the domestic sphere with which her subjectivity associates itself will soon be in need of novels whose heroines are represented learning, in struggles whose conclusions are almost always implicit in the way they begin, the value of submitting desire to the paternal law.

Of course the female authors and readers associated with the rise of the novel are not always willing to submit to this discipline. And in what is perhaps the most strongly argued critique of the institution of marriage to be written by a feminist before this century, "Milton" is prominently associated with the very ideological contradictions that get exposed. In *Reflections upon Marriage*, Mary Astell submits the notion of "subjection" to an analysis that is devastatingly sharp and in certain ways deconstructive, since she wants to undo the notion that subjection is synonymous with "natural" inferiority. Arguing, even if with heavy irony, by means of the very rationalist and individualist principles that came to prevail during the Civil War period, Astell urges women who are considering marriage to become fully conscious of the liberties they will have to surrender if they are to enter into this state of institutionalized domestic subjection. Her wry reference to Milton is fairly well-known: "For whatever may be said against Passive-Obedience in another case, I suppose there's no Man but likes it very well in this; how much soever Arbitrary Power may be dislik'd on a Throne, not *Milton* himself wou'd cry up Liberty to poor *Female Slaves*, or plead for the Lawfulness of Resisting a Private Tyranny."[35]

As I have suggested, the appearance, at least, of Active-Obedience is far more important to *Paradise Lost* and to Milton's rationalism than this remark would suggest. Might an awareness of this be registered in Astell's reflections on Genesis in the supplementary "Preface"? Like other feminists writing from within the Christian tradition, Astell finds 1 Timothy 2:11–14, with its unambiguous assertion of the Genesis Adam's priority over Eve, exceedingly troublesome: she offers a rather laboured allegorical interpretation, and then adds the caveat that if the "Learned" don't accept it, it will be because "Learning is what Men have engros'd to themselves."[36] Though less defensive, her remarks on Genesis itself are no less acerbic. After mentioning, approvingly though tentatively, the opinion that "in the

Original State of things the Woman was the Superior," Astell proceeds to this brilliantly savage rebuttal of the notion of woman's "inferior" secondariness:

> However this be, 'tis certainly no Arrogance in a Woman to conclude, that she was made for the Service of GOD, and that this is her End. Because GOD made all things for Himself, and a Rational Mind is too noble a Being to be Made for the Sake and Service of any Creature. The Service she at any time becomes oblig'd to pay to a Man, is only a Business by the Bye. Just as it may be any Man's Business and Duty to keep Hogs; he was not made for this, but if he hire himself out to such an Employment, he ought conscientiously to perform it.[37]

Like other feminist commentators, from participants in the "Querelle des Femmes" to Phyllis Trible and Mieke Bal, Astell here implicitly privileges "P" over "J." In overturning the view that woman was created "for" man, Astell, however, applies to the domestic sphere the historically determinate notion of contractual relations that Milton helps to articulate in his divorce tracts, political treatises and in *Paradise Lost*. With dazzling, Circe-like powers, Astell's analogy works to disabuse bourgeois "Man" of his delusions of grandeur. But in exploiting, however archly, a contractual notion of "Service," it also illustrates some of the hazards involved in the project – ongoing – of trying to call a spade a spade.

Notes

1. For this, see Barbara K. Lewalski, "Milton and women – yet once more" (*Milton Studies*, 6, 1974, 8). Other defenses have been written by Virginia R. Mollenkott, "Milton and women's liberation: a note on teaching method" (*Milton Quarterly*, 7, 1973, 99–102); Joan M. Webber, "The politics of poetry: feminism and *Paradise Lost*" (*Milton Studies*, 14, 1980, 3–24) and Diane K. McColley, *Milton's Eve* (Urbana, University of Illinois Press, 1983). Generally speaking, an apologetic tendency is a feature of much North American academic literature on Milton.
2. Quotations from Milton's poetry are from *John Milton: Complete Poems and Major Prose*, ed. Merritt Y. Hughes (New York, Odyssey, 1957).
3. Biblical quotations are from the King James version.
4. Phyllis Trible, *God and the Rhetoric of Sexuality* (Philadelphia, Fortress, 1978), 100–1. The discussion in chs 1 and 4 of this work revises and extends the influential "Depatriarchalizing in biblical interpretation" (*Journal of the American Academy of Religion*, 16, 1973, 30–48). For a fuller discussion of some of the exegetical issues touched upon here, see an earlier version of this essay, "Genesis, genesis, exegesis, and the formation of Milton's Eve," in *Cannibals, Witches and Divorce: Estranging the Renaissance*, ed. Marjorie Garber (Baltimore, Johns Hopkins Press, 1987), 147–208. The present essay is part of a full-length study on Genesis, gender, discourse and Milton to be published by Cornell University Press and by Methuen.
5. Mieke Bal, "Sexuality, sin, and sorrow: the emergence of the female character (a reading of Genesis 1–3)" (*Poetics Today*, 6, 1985, 21–42).

6. *Tetrachordon*, ed. Arnold Williams, in vol. II of *The Complete Prose Works of John Milton*, ed. Ernest Sirluck (New Haven, Yale University Press, 1959), 594. Subsequent references to this edition of *Tetrachordon* will appear parenthetically introduced by "*T*." See David Paraeus, *In Genesin Mosis Commentarius* (Frankfurt, 1609), 267, 293.
7. John Calvin, *A Commentarie of John Calvine, upon the first booke of Moses called Genesis*, tr. Thomas Tymme (London, 1578), 47.
8. Margo Todd argues persuasively for the importance of relating Protestant to humanist views in "Humanists, Puritans and the spiritualized household" (*Church History*, 49, 1980, 18–34). For a discussion of the distinctively Puritan development of this ideology see William and Malleville Haller, "The Puritan art of love" (*Huntingdon Library Quarterly*, 5, 1942, 235–72); William Haller, "Hail Wedded Love" (*English Literary History*, 13, 1946, 79–97); see also John Halkett, *Milton and the Idea of Matrimony: A Study of the Divorce Tracts and "Paradise Lost"* (New Haven, Yale University Press, 1970), and James T. Johnson, *A Society Ordained by God: English Puritan Marriage Doctrine in the First Half of the Seventeenth Century* (Nashville, Abingdon, 1970). For a negative evaluation of the impact on women of the development of bourgeois marriage doctrine, see Linda T. Fitz, "'What says the married woman?:' marriage theory and feminism in the English Renaissance" (*Mosaic* 13, Winter) 1980, 1–22. For a wide-ranging, comparatist discussion of these socio-economic and ideological changes as they affect the relations of the sexes, see the introduction to *Rewriting the Renaissance*, ed. Margaret W. Ferguson, Maureen Quilligan and Nancy J. Vickers (Chicago: University of Chicago Press, 1986), xv-xxxi.
9. Calvin, op. cit., 74. Latin cited from *Mosis Libri V, cum Johannis Calvini Commentariis* (Geneva, 1563), 19.
10. The political, legal and social contexts for Milton's tracts are discussed by Chilton L. Powell in *English Domestic Relations, 1487–1653* (New York, Columbia University Press, 1917), 61–100, and by Ernest Sirluck (ed.), vol. II of *Complete Prose Works*, 137–58. Milton's rhetorical strategies are examined by Keith W. Stavely, *The Politics of Milton's Prose Style* (New Haven, Yale University Press, 1975), 54–72, and by John M. Perlette, "Milton, Ascham, and the rhetoric of the divorce controversy" (*Milton Studies*, 10, 1977, 195–215). A relevant and illuminating study of the "crossing" of rhetorical, judicial and other discursive codes can be found in Pat Parker's "Shakespeare and rhetoric: 'dilation' and 'delation,'" in *Othello, Shakespeare and the Question of Theory*, ed. Patricia Parker and Geoffrey Hartman (London, Methuen, 1985), 54–74.
11. For a discussion of the title, see the preface by Arnold Williams, *Tetrachordon*, 571.
12. *The Doctrine and Discipline of Divorce*, ed. Lowell W. Coolidge, vol. II of *Complete Prose Works*, 240. Further references will be introduced by "*DDD*."
13. Calvin, op. cit., 72; *Mosis Libri V*, 18.
14. Rachel Speght, *A Mouzell for Melastomus, the cynicall bayter of, and foule mouthed barker against Evahs sex* (London, 1617), 6, 14, 16. Joseph Swetnam, *The Araignment of lewd, idle, forward, and unconstant women* (London, 1615). For further discussion of this controversy, see Coryl Crandall, *Swetnam the Woman-Hater: The Controversy and the Play* (Lafayette, Purdue University Studies, 1969), and Linda Woodbridge, *Women and the English Renaissance: Literature and the Nature of Womankind, 1540–1620* (Chicago, University of Illinois Press, 1984). The "Querelle des Femmes" has recently been studied by Joan Kelley, *Women, History and Theory* (Chicago, University of Chicago Press, 1984), 65–109. See also Ian Maclean, *The Renaissance Notion of*

Woman (Cambridge, Cambridge University Press, 1980), as well as the discussion of "feminist polemic" in *First Feminists: British Women Writers, 1578–1799*, ed. Moira Ferguson (Bloomington, Indiana University Press, 1985), 27–32.

15. Joan Sharpe, chapter VIII of *Ester Hath Hang'd Haman: A Defense of Women, Against The Author of the Arraignment of Women* by Ester Sowernam, reprinted in *First Feminists*, 81.

16. Speght, op. cit., 4, 5.

17. ibid., 11.

18. ibid., 14.

19. Alexander Niccholes, *A Discourse, of Marriage and Wiving: and of the greatest Mystery therein Contained: How to Choose a good Wife from a bad . . .* (London, 1615), 5.

20. ibid., 2.

21. See the influential discussion by Keith Thomas, "Women and the Civil War sects" (*Past and Present*, 13, 1958, 42–62). Phyllis Mack examines some female prophets and the ways in which their activities were "limited by traditional beliefs about woman's passivity, her low social position, and her basic irrationality," in "Women as prophets during the English Civil War" (*Feminist Studies*, 8, 1, 1982, 25). For a discussion of more overtly political interventions, see Patricia Higgins, "The reactions of women, with special reference to women petitioners," in *Politics, Religion and the English Civil War*, ed. Brian Stuart Manning (London, Edward Arnold, 1973), 177–222.

22. *Annotations Upon All the Books of the Old and New Testaments . . . By the Joynt-Labour of Certain Divines . . .* (London, 1645). For its insistence on the generic sense of Genesis "Man," the *Annotations* would seem to be indebted to the text ordered by the Synod of Dort and published in 1637, later translated as *The Dutch Annotations Upon the Whole Bible . . .*, tr. Theodore Haak (London, 1657).

23. *Colasterion*, ed. Lowell W. Coolidge, vol. 2 of *Complete Prose Works of John Milton*, 739–40.

24. Calvin, op. cit., 77–8.

25. Speght, op. cit., 2, 3.

26. Catherine Belsey examines the development and representation of liberal-humanist "Man" in *The Subject of Tragedy: Identity and Difference in Renaissance Drama* (London, Methuen, 1985). Francis Barker suggestively locates in the seventeenth century the emergence of a distinctively bourgeois subjectivity; see *The Tremulous Private Body: Essays in Subjection* (London, Methuen, 1984). Jean Bethke Elshtain critiques the rise of liberal ideology in *Public Man, Private Woman* (Princeton, Princeton University Press, 1981), 100–46. For a discussion of the divorce tracts that sees them expressing an alienated bourgeois individualism, see David Aers and Bob Hodge in their very important "'Rational burning:' Milton on sex and marriage" (*Milton Studies*, 12, 1979, 3–33).

27. J. M. Evans, *"Paradise Lost" and the Genesis Tradition* (London, Oxford University Press, 1968), 256.

28. If commented upon at all, the emphasis on procreation here is naturalized so that it becomes an expression of Raphael's character or situation. Aers annotates these lines by suggesting that Raphael is revealing a typically "distorted view of sexuality," *John Milton, "Paradise Lost:" Book VII-VIII*, ed. David Aers and Mary Ann Radzinowicz, *Cambridge Milton for Schools and Colleges*, ed. J. B. Broadbent (Cambridge, Cambridge University Press, 1974), 99. Halkett (op. cit., iii) points out that Raphael later (VIII.229–46) reveals that

he was not present the day of Eve's creation. But since both are supposed to take place on the same "Day," Raphael's absence obviously cannot explain the different treatment given Adam's creation and Eve's in his account. I would argue that such character- and situation-related effects are part and parcel of the ideologically motivated narrative distributions examined here.

29. In emphasizing the lines of continuity between the divorce tracts and *Paradise Lost*, I am questioning the position developed by Aers and Hodge, who see *Paradise Lost* gesturing towards "a more adequate view of sexuality and the relationship between women and men" (op. cit., 4). Like other readers, Aers and Hodge stress the importance of the following speech, suggesting that in it "Adam makes the equation Milton did not make in his prose works, the crucial equation between mutuality, equality, and delight" (23):

> Among unequals what society
> Can sort, what harmony or true delight?
> Which must be mutual, in proportion due
> Giv'n and receiv'd.   (VIII. 383–6)

In my view, however, this produces a mystifying view of "equality," since what Adam is here rejecting is the society of creatures belonging to a different species; Eve is "equal" only in the restricted sense of being a member of the human species. Although I do not here explore the various tensions and contradictions of Milton's views on gender relations in *Paradise Lost*, I make an attempt to do so in "Fallen differences, phallogocentric discourses: losing *Paradise Lost* to history," in *Post-Structuralism and the Question of History*, ed. Derek Attridge, Geoff Bennington, and Robert Young (Cambridge, Cambridge University Press, 1987).

30. Christine Froula, "When Eve reads Milton: undoing the canonical economy" (*Critical Inquiry*, 10, 1983, 321–47). That Derrida's *Supplement* can productively expose motivated contradictions in the not unrelated field of Renaissance rhetorical theory is demonstrated by Derek Attridge in "Puttenham's perplexity: nature, art and the supplément in Renaissance poetic theory," in *Literary Theory/Renaissance Texts*, ed. Patricia Parker and David Quint (Baltimore, Johns Hopkins University Press, 1986), 257–79.

31. For a sharp analysis of the ways in which, among the upper classes, the development of an affective domestic sphere served to reinforce masculinist modes of thought, see Susan Moller Okin, "Women and the making of the sentimental family" (*Philosophy and Public Affairs*, 11, 1981, 65–88).

32. Calvin, op. cit., 76–7.

33. Annotation on Genesis 2:22 in John Diodati, *Pious and Learned Annotations upon the Holy Bible*, tr. (R.G.), 3rd edn (London, 1651).

34. Cleanth Brooks, "Eve's awakening," in *Essays in Honor of Walter Clyde Curry* (Nashville, Vanderbilt University Press, 1954), 283–5. Brooks says that to the student of Freud, Eve's psychology may seem "preternaturally" convincing; he also remarks that Eve is "charmingly feminine withal"!

35. Mary Astell, *Reflections upon Marriage, The Third Edition, To Which is Added A Preface, in Answer to some Objections* (London, 1706), 27. Ruth Perry examines this work's political discourse in her recent biography, *The Celebrated Mary Astell: An Early English Feminist* (Chicago, University of Chicago Press, 1986), 157–70. See also Joan K. Kinnaird, "Mary Astell and the conservative contribution to English feminism" (*Journal of British Studies*, 19, 1979, 53–75); and see the discussion by Hilda Smith, *Reason's Disciples: Seventeenth-Century English Feminists* (Chicago, University of Illinois Press, 1982), 131–9.

36. Astell, op. cit., Preface, a2, a3.

37. ibid., A2.

6

DAVID QUINT

David's census: Milton's politics and *Paradise Regained*

The political allusions in Milton's poetry after 1660 are not always easy to detect; nor, perhaps, were they meant to be. It has not, to my knowledge, been noted that the temptation of Parthia in the third book of *Paradise Regained* is based in its larger outline upon an episode in Lucan's *Pharsalia*. After the defeat of his forces at Pharsalia, Pompey proposes (VIII.262f.) to seek the aid of the Parthian king in order to continue the war against Julius Caesar. He is dissuaded from this course by his followers who protest against an alliance with Rome's enemies and criticize the Parthians for their effeminacy and unreliability as soldiers.[1] This epic model suggests that the temptations of Parthia and Rome in *Paradise Regained* are really the same temptation: Pompey wants Parthian arms in order to regain possession of Rome.[2] It also explains the presence of Pompey at the opening of Book III among Satan's examples of youthful conquerors (35–6), his name followed four lines later by that of "Great Julius" (39). It colors the final verse (385) of Satan's peroration on the benefits of a Parthian alliance: "and Rome or Caesar not need fear." The enemy may be not so much Rome as Caesar or Caesarism.

For, most importantly, the model of Lucan's Pompey places Milton's Jesus in the position of a defeated republican, the loser of the civil war who now considers what form of resistance to pursue against the new Caesarian monarchy – that is to say, roughly in the same position of John Milton himself during the Restoration. The lost tribes of Israel which Satan calls upon Jesus to restore with Parthian arms (III.371–85; 414–40) have been associated by critics of *Paradise Regained* with Milton's backsliding compatriots, the adherents of the Good Old Cause who made their settlement with Charles II.[3] This association gains strength when in the ensuing temptation of Rome, Satan suggests that Jesus replace Tiberius and free a "victor people" from their "servile yoke" (IV.102): the Romans are to be restored to the liberty of their republic. Jesus' reply, that the Romans have fallen away from republican virtue – which he earlier praised in the figures of "Quintius, Fabricius, Curius, Regulus" (II.466) – and brought about imperial oppression, "by themselves enslaved" (IV.144), matches his denunciation of the ten lost tribes who "wrought their own captivity" (III.415). The idolatrous Israelites are paired with the politically degenerate Romans and their respective sins appear to be causally related. Jesus rejects any worldly political action to deliver these figures for the fallen citizens of the Commonwealth: they are left to God's "due time and providence."

The episode thus appears to affirm a withdrawal from collective political action in favor of individual acts of piety and passive resistance whose master model will be Jesus' own passion: this is the moral drawn by the chastened Adam at the end of *Paradise Lost* (XII.561–73), and it was presumably the attitude of the politically disappointed John Milton forced to lie low during the first decade of the Restoration and condemned to the internal exile of his blindness. Readers as different as Northrop Frye and Christopher Hill warn us not to confuse this attitude with a mere quietism.[4] Adam envisions "things deemed weak/Subverting worldly strong" (*PL* XII.567–8), and in *Samson Agonistes* the blind, defeated hero brings down ruin upon his enemies. Nonetheless, this inward turn to individual spirituality, even as it claims to subsume politics, appears to represent a turning away from the public spirit of Milton's controversialist prose: there is an especially pointed pathos when, during the temptation of Athens, Jesus rejects Satan's suggestion that he master the techniques of republican oratory and follow the models of Demosthenes and Pericles "whose resistless eloquence/ Wielded at will that fierce democraty" (*PR* IV.268–9) – those classical models whom Milton boasted he had equalled in his *Defenses* of the English people.[5]

And yet the great poems of Milton's captivity continue to inscribe many of the politico-religious polemics of his earlier prose. After a period when critics rather unpersuasively tried to demonstrate that Milton had turned against the Commonwealth in *Paradise Lost* and that his Satan was a kind of caricature Cromwell, more recent studies from a different ideological bias have shown the persistence of anti-royalist sentiments in the poem, voiced less explicitly by topical allusions and citations that connect Satan instead with Charles I and that echo Milton's pamphlets of the 1650s.[6] The model of Lucan's Pompey fits this latter pattern, for it identifies the Jesus of *Paradise Regained* with the Republican cause, even if his mission is much larger than that cause. The use of allusion and indirection to criticize the restored Stuart regime was no doubt conditioned by the problem of censorship, especially when the criticism came from an already marked man like Milton. The notorious ambiguity of its language makes poetry an appropriate medium for veiled political utterances; in this respect, Milton's turn to poetry from his controversialist prose may not have been such a drastic departure after all: it kept alive, if in disguised form, a dissenting voice against monarchy.[7]

The episode of the temptation of the kingdoms contains a further series of buried political allusions – clustered around the pivotal reference to David's census at the end of Book III. They point in this case not to the classical literary tradition in which Lucan is a republican touchstone, but to texts more contemporary with Milton: they suggest the extent to which the language and terms of *Paradise Regained* are in dialogue with the political writings, royalist and anti-royalist, of the first decade of the Restoration; they demonstrate Milton's continuing engagement in political controversy. It is pleasing to see Milton keeping his revolutionary faith in dark times, but new problems of interpretation arise: how are we to understand a poetry that expressly preaches withdrawal from worldly politics while, through indirect means of allusion, it criticizes the poet's political world? The temptation of the kingdoms is particularly double-edged in this regard, for Jesus' rejection of kingship is both a renunciation of all temporal force and carnal power and, at the same time, a pointed attack on the Stuart monarchy.

Critics have found it easy enough to square Milton's call for individual piety and passive witness with his supposed disillusionment and retreat from the political stage.[8] But the conventional image of Milton the defeated Commonwealth-man turning in upon himself and his spiritual resources must be supplemented, if not replaced, by an image of the same Milton carrying on as polemicist against the Restoration. The problem is to explain how these two, more contradictory images should co-exist: why should a still active opponent of monarchy espouse an extreme individualism – what amounts to a political renunciation. Perhaps this contradiction is not so surprising: other defeated revolutionaries have turned to protest without advancing an alternative political program. But it may be possible, once the political content and context of Milton's poetry are more exactly identified, to offer a tentative explanation of why he proposed no alternative except his individualist religious doctrine. For all its claims to a universality that would displace, transcend, or subsume the political, this doctrine may itself respond to a specific historical and political climate.

II

Like the allusion to Lucan's Pompey, Jesus' evocation of the sin of David's census provides a connecting link between the alternative temptations of Parthia and Rome.

But whence to thee this zeal, where was it then
For Israel, or for David, or his throne,
When thou stood'st up his tempter to the pride
Of numb'ring Israel, which cost the lives
Of threescore and ten thousand Israelites
By three days' pestilence? such was thy zeal
To Israel then, the same that now to me.
                                        (III.407–13)

It is to recover David's throne (I.240; III.153, 169, 357, 383; IV.108, 147, 379, 471) that Satan proposes the temptation of the kingdoms in the first place. This "royal seat" (III.373) connects the kingdoms imagistically with the earlier banquet temptation where Satan bids Jesus "only deign to sit and eat" (III.335), a scene which recollects, in turn, Spenser's Mammon and his treacherous golden fruit and silver stool (*Faerie Queene*, II.7.63);[9] in the wisdom temptation of Athens, this paralyzing seat becomes "Moses' chair" (IV.219). David's throne, which Satan offers as the goal of Jesus' mission, may become instead a worldly deviation into immobility and spiritual sloth: Jesus' true posture is to "stand" – "to stand upright/ Will ask thee skill" (IV. 551–2) – rather than to sit.

Jesus' recollection of the disastrous census of 2 Samuel 24 and 1 Chronicles 21 calls David and his kingship themselves into question and reaffirms that Jesus' own kingdom is not of this world: it is "allegoric" as Satan sarcastically concludes (IV.390). Placed between the offers of Parthia and Rome, the royal sin of "numb'ring Israel" reflects upon both. For the Parthians are the temptation of numbers itself, or raw military might, the "thousands" (III.304) and "numbers numberless" (310) who pour out of Ctesiphon. The gathering of the Parthian host may serve the same purpose as David's census, which, like the archetypal Biblical census of the Book of Numbers that records "all that are able to go forth to war in Israel" (Num. 1:3), is a military census: David learns of Israel's "thousand thousand and an hundred thousand men that drew sword" (1 Chr. 21:5). But the Parthian forces are "numberless" – only loosely ordered and organized. David's numbering is more properly aligned with the ensuing temptation of Rome, which is presented as the center of an administrative empire, its praetors and proconsuls crossing paths with embassies from its far-flung provinces (IV. 61–79).[10] It may thus recall a third Biblical census, the census ordered by Augustus to tax all the world at the time of the Nativity, during the rule of the proconsul Cyrenius (Luke 2:1–2).[11] Royal power is identified with the state's ability to place its population under bureaucratic scrutiny and control; and this power conduces to the sin of pride, David's reliance upon the military strength and human resources of his kingdom rather than upon God.

Davidic kingship itself thus becomes one, perhaps even the most important, of the kingdoms of the world which Jesus rejects. The best of all Biblical kings becomes difficult to distinguish from the "proud tyrannick power" of the Parthian and Roman rulers. Milton's target is monarchy itself, and his poem recalls his earlier polemics against a self-styled Davidic king. The author of *Eikon Basilike* had presented a chapter of penitential meditations and vows which Charles I had purportedly made during his "solitude" and captivity at Holdenby: these include a somewhat garbled version of the prayer (2 Sam. 24:17) which David raised when God sent a plague upon Israel to punish him for the census.

> And if Thy anger be not yet to be turned away, but Thy hand of justice must be stretched out still, let it, I beseech Thee, be against me and my father's house: as for these sheep, what have they done?[12]

Milton seized upon this passage in *Eikonoklastes* and accused the dead king of hypocrisy: "the vain ostentation of imitating David's language, not his life."

> For if David indeed sinn'd in numbring the people, of which fault he in earnest made that confession, & acquitted the whole people from the guilt of that sin, then doth this King, using the same words, bear witness against himself to be the guilty person; and either in his soule and conscience heer acquitts the Parlament and the people, or els abuses the words of David, and dissembles grossly eev'n to the [very] face of God.[13]

Charles, Milton concludes, has not understood or chosen not to understand the implications of his Davidic imposture: for David was a sinner, and was justly punished. The king, in fact, has brought "a curse upon himself and his Fathers house (God so disposing it) by his usurp'd and ill imitated prayer."[14] David's census is the type which Charles has himself invoked for his own irrefutable crimes. Its reappearance in *Paradise Regained* continues to affirm the guilt of the king, self-condemned by his scriptural analogy.

But Charles I was not the only Stuart to present himself as a second David; the Davidic analogy figures even more prominently in the propaganda of his son, whose restoration was frequently compared by his apologists to David's return to the throne after the revolt of Absalom: this typology would later be reworked by Dryden at another period of royal crisis.[15] Sermons of 1660, written and published to celebrate the birthday of Charles II and upon national days of thanksgiving for his return, devoted themselves to spelling out the king's resemblance to David. Analogies, however, multiply in these texts. In *David's Devotions upon his Deliverances*, Joseph Swetnam, a preacher in Derby, sees typological significance in Charles' age.

> Here is no *childe*, to bee carried to and fro by the breath of self-seeking sycophants, but of that age the Lord Christ was, when he undertook his spiritual kingship, and David his temporal, thirty years old.[16]

Swetnam suggests that the years of the interregnum and of Charles' exile have been a period of preparation and maturation; Dryden describes it in *Astraea Redux*, also of 1660, as the time of Charles' political education, when, like the "banish'd *David*" (79) he examined the workings of foreign governments and viewed the "Monarchs' secret Arts of sway" (77).[17] The period also resembles the "hidden" life of the child Jesus, who "grew, and waxed strong in spirit, filled with wisdom" (Luke 2:40), between his debate with the doctors in the temple and his baptism, the starting point of his ministry and the starting point of *Paradise Regained*. Milton's poem about the inauguration of the career of Jesus thus reverses and rejects Charles' inaugural typology: for Swetnam Charles is like David who is like Christ, but Milton's Jesus declines David's model and a kingship for which, as Satan reminds him, his years "are ripe, and overripe" (III.31). Satan's temptation of the kingdoms begins (III.236–50) as an offer to instruct Jesus "in regal arts/ And regal mysteries" (III.247–8), a kind of catch-up course for a student who has spent his school-time on other subjects.[18]

Swetnam develops other Christological parallels for Charles:

> Heresie and blasphemy like *Apolloes* oracles at Christ his birth being silenced, *oracula cessant*, as Juvenal said A canting *Augustus*, as Suidas hath it, enquiring about his successor, might if hee could return, write *hic est ara primogeniti dei*; this is hee whose right is from God; in a sound sense I may say, the son of God, the sonne of his care, and delight, witness those wonderful providences in his preservation, and restauration.[19]

Suidas recounts that when Augustus asked the oracle at Delphi who was to reign after him, the oracle ceased to prophesy altogether; the astonished emperor built an altar to the first-born son of God, an intimation of the coming of Christ.[20] In Swetnam's version, Charles-as-Christ becomes Augustus' true "successor." There is an evident parallel – with a difference – in *Paradise Regained*, where a Jesus who has announced the cessation of oracles (I.456–64) rejects Satan's proposal that he replace Tiberius, Augustus' heir. Milton's objection to an Orosian linking of Christ and Caesar is that it leads, by a somewhat roundabout historical route, to the kind of claim which Swetnam makes for the divine right of kings.

Were Jesus to succumb to the temptation of Rome and the inheritance of Caesar, it would suggest that he had placed his Church under the Roman jurisdiction of the papacy.[21] Further, it would allow the Roman Church to claim – as it did – the temporal goods and power of the Empire, what it claimed to receive from the infamous Donation of Constantine; in *Of Reformation in England* Milton saw Constantine's enrichment of the Church as the primary source of Christianity's corruption, a confusion of temporal and spiritual power that was the worst of the papacy's errors and one which had been communicated to reformed churches as well.[22] When the Jesus of *Paradise Regained* rejects the gift of the kingdoms of the world which Satan proffers him, he pointedly contests Satan's claim to ownership.

> The kingdoms of the world to thee were given,
> Permitted rather, and by thee usurped,
> Other *donation* none thou canst produce.
>
> (IV.182–4; my italics)

The imperial papacy, moreover, by accepting the structures of pagan kingship within the Church, has, in turn, made itself the model and prop for monarchy: especially, perhaps, for the English monarchy whose king is head of both state and Church. So Milton implies in *The Ready and Easy Way to Establish a Free Commonwealth*.

> All Protestants hold that Christ in his church hath left no viceregent of his power, but himself without deputie, is the only head thereof governing it from heaven: how then can any Christian-man derive his kingship from Christ, but with wors usurpation then the Pope his headship over the church, since Christ not only hath not left the least shaddow of a command for any such viceregence from him in the State, as the Pope pretends for his in the Church, but hath expressly declar'd that such regal dominion is from the gentiles, not from him, and hath strictly charg'd us, not to imitate them therein.[23]

Monarchy and the papacy are unholy, mutually dependent twins, each upholding the other's claim to derive its authority from God. Milton hints that the king's return may open the way for Catholicism in England, for Charles was "traind up and governd by *Popish* and *Spanish* counsels, and on such depending hitherto for subsistence."[24] His poem's dissociation of Jesus from Rome and her emperor attempts to redress the historical error by which kingship has received a false Christian legitimation: it attacks the Christological pretenses of the Stuart monarchy.

Striking as the coincidences are between the scriptural figures of *David's Devotions* and of *Paradise Regained*, I am not arguing that Milton knew Swetnam's sermon: these figures were commonplaces. It is important to note, however, that they were contested ground, that they could be invoked to support the Restoration monarchy as well as to condemn it. Milton's task is partly to reclaim these figures and "purify" them of their royalist associations. This is even true of the larger subject of the temptation of the kingdoms itself. An anonymous tract, published in 1659 and reprinted the following year, *A Character of King Charles II, Written by a Minister of the Word*, closes with a meditation on Christ's temptation that turns rather surprisingly into an apology for kingship.

> The *Tempter* in the Gospel *presented* unto our Blessed Saviour the *sight* of the *Kingdoms* of the *world* and the *glory* of them: The Kingdoms and their glory! and we may *confess* that there is no such Beauty, Splendor,

Bravery, Riches, Pleasures, Majestie to be found in the world as in the *Courtes* of Princes, who are Gods *Deputies* here on *earth*; there is *soft rayment*, there are sumptuous Feasts, rich Jewels, glorious Triumphs, royal State; there is honourable Attendance, and what not? And all those (no doubt) Satan presented on their *fairest side*, to their best *advantage*: But he did not tell him how many *Cares* and anxieties attend *Greatness*: He did not *acquaint* him with the abundant troubles and great disquiet, and marvellous perplexities; which usually attend *earthly Crowns*; all these Satan *hides* out of the *way*, nothing may be *seen* but what might both *please* and *allure*. But most certain it is, that the *Crowns* of *Gold* that adorn the *heads* of *Kings*, though they shine and glister all is not gold in *them*, because they are *in-layed* with *Bryars* and *Thorns*. High *Seats* are always *uneasie*: And there is no good *Prince* who desires to manage his *Scepter* well, if he could view it round on all *sides*, but shall find that there is a great deal more attending earthly *Diadems* beside *Pomp* and *Glory*. And for this *reason*, First, *Prayers must be made for Kings* that desire to rule well, because their troubles, cares, and fears are greater than other *mens*. *Secondly*, their *Temptations* are likewise *greater* than those of private *Persons*, and therefore they stand more in need of joynt, publick, and private *Prayers*. And, *Lastly*, they must in a special manner be prayed for by their *people* upon the account of *good* which may be received under them; *that they may lead a quiet and peaceable life in all godliness and honesty.*[25]

It is not quite clear just what the "minister of the Word" takes to have been the source of temptation in Satan's offer of the kingdoms. Presumably Christ was tempted to accept the material comforts and personal prestige of kingship – for which the Minister nonetheless cannot conceal his admiration, even his sense that they are the due of "Gods *Deputies*" – without assuming its cares and responsibilities. Such duties, as the conceit of the crown "*in-layed* with *Bryars* and *Thorns*" suggests, transform the conscientious king into a Christ-like suffering servant for his people: here, too, kingship becomes confused with the office of Christ, from whom the king claims deputyship or "viceregence." The terms of this apology for monarchy are conventional, and Milton's Jesus goes to some pains to discount them.[26]

> What if with like aversion I reject
> Riches and realms; yet not for that a crown,
> Golden in show, is but a wreath of thorns,
> Brings dangers, troubles, cares, and sleepless nights
> To him who wears the royal diadem,
> When on his shoulders each man's burden lies:
> For therein stands the office of a king,
> His honour, virtue, merit, and chief praise,
> That for the public all this weight he bears.

> Yet he who reigns within himself, and rules
> Passions, desires, and fears, is more a king;
> Which every wise and virtuous man attains.
> (II.459–67)

Jesus makes it clear that he does not shun kingship for lack of public spirit, or an unwillingness to sustain the ruler's burdens. He prefers a spiritual leadership, "to guide nations in the way of truth/ By saving doctrine" (473–4), over the king's reign "oft by force" over the bodies of his subjects. And he notes that it has been thought nobler "to give a kingdom" (481) and "to lay down" (482) rulership: this last bit of moral wisdom probably recalls Cromwell's several refusals of the crown. At the same time, Jesus redefines true kingship as an interior self-mastery that is available to all men of virtue and is independent of any political institution. This passage at the end of Book II of *Paradise Regained* actually precedes the kingdoms temptation proper: Jesus turns down worldly kingship before it is even offered him, and the example of David's census at the corresponding end of Book III merely confirms the wisdom of his choice.

David's census was punished by God with a plague that cost 70,000 Israelite lives. The idea that plagues are divine visitations for political sins had acquired a new currency in the 1660s. Writing in his *Natural and Political Observations Made upon the Bills of Mortality* in 1662, John Graunt notes that the return of Charles II had restored health to a blighted England.

> As to this year 1660, although we would not be thought *Superstitious*, yet is it not to be neglected that in the said year was the *King's Restauration* to his Empire over these three Nations, as if God Almighty had caused the healthfulness and fruit fulness thereof to repair the *Bloodshed*, and *Calamities* suffered in his absence. I say, this conceit doth abundantly counterpoise the Opinion of those who think great *Plagues* come in with *Kings* reigns, because it hapned so twice, *viz. Anno* 1603, and 1625, whereas as well the year 1648, wherein the present *King* commenced his right to reign, as also the year 1660, wherein he commenced the exercise of the same, were both eminently healthfull, which clears both *Monarchie*, and our present *King's Familie* from what seditious men have surmised against them.[27]

Graunt writes against the opinion of certain "seditious men" who had linked pestilence with monarchy, particularly with royal accessions. Who were these seditious men? One was John Milton who at the close of *The Ready and Easy Way* admonished his compatriots not to give up their freedom for false hopes of greater commercial prosperity.

> But if the people be so affected as to prostitute religion and libertie to the vain and groundless apprehension that nothing but kingship can restore

trade, not remembering the frequent plagues and pestilences that then wasted this citie, such as through God's mercie we never have felt since;[28]

The Commonwealth rescued England from plague, which, Milton implies, will return again with the monarchy. And when Graunt's *Observations* were reprinted in 1665, his words had acquired a new relevance, for the Great Plague had visited London and the rest of England. It produced murmurings among the old republicans, as John Burnet testified in his *History of His Own Time*.

All the King's enemies and the enemies of monarchy said, here was a manifest character of God's heavy displeasure upon the nations, as indeed the ill life the King led, and viciousness of the whole court, gave but a melancholy prospect. Yet God's ways are not as our ways. What all had seen in the year 1660 ought to have silenced those who at this time pretended to comment on providence.[29]

Contemporaries found a scriptural analogy for the plague in the pestilence that followed David's census. In *A Memorandum to London* (1665), the aged satirist George Wither recollected how

> King David's pride, made manifest in him
> (By numbring of the people) brought on them
> A *Pestilence*.[30]

Wither had been imprisoned for three years at the Restoration and his sympathies, although disguised, belong fairly clearly to the Good Old Cause. By contrast, Royalist writers shifted the blame for the plague to the killing of Charles I and the sins of the Commonwealth. This is the strategy of John Tabor's version of the plague of 2 Samuel 24 in his *Seasonable Thoughts in Sad Times* (1667).

> In *David's* time, a Plague on *Israel*
> For what *Saul* did to th' *Gibeonites* befel.[31]

Tabor drastically rewrites scripture so that the plague falls as a divine punishment not upon Royal David and his census, but upon the bloodstained career of his predecessor Saul – a transparent figure for Cromwell. Here, too, the text of the Bible becomes open to the manipulation of competing propagandists, disputing over precisely whose political sins had occasioned the Great Plague. By its evocation of David's census, *Paradise Regained* appears to echo and enter into these contemporary disputes; it sees Milton's earlier prophetic warnings confirmed and points an accusing finger at the restored king.

III

Paradise Lost had already coupled disease and kingship in two parallel passages (XI.471–525; XII.79–104) in Michael's narration to Adam; both are the results of the Fall and of an inner servitude to the lower appetites: sickness is "inductive mainly to the sin of Eve" (XI.519), while monarchy follows Adam's "original lapse" (XII.83). The juxtaposed passages suggest that kingship is a kind of disease of the body-politic.[32] But here, too, in the idea that kingship is a product of sin, is the basis of the Miltonic position that political reform can only be founded upon, and hence must give way to, individual spiritual regeneration. *Paradise Regained*, inscribed in a whole web of contemporary political discourse, demonstrates that the poet has not given up the fight against monarchy. But if Milton did not opt for simple quietism, neither did he find a formula for political action that goes beyond individual acts of piety. Christopher Hill may be correct when he argues that Milton's political thought "represents a dead end, with its blind assertion that good will triumph," though Hill also acknowledges Milton's crucial importance in the formation of a nonconformist conscience whose effects on British political history have not been negligible.[33] The reasons for the impasse in Milton's thought need to be sought in the larger historical factors and patterns that Hill has done much to outline and clarify: these may perhaps be suggested by one more look at David's census.

The census, we remarked earlier, is the sin of the king as the head of a statist power. The regime's ability to know its resources, human and material, allows it to organize them to its own ends. It was precisely in Milton's own time that the first scientific population studies were being developed, and these were expressly allied to statist projects. John Graunt's *Natural and Political Observations* of 1662, mentioned above, was a pioneering work of modern demography. Graunt confesses to his initial reluctance to undertake an estimate of the population of London.

> I had been frighted by that mis-understood Example of *David* from attempting any computation of the People of this populous place; but hereupon I both examined the lawfulness of making such enquiries, and, being satisfied thereof, went about the work.[34]

Having argued away the scruples which David's census caused him, Graunt began his study. Nonetheless, the Biblical example and the fear of divine displeasure and visitation continued to be cited in the following century by parliamentary opponents to a national census; the Census Act was not, in fact, passed until 1800.[35] Graunt presents his findings as an instrument of royal policy, and Charles II seems to have appreciated the offer, for the King himself recommended the election of Graunt, a London merchant and shopkeeper, to the aristocratic Royal Society. He added, according to Thomas Sprat, "this particular charge to His Society, that if they found any more such Tradesmen, they should be sure to admit them all, without more ado."[36] Graunt's concluding remarks spell out the utility of population studies for his sovereign.

> It is no less necessary to know how many People there be of each Sex, State, Age, Religion, Trade, Rank, or Degree &c by the Knowledg whereof Trade, and Government may be made more certain, and Regular.[37]

This census would do much more than count: it would be a form of state scrutiny that would permit greater control over a population that, as Graunt describes it, is underemployed in productive pursuits.

> how many Women, and Children do just nothing, onely learning to spend what others get? how many are meer Voluptuaries, and as it were meer Gamesters by Trade? how many live by puzzling poor people with unintelligible Notions in Divinity and Philosophie? how many by perswading credulous, delicate, and Litigious Persons, that their Bodies or Estates are out of Tune, and in danger? how many by fighting as Souldiers? how many by Ministeries of Vice, and Sin? how many by Trades of meer Pleasure, or Ornaments? and how many in a way of lazie attendance, &c upon others? And on the other side, how few are employed in raising, and working necessary food, and covering.[38]

The tradesman Graunt's horror at idleness and parasitism contains an implicit call upon the state to use his new *statistical* methods to intervene and monitor economic activity: to increase the country's level of production. The gathering of information about the citizenry would not only promote trade, but regularize the administrative processes of government. Graunt earlier suggests that his figures would have corrected and facilitated the gathering of the poll-tax, ordered by Charles II in 1660 and repeated again in 1666: "the number of Heads is such, as hath certainly much deceived some of our *Senatours* in their appointments of *Pole-money, &c.*"[39] Here Graunt's friend and colleague, Sir William Petty, concurred. In his *Treatise of Taxes and Contributions*, which was also published in 1662 and which at several junctures cites the *Natural and Political Observations*, Petty similarly commented on the shortcomings of the 1660 taxation.

> Ignorance of the Number, Trade, and Wealth of the people, is often the reason why the said people are needlessly troubled, *viz.* with the double charge and vexation of two, or many Levies, when one might have served: Examples whereof have been seen in late Poll-moneys; in which (by not knowing the state of the people, *viz.* how many there were of each taxable sort, and the want of sensible markes whereby to rate men, and the confounding of Estates with Titles and Offices) great mistakes were committed.[40]

As Petty's remarks suggest, Charles' poll-taxes were unpopular measures, and when Parliament threatened to add to the tax bill of 1666 a proviso that called for a commission to oversee how the tax revenue was spent, it must have seemed as if the struggles of the 1640s over royal taxation were about to repeat themselves.[41] Petty's and Graunt's proposals to improve the efficiency of the tax collection through better studies of the population probably only increased resentment at a government that would inquire too closely into its subjects' affairs. Petty answers an imaginary critic:

> The next objection against this so exact computation of the Rents and works of lands, &c is, that the Sovereign would know too exactly every man's Estate; to which I answer that if the Charge of the Nation be brought as low as it may be, (which depends much upon the people in Parliament to do) and if the people be willing and ready to pay, and if care be taken, that although they have not ready money, the credit of their Lands and Goods shall be as good; and lastly, that it would be a great discommodity to the Prince to take more than he needs, as was proved before; where is the evil of this so exact knowledge?[42]

Petty's argument rests upon an idea of economic rationality that governs king and subject alike. This rationality sanctions in its name a total, scientific organization of state finances; Petty dismisses any objection which the citizen might have to becoming a numerical figure in what he would later call "political arithmetick." It is precisely the impersonal and objective nature of the tax survey that should allay the loyal citizen's qualms about the state's invasion of his privacy – even though the issue of privacy may be really one of local privilege and traditional prerogative resisting the fiscal encroachments of a centralized and rationally uniform state power. Petty was in a position to know how individuals did in fact react to measures of government scrutiny, for he had been in charge of the enormous and astonishingly efficient Down Survey of army lands in Ireland from 1655 to 1656, and he also completed an unpublished census of the Irish population in 1659. These colonialist surveys – which were not carried out without controversy – were what he proposed to transfer and apply to the home country.[43]

In Ireland, Petty had been the servant of Cromwell and the Commonwealth. His and Graunt's ideas belonged to a tradition of Baconian thought developed by Puritan reformers, particularly by the circle of Samuel Hartlib; the young Petty was Hartlib's protégé. These savants sought to place science and technology in the service of economic progress and national greatness; they were loyal to the new republican regime which they also saw as an instrument to further their projects.[44] Hence they favored a strong central government to regulate trade and to carry out an aggressive foreign policy of empire and expansion. These policies also found special support during the first years of the Commonwealth from members of a newly emergent sector of the London merchant community that had originally risen to wealth through trade to the western colonies and which now sought its share of the East Indian market as well.[45] Together with the scientific reformers, these mercantile interests contributed in 1650 to the formation of the Council of Trade which, though shortlived, produced the landmark Navigation Act of 1651; these two groups, whose membership sometimes overlapped, variously supported the other notable efforts of the Cromwellian government's pursuit of commercial expansion: the Western Design, the conquest and colonial resettlement of Ireland, and the Dutch War of 1652–4. When viewed in light of these developments of the 1650s, then, Graunt's and Petty's writings of the 1660s appear to be not so much royalist as more generally statist: their plans to rationalize government and the national economy through statistics had grown out of the Puritan Commonwealth's own intellectual circles, and their implicit ideal of a powerful, interventionist state had been partly realized in Cromwell's policies. Nonetheless, these statist policies – and the allegiances of the scientist-projectors – were soon appropriated by Charles II. The renewed and revised version of the Navigation Act in 1660 was part of the Restoration settlement, and the king embarked on two further Dutch Wars.[46]

Milton had seen this coming, this easy transition and slide from republican to royalist statism, just as he saw his countrymen's hunger for trade as a threat to their freedom. As early as 1654, he had closed his *Second Defense of the English People* with a warning to his fellow citizens not to fall from true liberty into a worship of the state and its workings.

> For if the ability to devise the cleverest means of putting vast sums of money into the treasury, the power readily to equip land and sea forces, to deal shrewdly with ambassadors from abroad, and to contract judicious alliances and treaties has seemed to any of you greater, wiser, and more useful to the state than to administer incorrupt justice to the people, to help those harassed and oppressed, and to render to every man promptly his own deserts, too late will you discover how mistaken you have been. . . . If you begin to slip into the same vices, to imitate those men, to seek the same goals, to clutch at the same vanities, you actually are royalists yourselves, at the mercy either of the same men who up to now have been your enemies, or of others in turn. . . .[47]

The language is that of Biblical prophecy – compare Hosea's condemnation of foreign alliances (5:13; 8:8–10) and Isaiah's call for justice and reform (1:17) – but the application is contemporary. Milton polemicizes against Commonwealth statesmen who are devoted to the state as an end in itself. A friend of Hartlib and familiar with the ideas of his scientific circle, Milton singles out first of all those projectors, as Graunt and Petty were later to be, of schemes for the nation's fiscal management. The efforts of statist politicians to build England into an economic and military power, engaged in a dynamic foreign policy, would transform the republic into a mirror-image of the deposed monarchy – and, Milton implies, would pave the way for the king's return. He equates with royalism a preoccupation with statecraft that places the aggrandizement of state power above individual considerations of justice: the centralizing tendency of that power is opposed to what is due to "every man" according to "his own deserts." When, later, on the eve of the Restoration, Milton outlined his own utopian political plans in *The Ready and Easy Way*, he proposed a federation of local county governments, partly modeled on the United Provinces. Each county was to be "a kinde of subordinate Commonaltie or Commonwealth" with relative judicial autonomy: "they shall have none then to blame but themselves, if it be not well administered: and fewer laws to expect or fear from the supreme autoritie."[48] This fear of central state authority is linked with – to the point of being the reflection of – Milton's religious politics: his opposition to Presbyterianism, to tithes and a stipendiary clergy, to censorship, to a state religion, even one constituted by the Independents themselves. When the Jesus of *Paradise Regained* rejects the use of fear (I.223) and of force (II.479) to build his kingdom, it is especially the forcing of conscience that is at stake.[49] The more powerful the state, the more developed its instruments of scrutiny and control, the greater will be its ability to impose conformity. Rather ominously, Graunt's population survey seeks to learn the religion of every citizen as well as the citizen's sex, state, trade, rank, and degree.

If the allusion to David's census contains specific attacks upon the Stuart monarchy, it may also attack that monarchy as part of the larger configuration of the modern nation-state, the sponsor, whether in royalist or republican guise, of a new statistical science and instrumental rationality. This double perspective – the convergence of related but not fully congruent ideas in Milton's political thought – might help to account for, if not resolve, the political contradiction of his great poetry: its persistent, genuinely subversive criticism of kingship, its lack of any political alternatives to kingship beyond individual spirituality. The Commonwealth alternative had produced its own forms of statism which, Milton seems to have thought, contributed to its drift back to monarchy. Milton's refuge in a passive individualism may thus have been an antithetical response to the very idea of the state, especially to the modern Leviathan that drew power to its center and constantly expanded its spheres of government control. He was, perhaps, responding to a state that did not yet exist: for all the achievements and schemes of the English projectors, it was in France and Prussia, rather than in Britain, that seventeenth-century governments began to run along comprehensive, scientific principles of organization. And Milton may well, as Hill suggests, have been swimming against the historical tide. In the 1670s resistance to royal absolutism would be effected by the emergence of political parties: individuals could join shifting coalitions in order to influence and guide state policy.

Yet if Milton could foresee little political role for the individual against the authoritarian state and urged a withdrawal to inward piety, this recourse may not have been a wholly negative gesture. It maintained an area of personal autonomy from a state that seemed increasingly to intrude upon local and private reserves. One such reserve may be figured in the domestic bower of Adam and Eve trespassed upon by a voyeuristic Satan who, like a government surveyor, takes the measure of Eden.

> But first with narrow search I must walk round
> This garden, and no corner leave unespied;
>
> (*PL* IV.548–9)

After this Eden of privacy (and property) has been invaded and desecrated by satanic forces, the dispossessed Adam and Eve fall back upon a "paradise within," its boundaries contracted into the individual conscience. In Milton's sequel poem, Satan will attempt to penetrate this latter paradise as well with his "nearer view/ And narrower scrutiny" (IV.514–15), as he tries to learn the true nature of God's Son. The Prince of this world seeks ever more detailed information on those he would make his subjects and his field of knowledge would include the inner realm of identity itself. But Jesus keeps his adversary guessing until true knowledge comes too late to help him. The hero of *Samson Agonistes* similarly reveals his returning strength only at the moment when he brings his enemies down. But the fallen Samson had earlier yielded up his "capital secret" (*SA* 394) to Dalila and the Philistine authorities; he has to endure the continuing probing of Harapha who comes "to survey" him (1089; 1227–30), in a scene which suggests a blind man's horror of being observed by those he cannot see. Milton's last two poems share a common concern with maintaining inwardness under the scrutiny of others, even when, in the case of Samson, one is made into a public spectacle. Milton's Jesus defends his individuality from the observation and reckoning of external power and shows the way that paradise can be regained.

IV

Having placed Milton towards the beginning of a modern conflict between individual and state, I have inevitably evoked the figure of his contemporary Hobbes. It was Hobbes, the apologist for royal sovereignty and religious uniformity, who defined individuality as a proprietary selfhood that could only come into being through a prior contractual relationship with the state. And of Hobbes' Baconian turn of mind John Aubrey wrote: "He turned and winded and compounded in philosophy, politiques, etc., as if he had been at Analyticall [i.e. mathematical] worke."[50] I cite as a coda a well-known passage in Aubrey's brief life of Milton.

> His widowe assures me that Mr. T. Hobbes was not one of his acquaintance, that her husband did not like him at all, but he would acknowledge him to be a man of great parts, and a learned man. *Their Interests and Tenets did run counter to each other*. (My italics)[51]

Aubrey is succinct. "Hobbes" could be the name for that which all the various political strategies of *Paradise Regained* converge to resist.

Notes

1. Pompey's captains accuse the Parthian kings of mother–son incest, the crime of Oedipus: "Damnat apud gentes sceleris non sponte peracti/ Oedipodionas infelix fabula Thebas:/ Parthorum dominus quotiens sic sanguine mixto/ Nascitur Arsacides!" (VIII.406–9). This passage may reinforce the Oedipal themes that surround Jesus in *Paradise Regained* and culminate in the simile at IV.572–5; these have been discussed by James Nohrnberg in "*Paradise Regained* by One Greater Man: Milton's wisdom epic as a 'fable of identity,'" in E. Cook *et al.* (eds), *Centre and Labyrinth: Essays in Honour of Northrop Frye* (Toronto, 1983), 83–114.
   All citations from Milton's poetry in this essay will be taken from *The Poems of John Milton*, ed. John Carey and Alastair Fowler (London and New York, 1968). Citations from Milton's prose will be taken from the Yale edition of the *Complete Prose Works of John Milton*, ed. Don M. Wolfe, 8 vols (New Haven, 1953–82), hereafter referred to as *CPW*; a second reference will indicate the corresponding location of the passage in the Columbia edition of *The Works of John Milton*, ed. Frank Allan Patterson *et al.*, 20 vols (New York, 1931–8), hereafter referred to as *Works*.
2. For readings of the relationship between the temptations of Rome and Parthia, see Northrop Frye, *The Return of Eden* (Toronto, 1965), 130–3; Barbara Kiefer Lewalski, *Milton's Brief Epic* (Providence and London, 1966), 265–80; Arnold Stein, *Heroic Knowledge* (Minneapolis, 1957), 78–93. These scholars generally view Milton's Parthia as a figure for militant Genevan Protestantism: this view was earlier developed by Howard Schultz in "Christ and Antichrist in *Paradise Regained*" (*PMLA*, 67, 1952, 790–808).
3. Frye, op. cit., 132; Lewalski, op. cit., 270. The parallel between the lost tribes of Israel and the self-enslaved Romans has been noted by Stein, op. cit., 89, and, more recently, by Andrew Milner in *John Milton and the English Revolution* (Totowa, NJ, 1981), 174–5.
4. Frye, op. cit., 112–14; Christopher Hill, *Milton and the English Revolution* (New York, 1977), 421. Milner, op. cit., 174, makes the attractive suggestion that Milton's endorsement of a quietist withdrawal from politics should be understood as a temporary strategy rather than as a long-term solution. It is important to remember the extent of the persecution meted out upon dissenters by the Restoration regime: see Gerald R. Cragg, *Puritanism in the Period of the Great Persecution 1660–1688* (Cambridge, 1957).
5. "nor were the expressions both of armie and people, whether in thir publick declarations, or several writings, other than such as testifi'd a spirit in this

nation, no less noble and well-fitted to the liberty of a commonwealth, than in the ancient *Greeks* or *Romans*. Nor was the heroic cause unsuccessfully defended to all Christendom, against the tongue of a famous and thought invincible adversarie . . . in a written monument likely to outlive detraction, as it hath hitherto convinc'd or silenc'd not a few of our detractors, especially in parts abroad." *The Ready and Easy Way to Establish a Free Commonwealth*, 2nd edn, *CPW*, VII.420–1, *Works*, VI.116.

6. Stevie Davies has succinctly sketched this history of Milton criticism in *Images of Kingship in Paradise Lost* (Columbia, 1983), 3–5. Davies' book is one of several recent studies that have re-examined Milton's poetry for anti-royalist allusions; see also Joan S. Bennett, "God, Satan, and King Charles: Milton's royal portraits" (*PMLA*, 92, 1977, 441–57), and Hill, op. cit., 341–448.

7. The allusion to the *Pharsalia* may point to a parallel case. Frederick M. Ahl has remarked on how Lucan and other imperial poets managed to veil their criticism of the regime; see Ahl, *Lucan* (Ithaca and London, 1976), 25–35. For the seventeenth-century situation and the indeterminability of political poetry, see John M. Wallace, "'Examples are best precepts': readers and meanings in seventeenth-century poetry" (*Critical Inquiry*, 1, 1974, 273–90).

8. This critical tradition is represented at its best by Tillyard, who offers a complicated and sympathetic assessment of Milton's spoiled political hopes and the inward turn of his poetry; see E. M. W. Tillyard, *Milton* (1930; rev. edn, New York, 1967), 249–51. Stein, op. cit., 63–93, finds the political issues of the poetry more persistently problematic and unresolved.

9. Cf. Frye, op. cit., 126, for the recollection of Spenser's Mammon. The motifs of throne, chair, and sitting can thus be related to *Paradise Regained*'s themes of retirement, examined by Nohrnberg, op. cit., 104.

10. *Paradise Regained* carefully contrasts the Parthian troops which the "city gates outpoured" (III.311) from Ctesiphon with the "conflux issuing forth, or entering in" (IV.62) the gates of Rome. The two-way traffic of Roman administration is seen as an imperial advance over unidirectional Parthian conquest.

11. The census of Augustus figures prominently in two Neolatin nativity poems that Milton surely knew, Mantuan's *Primae Parthenices*, III.1–26, and Sannazaro's *De partu virginis*, II.116–234. For the importance of the *De partu virginis* as a model for the epic form of *Paradise Regained*, see Stewart A. Baker, "Sannazaro and Milton's brief epic" (*Comparative Literature*, 20, 1968, 116–32). In *The Descent from Heaven* (New Haven and London, 1963), 161–2, Thomas M. Greene points out that the census of Augustus in Sannazaro's epic is treated as a figure for the universal, global claims of the Roman Church. The idea governs Catholic interpretations of Luke 2:1–2 which, following Orosius, not only viewed the Pax Augusta as the preparation for the birth of the Prince of Peace, but also regarded the census as the means for Jesus – and, by inference, all future Christians – to be enrolled as Roman citizens. See, for example, the great early seventeenth-century compendium commentary of Cornelius a Lapide, the *Commentaria in Scripturam Sacram*, ed. A. Crampton (Paris, 1876), XVI.53–6. By contrast and in reaction to this line of interpretation, Calvin argued that the census was merely a further extension of Roman tyranny that signified the total temporal servitude of the Jews: see Calvin, *Commentary on a Harmony of the Evangelists, Matthew, Mark, and Luke,* tr. William Pringle (Edinburgh, 1846), I.110. The Geneva Bible of 1560 comments that by the Roman census "the people were more charged and oppressed." Milton's allusion to David's census may thus contain a critique of Augustus' census as it is celebrated in the poems of Milton's Catholic predecessors.

12. *Eikon Basilike: the Portraiture of His Majesty King Charles 1st* (London, 1879), 181 (ch. 25).
13. *Eikonoklastes*, 25, *CPW*, III.555, *Works*, V.266.
14. ibid., *CPW*, III.555, *Works*, V.265.
15. For a discussion of the Davidic propaganda of Charles II, see Richard F. Jones, "The originality of *Absalom and Achitophel*" (*MLN*, 46, 1931, 211–18).
16. Swetnam, *David's Devotions upon his Deliverances* (London, 1660), 9.
17. Dryden, *Astraea Redux*, *The Works of John Dryden*, ed. Edward Niles Hooker and H. T. Swedenberg, Jr (Berkeley and Los Angeles, 1956–79), I.24.
18. Satan's offer to bring Jesus to the foreign monarchs' "radiant courts/ Best school of best experience" (III.237–8) thus links the temptation of the kingdoms to the ensuing temptation of Athens and her "schools of ancient sages" (IV.251). Jesus is tempted to continue his studies "Till time mature thee to a kingdom's weight" (IV.282). In *Commentary on a Harmony of the Evangelists*, I.165–72, Calvin discusses the hidden life of Christ and concludes that the child Jesus already possessed a fullness of knowledge and could not be said to learn as he grew older. For the parallel to Milton's own long sojourn as a scholar in his father's house, see Nohrnberg, op. cit., 86–7.
19. Swetnam, op. cit., 8.
20. Suidas, *Historica cateraque omnia . . . opera* (Basel, 1581), 151. See also Samuel Clarke, *The Life and Death of Julius Caesar, the first Founder of the Roman Empire, as also the Life and Death of Augustus Caesar* (London, 1665), 93.
21. Lewalski, op. cit., 273–80; Schultz, op. cit., 803. See note 11.
22. *Of Reformation in England*, Book 1 *CPW*, I.552–60, *Works*, III.22–8.
23. *The Ready and Easy Way*, *CPW*, VII.429, *Works*, VI.142.
24. ibid., *CPW*, VII.457, *Works* VI.142.
25. *A Character of His most Sacred Majesty King Charles II* (London, 1660), 33–4.
26. One can compare the prefatory letter of James I to Prince Henry at the beginning of *Basilikon Doron*: "being rightly informed hereby of the waight of your burthen, ye may in time beginne to consider, that being borne to be a king, ye are rather borne to *onus*, then *honos*: not excelling all your people so farre in ranke and honour, as in daily care and hazardous paines-taking, for the dutifull administration of that great office, that God hath laide upon your shoulders." *The Political Works of James I*, ed. Charles Howard McIlwain (Cambridge and London, 1918), I.3.
27. John Graunt, *Natural and Political Observations Made upon the Bills of Mortality*, ed. Walter F. Willcox (Baltimore, 1939), 51.
28. *The Ready and Easy Way*, *CPW*, VII.461, *Works*, VI.147.
29. John Burnet, *History of His Own Time* (Oxford, 1833), I.397. For the political charges and countercharges surrounding the Plague and Great Fire, see Michael Mckeon, *Politics and Poetry in Restoration England* (Cambridge, Mass. and London, 1975), 138–46.
30. Wither, *A Memorandum to London* (London, 1665), 13. For Wither's poetry of the Civil War and Restoration, see Charles S. Hensley, *The Later Career of George Wither* (The Hague and Paris, 1969).
31. John Tabor, *Seasonable Thoughts in Sad Times* (London, 1667), 45.
32. Kingship and plague are also equated in a passage commenting on the *Iliad* in chapter 5 of the first *Defense of the English People*, *CPW*, IV.441, *Works*, VII.312–13: "Achilles Agamemnonem, postquam eum ipsum esse pestem populi pestilentia tum laborantis comperisset. . . ." [Achilles, having found that Agamemnon was himself a pestilence unto his people who were then suffering under a pestilence. . .]
33. Christopher Hill, *The Experience of Defeat* (London, 1984), 318, 327.

34. Graunt, op. cit., 67.
35. See Hyman Alderman, *Counting People: The Census in History* (New York, 1969), 41–2.
36. Thomas Sprat, *History of the Royal Society*, ed. Jackson I. Cope and Harold Whitmore Jones (St Louis, 1958), 67.
37. Graunt, op. cit., 78–9.
38. ibid., 79.
39. ibid., 4.
40. *The Economic Writings of Sir William Petty*, ed. Charles Henry Hull (1899; rpt. New York, 1963), I.34.
41. See Ronald Hutton, *The Restoration* (Oxford, 1985), 255–7. A contemporary view of the Poll-tax dispute is found in the December 8, 11–12, 1666 entries in Pepys's diary. See *The Diary and Correspondence of Samuel Pepys, F.R.S.*, ed. Richard, Lord Braybrooke (London, 1929), II.458, 460–1.
42. Petty, op. cit., I.53.
43. For Petty's own account of the Irish survey, see *The History of the Survey of Ireland Commonly Called the Down Survey by Doctor William Petty* (1851; rpt. New York, 1967). See also Charles Webster, *The Great Instauration: Science, Medicine and Reform 1626–1660* (New York, 1976), 436–44.
44. See Webster's comprehensive study, especially 355–60, 369–84; for Graunt's parliamentary allegiance and friendship with Hartlib, 445.
45. R. Brenner, "The Civil War politics of London's merchant community" (*Past and Present*, 58, 1973, 53–107). See also Webster, op. cit., 462–5, and J. P. Cooper, "Social and economic policies under the Commonwealth," in *The Interregnum: The Quest for Settlement 1646–1660*, ed. G. E. Aylmer (London, 1972), 121–42.
46. See Gordon Jackson, "Trade and shipping," in *The Restored Monarchy 1660–1688*, ed. J. R. Jones (Totowa, NJ, 1979), 136–54; David Ogg, *England in the Reign of Charles II* (Oxford, 1955), I.234–51.
47. *Second Defense*, CPW, IV.681, *Works*, VIII.242–5: "nam pecuniae vim maximam in aerarium inferendi rationes posse calidissimas excogitare, pedestres atque navales copias impigrè posse instruere, posse cum legatis exterorum cautè agere, societas & foedera peritè contrahere, si qui majus utulius ac sapientius in republica existimavistis esse, quàm incorrupta populo judicia praestare, afflictis per injuriam atque oppressis opem ferre, suum cuíque jus expeditum reddere, quanto sitis in errore versati, tum serò nimis perspicietis. . . Si vos in eadem vitia prolabi, si illos imitari, eadem sequi, easdem inanitates aucupari ceperitis, vos profecto regii estis, vel eisdem adhuc hostibus, vec aliis vicissim opportuni. . ."
48. *The Ready and Easy Way*, CPW, VII.458–9, *Works*, VI.144.
49. These are the concerns of *A Treatise on Civil Power in Ecclesiastical Causes* (1659), CPW, VII.239–72, *Works*, VI.1–41.
50. *Aubrey's Brief Lives*, ed. Oliver Lawson Dick (London, 1950), 153. I am grateful to Theodore Rabb for pointing this passage out to me.
51. ibid., 203.

7

JOHN GUILLORY

The father's house: *Samson Agonistes* in its historical moment

Neque enim, pater, ire iubebas
Qua via lata patet, qua pronior area lucri,
Certaque condendi fulget spes aurea nummi . . .
("Ad Patrem")

Life-narratives

The argument of this essay takes as its point of entry the long-standing conviction of Milton's readers that the narrative of *Samson Agonistes* does not yield to interpretation unless it can be made to stand quasi-allegorically for some other story whose constituent concerns and characters belong to the time and place of the drama's composition. The difficulty of producing this other narrative raises in an acute form the most general of theoretical questions concerning the historical specificity of any literary text; yet it may be that the very resistance to this specificity thrown up by the code-like narrative of *Samson* (extending even to the date of composition, which has never been fixed) is an interesting arena upon which to engage the theoretical question. I propose to read the narrative in its historical moment, but I do not mean that I shall decode the drama by establishing once again, or for the first time, its proper historical context. I intend rather to argue that the relation of text to context (as though to bring the historical "background" a little closer) is a false problematic and has produced in this instance an illusion of narrative intelligibility. The problematic I would advance in its stead recognizes the text as itself a historical event, in the sense that Milton's choice of the Samson story is a determinate choice, not the neutral vehicle of meaning but an event whose significance is enabled and conditioned by a particular configuration of the total social formation.

The difference such a reading would make can be suggested by glancing briefly at the three contextual decodings of the narrative heretofore governing criticism. These are, first a *political* context, in which Milton's redaction of the Samson story records a certain response to the failure of the Commonwealth and the restoration of the monarchy. Second, an *autobiographical* context, in which the life of Samson is identified with the professional, literary, or domestic life of Milton. And third, a *theological* context (currently the most favored), in which the narrative recapitulates the stages leading up to the "regeneration" of the "elect" Protestant.[1] None of these contextual readings, or their many variant or combined forms, is without explanatory power, nor are they mutually exclusive. Yet they produce their intelligible translations of the Samson story at the cost of isolating the dyad of text and context from the social formation within which both text and context are significant events. Here I would pose the question not of context but of *mediation* (scarcely a new concept, but one seldom enough employed in Renaissance criticism). The problematic of mediation, which addresses the relation between a field of cultural production and the whole of social life, has been developed most rigorously within a materialist concept of history and it is ultimately a materialist reading I shall attempt. I offer as a useful and certainly not tyrannical formula for the materialist problematic a sentence from Theodor Adorno's critique of Benjamin: "Materialist determination of cultural traits is only possible if it is mediated through the *total social process*."[2] Milton's choice of the Samson story signifies as a determinate choice within nothing less than this totality.

Nevertheless it will be necessary to begin with a rather more limited and specific hypothesis about mediation between social levels in the early modern period: Max Weber's still crucial argument in his *The Protestant Ethic and the Spirit of Capitalism*. Weber differs on some significant points with what would presumably be a thoroughly materialist account of the relation between religion and economy, but his work has provided the terms and evidence for virtually every concept of mediation specific to the early modern period and to Protestant Europe. For Weber the hinge of the social levels represented by Protestantism and capitalism is the practice of "vocation," which operates as both a focus of theological controversy and as a discourse of the working life. Weber traces this polyvalence to the early Reformation rejection of "good works" and the later emergence of a doctrine of election, a doctrine which in practice imposed a structure upon life itself. Calvin's God demanded "not single good works but a life of good works combined into a unified system."[3] Thus the Catholic organization of everyday life, wherein every moment is referred to eternity as the potential moment of death, is replaced by a *narratable* life, a structured life determined as "elect" or "reprobate" only as a whole. There is good prima-facie evidence for situating *Samson* as an intervention into this history in the very fact that current contextual decodings of the narrative have invariably sought out a context in which a life-narrative is at issue. Even the political reading of the drama is contingent upon the conventional figuring of the nation's history as the life of the heroic individual.[4] Moreover, Milton seems to have designed the narrative precisely in order to problematize the structured life, as the confirmation of the providential plan governing the isolated episodes of Samson's life is suspended until the crisis of retrospective validation in the temple.[5]

At certain points Milton more openly attaches the life of Samson to the history of Protestant election or vocation, as when the Chorus, addressing God, says that Samson is

> such as thou hast solemnly elected,
> With gifts and graces eminently adorn'd
> To some great work, thy glory.
>
> (678–80)[6]

Yet we know that in fact the sense of election in such a passage cannot be strictly Calvinist because Milton himself was a believer in the Arminian revision of Calvinist doctrine, which affirmed the freedom of the will over predestination. If at this moment the history of election appears in the margin of the drama merely as a problem of definition, or of the theological context, that impression will be dispelled as soon as we measure what is at stake in Milton's deployment of the received discourse. A better sense of what such discursive maneuvers mean is given by Foucault's conception of "genealogy," a process he describes as "the violent or surreptitious appropriation of a system of rules . . . in order to impose a new direction, to bend it to a new will, to force its participation in a new game."[7] Milton's drama undertakes the "surreptitious appropriation" of that Calvinist system or plan for the ordering of life whose cardinal principle is predestination. This system of rules is given a new direction in the Arminian heresy, to which *Samson Agonistes* lends its particular force. Such interventions take their place and have their effects within the long sequence of discursive practices by which the vocation is dislocated from the medieval ecclesiastical lexicon in order first to be identified with the radical Protestant concept of election, and later, in equally critical circumstances, to be extracted from its theological matrix. By the later eighteenth century the vocation functions as the key term in the bourgeois ideology of industriousness Weber finds exemplified in the writings of Benjamin Franklin. The current sense of vocation is therefore not the lineal descendant of some original discourse but the fossil record of successive upheavals. Its very sedimentation makes it capable of inflecting the working life both positively and negatively, as the déclassé "vocational training," or as the vocation which transcends the venal motives of careerism.

The narrative of *Samson* belongs in another demonstrable respect to the genealogy of Weber's Protestant ethic, namely to that epistemological crisis of proving one's election which racked the soul of the Calvinist. Just as the dilemma of *certitudo salutis*, according to Weber, gave rise to an identification of *success* with the proof of salvation, so Milton's Samson suffers from a persistent doubt about his success, a doubt that cannot be reduced only to a question of salvation or "regeneration." The real historical dilemma of election, the gulf between the private assurance of election and its public exhibition, is carried over intact into Milton's drama, even though election itself is drained of its Calvinist rigor. What remains of that doctrine is precisely its ideological effect, its participation in the constitution of a new subject with a new name: the "individual." Only the individual can be saved or damned, and *in the same way*, only the individual can succeed or fail at a vocation. Current readings of *Samson*, if they remark just the problematic relation between the inner narrative of conviction or doubt and the outer narrative of success or failure in the struggle against the Philistines, tend to privilege the internal narrative in a reduction of the drama to the operation of a psychic economy, an economy in which the ebbing and flowing of Samson's physical strength can be correlated to the conviction of providential vocation, the inner state Protestant theology calls "faith."

From works of law to works of faith: the Pauline doctrine enables for Calvinism the transformation of religious practice into a psychic economy, a spiritual accounting that constitutes the individual in a new way, over against the juridical constraints of the social, the "law." Clearly the homeostatic psychic economy of Calvinism permitted the achievements of the working life, in a fatal slippage from "works" to "work," to be entered as credits in the ledger of the soul. Weber's study documents the emergence of this psychic economy, which he calls an "ethic," and which for him mediates between the major social structures of Protestantism and capitalism. I shall argue that the putative homeostasis of the individual psyche is geared to a *general* economy of social relations, an economy in which the vocation (in the sense of "working life") is not merely a redundant confirmation of a purely interior certainty, nor the state of faith merely the warm glow of material success. If the historical problem of the vocation can be conceived alternatively as the relation between an inaccessible inner state and a narratable life, then the problematic of mediation underlying Weber's study can be addressed as the question of how certain narratives – "accounts" of individual lives – emerge and function within a specific historical conjuncture.

To be sure, this is a question of ideology and the means of its critique, but here it would seem that the most readily available apparatus for examining the narrative of the inner life – psychoanalysis – is itself another version of the same kind of ideological discourse. There are nonetheless good reasons for moving beyond Weber initially (if not finally) in the direction of Freud, not the least of which is that ideology-critique (as it has been developed from Marcuse to Althusser) is as yet dependent in its formulations upon the very psychoanalytic vocabulary that is the latest and finest product of ideology.[8] Yet it may well be the case that ideological discourses provide the means of their own critique in failing to erase their genealogies; in this sense, the Protestant vocation belongs to what Foucault calls the "history of the present," the history of psychoanalysis itself.

In the final section of this paper I hope to move beyond an ideology-critique in psychoanalytic terms and onto the ground of materialism by locating the point at which the homeostatic economy of the psyche disintegrates and the vista of the general economy appears beyond the life of the individual. With reference to the narrative of *Samson*, this point is the moment of Samson's death, when his life becomes fully narratable, or when that life-narrative begins to circulate. From this retrospective vantage, it can be shown that the psychic economy generating the serial episodes of the life-narrative has all along been determined by a contradiction between the demands emanating from the poem's two fathers, Yahweh and Manoa; the distinction between these two fathers marks the *difference* between the psychic and the social. The Hebrew God demands a "great work," while the earthly father demands, as I shall show, "labor in a calling." Both demands can be identified with the concept of vocation, but this is no longer an instance of polyvalence so much as contradiction. Samson arranges the disposition of his resources – the psychic, symbolic, or material capital represented by "strength" – in order to satisfy the demands of both fathers; and this he is able to do not by a labor of production, but by a single, fantasmatic "great work" of destruction. The fact of a deviant *labor of destruction* expending the whole of a capital endowment situates the drama historically within a specific economic order, but signifying by its narrative of destruction the antithesis of that order. To read *Samson Agonistes* in its moment is to understand first, its discordant relation to the normative vocational narrative of the bourgeois Protestant, and second, the meaning of such a counter-narrative, its capacity to circulate and to give pleasure, within a social order exalting at every level the principle of production.

Extraordinary calling

To begin with Weber's question, then, is to set before us the task of fixing the typical thematization of the Samson story in Judges within the field of Protestant writings. Consider, for example, this text by the well-known theologian, William Perkins, from *A Treatise of the Vocations, or Callings of Men*:

And if we marke it well, the work of God shewes evidently to what dangers they are subject, that doe anything either without or against their callings. Sampson's strength lay not in his haire (as men commonly thinke) but because hee went out of his calling, by breaking the vow of a Nazarite, when he gave occasion to Dalilah to cut off his Haire, therfore he lost his strength; for God promised strength but with a commaundement, that hee should be a Nazarite to the end.[9]

Judges provides an illustrative tale of what happens when a man falls away from his calling; indeed, the calling is defined here by what diverges from it, just as it would seem to be defined in Milton's redaction of the story. Yet this definition does not distinguish Samson from any other follower in the Nazarite path; he was called to much *more* than obedience to vows. In Perkins' text the story is partially depleted of its meaning in order that the situation of Samson might be read as normative. The same tactic of normalization is adopted by the marginal annotators of the Geneva Bible, who also interpret the narrative from Judges as a moral fable of "vocation." Such an allegory is developed during Samson's final moments, as here the uniqueness of his situation tends to escape the net of circumscriptive thematization. Hence, Samson's coerced "sport" before the Philistine lords (16:25) calls forth this comment: "Thus by Gods iust judgements they are made slaves to infidels, which neglect their vocation in defending the faithful." Not quite consistently, Samson between the pillars (16:29) is glossed: "According to my vocation, which is to execute Gods iudgements upon the wicked," a statement that would seem to acknowledge a specific rather than a general concept of Samson's task. The more disturbing suicidal exclamation ("Let me die with the Philistines") is accompanied by a somewhat evasive return to a normative theme: "He speaketh not this of despaire, but humbling himself for neglecting his office and the offense thereby given." Samson's "suicide," which is conventionally explained away, is least of all compatible with a "vocational" reading.

The texts from Perkins and the Geneva commentators, with which Milton would have been familiar, record an incapacity to fix a boundary between the two senses of vocation, as calling and as work. Yet such a distinction was frequently attempted, and it usually took the form adopted by Perkins in the following passage:

The generall calling is the calling of Christianity, which is common to all that live in the Church of God. The particular, is that special calling that belongs to some particular men: as the calling of a Magistrate, the calling of a Minister, the calling of a father, of a childe, of a seruant, of a subiect, or any other calling that is common to all.

(I.752)

Perkins' category of the special calling is scarcely exclusive, but it is evident from the remainder of the treatise that he is primarily interested in those callings which we would call "occupations." The relative poverty of Perkins' vocabulary reproduces the same paronomasia that is the subject of Weber's researches in *The Protestant Ethic and the Spirit of Capitalism*. The discursive problem to which Milton's version of the Samson story responds can now be more narrowly defined and examined: it concerns the distinction between general and particular vocation, as that unstable distinction conditions subsequent deviations from Calvinism.

Weber initially addresses this problem by tracing the emergence of the modern sense of *Beruf*, "which undoubtedly goes linguistically back to Bible translations by Protestants" (207). His major example is Luther's translation of the apocryphal book of Jesus Sirach 11:20 as "bleibe in deinem Beruf," where the Vulgate had "opus." German Bibles had, formerly, "Werk," or "Arbeit." The Latin term synonymous with *Beruf* was of course *vocatio*, but that had referred to the *religious* life, particularly to the life of the cloister. Luther also translates a similar crucial verse, 1 Corinthians 7:20, as "Let each man abide in that calling wherein he was called" (translating the New Testament *kleesis* as *Beruf*). More accurate translations would be, for the Latin, *status*, and the German, *Stand*. The alterations are small volleys in the polemics of Protestantism, aimed specifically at the *consilia evangelica* of the monks. The latter is replaced by a new "valuation of the fulfillment of duty in worldly affairs" (80), the Weberian *idée reçue* that is in fact only a premise of Weber's argument. Protestant theologians such as Perkins, who condemn the monks themselves for idleness, are able to say that the monks have no *vocation* (I.755), impressive testimony to the effectiveness of the appropriated term, if only as a device of polemic. However, several intervening circumstances have to be remarked, and they are, according to Weber, even more significant than the revaluation of labor inaugurated by the early Protestants.

According to Weber, the sanctification of work did not necessarily imply its rationalization, which he associates with Calvinist rather than Lutheran forms of Reformation. In fact, Luther's sense of labor is in some ways thoroughly traditional; he believed, as Weber remarks, that "the individual should remain once and for all in the station and calling in which God had placed him, and should restrain his worldly activity within the limits imposed by his established station in life" (85). Along with its newer resonances, *Beruf* retained the meaning of *status*. Luther's innovation might be simply irrelevant to any post-Calvinist conception of labor, were it not for the fact that he uses *Beruf* frequently also to mean "the call to eternal salvation through God." Calvin's sense of a "call to eternal salvation" is only too clear; yet the machinery of predestination yields another distinction authorized by the cryptic final sentence of the marriage parable in Matthew: "For many are called (*kleetos*) but few are chosen (*eklektos*)." This is the text by which Calvin expounds his distinction between a general and a special calling:

The statement of Christ "Many are called but few are chosen" [Matt. 22:14] is, in this manner, very badly understood. Nothing will be ambiguous if we hold fast to what ought to be clear from the foregoing: that there are two kinds of call. There is the general call, by which God invites all equally to himself through the outward preaching of the word – even those to whom he holds it out as a savor of death [cf. II Cor. 2:16], and as the occasion for severer condemnation. The other kind of call is special, which he deigns for the most part to give to the believers alone, while by the inward illumination of his Spirit he causes the preached Word to dwell in their hearts. Yet sometimes he also causes those whom he illuminates only for a time to partake of it; then he justly forsakes them on account of their ungratefulness and strikes them with even greater blindness.[10]

The general call is at best vacated of its meaning, and at worst it becomes what Empson would have called one of God's "grisly jokes." More important, the distinction is drawn entirely within the soteriological problematic. Whereas Luther had defined a special calling as the particular employment or labor of an individual life, Calvin identifies the same structural category with the *elect*. It might be supposed that the more radical and powerful Calvinist scheme would simply displace the Lutheran distinction, but that is not what happens. Weber shows that precisely the problem engendered by the discrimination of the elect from the reprobate is responsible for the retention of Luther's pun on *Beruf*: "It was only as a result of the development which brought the interest in proof of salvation to the fore that Luther's concept was taken over and then strongly emphasized by [the Calvinists]" (210).

After Calvin, then, "calling" and "vocation" continue to be used indiscriminately on both sides of the distinction between *vocati* and *electi*. The indeterminacy of this conceptual complex is the condition for the semantic link between Calvin's election, which has nothing to do, after all, with labor *per se*, and Luther's *Beruf*. Milton inherits these distinctions, along with their instability. An irresolvable ambiguity of terms is especially characteristic of the Arminian heresy, whose aim is scarcely to discard the technical apparatus of Calvinism; on the contrary, the terms remain in place, but their relations are altered, and another bifurcation appears. For Milton, as an Arminian, the distinction between *vocati* and *electi* cannot have quite the same force as it must for the Calvinist, since he no longer accepts a decree of reprobation. More than that, *De Doctrina* undertakes to remove election completely from its context of predestination; but then what content might it have? Would it not simply be absorbed by the secondary meanings of vocation, because, against its now conventional meaning, it would refer to *choosing* rather than *being chosen*? "Whence I infer," Milton writes, "that 'the elect' are the same as 'believers,' that the terms are synonymous" (VI.180). God chooses those who choose themselves. Milton has no need for a purely soteriological distinction between a general and a special election. All election is general: "It seems, then, that predestination and election are not particular but only general: that is, they belong to all who believe in their hearts and persist in their belief" (VI.176). Finally Milton is careful to distinguish the general election from the idea of the particular, individual task: "nor do I mean the election by which he chooses an individual for some employment [ad munus]" (VI.172).

But is the latter notion in any other way an example of election? Elsewhere in *De Doctrina* Milton refers to a similar idea as *special vocation*:

> Special vocation means that God, whenever he chooses, invites certain select individuals, either from the so called elect or from the reprobate [sive electos quos vocant sive reprobos], more clearly and more insistently than is normal.
>
> Certain selected individuals: he called Abraham, for example, out of his house, when he probably had not the slightest idea that such a thing would happen, Gen. xxi. 1, etc. and when, in fact, he was an idolator.
>
> (VI.455)

A distinction between election and vocation is very difficult to maintain, both here and in the chapter on "Predestination." Samson is unquestionably an example of "special vocation," like Abraham, called out of his house [domo sua evocavit] to do the work of God; but a much larger point emerges from this analysis: Milton's concept of special vocation is the *return* of election, the return of being chosen rather than choosing. The now orthodox interpretation of Samson's "regeneration" misses this point by attaching his internal narrative to the *general* vocation, the spiritual progression Milton adopts in his Arminian version of the Calvinist paradigm: vocation–regeneration–repentance–faith–justification. The application of such a paradigm to Samson's story falsifies precisely Milton's attempt to suppress the Calvinist residue of his theology, which nevertheless returns in *De Doctrina* with the nervous "sive electos quos vocant sive reprobos," and in *Samson* with every meditation, however finally exculpatory, on the justice of God. Much as the Geneva annotators accommodated the violence of Judges, current advocates of Samson's "regeneration" have normalized Milton's redaction, reducing the extraordinary call to merely typical status.[11]

Unprofitable servant

Samson, Manoa, and the Chorus allude frequently to Samson's unique calling, and it is these passages I hope to have located precisely within the region of theological controversy. I would now like to consider in greater detail the key passage from *Samson* quoted above, with the intention of probing the limits of Weber's conceptualization of the Protestant vocation. The passage is excerpted from a longer rumination by the Chorus on what must have seemed to Milton an affinity of the *Samson* narrative with the story of Job:

> Nor do I name of men the common rout,
> That wand'ring loose about
> Grow up and perish, as the summer fly,
> Heads without name no more remember'd,
> But such as thou hast solemnly elected,
> With gifts and graces eminently adorn'd
> To some great work, thy glory,
> And people's safety, which in part they effect:
> Yet toward these, thus dignifi'd, thou oft,
> Amidst thir height of noon,
> Changest thy count'nance and thy hand, with no regard
> Of highest favors past
> From thee on them, or them to thee of service.
>
> (674–86)

If election seems here to be an *ironic* predestination, a "grisly joke," it is in this and several other ways a transformation rather than a transcendence of the Calvinist scheme. As a "solemnly elected" individual, Samson stands against not a spiritually reprobate majority but the *nameless*, "the common rout . . . Heads without name no more remember'd." The antinomies of election and reprobation are redefined as election and *obscurity* – the "invisible" church has become, precisely, the *most* visible. These "elect" can be figured as visibility itself; they are most conspicuous at "thir height of noon." The pressure of Milton's own obsession is evident here; certainly he feared obscurity more than any discredited reprobation, but then he has gone a long way toward identifying the one with the other. The obsession of the drama with fame, itself an ethically suspect motive, compounds with the Calvinist soteriology to produce a socially advanced valuation of individual fate. We shall return to this notion when we follow Samson into the temple, at his height of noon ("noon grew high").

The homology of election and fame suggests a modification of election to respond to a newly defined élite, one which *emerged* from the Calvinist elect. Hence Milton is intent to dissociate Samson from a hereditary nobility (171) just as much as from the common rout. In the biblical text these discriminations are not made. At the same time, it is rather difficult to specify any group to which Samson might belong as a representative figure. It is easier to locate a referent for the obscure multitude in the egregious interjection, "That wand'ring loose about." Such wandering is not entailed by the distinction between those who are elected to a conspicuous fame and those who are not. "Wand'ring loose" implies a hypothetical antithesis, a quality of fixity in the character of Samson, but that idea is not to be found in the passage itself. Rather it generates a series of oppositions from beneath, operating as a covert thematic which is elsewhere openly acknowledged in the phallic narrative of Samson's castration by Dalila, signifying among other things a slackening of vocational rigidity. Resolute application to an ordained task is demanded by the "special vocation" that Milton distinguishes from mere labor on the one hand, and predestination on the other. If that *idée fixe* fails to maintain its distinction from Calvin's predestination, I will now argue that it also fails to remain uninvaded by the fact of "mere" labor.

"Special vocation" in the sense of the "working life" is signalled by what is probably the most active subtext in the drama, the parable of the talents (Matt. 25:14–30). Milton has already linked both his blindness and his "one talent" to this parable in Sonnet XIX, and it is unsurprisingly evoked by Samson, who possesses the singular talent of strength. Just as critical is an unmistakable affinity with the parable of the workers in the vineyard (Matt. 20:1–16); both parables conceive of the relation between God and man as that of a master-employer to a servant-employee. In *Samson*, any recollection of the parable of the workers in the vineyard would seem to cancel the elective assurance of the parable of the talents. Yet we hear in the protest of the Chorus against the (apparently) arbitrary master who remunerates his servants with ironic even-handedness ("just and unjust, alike seem miserable") the complaint of the workers in the vineyard. The contest of the two parables occurs more familiarly in Sonnet XIX: "Doth God exact day-labor, light denied?" When Samson's "one talent which is death to hide" does not yield a profit, his labor is mere wage-labor; he merely gets what he deserves. And getting what one deserves is of course the economic formula for *reprobation*, which can only be transcended by the absolute gift of election, the absolute transcendence of economy itself. The lament of the Chorus, "[Thou] throws't them lower than thou didst exalt them high," is thus heavily charged with the same Calvinist irony that retroactively contaminates the parable of the workers in the vineyard: "So the last will be first, and the first last." The psychic economy governing Samson's "special vocation" can be described as an attempt to affirm the economy of the parable of the talents against the economy of the parable of the workers in the vineyard (as though the economic form of talent/profit were not in fact mediated in the real world by the form of wage-labor).[12]

The logic of Milton's economy requires not the equal remuneration of labor but the production of a *profit*. We will see that for Samson, if that profit does not appear "in the close," labor is degraded to "day-labor, light denied," or worse, to "idleness," the condition of the "common rout . . . wand'ring loose about." That is to say, Samson will have no vocation. In its contempt for "wand'ring," the Chorus speaks in unison with Perkins and his colleagues, when they condemn "rogues, beggars, vagabonds" for idleness, for not taking up a vocation in life.[13] Their vagrancy is of course a consequence of their mass expropriation, but the social fact of vagrancy is volatilized in the crucible of Puritan ethics and rematerializes as a schematic counterpart to the valorization of labor undertaken by all those theologians from Perkins to Baxter who imported the categories of election and vocation into the representation of everyday working life. Hence Samson prefers even a degraded form of labor, the "servile toil" of the Philistine mill, to the idleness that is the antinomy of calling:

> To what can I be useful, wherein serve
> My Nation, and the work from Heav'n impos'd,
> But to sit idle on the household hearth,
> A burdenous drone.

> (564–7)

Such a "drone" could not be distinguished from the "summer flies" dismissed by the Chorus. Samson's calling, which has consisted hitherto of isolated acts of destruction, is nevertheless an *occupation*. His vocational failure leaves him with nothing to do, an "unprofitable servant" (Matt. 25:30) who has fallen out of his class and into the horde of the socially reprobate, the expropriated, the unemployed.

Intimate impulse

Labor is the shadow cast by all of Samson's actions; yet the objective form of his vocation, his apparently random acts of destruction, prevents us from finally assimilating his narrative to a normative ideology. This problem, which is not accessible to a Weberian analysis, can be approached from another direction as the problem of the discrepancy between the demands of Samson's two fathers, God and Manoa. If Manoa disapproves of Samson's "nuptial choices," he also remains skeptical of those divinely inspired "intimate impulses" which we know to be both the justification of Samson's object choices and the form taken by his calling. What does Manoa want of and for his son? The question might be rephrased to highlight Manoa's contemporaneity with Milton: "What might the seventeenth-century middle-class father want of his male child?" Many things, of course, but at the least he might claim the right to control both marital and occupational choices. In his divorce tracts, Milton rejects the coerced choice of marriage partners as a "savage inhumanity" (II.275). As for the second "right," the evidence (for example, of "Ad Patrem") points to its rejection as well. On this point Milton was as usual advanced for his time. The period of transition is epitomized by one historian of the family, Jean-Louis Flandrin, as follows:

> In the sixteenth century, the only recognized vocation had been the religious one; apart from that, parents were left free to choose the

occupations of their children. By the end of the seventeenth century, however, every estate had become a "profession" and required a "vocation," which parents were forbidden to thwart.[14]

It would be very difficult to believe that this reversal was effected without trauma; we know that Milton's own father was perplexed by the occupational vagueness of his son's life. If Samson's activity scarcely has the appearance of an occupation, its structurally "vocational" features are determined by the father's demand for a certain regular activity, for rational labor. At the same time, this activity must answer to the demand of the Father God, which Milton rather coyly implies is quite beyond Manoa's comprehension.[15] This contradiction is focused (if not resolved) by the repetition of the "intimate impulse," a paradoxical rationalization of an act itself anarchic and eruptive.

The problem of the iterability of the "intimate impulse" arises crucially in the recounting of Samson's decision to marry a second Philistine woman: "I thought it lawful from my former act" (231). The absence of any narrative confirmation of divine guidance leaves the impulse stranded in the psyche, reduced merely to a *feeling*. The possibility of doubt has the effect of producing a fully Cartesian meditation on the privacy of thought. Samson does not attempt to assimilate his second marriage to the earlier impulse, which he "knows" to be from God, but rather elevates that impulse into a principle of legitimation. The "feeling" remains inaccessible but the concept of the impulse functions as a legal precedent, and so displaces the epistemological problem of a private experience onto an already legitimized social structure. In this way the act that needed to be justified because it transgressed the law itself becomes the justification of future transgression. The Chorus accepts this argument, after some vigorous attempts at self-persuasion ("He with his Laws can best dispense") that conclude at the *expense* of a "rational" principle ("Down Reason, then, at least vain reasonings down"). At this point Manoa enters, and the narrative sequence makes explicit the antinomies governing the drama: the father, the law, rationality, and iterability must be ranged against God, transgression, irrationality, and a convulsive mode of action. Narrative repetitions in *Samson* appear as singular, unstructured acts of impulsion, or as a "compulsion to repeat." Samson's marriages, his failures to contain his several secrets, his acts of destruction; everything must be done at least twice. Milton would have been sensitized to this pattern even by the current etymology of Samson's name, "there the second time." The narrative invokes a pervasive polarity between the law, as representative of social relations, and the impulse, as representative of an overruling psychic economy. At this point we are prepared to consider the question of why Samson's vocation takes the form of a compulsion to repeat, which is precisely a compulsion to transgress the law.

That the question of the law arises here (and even more crucially at the climax of the drama) has the effect of opening up the relation of the psychic to the social just at the moment when the social seems to be disappearing into the psychic. I would like to set this relation in apposition to several texts of Freud, with the intention of reconstructing that recurrent structure of ideology by which psychic economies, whether Calvinist, Freudian, or anything in between appropriate and displace the mechanism of the economic *per se*. A hypothetical "psychic economy" governing the internal narrative of *Samson* therefore does not leave behind the prehistory of election, its complicity with Calvinist ideologies of labor, but rather follows the track of that ideology as it displaces the scene of action to the "mind." If Manoa can be seen to represent the familial interests of the contemporary bourgeoisie, it is Samson who refuses the representative function, who offers instead a unique and interesting *internal* drama. It will also be helpful to observe in the typical strategies of psychoanalysis the analogue of Samson's private justification of his public actions (founded upon a communication between himself and God); election is here performing the quasi-analytic function of inducing introspection, of displacing compulsion to a domain of interiority. Samson exhibits what Freud calls a *Schicksalszwang*, a "fate compulsion," described in *Beyond the Pleasure Principle* as "being pursued by a malignant fate or possessed by some 'daemonic' power." The mythological terms are then smoothly translated into analytic language: "but psychoanalysis has always taken the view that their fate is for the most part arranged by themselves and determined by early infantile experiences" (XVIII.21). In order to translate the *daemon* into *Zwang*, Freud overleaps several centuries, the whole period of the "disenchantment of the world," in which neither the *daemon* nor the *Zwang* are available terms of explanation. For Milton's Samson, it is an open question whether his fate is determined by an external agency or arranged by himself ("Whether prompted by God or by his own valor").[16] Fixing upon one or the other alternative will depend, precisely, upon whether and how external agencies are internalized, that is upon a *psychologizing* move. In his metapsychology, Freud attempts to demonstrate that the external *Zwang* is so transformed by the psychic economy as to become virtually supernumerary to its operation, reduced, as it were, from an agency of predestination to an impotent foreshadowing. I propose, then, something more than an analogy to this metapsychology: that if late Calvinist theology defines a psychic economy, the relation of economy to psyche, or of labor to election, can be theorized in a preliminary way as the relation of (external) *Zwang* to (internal) *Schicksal*.

Consider, for example, the analytic account of that external compulsion known as the "law" given in *The Future of an Illusion*. In place of the Hebraic etiology of law as God-given, Freud posits as the founding institutions of civilization two forms of social coercion: "But with the recognition that every civilization rests upon a compulsion to work [*Arbeitszwang*] and a renunciation of instinct [*Triebverzicht*], it has become clear that civilization cannot consist principally and solely in wealth itself and the means of acquiring it and the arrangement for its distribution" (XXI.10). The *Arbeitszwang* is soon left aside, since it is a universal necessity, and (at least at this point in the argument) does not undergo internalization. Freud is concerned only to explain the renunciation of instinct, and it is that "external compulsion" [*äusserer Zwang*] which "gradually becomes internalized" (XXXI.11).

In the major study to follow, *Civilization and its Discontents*, work appears again as a result mainly of the "stress of necessity," but in addition an attempt is made to articulate the two founding coercions of civilization in relation to a single defense mechanism, sublimation. Still, the most significant comment is relegated to a footnote:

> It is not possible, within the limits of a short survey, to discuss adequately the significance of work for the economics of the libido. No other technique for the conduct of life attaches the individual so firmly to reality as laying emphasis on work; for his work at least gives him a secure place in a portion of reality, in the human community. The possibility it offers of displacing a large amount of libidinal components, whether narcissistic, aggressive or even erotic, on to professional work and on to the human relations connected with it lends it a value by no means second to what it enjoys as something indispensable to the preservation and justification of existence in society. Professional activity is a source of special satisfaction if it is a freely chosen one – if, that is to say, by means of sublimation, it makes possible the use of existing inclinations, of persisting or con-stitutionally reinforced instinctual impulses.
>
> (XXI.80)

It is only rarely in Freud's work that the "economics of the libido" touches upon the economy in the restricted sense, here as the re-entrance of libido into economy. Freud's note does not argue that work actually absorbs a considerable quantum of frustrated *erotic* libido – he only adds a tentative "even erotic" to his list of possible sublimations. In this formulation, certain kinds of work, "freely chosen activity," provide the opportunity of sublimating *aggression*.[17] The activity resulting from such a sublimation can again be described as *Arbeitszwang*, but this would mean something new, an *internalized* compulsion. Joan Rivière, the translator of this work in the *Standard Edition*, gives us "professional work" for the word *Berufsarbeit*, which should make very clear historically, what kind of work Freud has in mind. The history sedimented in the word Freud employs recalls the same contradiction discovered in the Protestant *Beruf*, work as "freely chosen activity" (vocation) and as being chosen (election).

Nevertheless the implications of this sedimented history are only ancillary to Freud's argument, which is concerned in the body of text with accounting for the "discontent" of that instinctual renunciation which is a consequence of aggression, the major derivative of the "death-drive." The subtleties of the theory are less pertinent at the moment than the central thesis of an aggressivity placed in the service of the super-ego, which becomes a kind of breeder-reactor of renunciation and further aggression. It would seem that in this context the question of work would no longer be problematic, that the compulsion to repeat (*Wiederholungszwang*), as the major representative of the death-drive, would sum up every lesser example of compulsion. Nevertheless, the "compulsion to work" does reappear later in the book, having ascended from the footnotes to a very prominent place in the argument – this time as a mythological complement to the sexual drive: "The communal life of human beings had, therefore, a twofold foundation: the compulsion to work, which was created by external necessity, and the power of love. . . . Eros and Ananke have become the parents of human civilization too" (XXI.101). The identification of Ananke with the "compulsion to work" (*der Zwang zur Arbeit*) is surprising; why is there no theoretical relation between this *external* necessity and the internal aggression that is everywhere else in Freud's later work the complement to Eros? Elsewhere the dyad is, as we know, Eros and Thanatos, the death-drive. The relation between Thanatos and Ananke can be brought to the fore by reconnecting the ligaments of the argument as follows: An internalized *Arbeitszwang* is the sublimation of aggression, which is a derivative of the death-drive, whose representative is the *Wiederholungszwang*. If work is indeed the sublimation of aggression according to the later theory of the drives, it is unfortunately also true that sublimation was never successfully integrated into the economic scheme of the metapsychology. It is just this failure of integration that allows Freud to idealize a certain kind of labor, the *Berufsarbeit*, and in fact to model the psychic economy of labor on two quite atypical examples, "intellectual work" and "artistic creation" (XXI.79). In this kind of labor, an *impossible* psychic economy obtains, one in which nothing is lost in expending energy.

If Calvinist theology can be said to function as a psychology, a system for inducing and representing psychic events, this psychology, like Freud's, also fails to represent labor except in idealized form, as extra-economic, as a sublimation or internalized *Ananke*. Indeed it is the conception of a *Zwang* subtending the ideology of the bourgeois vocation – a *compulsion to work* which is attested in myriad documents of the early modern bourgeoisie – that allows us to reconstruct something like a psychic economy of Calvinism. The *Berufsarbeit* of the Calvinist is also a sublimation of aggression (competition), which is a derivative of his fate (election), whose representative is the compulsion to repeat (as we shall see, accumulation of profit). Samson acts out the psychic economy of the Calvinist, but in a deviant form: his vocation is a *desublimation* of aggression, a crucial

163

difference marking the discrepancy between the divine and earthly father's demands as the recto and verso of destruction and production.[18]

Like the bourgeois vocation, Samson's acts seem to escape the stress of necessity when they are no longer compelled from the outside, and this is to say that the individual is constituted as such ("Samson hath quit himself like Samson") at the moment when the vocation is proven, election confirmed. Of course the constitution of the individual as an autotelic mind, free in its interiority, completes a process of identification that is for Freud the original determinism of psychogenesis. "Individuality" is a dialectical successor to the law of the Father, and it is asserted (as we know in Milton's case as well as Samson's) most conspicuously when the choice of vocation comes into conflict with the will of the Father. Clearly the choice of vocation can be made the terrain of renewed Oedipal conflict, but it is scarcely surprising that Freud has so little to say about this second battle between fathers and sons. The *Berufsarbeit* is always removed from the reductive reach of the metapsychology.

If the crucial point for Milton in placing Samson between the pillars is precisely his freedom ("Now of *my own accord* such other trial/I mean to show you of my strength, yet greater"), that freedom might nevertheless be read by the demystifying theory of either Calvin or Freud as the internalization of the law, the will of the Father. Milton is finally as undecided as Freud about the extent to which he will permit such a demystification, and thus the source of the "rousing motions" is itself left undecided: "And eyes fast fixed he stood, as one who prayed,/Or some great matter in his mind revolved." The distance that produces the indeterminable option produces a fully privatized individual, who therefore acts of his "own accord," that is, in accord with his interiority. From the strategically distanced position of audience to the messenger, we can only speculate that inside the black box of Samson's mind there "revolves" a gyroscope of motivation, whose external expression is a sudden, unpredictable *motion*, the convulsing to and fro that brings the temple down. As the verse turns to its second option, not of prayer but of constituting "other minds," the Arminian heresy assumes a larger ideological function of identifying freedom with individuality. Such an identification is an unforseen consequence of the very theology that administered so apparently final a rebuke to human volition. Late Calvinism, which typically weakens the doctrine of predestination to an ethic of self-determination, is locked into place as one possible ideological buttress of the bourgeois vocation. God wants us to do what we want to do.

Just as the "impulse" can signify both compulsion and volition, its complex form, the compulsion to repeat, can be construed as the conjuncture between the repetitional structure of social constraint – namely, the law – and the matter of what is repeated in the *Samson* narrative – a transgressive violence. The impulse both embodies and transgresses the law

("I thought it lawful from my former act"). In this context, it is significant that Samson's "rousing motions" are preceded by the recollection that God has the power to "dispense" whom he will from a strict obedience. There can be no doubt that the idea of *dispensation* and the plan of *destruction* are linked in Samson's mind – but what is a dispensation? Milton's discussions of the term are mainly to be found in the divorce tracts, where dispensation is defined as "some particular accident rarely happ'ning and therefore not specify'd in the Law, but left to the decision of charity, ev'n under the bondage of Jewish rites, much more under the liberty of the Gospel." He gives the example of David's eating the "Shew bread . . . which was ceremonially unlawful" (II.299). However, the dispensation does not abrogate the law. Samson claims that he will do nothing "scandalous or forbidden to our Law," yet he does what the Philistines command, attend at their religious rites. Let us for the moment refocus the instrument of the inquiry and ask what really was "dispensed" when Milton displaced the action fully into Samson's mind, when it became inaccessible to our perception. We confront immediately what appears to be a contradiction, as the foregoing analysis would lead us to suppose that Samson's final act of freedom should be interpreted as internalization of the law, whereas now we must regard the same moment between the pillars as a *dispensation*.

The contradiction results from the projection of the former complement of compulsion–volition upon the latter, of law–dispensation. Of course any declaration of freedom can be understood as, and reduced to, an internalized necessity, but I am inclined to take seriously the insertion of Samson's act into a category of dispensation. For once Milton has not defined freedom trivially as the alternative of obeying or disobeying the law, but rather located it in those hypothetical moments when the law is set aside. With this hypothesis in mind, we can be properly impressed that Samson is dispensed first from the law of endogamy (marriage within the tribe), and last from the corresponding prohibition in the ritual sphere, of participation in extra-tribal worship. He is dispensed from the *constituting prohibitions* of Hebraic culture. Milton poses, in heterodox theological terms, a radical question about the founding coercions of culture. It will not do, therefore, to recuperate the law wholly as an internalized necessity, by however sophisticated an articulation of an intervening "third term," a primal or symbolic father. There is an irreducible contradiction between the possible meanings of Samson's final act, as a determinate compulsion to repeat, and as the "free" indulgence in the absence of the law, of what the law forbids to the individual – violence.

By the latter alternative I mean to confront the fact of aggression directly; it has for the most part been evaded in criticism of the drama, or reduced to the merely contingent circumstance of Samson's regeneration.[19] If the fact of legitimated aggression is as central to *Samson Agonistes* as it is to any revenge drama, that assumption of legitimacy must be read in the framework of a psychic economy as a fantasy of desublimation.[20] Such a fantasy is an exact inversion of the bourgeois ideology in which the *Berufsarbeit* is the sublimation of aggression. The concept of desublimation brings into focus that contradiction by virtue of which Samson's acts become the labor of violence, that is, both rational and dispensed from what will prove to be not the economics of the libido but a specific class rationality.[21]

The fantasized character of aggression in the drama must be insisted upon, because the law is only temporarily set aside. Its representative, Manoa, remains very much onstage, and his presence betrays the immanence of very particular historical conditions. The transcendent Father-God, in contradistinction, has the dogmatic privilege of a trans-historical potency: "He with his laws can best dispense." Samson is returned "Home to his father's house" in the recognition that the family is the agent of the law. Most importantly for the operation of the psychic economy, the destruction of the temple satisfies both Manoa and the Father-God, rather an unlikely achievement. The extraordinary calling is much more likely to conflict with the father's demand, as it did with Milton and his own father. Milton often has it both ways, but never more exorbitantly than in the final images of Samson as both "self-killed" and "self-begotten" ("Like that self-begotten bird"). If in dispensing with his law, the father *absents* himself, that absence must be read as both punishment and reward (or in the imagery of the drama, as the complex of blindness and a compensatory "inward illumination"). The psychic economy defined by this complex is further condensed into the *complicatio* of the phoenix, an image of maternal succession ("from out her ashy womb now teemed") and so of the absence of the father; but also a "Christian" typological image, certainly threatening to Milton, of the Father's sacrifice *of* the Son.[22] It is not possible, it seems to me, to put these images together, except in the sense in which Samson is "tangled in the fold;" that is, the images can be laid atop one another along with the general antinomian wreckage. Inasmuch as the phoenix achieves a genealogy that evades the necessity of paternal succession, indeed, of the "paternal metaphor," the image embodies the paradox of the castrated male, who becomes limitlessly powerful because *beyond the law.* The psychic economy evinced by Samson eventuates in this paradox, however, only provided the psyche is conceived to be autonomous and self-contained. That economy can now be reinserted into a general economy of exchange by raising the question of what profit accumulates, and to whom, when the agent of exchange destroys himself, or offers himself in a *total* exchange. This question concerns the economic relation between production and destruction, within what we must now recognize as the historical regime of a specific mode of production. The significance of the narrative of destruction is mediated by nothing less than this "total social process."

Symbolic capital

The destruction of the Philistine lords serves the immediate purpose of seeming to overturn a relation of domination that has become structural in the perception of the dominated. As Milton knew, Philistia continued to rule until the period of the Kings. No national victory is claimed at the end of *Samson*. Rather Milton asserts the exemplary status of Samson's life and death, valued above even the providential history of the Israelites. The disappointed millennialism of the major works is thus countered by the consolation of the "one just man," a theme frequently enough evoked by collective failures. But what kind of consolation is this? How can it be said that an image of destruction compensates for the renewal of domination? The effective redress (an *imaginary* revenge) is possible because the image is an image of *excess*, of what would be called in the lexicon of contemporary ideology, "terrorism." The political allegory in *Samson Agonistes* mistakes the particular forms of domination (whatever they may be at the time of the play's composition) for an immutable structural domination from which there is no release except in fantasy. What emerges at the end of *Samson* is thus an intersubjective exchange, bypassing the polis, between Samson and the Hebrew youth who "inflame their breasts/To matchless valour, and adventures high" with the memory of Samson's deed. The political has the status of an "occasion" for the individual agon, a narrative condition which has successfully frustrated political interpretations of the drama, or opened it to the most facile of allegories. The historical moment of the drama, if it is indeed bounded by the failure of the Commonwealth, is also the moment of that class *victory* consolidated by the alliance of aristocratic and bourgeois property, when Weber's "ethic" of individual success establishes ideological hegemony.

The narrative of *Samson Agonistes* acknowledges the victory of this class rationality by negating it in the fantasy of desublimation, of "terrorism," which is nothing other than an image of the abolition of all structural domination, the whole of political economy, in the face of its actual continuance.[23] Hence the law is dispensed, not abrogated. Milton's first and still in some respects his subtlest critic, Andrew Marvell, recognized just this terrorist hyperbole in his sly identification of Milton with the Samson of *Samson Agonistes*: "(So *Sampson* grop'd the Temple's Posts in spite)/The *World* o'erwhelming to revenge his sight" (italics mine). Samson's act of destruction extends beyond the Philistine temple to the world itself. "Disestablishment" proceeds unchecked; all temples are demolished, all states, all societies. At the threshold of a new social formation, the bourgeois Canaan whose terrain can be mapped in the excesses and deformations of the pseudo-biblical narrative – at the moment of this Pisgah vision, there appears in the distance an apocalypse in which even the "free" relations of production (which we know to be objectively the rule of discipline, of "labor in a calling") are utterly undone. This moment is folded back upon the destruction of the temple and the obsolete order it represents, in a collapsed temporality whose import is the possibility of destruction always present as a complement to production itself.

That this complementary fantasy of destruction is itself a function of the social economy is attested by the final lines of the drama, where the "servants" of the lord are dismissed, having drunk in the scene of destruction, with a greater accumulation ("acquist") of "experience," that is to say, a kind of usable *talent* as well as a *vocational* paradigm:

> His servants he with new acquist
> Of true experience from this great event
> With peace and consolation hath dismist,
> And calm of mind, all passion spent.
>
> (1755–8)

The closing of the psychic account with both a surplus and an absolute expenditure argues that Milton's deepest protest was not against the Philistines (or the Stuarts) but against the very law of rational calculation, against the ceaseless counting of profit and loss. That protest is voiced by Peter in the first gospel: "We have forsaken all, and followed thee; what shall we have therefore?" (Matt. 19:27). Calvin believed that Jesus answered Peter's question with the parable of the workers in the vineyard. This is of course not the answer that Milton would have wanted; he would surely have replied with the parable of the talents, by which he answered his own version of Peter's question, "Doth God exact day-labor, light denied?" And it is surely the parable of the talents to which Milton returns in the Chorus' final speech. I propose now to translate the concept of desublimation into a more historically specific economic cognate, which would comprehend Milton's transformation of Matthew's "talent" into what Pierre Bourdieu calls "symbolic capital" (preeminently, "honor" or "fame").[24] Such a translation is intended not to reduce talent to capital but to recognize the specificity of that capital which goes by the name of talent.

The concept of "symbolic capital" acknowledges the distance that has opened up in theory between the "economy" in the restricted sense, and the general economy of such practices as the religious, the erotic, the aesthetic. Bourdieu does not describe the latter practices by analogy to the economy of production and exchange; on the contrary, he argues that "a *restricted definition of economic interest . . .* is the historical product of capitalism" (177). There are important consequences in thus shifting the perspective upon economic interest from a restricted to a general "economy of practices," not the least of which is that the practice of Protestant vocation studied by Weber can be made more fully legible *as* a practice. For Bourdieu, a general theory of economic practice yields a concept of "symbolic capital," which is defined as "*credit*, in the widest sense of the word, i.e. a sort of advance which the group alone can grant those who give it the best material and symbolic *guarantees*" (181). The problem of the Calvinist *certitudo salutis*, of justification by *faith*, in so far as it is "surreptitiously appropriated" in the agon of Samson's election, is expressed as an operation of symbolic capital: his final act is the conspicuous guarantee of that "credit" which his group had been holding in abeyance, and which confirms the meaning of the sign of his election, his physical strength. Samson's symbolic capital is thus a complex structure of reciprocal interests (or "credit") flowing between himself, his society, and his two fathers, Manoa and God. The restoration of credit, the actual "regeneration" in the narrative, produces an immediate (posthumous) profit of "honor" and "fame," and this profit is returned with Samson's body "to his father's house." As a form of symbolic capital, this honor or prestige might well be converted at some point into material capital. The interconvertibility of capital is attested in the narrative, although in the mode of denial, by a belated shadow plot of material capital, Manoa's plan to ransom Samson. Another kind of expenditure completes the circuit of exchange, the expenditure not of money but of the body itself ("dearly bought revenge").

The signal feature of the transaction defined by the sacrifice of the body can be identified, in Bourdieu's words, as "the exhibition of symbolic capital . . . one of the mechanisms which (no doubt universally) make capital go to capital" (181). As an economic practice, Calvinist election is organized in exactly this way; it has its mystery of primitive accumulation, a primal decree of election, which is nothing other than the arrogation of symbolic capital. Such capital is "exhibited" by the further accumulation of symbolic or material capital. Calvin's God declares, like the master of Matthew's parable, "For unto every one that hath shall be given, and he shall have abundance" (25:29). Samson's election shares this much with its Calvinist precursor: strength returns to strength, election cannot be withdrawn. Nevertheless, the formula "capital goes to capital" leaves out of the accounting the "great work" itself, or the particular form of symbolic capital's exhibition. The distinction of Milton's redaction of Matthew's parable is not that it conforms to an economic paradigm but rather that it makes of the *denial* of rational calculation the most profitable of economic practices. As an economic figure for Samson's violent end, the image of the phoenix expresses this impossibly calculating denial of calculation: everything is sacrificed and everything is returned. More precisely, the phoenix represents an unlimited return (fame) upon an absolute investment (the body): "though the body dies, the fame survives." Here finally desublimation can be named for what it is, *spending*, the expenditure of "energy" or "libido" or "capital." Milton is able to acknowledge this expenditure by invoking its negative reflection in the stream of the narrative, the theory of tragic catharsis ("all passion spent"). Nevertheless the phoenix image, as the embodiment of that cathartic expenditure, does not tell us why we need not count the loss of the body as an absolute loss; rather, the infinitude of expenditure works a kind of mathematical magic: spending everything is getting everything.

At this point it becomes difficult, if also quite necessary, to distinguish categorically between desublimation and sublimation, especially as the latter is for Freud the patient, disciplined investment (*Besetzung*) of psychic capital in the form of desexualized libido. Investment, of material or symbolic capital, is also a mode of spending. The significance of spending as such in the history of economic exchange has been well established by Mauss and Bataille; primitive economic exchange is founded on "expenditures," gifts, sacrifices, ritual destructions.[25] Hence it is possible to figure the transcendence of economic motives by recurring to the practice of the gift or the sacrifice, but this entails repressing the fact that these are economic transactions. The rational economy of capital accumulation is shadowed always by another, atavistic system of exchange. In Milton's *Samson*, the atavistic economy appears in the form of the narrative itself, the narrative of sacrifice, while the rational economy falls to the level of subtext and figuration. Samson's sacrifice is then both the repayment of a debt, his original "credit," and the *overpayment* of that debt. Only as such does it have the power to produce a profit, either for himself or his creditor.

Like desublimation, expenditure occupies a realm of fantasy set against the reality of rational calculation. The *discipline* of spending in the practice of investment makes all the difference historically; it has made a different world. That is not to say, however, that the fantasy of expenditure cannot be acted out, or that the acting out does not have real economic consequences. The transcendent economy of expenditure is not the survival of primitive exchange within an uncolonized territory of the capitalist economy; it is an atavism functionally integrated into the same economy. Just as investment seeks to conceal the labor that transforms capital into profit (in such "surplus labor," energy is absolutely expended), "sacrifice" denies that what is absolutely lost or ritually destroyed can be expressed as an *economic* value. Hence the very body that Manoa intended to purchase from the Philistine is, when sacrificed, the occasion for no grief at all, no accounting of loss ("Nothing is here for tears"). Manoa's position is that of spokesman for the restricted economy. He will not recognize the secret table by which material and symbolic capital are converted into one another, the body converted into fame, or Matthew's "talent" into Milton's. In this he makes possible a certain mystification Bourdieu describes as follows:

> Economic calculation has hitherto managed to appropriate the territory objectively surrendered to the remorseless logic of what Marx calls "naked self-interest" only by setting aside a "sacred" island miraculously

spared by the "icy waters of egotistical calculation" and left as a sanctuary for the priceless or worthless things it cannot assess.

(178)

That island has been for several hundred years the domain of art, but its appearance was prepared for by the segregation of the sacred itself, the religious life that Protestantism claimed to set apart not from everyday life but from the economic domain of legitimate self-interest. In the doctrine of election, the soul itself is beyond price, beyond any human effort to redeem it, and so relegated logically to the domain of the priceless or the worthless. At the same time Calvinism established a most rigorous program of psychic accounting, which, if it did not institute the discipline of everyday life, provided that discipline with its system of symbolic book-keeping.[26] In retrospect, it would seem that the logical relation between the priceless and the worthless is the mechanism by which the concept of vocation is reduced historically to the legitimation of the bourgeois vocation, the end of which is the constant accumulation of material or symbolic capital. Milton enacts this peculiar derivation not by idealizing productive labor, but by indulging a fantasy of release from the calculus of economic rationality, a fantasy taking the narrative form of violent expenditure or ritual destruction. The interlocking laws of the psychic, domestic, and political economies project into fantasy their undoing, as desublimation, expenditure, or terrorism. The freedom constituting the individual as such is grounded in this fantasy; it is freedom from the law.

Milton sets an image of the law's undoing at the end of his poetic career, not as its telos but as its coda; the title page of his last book reads: "*Paradise Regained*, a poem in IV books, to which is added *Samson Agonistes*." The drama stands in relation to Milton's poetic *œuvre* as Samson's final act stands in relation to his life, a coda in which the life of creation is signified by the life of destruction. The ambiguity of such a gesture has passed beneath the notice of Milton's critics, who see, where Milton places the rubble of the Philistine temple, the completed edifice of his *œuvre*. Nevertheless by means of just such a narrative of destruction or "sacrifice" Milton transforms a life Perkins might have condemned as no calling at all into a vocation at once rationalized in economic terms, and yet transcending economy because not calculable in "species." Self-sacrifice, exceeding the motive of revenge, is no less the meaning of Milton's identification with Samson than the *ressentiment* of blindness or defeat. The suicide of Samson is the proto-typical self-sacrifice of the artist, a fantasy capable of realization when there comes to prevail in late capitalism a relentless distinction between the worthlessness of the artist's life and the pricelessness of art.[27] Post-artisanal "artistic labor" is neither undervalued nor overvalued, but rather *unvalued*. In the life and death of Samson a paradigmatic life-narrative emerges, founded no doubt on the "Christus Patiens" Milton never wrote, but sliding over that narrative, mutating into a new story, "the life of the poet." In this important sense, as Milton's readers have rightly intuited, Samson is a type not of Christ but of Milton, the Milton who, in Marx's famous phrase, "produced *Paradise Lost* as the silkworm produces silk," the inverted image of the figure who destroys the Philistines "as an Eagle."

Lodged between the narratives of saint and artist, the narrative of Samson's life records for Milton the transformation of the father's talents, the money-lender's material capital ("Fathers are wont to lay up for their sons"), into "talent," symbolic capital. The narrative that enacts this transformation has its historical moment on the threshold of the new order; no other story will do. In the determinate choice of the Samson story, the distinction between material and symbolic capital is magnified, projected onto the largest possible screen, in the distinction between the conflicting demands of the two fathers, earthly and heavenly. So Milton himself scorns the material capital by which his career is made possible, while taking up as the deep paradigm of his poetic calling that relation between investment and profit which *was* his father's business. The poet reappears in his own narrative as the vocational double of the rational investor, the very figure with whom he is thought to have nothing in common. But "relation stands:" the poet is the "son" of the scrivener, the life of expenditure and sacrifice is the complement of investment and accumulation. Like Samson, Milton makes a return, with interest, upon his father's investment: "to himself and Father's house eternal fame." But within the drama, with its fantasmatic doubling of paternal figures, the final recognition of "talent" is reserved for the heavenly father, whose function is to foreshadow the accounting of those "sacrifices" constitutive of the artist's life-narrative as he once reckoned the value of the saint's. Such value is supposed to be beyond measure, whether or not the products of the sacred island are exchanged in an antithetical mainland economy, at whatever price. By means of such narrative fictions, capital marks off the boundaries of an aesthetic kingdom, within which it reappears disguised as the opposite of itself.

Notes

1. *De Doctrina Christiana* defines regeneration as follows: "Regeneration means that the old man is destroyed and that the inner man is regenerated through the word and the spirit so that his whole mind is restored to the image of God, as if he were a new creature. Moreover, the whole man, both soul and body, is sanctified to God's service and to good works." *Complete Prose Works of John Milton*, ed. Don Wolfe *et al.*, 8 vols (New Haven, Yale University Press, 1973), VI.461. Further references to the Yale edition of the prose works will be included in the text. The linking of this passage to *Samson Agonistes* was made by William Riley Parker in *Milton's Debt to Greek Tragedy in Samson Agonistes* (Baltimore, Johns Hopkins University Press, 1937), 235ff., and elaborated in an essay by Arthur Barker, "Structural and doctrinal pattern in Milton's later poems," in *Essays in English Literature from the Renaissance to the Victorian Age*, ed. Millar MacLure and F. W. Watt (Toronto, University of Toronto Press,

1964), 169–94. In the last several decades, Samson's "regeneration" has become a given of criticism; it is assumed to structure the narrative even where the context of *De Doctrina* is only distantly invoked.

2. *Aesthetics and Politics*, ed. Ronald Taylor (London, New Left Books, 1977), 129.

3. Max Weber, *The Protestant Ethic and the Spirit of Capitalism*, tr. Talcott Parsons (New York, Scribner's, 1958), 117. The distinction Weber is making is crucial to his argument and should defuse the misunderstanding of his position on the question of the specific relation between Protestantism and capitalism. The "structured life" is first of all an ideological practice, a retrospective or prospective working up of a life-narrative out of life-experience. At the same time such a narrative represents a genuinely material practice, since it comes to constitute a condition (not a cause) for other practices as well. For an extended discussion of the Weber controversy, see Gordon Marshall, *In Search of the Spirit of Capitalism: An Essay on Max Weber's Protestant Ethic Thesis* (New York, Columbia University Press, 1982).

4. This is Milton's typical use of the Samson figure in his polemical prose, for example, in the *First Defense* (IV.402), in *Areopagitica* (II.558) and the *Reason of Church-Government* (I.858).

5. Hence the perennial dissatisfaction with the construction of Milton's plot, first voiced in Dr Johnson's complaint that the drama has a beginning and an end, "but it must be allowed to want a middle."

6. All quotations from the poetry are cited from *John Milton: Complete Poems and Major Prose*, ed. Merritt Y. Hughes (New York, Odyssey, 1957).

7. Michel Foucault, "Nietzsche, genealogy, history," in *Language, Counter-Memory, Practice*, tr. Donald F. Bouchard and Sherry Simon (Ithaca, Cornell University Press, 1977), 151–2.

8. See Herbert Marcuse, *Eros and Civilization: A Philosophical Inquiry into Freud* (Boston, Beacon Press, 1955), and Louis Althusser, "Freud and Lacan," in *Lenin and Philosophy*, tr. Ben Brewster (New York, Monthly Review Press, 1971).

9. William Perkins, *The Works of that Famous and Worthy Minister of Christ*, 3 vols (London, John Legatt, 1612), I.751.

10. John Calvin, *Institutes of the Christian Religion*, ed. John T. McNeil, tr. Ford Lewis Battles, 2 vols (Philadelphia, Westminster Press, 1960), II.974.

11. That Milton tended to reserve the term "election" for what he elsewhere called "special vocation" or "special calling" is supported by the usage in *Paradise Lost* III.183–4 – "Some I have chosen of peculiar grace/Elect above the rest" – where "the rest" are then immediately defined as those for whom repentance is still possible. Milton uses the term "elect" to make a distinction within the category of the saved or within the category of the reprobate but not between the saved and the reprobate.

12. Milton works out such a poetic economy in the Preface to Book II of *The Reason of Church-Government* (I.801ff.), again founding his economy on the parable of the talents: "remembering also that God even to a strictnesse requires the improvement of these his entrusted gifts." Later in the Preface the economy takes the specific form of a legal contract between creditor and debtor: "Neither doe I thinke it shame to covnant with any knowing reader, that for some few years yet I may go on trust with him toward the payment of what I am now indebted" (820). It will be worth noting in this context, the curious "Letter to a friend," in which the young Milton defends his leisurely years of study against a charge of idleness. The priority of talent to labor is argued by the radical means of transforming the parable of the workers of the vineyard, or the wage form of labor, into an allegory of investment (of talent):

Lastly if the Love of Learning as it is be the persuit of something good, it would sooner follow the more excellent & supreme good knowne & praesented and so be quickly diverted from the emptie & fantastick chase of shadows & notions to the solid good flowing from due & tymely obedience to that command in the gospel set out by the terrible seasing of him that hid the talent. It is more probable therefore that not the endlesse delight of speculation but this very consideration of that great commandment does not presse forward as soone as may be to undergoe but keeps off with a sacred reverence, & religious advisement how best to undergoe not taking thought of beeing late so it give advantage to be more fit, for those that were latest lost nothing when the maister of the vineyard came to give each one his hire.
(*The Works of John Milton*, ed. Frank Allan Patterson *et al.*, 20 vols (New York, Columbia University Press, 1931–8), XII.324)

Here Milton attempts to justify what appears to be his condition of idleness (his lack of a "credible employment") by linking himself both to the holder of the talent and the latest of the workers in the vineyard. The design of the argument is clearly to transform Milton's apparent idleness into an actual investment (an investment of time as opposed to a hoarding of talent). Similarly, Samson's apparent idleness before his final burst of activity in the temple evokes investment, the quiet accumulation of strength.

13. Perkins, op. cit., I.757: "it is a Foule disorder in any Common-wealth, that there should be suffered rogues, beggars, vagabonds. . . . Againe, to wander up and downe from yeare to yeare to this end, to seeke & procure bodily maintenance, is no calling, but the life of a beast."

14. Jean-Louis Flandrin, *Families in Former Times: Kinship, Household, and Sexuality*, tr. Richard Southern (Cambridge, Cambridge University Press, 1979), 139.

15. William Kerrigan, in *The Sacred Complex: On the Psychogenesis of Paradise Lost* (Cambridge, Mass., Harvard University Press, 1983), discerns in the contradiction between the natural and the heavenly father's will a religious version of the Oedipus complex. In the "sacred" complex, the wish to obey and the wish to disobey the father are both gratified. At a later point, I will argue the relation of what Kerrigan calls the sacred complex to what Milton perceives as the Father's "sacrifice" of the Son in the Crucifixion.

16. The quotation is from the *First Defense* and reads in full: "[Samson] still made war single-handed on his masters, and, whether prompted by God or by his own valor, slew at one stroke not one but a host of his country's tyrants, having first made prayer to God for his aid" (IV.402).

17. All quotations from Freud are cited from the *Standard Edition of the Complete Psychological Works of Sigmund Freud*, ed. James Strachey *et al.*, 24 vols (London, Hogarth Press, 1953–74). Freud is speaking rather loosely in equating the narcissistic, the aggressive, and the erotic as libidinal components, and I am both criticizing and following this loose procedure in proposing a theoretical "sublimation of aggression." As the concept of sublimation is worked out in the earlier theory of the drives, it is always closely allied to a process of "desexualization" in which, nevertheless, libidinal instincts are satisfied. The deficiency of that theory from an economic point of view is manifest and has been frequently remarked (for example, by Jean Laplanche and J. B. Pontalis in *The Language of Psychoanalysis*, tr. Donald Nicholson-Smith (New York, W. W. Norton, 1973), 431–3; and by Jacques Lacan, in *The Four Fundamental Concepts of Psycho-Analysis*, tr. Alan Sheridan (New York, W. W. Norton, 1977), 165–6). Evidently Freud found no real use for sublimation until the later

theory of the drives, when he was then able to find a place for the concept in the theory of aggressivity. An unexpected result of that revision of the metapsychology is the kind of marginal suggestion about the libidinal economy of work quoted above. "Professional work" is then conceived to sublimate aggressive instincts, no doubt by fusion with "desexualized libido" or narcissistic ego-libido, because "the death instincts are by their nature mute." Hence the pleasure of certain kinds of labor, not unlike the puzzling "economy" of sadism or masochism. Freud is very close here to recognizing the legitimated competition (the actual and symbolic violence) of bourgeois labor, where work is not only the reproduction of the material conditions of existence, but the production of a profit (and the simultaneous production of a scarcity for others). Despite the brief for sublimation in the service of Eros, even "intellectual work" is agonistic, as François Roustang has shown so persuasively in the case of Freud's own life work. See Roustang's *Dire Mastery: Discipleship from Freud to Lacan*, tr. Ned Lukacher (Baltimore, Johns Hopkins University Press, 1976).

I am much indebted to Marcuse's discussion of the libidinal economy of labor in *Eros and Civilization*, 81ff., although I am reluctant to take at face value, as Marcuse seems to, the later theory of the drives, much less a "dialectic" of Eros and Thanatos. A theoretical sublimation of aggression is significant because only at this weak point of the metapsychology and in this "ideological" way does Freud approach the social reality of labor, either coerced or "freely chosen."

18. In the following argument I extrapolate from Marcuse's concept of "repressive desublimation," elaborated in *One-Dimensional Man* (Boston, Beacon Press, 1964), and Jean Baudrillard's similar use of the term in *The Mirror of Production* (St Louis, Telos Press, 1975).

19. On this subject Kenneth Burke's discussion of the drama redresses the balance of criticism. See *A Rhetoric of Motives* (Berkeley, University of California Press, 1969), 3ff. It should finally be possible to take up the question of why aggression, self or other directed, is so crucial to the drama as a motivated act of writing (language for use, as Burke would say).

20. In deploying the concept of desublimation, I do not mean conversely to credit the theoretical validity of sublimation in the Freudian metapsychology. On the contrary, sublimation names the same specifically ideological assemblage as Weber's "rationalization;" sublimation names the disciplining of the drives in the service of what is "finer and higher." The theory of sublimation is therefore perfectly adequate to its ideological function, which is to prevent any form of the *Berufsarbeit* from being assimilated into the critique of culture-as-repression. For Freud it is only important that sublimation provide this area of shade, where the drives can be satisfied even though "aim-inhibited." Hence the concept of sublimation remains theoretically unincorporated and functions liminally as a zone of legitimation between the more critical elements of psychoanalytic and sociological theory.

21. The analysis of the psychic economy governing the narrative can be generalized at this point to enclose the marriage of Samson and Dalila within the purview of its terms. Samson's marriage is both a submission to the disciplining of sexuality and a fantasized release from this discipline. The contradiction within the domestic economy is resolved by the institution of divorce, which reinstates discipline fully by dissolving the marital bond. Just as there would seem to be only a dubious sublimation of erotic drives, so the domestic sphere offers only a limited possibility of desublimation. Here we merely acknowledge a very

mundane truth, that in the bourgeois distinction of public and private, as that distinction co-operates with the sexual division of labor, the private functions ultimately to block a complete relaxation of discipline, to drive the male back into the public arena. What appeared first as the realm of seduction and desublimation, seems in the end to be a surface of deflection.

22. Milton's subordinationism has the effect of forcing him to reconstrue the event of the Redemption as the Father's sacrifice of the Son, a consequence that would not follow from orthodox trinitarian theology. While Milton was evidently troubled by the primitive scene his theology placed at the center of Christianity (he seems unable, from "The Passion" onwards, ever to envision poetically the scene of the Crucifixion), that scene is in another sense the engine of his life and work, since it is the point at which his theology and his Oedipal conflicts converged.

23. See Baudrillard, op. cit., 41: "Although the concept of non-labor can thus be fantasized as the abolition of political economy, it is bound to fall back into the sphere of political economy as the sign, and only the sign, of its abolition."

24. Pierre Bourdieu, *Outline of a Theory of Practice*, tr. Richard Nice (Cambridge, Cambridge University Press, 1977), 171ff.

25. See Marcel Mauss, *The Gift: Forms and Functions of Exchange in Archaic Societies*, tr. Ian Cunnison (New York, W. W. Norton, 1967), and Georges Bataille, "The notion of expenditure," tr. Allen Stoekl (*Raritan*, III, 1984, 62–79), particularly Bataille's comment on the major "unproductive value," glory.

26. The "spiritual accounting" metaphor is conventional, if also extremely popular with Protestant writers. My argument is intended to show that such accounting is not merely an economic metaphor – it represents an actual, economic practice, the disposition of symbolic capital. The "final account" to which Perkins refers, when "the bill of our receipts and expenses" is drawn out (I.777), thus has its referent in practice not only in the Last Judgment, but also the everyday accounting to which Protestants subjected their souls in those diaries that were kept as faithfully as business ledgers. In *The Rise of Puritanism* (New York, Columbia University Press, 1938), William Haller quotes the typical diary of John Beadle, published in 1656: the godly man should "keep a strict account of his effectual calling" (96).

27. To summarize (very roughly) a condition prevailing after the decline of the artist-artisan and the disappearance of the patronage system: When the work of art (whether or not it is fully commodified, as are paintings and novels) no longer has what Baudrillard calls the "alibi of use-value," the artist cannot be remunerated for labor whose value cannot be assessed. Without material capital, the artist faces as an always dire circumstance the problem of reproducing the conditions of daily existence. Conversely, the exchange-value (material or symbolic) of the artwork becomes subject to extreme fluctuation, the mark of its "pricelessness." Should the artist become "famous" the worthless life of unremunerated labor can be recuperated in narrative as "sacrifice," that is, as the priceless correlative of the artwork itself. (Hence the material worth of artifacts such as manuscripts and letters, artifacts of the life-narrative.) Such a sketch is necessarily very rough, but it is intended only to throw into some relief the configuration of life, labor, and art which seems first clearly visible in the seventeenth century. On the function of "aesthetic values" in the fully developed capitalist system, see Jean Baudrillard, "The art auction," in *For a Critique of the Political Economy of the Sign*, tr. Charles Levin (St Louis, Telos Press, 1981), 112–22.

III
The written word

8

RICHARD BRADFORD

Milton's graphic poetics

The formal dispositions of Milton's language have been subjected to a series of minute investigations and irritated dismissals unique in literary history. Some eighteenth-century editors and commentators valorized the verse form of *Paradise Lost* as relocating English metre and poetry in a classical tradition, while others attacked it as neither metrical nor English. Samuel Johnson's famous declaration that the poem "seems to be verse only to the eye" was no more than a perfunctory acknowledgement of a well-established contemporary attitude which regarded rhyme or the syntactic acknowledgement of the line ending as a token of a poem's formal autonomy: as early as 1679 a little-known country parson, Samuel Woodford, had suggested that the "poem" might suffer little if printed as prose.[1] Milton's abjuration of rhyme might seem, to a twentieth-century reader, to be simply a matter of creative choice, but in the seventeenth and eighteenth centuries the blank verse of *Paradise Lost* was seen as an experiment which went far beyond the mere flouting of metrical prescriptions. Milton's statement in the note on "The Verse" that he had replaced rhyme with "sense variously drawn out from one verse into another"[2] involved rather more than an exercise in metrical tinkering. By removing the aural signal of the line ending and slackening its syntactic boundary his verse accommodated what its detractors saw as an interlineal syntactic promiscuity, with its inversions, extended parentheses, delayed verbs and other deviations from the usual orderly disposition of language. Johnson thought the verse based on "a perverse and pedantick principle," a desire "to use English words with a foreign idiom."[3] But there were also attempts made, notably by the editors "Jonathan Richardson, Father and Son" and Thomas Newton, to see the style as pursuing its own internal logic, intermittently engaging and disrupting grammatical expectations and forcing the reader to recognize subtleties which might be swamped by a more familiar "idiom."[4]

The debate has continued into this century. F. R. Leavis attacked the verse form of *Paradise Lost* in a famous essay, "Milton's verse," published in *Scrutiny* in 1934. Of the style he said that "the pattern, the stylised gesture and movement, has no particular expressive work to do, but functions by rote, of its own momentum in the manner of a ritual," and of the metre that the reader is "brought inevitably down with the foreseen thud in the foreseen place."[5] T. S. Eliot, in an essay published in 1936, and now usually referred to as "Milton I," states that in the poem, "a dislocation takes place ... so that inner meaning is separated from the surface, and tends to become something occult, or at least without effect upon the reader until fully understood."[6] As well as sharing Leavis' opinion of the poem as gorgeous but gratuitous word-play Eliot neatly articulates the principal argument of the "Anti-Miltonist" critique – the notion that the language maintains a surface complexity which effectively detaches it from coherent, sequential thought. Christopher Ricks in *Milton's Grand Style* has triumphantly counterattacked the Leavis–Eliot position by practising a strategy of reading which produces a depth of texture and alternative localized meanings ultimately cohering as functions of a larger thematic unity. Ricks's approach is in no sense novel: he eagerly exploits the suggestions and more adventurous perceptions of those eighteenth-century editors who found the style subtly expressive.

Central to his, and their, critical practice is a continual rewriting of the poem. Neither Ricks nor his eighteenth-century predecessors attempt immediately to resolve the ambiguities or close the gaps left by the poem's stylistic peculiarity, but rather they encourage the proliferation of readings and codify them as germane to some greater epic intention. Roland Barthes has made a distinction between works *lisible* and *scriptible*, works respectively parsimonious and generous in offering a plurality, a polyperversity of readings, and, superficially, Ricks's procedure seems to recognize *Paradise Lost* as a *scriptible* or "writerly" text.[7] But it must be made clear that Ricks differs significantly from the sort of critic, usually termed post-structuralist, who would associate *scriptible* with the systematic avoidance of the pursuit of origins or centres and from the sort of criticism whose reference points may be located in Jacques Derrida's *L'Ecriture et la différence* (1967) and in Barthes's exorbitant deconstruction of Balzac's *Sarrasine* in *S/Z* (1970). It has often been remarked that deconstruction is merely an extension of the New Critical search for structures of "irony," "paradox" and "ambiguity" as tokens of the linguistic autonomy of poetry, but Ricks's book on Milton, as with many of the stylistic and metrical analyses which followed it, illustrates the nature of the difference. Ricks dislocates Milton's language by revealing it as a set of alternatives; in a phrase he quotes from Donald Davie, "[Milton's] language operates through time, in terms of successive events, each new sentence a new small action in its sometimes complicated plot."[8] The metaphor is precise and misleading. Each puzzling twist and turn in which a phrase is revealed as first working in one way and then in another is eventually assimilated to the operation of the "Grand Style," an epic writing capable of absorbing and tolerating earthbound linguistic betrayals of moral or perceptual confusion – Holmes and Homer. If the "events" or linguistic moments are "successive" and part of a "plot" – a term which inevitably implies a hidden truth – it is curious that, as I shall show, each critical elaboration produces a plenitude of meanings which are realigned according to some thematic paradigm established prior to the critical engagement. In what follows I want to examine the process by which meanings are habitually generated from the shifting surface of *Paradise Lost* and then neutralized by reference to a point of fixity, a centre. It is a process brilliantly enacted by Ricks in his redefinition of style but it is a process contemptuous of its own method. The *scriptible* text is discovered but made *lisible* by the certainty that each "discovery" will contribute to what it is already assumed that the poem is "about."

One of the most striking successes of Ricks's book lies in his ability to intervene like a cool judicial sage in the arguments of the eighteenth-century critics, frequently playing off the intolerant rationalism of Richard Bentley against the more lambent perceptions of Pearce, the Richardsons or Newton.[9] The following is typical: "An interchange between Bentley and Pearce brings out that flexible syntax in Milton can be mistaken for careless syntax" (88). One illustration of this flexibility is especially interesting:

> Thus saying, from her Husband's hand her hand
> Soft she withdrew.
>
> (*PL* IX.385–6)

Ricks points out that an initial reading of "Soft" as an adverb, "softly" or "yielding," can be modified first by the implication of lines 319–21 and 376–7 that Eve is persistent as well as meek, and second by the possibility that "soft" might contain traces of an adjectival meaning through a typically Miltonic reversal of adjective and noun, "hand/soft,"

> so that the total effect is "her soft hand softly she withdrew" with *soft* sounded much more quietly than *softly*. And with the delicate fusion of two points of view, since the adverb has the neutrality of an onlooker, while the adjective puts us in the place of Adam as he feels Eve's hand.
>
> (90)

Ricks's method produces a number of thematic alternatives from the syntax, but far from creating incoherence, the results are neutralized as components of a single, if more complex, stylistic intention. But there is something rather odd about his implication that the "total effect," the "delicate fusion of two points of view," is something that occurs in the sphere of oral performance – "sounded much more quietly than" – because the production of textural depth depends upon two *separate* oral performances. When the word "soft" is spoken with its primary signification as an adverb, the "metrical" or "spatial" pause after "hand" corresponds neatly with a rhetorical or performative pause, but in order for an oral performance to convey the secondary adjectival resonance the gap must be closed considerably to move the modifier away from the verb "withdrew" and closer to the substantive "hand." Moreover, although the basic iamb/trochee sequence "her hand/ Soft she" is maintained, there would have to be a quite notable shift of stress from "hand" to "soft" in order for the adjective/noun possibility to be recognized. I don't think that all of these pause and stress variations could possibly occur in a single oral performance.

But Ricks's implication that they can is hardly surprising given the influence of linguistic metrics developed since the *Kenyon Review* symposium of 1956. This programme is founded upon the identification of separate and diverging intonational sequences to account for the full metrical identity of a poetic line, or in Ricks's terms "total effect." Linguistic metrical analysis is essentially a reaction against the traditional classically based notation of stress and unstress. This began with Trager and Smith's "discovery" that there are more than two levels of stress in English (they generously decided on four instead).[10] Seymour Chatman was the first to apply this broader notation to poetry in a special *Kenyon Review* issue (1956) containing a number of essays on metre.[11] He envisages a tension between two systems, the abstract, usually iambic, metrical pattern and the more contingent stress, pitch and pause variation of spoken language. His chief point is that a performance of a line in some way incorporates both. Probably the most sophisticated and comprehensive summation of linguistic metrics' contribution to criticism is Derek Attridge's *The Rhythms of English Poetry*. In an eloquent defence of the concept of metrical tension he states that,

> If you prefer to emphasize the regularity of the metre, the resolute irregularity of the language will be felt pulling against you; if you let speech rhythms have their head, the periodicity of the beat will exercise a counter claim: both readings, however, will register the inherent tension of the line.[12]

His point is that metrical tension is a matter of having one's cake and eating it. He would presumably regard the alternative oral readings of "hand/Soft" as each capable of containing traces of the other, as acknowledging one another's presence in the "inherent tension of the line," or in this case "lines." Attridge's structural model is predicated upon the langue/parole, system/performance differential that is the basis of practically all literary linguistics. Linguistic metrics adapts the conceptual structure of transformational grammar as a model for poetic metre, with the abstract metrical pattern representing the deep structure, and the actual poetic line the surface structure of the verse. But in Ricks's example the variation occurs across the line ending and thus compromises the line itself as the unit of deep structure. The identity of the two lines is both dissolved and reassembled in the service of varied meaning. His reading of "Soft" as adjective and adverb creates two metrical structures and two different sentences. It is difficult to reconcile Attridge's claim that different performances of a poetic sequence will always acknowledge some underlying pattern with his later assertion that "metre, by freeing the spoken language from its univocal straight jacket, invests it with the kind of openness and multiplicity that is normally the special prerogative of the written text" (314). It is surely the visual isolation of "hand" and "Soft" as part of the signifying potential of the written text which effectively destroys the concept of an abstract foundation, the line, against which variation could take place.

There is a close connection between Ricks's assumption of a "total effect" and the dependence of linguistic metrics on the anchoring function of deep structure or abstract metrical pattern. Both are ways of allowing poetic language metrical tension or, in terms of meaning, "ambiguity," whilst preserving the notion that there is still a unitary relation between written signifier and transcendent signified, between "ambiguity" and "total effect."

Ricks's analysis involves treating the text as writing but recuperating his findings as speech. Milton tells us something about how Adam feels but he does so in silence, in a communicative system where graphic signifiers can be shifted around on the page to open and close gaps and produce new meanings. In a 1971 essay on Wordsworth, Ricks uses the phrase "white space" to account for the moment at the line ending where sequential meaning is momentarily suspended, the moment at which the critic is able to move in and begin to write the text.[13] And this seems closely related to a term applied by Denis Donoghue in his *Ferocious Alphabets* to the reading strategies of post-structuralism: graphireading. "From GREEK *graphos*, writing. Hence the graphireader deals with writing as such and does not think of it as transcribing an event properly construed as vocal or audible."[14] Donoghue opposes graphireaders with what he calls epireaders, who "read or interpret – the same act – in the hope of going through the words to something that the words both reveal and hide. . . . Epireaders say to poems: I want to hear you. Graphireaders say: I want to see what I can do, stimulated by your insignia" (151–2). It is clear that Donoghue regards graphireaders as rather squalid, childish individuals who merely want to play around with signs. But this is precisely what Ricks (whom Donoghue would regard as a grown-up epireader) does. He also, as Donoghue puts it, goes through "the words to something that the words both reveal and hide." But Donoghue's assertion that the "going through" is the natural process of reading seems to ignore the variety of resistances and diversions offered by the medium. It cannot account for the fact that Ricks, and others, celebrate the poem as writing, as a silent configuration of written signifiers, but at the same time want it to *speak* to them. In a chapter called "Liquid texture" Ricks examines three lines from Book IX:

> Cover me ye Pines,
> Ye Cedars, with innumerable boughs
> Hide me. . .
>
> (*PL* IX.1088–90)

"The cry is not made less simple if one points out that here . . . the syntax is curiously fluid, that one may divide it at all sorts of places" (83). And he does, four times (Pines,/Ye; me/ye Cedars,/with; boughs/Hide). One cannot argue with Ricks about the abundant variety of effects generated by such an experiment, but his emphasis upon the idea that it is the syntax which changes in each case is rather odd. Later on in the chapter he offers a specific definition of syntactic and non-syntactic effects: "E. E. Cummings might achieve such effects through typography and punctuation – Milton uses syntax" (90). This is an exceedingly fine distinction. Given the clear similarity between what Ricks does to Milton's lines and what Cummings tends to do with language it is difficult to see how mere "typography" can be regarded by the critic as playing so small a part in the Milton lines. But the comparison between Cummings and Milton also contains the implication that what the former does is to play around with language, whilst the poet of the "Grand Style" renders the "speech" of a character in a compelling dramatic situation – typography versus syntax. I shall return to the connection between Milton and modernist poetry later in this essay but for the moment let us see what Ricks can tell us about Adam. "But the effect of the (original) two lines is as of innumerable trees – all of which telescope into one terrifyingly simple cry" (84). This is really what Donoghue's "going through" the words means then. The *visual* isolation of the phrase "Hide me" is *heard* with confident clarity.

On the matter of silence and noise in poetic texts John Hollander must be regarded as the critical eminence. In his important essay "The poem in the eye" he suggests that hearing and seeing poems are separate engagements analogous to the Saussurean division of language into a system of differences and speech events.[15]

> It is on the second of these axes that I would pose the ear, the individual talent, the voice, the *parole*; on the first are ranged the eye, the tradition, the mask through which the voice sounds, and the *langue*. The ear responds to the dimension of natural experience, the eye to that of convention.
>
> (248)

The offer of stability made by this formulation is tempting and persuasive and it does provide the ground for some of Hollander's most striking critical insights. For instance, his exploration of the ability of enjambment to generate new levels of meaning from the syntax of certain poems depends upon his recognition of the typographical poetic line as an extra-grammatical intrication of meaning established by literary convention. In structures such as Milton's blank verse, where aural signals like rhyme or rhythmic inversion are absent or ambiguous, the reader recognizes this effect through the conventional significance of the line ending on the page. But, as has been seen, there is a powerful tendency in criticism to then assimilate enjambments of this kind to the category of written marks, such as commas or full stops, which are assumed to be merely typographic stage directions to oral performance. This process is an attempt to assert the priority of the poem's oral status over the shapes and marks which seem merely an artificial representation of a representation. Hollander's differential axes of ear and eye reveal a prejudice, an ascription to the eye of client status: the visual format is "the mask *through which the voice sounds.*"

The drive towards the privileging of the spoken poem by treating the typographic object as a mediating pragmatic necessity is endemic to criticism and the *ex cathedra* theorizing of poets; it is an attempt to set aside, as what Derrida in *Of Grammatology* calls a "supplement" to speech, the most tangible and durable manifestation of language's materiality.[16] Poems tend to be talked about as if they were invulnerable to paraphrase, to the extent that the secondary text should never be allowed to overwhelm the original; linguistic depth and intrications of meaning are regarded as properties of the poem to be disclosed by criticism. Earlier I considered the question of how Ricks is able to synthesize variations of meaning as properties of a single, albeit epic, voice. That question may be answered by revealing that dark area of criticism where the critic is momentarily transformed from seeker after truth into rhetorical conjurer, where the exploitation of the text as a visual structure allows strategies of reading which question the stability of the relationship between poetry and criticism. John Hollander is admirably uncomplaisant about the validity of his critical techniques and it is in his own revealing reflections on this activity that there emerge a number of pointers to the hidden protocols of graphireading.

Hollander's Saussurean analogy between eye/ear and langue/parole becomes even more interesting when it is extended to Saussure's other most celebrated contribution to theoretical linguistics, the statement that "in the linguistic system there are only differences, without positive terms."[17] A differential system of arbitrary signs can involve, as Derrida puts it, "synthesis and referrals that prevent there from being at any moment or in any way a simple element that is present in and of itself and refers [sic] only to itself."[18] Saussure sought to preserve his concept of the linguistic sign from its own implications by allowing for the possibility of intelligible signifieds to which each signifier provides access. Most importantly, he did this by asserting that the object of linguistic analysis is speech, where signifier and signified seem spontaneously fused, rather than a written language at the prey of absence and anonymity (*Course*, 23–4). Similarly, Hollander asserts the priority of the spoken poem over the written text by identifying the eye as responding to the *langue*, the differential system *through* which the "individual talent" is heard to speak. Just as Saussure created his hierarchy of speech/writing to support a logocentric bias so Hollander needs to categorize the effects he identifies as the products of speech rather than writing, or more importantly the products of an author rather than those of a critic manipulating a system of literary conventions.

The signifier "clear" contains within itself the traces of a number of separate signifieds. A pragmatic resolution of any ambiguity that this word might produce could, it may be argued, be achieved by creating a hierarchy of meanings from its textual and grammatical context. But the spatial arrangement of signifiers on a page produces new and more problematical contextual relationships. This is Eve "speaking" in *Paradise Lost*, Book IV:

> a murmuring sound
> Of waters issued from a cave and spread
> Into a liquid plain, then stood unmoved
> Pure as the expanse of heaven; I thither went
> With unexperienced thought, and laid me down
> On the green bank, to look into the clear
> Smooth lake, that to me seemed another sky
> (IV.453–9)[19]

At line 458 "clear," cut off from "smooth lake," seems to take on a substantive form. The effect is to suggest a sense of infinite space consistent with Eve's apparent perception of sky and water as an unbroken continuum. Consider this *OED* usage from 1694: "Between nine and ten o'clock there was a fine clear, by which I saw the land very plainly."[20] It is interesting that the only other example of this substantive form given by the dictionary is also concerned with clarity of vision at sea.[21] To a contemporary *ear* any unwonted pause at "clear" would suggest a potential narrative contradiction. Why would Eve use a word of such familiar nautical currency when she is supposed to have no acquaintance with expanses of water and, more specifically, how can she have such a firm grasp of the phenomenon presented by the lake when, as the succeeding lines reveal, it is the delusive, incomprehensible qualities of water which provide the keynote of the episode?

> As I bent down to look, just opposite,
> A shape within the watery gleam appeared

Bending to look on me, I started back,
It started back, but pleased I soon returned.
(IV.460–3)

According to the critical method practised by Ricks and Hollander this
disruption of linear meaning could easily be accommodated within the
interpretative model where contradictions and discontinuities can be
transformed into purposive manifestations of a greater thematic coherence.
Eve is relating an earlier instance of her consciousness in contact with
reality; it is a retrospective relation. Adam and Eve, when they appear in the
poem, possess a vocabulary not dissimilar to that of mid-seventeenth-
century English. It is therefore plausible that her double usage of "clear"
could be an example of language in the process of closing the gap between
the event and the memory of the event. What was then an intractable
phenomenon is now "clear."

But in this instance, as in others, the critical resolution depends upon a
psychological or intentionalist model of textual signifying to support its
claim of access to a more complete "meaning." Ricks assumes in his
examples from Book IX that the poet finds a subtle way of telling us about
how Adam feels and that Adam's "terrifyingly simple cry" has a precise
textual equivalent. In the same way, the double signification in "clear" and
the information it seems to give us about Eve has to be seen as part of the
parataxis of her speech. This economy of critical procedures provides a way
of reconciling the recognition of a destabilized signifier ("clear," "soft") at a
point of spatial fissure, with the presumption of access to a signifying
intention behind it – a double mastery of text and context. I intend to
demonstrate that this double mastery contains within its assumed monadic
totality the actual fragmentation of the categories of the referential and the
rhetorical. But first there must be an examination of how these categories
have been established in relation to the textual identity of *Paradise Lost*.

The establishment of an authoritative and, by implication, unproblematic
meaning within the occasional opacities and apparent contradictions of
Milton's verse form is a critical process almost as old as the poem itself.
Paradise Lost offered a challenge to the reading practices and formal
expectations of the eighteenth century because its unrhymed enjambments
engaged a convention of reading, the acknowledgement of the poetic line as
a formal effect, without satisfying the criteria on which the convention
operated; many lines could be seen but not *heard* as discrete units. Thomas
Sheridan in *Lectures on the Art of Reading* (1775) attempted a solution by
proposing that the spatial gap at the line ending was a signal, inserted by
Milton, of an extra grammatical intrication of meaning capable of
generating textual depth; in effect, a key to unlock hidden meanings
inherent in the spoken poem and *located through* the written text.[22]
Sheridan's naturalization of the visual status of the poetic line as a function

of the structure of the original oral poem has become quietly institutionalized in the reading strategies of the past two hundred years. In a 1785 essay by one Thomas Barnes, the assimilation of Sheridan's readings to the contemporary attitude to the written poem is acknowledged.

> But when *read with the eye only*, without the accompaniment of the voice, there is a *fainter association* of the sound, the *shadow of the music*, as it were, connected with the words; so that we can judge exactly of the composition as if it were audible to the ear.[23]

Barnes gives a perfect description of the critical procedure. The reader is able to "judge exactly" the meaning of this silent configuration of signs as if he were listening to Milton himself.

The tendency to reduce writing to a function of speech is characterized by Derrida as a will to preserve the ideal of truth and authority through unmediated expression. He quotes Hegel, "the visible language is related only as a sign to the audible language; intelligence expresses itself immediately and unconditionally through speech," and comments, "What writing itself in its non-phonetic moment, betrays, is life. It menaces at once, the breath, the spirit, and history as the spirit's relationship with itself."[24] In the third chapter of *Grammatology*, "Of grammatology as a positive science," Derrida postulates a "necessary decentring," a "dislocation of the founding categories of language, through access to another system linking speech and writing." This system is not philosophical or linguistic, but poetic. "This is the meaning of the work of Fenellosa [*sic*] whose influence upon Ezra Pound and his poetics is well known: this irreducibly graphic poetics was, with that of Mallarmé, the first break in the most entrenched western tradition" (92). The poetic of Fenollosa and Pound is notable for its obsessive shifts between the graphic and the phonetic, orient and occident, eye and ear.[25] The poetry of "juxtaposition," with the literal and thematic "gap" in place of the tyranny of verb and modifiers, has not coexisted happily with the habits of reading which persist within the academic and critical institution, and one might draw an analogy between the critical reception of modernist free verse with its discontinuities and dependence on typography, and the reaction to *Paradise Lost* in the eighteenth century. In both cases criticism shifted its ground slightly and began to evolve techniques of naturalization. It is no coincidence that in Jonathan Culler's chapter "Poetics of the lyric" in *Structuralist Poetics*, there is an initial emphasis on the construction of poetic meanings from typographically rearranged prose and that the poems which respond most successfully to this sort of attention are drawn from the clipped lyrics of Pound and Williams and the blank verse of Milton.[26] Derrida's "irreducibly graphic poetics" may seem to emerge most consistently with modernism but they are also a property of *Paradise Lost*. And they are not, as the strength of the "western tradition" in the form of literary criticism has ensured, "irreducible."

The idea of *Paradise Lost* as in some way the precursor of certain features of modernism is one that most people would only entertain with a good deal of scepticism, but the most striking parallel is undeniable. Milton, like Pound, Williams and many of the Imagists and vers librists, compromised the stability of the relationship between text and interpretation by foregrounding certain key aspects of conventions through which poetry is made intelligible. And just as Fenollosa's emphasis upon western language as an arbitrary, contingent and, in his view, fundamentally perverse system of mediation emerged in poems as a threat to the accepted notions of linear meaning and comprehensibility, so Milton's rejection of traditional metre, and his freedom with the "natural" order of and relationship between words, threatened the assumption of transparency upon which an empiricist milieu so closely depended. "So many *things* in an equal number of words" was a dictum that appeared to be wilfully flouted when the system of interpretation which it underpinned failed to cope. Lord Kames in his *Elements of Criticism* (1762) assumes that there is an organic relationship between the unitary correlation of language and reality and the formal demarcations of poetic structure. The evocative logic of a line must, according to Kames, mirror and support its formal prosodic integrity. "Colour, for example, cannot be conceived independent of the surface coloured" (II.130).

Kames's anxiety about language coming adrift from things is fuelled by such lines as the following from *Paradise Lost*:

> Now in loose garlands thick thrown off the bright
> Pavement
>
> (III.362–3)

The structure is immensely close to a more recent piece of work by William Carlos Williams, "The Red Wheelbarrow:"

> so much depends
> upon
>
> a red wheel
> barrow
>
> glazed with rain
> water
>
> beside the white
> chickens[27]

If anyone should doubt the significance of this "coincidence," I would refer them to two critical texts which seek to join what Kames believes has been put asunder. This is Thomas Sheridan (1775) on Milton's line:

> now here by finishing the verse with the adjective *bright*, it is separated from its substantive, *pavement*, contrary to the genius of our tongue. And

yet in the right manner of repeating it, there appears to be no defect, but rather the idea seems to acquire a new force from this very circumstance. . . . But this separation in point of sound between the quality and its subject, gives time for the quality to make a stronger impression on us; and therefore should never be used, but when the poet means that the quality not the subject, should be the principal idea; which is the case in the above instance; where the intention of the poet is, to fix our thoughts, not on the pavement itself, but on the brightness of the pavement.[28]

Similarly discussed are "cold/Climate," "sweet/Recess" and "pure/Intelligence." This is John Hollander in his essay "'Sense variously drawn out:' on English enjambment" on Williams:

the line termini cut the words "wheelbarrow" and "rainwater" into their constituents, without the use of hyphenation to warn that the first noun is part of a compound, *with the implication that they are phenomenological constituents as well*. The wheel plus the barrow equals the wheelbarrow, and in the freshness of the light after the rain (it is the kind of light which the poem is about, although never mentioned directly), things seem to lose their compounded properties [italics in original].[29]

After permitting oneself a sagacious reflection on the reassurances of continuity one might proceed to examine these analyses more closely. Both rest on the assumption that what is generated by the spatial configurations of the text provides access to an oral event, an original intention behind it. And just as they inhabit the same critical tradition, the texts upon which they focus are similarly related.

This is a form of criticism where the critic takes advantage of silences and gaps in the text which prevailing ideas about the nature of literary communication allow to occur. It began in the eighteenth century with students of logic and grammer like Bentley, Pearce and Richardson and theorists of verse form and reading such as Sheridan. But most importantly it began because of *Paradise Lost*. The revival of it in this century occurred in response to the comparable stylistic disruptions of modernism. Hollander's reduction of Williams' experiment to the status of being "about" the quality of the light is, in a way, inevitable because of the institutional pressure of an author-centred theory of communication. In the same way when critics come across that characteristic moment in Milton's style, the "disturbance of expectation," there is an immediate assumption that things have to be resolved according to some imperative of organicism and consistency. But there is a difference. The discontinuities of spatial juxtaposition in modernist poems tend to compromise the illusion of a voice *in* the text. The reconstruction of an author's intention *behind* it is a critical operation which might, on its own terms, seem to be rather contemptuous of the status of the poem itself, but it is at least based on the teleological assumption that it is only the text which stands between author and reader. And it is here that a problem arises: *Paradise Lost* is a poem of many "voices," Milton's, God's, Satan's, Adam's, Eve's. . . . If a partial graphireading can provide access to a coherent centre it seems rather odd that the textual features upon which it operates are consistently evident in several differentiated discourses. In Book I the poet describes Satan's condition.

> At once as far as angels ken he views
> The dismal situation waste and wild
> (I.59–60)

In the space after the verb it is the range of Satan's vision that is evoked rather than its immediate object. This throws up an interesting tension between the contours of his perceived reality and the "dismal" nature of that reality. Thus "views" becomes a key pivotal word: it is a hinge between the almost complete grammar of the limits of perception and the continued revelation of desolation.

This reading would probably be approved of by Donoghue as "going through" the words to the meaning – the "meaning" being that Milton is able to convey to us the distressingly gradual process of Satan's recognition of his state. I have thus, it seems, gained access to Milton's hidden intention. In the same way Milton is able to tell me, or rather Ricks, what Adam feels at the moment of leavetaking in Book IX and, in Book IV, he tells us, through Eve, what she remembered of her first moments of consciousness and of her later reflections on this memory. Later on in that section from Book IV yet another voice is introduced, presumably that of God, who disabuses Eve of her narcissistic delusion.

> follow me,
> And I will bring thee where no shadow stays
> Thy coming
> (IV.469–71)

Alastair Fowler, in his edition, quite correctly suggests that "stays" should be read as "awaits" since the sentence moves on to reveal the more substantial presence of Adam ("no shadow"), the proper object of Eve's affections. But reading as Ricks or Hollander and according the white space after "stays" some significance, one is struck by the visual phenomenon of a transitive verb left dangling without its object. "Stays" can mean "restrains" as well as "awaits." Is this gap made available for the reader to write in another notional sentence with something like "Thy desire" as the object? The "meaning" of all this would probably be the recognition that Eve, in relating these lines, is again interpreting her memory of the event, only this time doing so unconsciously, with the spatial hesitation a token of her residual narcissism and an anticipation of her precipitation of the Fall.

Donoghue in his sustained critique of graphireading paraphrases Mallarmé whose "irreducibly graphic poetics" Derrida celebrated. "The purity of the poem is available only in space: no breath is allowed to effect a continuous presence between the words. The inequality of the words depends upon the equality of the spaces between them on the page" (153). Donoghue sees this as a perverse and obsessive unbalancing of writing and speech: "Only the written word could feature in Mallarmé's ideology. If the word were to be defined as spoken, the sovereign author could not suppress himself in its favour; he would be dragged into the poem with every audible breath" (155). But at the point at which the critic "goes through" the words and drags the author into the poem those words cannot be defined as spoken. Whether it is the voice of Eve relating the voice of God or the voice of the poet telling us about the poem, the gaps which emerge to allow us to "go through" are part of the overall silence of the written text. Or in other words, if each textual effect attests to the presence to consciousness of the signifying intention of a particular voice at a particular moment, how is it that each effect, such as the white space at the line ending, is part of the signifying potential of the whole text?

In modernist lyrics like Williams' "The Red Wheelbarrow" it is usual to assume that the broken syntax is part of a single textual strategy operating throughout the poem, but in *Paradise Lost* we are asked to accept that there is a distinction between the overall textual identity of the poem and its particular internal dramatic contexts. But when Ricks or Hollander examine meanings produced by the text, the written artefact, they must simultaneously locate them within a dramatic context. There is a striking connection between the text/context distinction in *Paradise Lost* and the categories of iterability considered in a recent debate between Derrida and John Searle on J. L. Austin's theory of speech acts. In his book *Speech Acts: An Essay in the Philosophy of Language* Searle argues that the illocutionary force, or the truth, of an utterance can be guaranteed by the intention of the speaker and by the context of the utterance. He says that as one of the conditions of promising, "if the purported promise is to be non-defective, the thing promised must be something the hearer wants done, or considers to be in his interest."[30] Derrida has pointed out that if unconscious desire on the part of the listener is also part of these conditions then the status of certain promises is actually threatened by their context.[31] Hollander in the essay "'Sense variously drawn out:' on English enjambment," discusses an instance of Eve, in effect, "promising" Adam that she is devoted to him.

From Book IV again, Eve's account of her displacement of narcissistic admiration onto a recognition of Adam as an objectified beauty, concludes "and from that time I see/How beauty is excell'd by manly grace" (ll. 489–90), where the literal sense of "see" dissolves into a figurative one ("see how" as "understand that"), with a lingering hedging of her commitment. (98)

Now, is Hollander's "lingering hedging" an "unconscious desire" on his part to see Eve's promise as "defective"? If so what is it that allows him to suspect (desire?) this, but which apparently does not occur to the person to whom the promise is originally addressed, Adam? I would say that it is his mastery of the text, his ability to see the written signifiers as Eve's words, that allows him to project his reading onto Eve; a reading which is, of course, denied to Adam who doesn't have a copy of the poem.

The chief distinction amongst the voices, the contexts, of the poem must lie in the separation of the poet from his characters, and in my essay emphasis has been upon what the poet says and what Eve says. The reading of the poet's discourse as laced with purposive textual gaps, "new small actions in a sometimes complicated plot," depends upon the critic positioning himself as listener in a communicative circuit where the "graphic poetics" of the written poem are transparent and unproblematic. But Eve and the rest of the cast "speak" primarily to each other. We are therefore asked to accept that the form of what they say is hidden from the people they talk to within the poem. For were this not so the "sometimes complicated plot" would not exist. Adam and Eve would be able to "read" their own speeches just as Ricks and Hollander do.

Graphireading must acknowledge its positioning of the text as an instrument of communication. *Paradise Lost* is full of instances where the signifier is contemplated in its most contingent and material form, but there is something dishonest in assuming that the different contexts in which these occur do not create serious disruptions of the relationship between text and context. If Eve is, in Book IV, systematically giving herself away to the reader on one level of interpretation but not to Adam on another, then the status of "voices" within the poem as separate from the formal features of the verse itself is in doubt. A shift toward the signifying procedures of the text and away from the phonocentric psychology of character ought to produce a more plural, genuinely *scriptible* work, yet it has so far only provided the partisans of closure with an opportunity to collect more evidence to support what "the words both reveal and hide."

If there is to be a serious reassessment of the relationship between author, text and reader in *Paradise Lost*, then it must be acknowledged that the stylistic features of the poem represent a fundamental challenge to the assumptions of critical practice, from the techno-sophistication of the new metrists to the sensitive close readings of Ricks. A corrupt form of graphireading has been practised on the poem since the early eighteenth century, as a way of elucidating it in the traditional sense of attempting to grasp a unifying context or theme. I propose graphireading not as a route to a rival governing interpretation but as a way of looking at what *Paradise Lost* says about the activity of reading verse. In his speech at the beginning of Book III God says of Adam and Eve

for so
I formed them free, and free they must remain,
Till they entrall themselves: I else must change
Their nature

(III.123–6)

Hollander's recognition of a "lingering hedging" at Eve's line ending should be remembered here because God appears to be doing something similar. God's consideration of an alternative, "I else must change," is a reaffirmation of his power to do what he likes with Adam and Eve. But the spatial gap might just allow a suspicion of self-doubt ("I must change myself"). The syntax "resolves the ambiguity" but the moment forces the reader to see that his comfortable contemplation of Eve's paratactic slips is made available not by his listening to Eve but by his intervention in the play of textual figures and relations. Because just as there is a gap between our reading of Eve and Adam's understanding of her, so at this point must there be a similar gap between our reading of God and the Son's understanding of him. It might be argued that it is a condition of dramatic contexts in literature that a possibility exists for the reader to understand characters better than they do each other. But the disjunction between written text and dramatic, spoken context is so radical in *Paradise Lost* that the work of the reader can, as has been shown, act as the arbiter of meaning.

Derrida has said that the non-phonetic moment "menaces at once, the breath, the spirit." Elements, such as the non-phonetic moment, that a unified understanding has repressed, work to undo the structures to which they seem marginal. This undoing must not be "repaired" as a way to reveal a rival unity (God is more confused than Eve); this again involves a forgetting of the dynamics of the text. The reading strategies that I have pointed to in *Paradise Lost* should be conducted in an intertextual space, to explore forces and structures that recur in reading and writing. The energies and signifying complexes of modernist verse forms and the disjunctions between written text and spoken context in *Paradise Lost* can "read" one another. When the Son answers the Father in Book III and says "gracious was that word which closed/Thy sovereign sentence" (144–5), his hesitation announces the radical "unclosure" of poetic sentences.

Notes

1. Samuel Johnson, "Life of Milton," in *Lives of the English Poets*, ed. G. Birbeck-Hill (London, Oxford University Press, 1905), I.193, and Samuel Woodford, *Paraphrase upon the Canticles* (1679), sigs B6ʳ-B6ᵛ.
2. See Milton's prefatory note to *Paradise Lost*, "The Verse."
3. Johnson, "Life of Milton," 190.
4. J. Richardson, Father and Son, *Explanatory Notes and Remarks on Milton's*

Paradise Lost (London, 1734). Thomas Newton, *Paradise Lost . . . A New Edition with Notes of Various Authors* (London, 1749).

5. F. R. Leavis, "Milton's verse" (*Scrutiny*, 2, 1934, 123–36).

6. Reprinted as "Milton I" in *Selected Essays of T. S. Eliot*, ed. F. Kermode (London, Faber & Faber, 1975); quotation is from p. 263.

7. Christopher Ricks, *Milton's Grand Style* (Oxford, Clarendon Press, 1963). R. Barthes, *S/Z* (Paris, 1970; English translation, New York, Hill & Wang, 1974).

8. Ricks, *Milton's Grand Style*, 42. Donald Davie, "Syntax and music in *Paradise Lost*," in *The Living Milton*, ed. F. Kermode (London, Oxford University Press, 1960), 73.

9. Richard Bentley's *Milton's Paradise Lost. A New Edition* (1732) is notable for the editor's assumption that the extant poem is corrupt, and for his rewriting of apparent stylistic inconsistencies. For a more complete discussion of the eighteenth-century editors and "The Milton controversy" in general, see chapter 1 in Ricks, *Milton's Grand Style*.

10. G. L. Trager and H. L. Smith Jr, *An Outline of English Structure*, Studies in Linguistics Occasional Papers, no. 3 (Oklahoma, Battenburg Press, 1951).

11. Seymour Chatman, "Robert Frost's 'Mowing.' An inquiry into prosodic structure" (*Kenyon Review*, 18, 1956, 421–38). The articles in this issue are acknowledged as the starting point of the linguistic analysis of metre. Contributors include Harold Whitehall, John Crowe Ransom and Arnold Stein. An excellent bibliography and commentary may be found in T. V. F. Brogan, *English Versification 1570–1980* (Baltimore, Johns Hopkins University Press, 1981), 290–318.

12. Derek Attridge, *The Rhythms of English Poetry* (Harlow, Longman, 1982), 313.

13. Christopher Ricks, "Wordsworth: 'A pure organic pleasure from the lines'" (*Essays in Criticism*, 21, 1971, 1–32).

14. Denis Donoghue, *Ferocious Alphabets* (London, Faber & Faber, 1981), 151–2.

15. Published in John Hollander, *Vision and Resonance: Two Senses of Poetic Form* (New York, Oxford University Press, 1975), 245–87.

16. Jacques Derrida, *Of Grammatology*, tr. Gayatri Chakravorty Spivak (Baltimore, Johns Hopkins University Press, 1977).

17. Ferdinand de Saussure, *Course in General Linguistics*, tr. Wade Baskin (London, Owen, 1960), 120.

18. Jacques Derrida, *Positions*, tr. A. Bass (Chicago, University of Chicago Press, 1981), 26.

19. Other than where secondary quotations are cited my references are to *Paradise Lost*, ed. Alastair Fowler (London, Longman, 1968).

20. Sir John Narborough, *An Account of Several Late Voyages and Discoveries . . . 1694*. Reference from 1711 edition, 22.

21. "The wind shifted . . . accompanied with a clear" (*Naval Chronicle*, 1804, XI.168).

22. See Richard Bradford, "'Verse only to the eye?' Line endings in *Paradise Lost*" (*Essays in Criticism*, 3, 1983, 187–204).

23. Thomas Barnes, "On the nature and essential characteristics of poetry as distinguished from prose" (*Memoirs of the Manchester Literary and Philosophical Society*, I, 1785, 54–71; 70).

24. Derrida, *Of Grammatology*, 25.

25. Ernest Fenollosa, *The Chinese Written Character as a Medium for Poetry*, ed. Ezra Pound (1919). Reprinted in *Prose Keys to Modern Poetry*, ed. K. Shapiro (New York, Harper & Row, 1962), 136–55.

26. Jonathan Culler, *Structuralist Poetics* (London, Routledge & Kegan Paul, 1975).
27. From "Spring and All" (1923) reprinted in William Carlos Williams, *Collected Earlier Poems* (New York, New Directions, 1938).
28. Thomas Sheridan, *Lectures on the Art of Reading* (London, 1775), II.257–8.
29. Hollander, op. cit., 111.
30. See Jacques Derrida, "Signature event context" and John Searle, "Reiterating the differences: a reply to Derrida" (*Glyph*, I, 1977, 172–208); John Searle, *Speech Acts: An Essay in the Philosophy of Language* (Cambridge, Cambridge University Press, 1969), 59.
31. "Limited Inc." (*Glyph*, 2, 1977, 162–254; 215).

9

ELEANOR COOK

Melos versus Logos, or why doesn't God sing: some thoughts on Milton's wisdom

> The Word was from the first . . . I have called Him a New Song.
> (Clement of Alexandria)
>
> Music was the negation of sentences, music was the anti-word.
> (Milan Kundera, *The Unbearable Lightness of Being*)

I am wrong, of course. God does sing, as witness my first epigraph. Or at least, he sings (or is Song) occasionally. But he does not sing within the canonical text of the Bible: he speaks, and his word comes, saying.[1] Perhaps, of course, he no more speaks than he sings, since "everything [was] wrought by God through the Son [Logos] in the Holy Ghost," to follow the much-used formula of Athanasius.[2] This means that I should rephrase my question and ask why the Logos, the second Person of the Trinity, speaks and does not sing. Or (moving out from canon to tradition) why it speaks so much and sings so little. Why are its creating and authoritative acts conceived as speaking acts and not singing acts? God composes, of course: he composes eternal harmony, and he plays upon the instrument that the universe is, metaphorically, in his hands. But others make his music, while he speaks his word. And he *is* the Word or the Logos, while he is not canonically, and seldom elsewhere, the Melos, not the Sound or Note or Song.

The question may sound trivial. Yet if the human logos or word can have, by analogy (or by whatever means, and the means are disputed and important) – if the human word can have by analogy some relation with a divine Word, then it has a significance that other terms, such as melos or song, lack in lacking this relation. And if one is a musician or a poet, and also a Christian in the Augustinian tradition, this matters a great deal. (Singing, by metonymy, may be poetry, as in Milton's "my advent'rous Song.") My question may sound both trivial and churlish to a strongly Platonic tradition, with its fine meditations on *musica speculativa* and its sense of world harmony. To such a tradition, Augustine is troublesome, since, for all his love of Platonism, he decisively rejects it.

Nowadays, we hear a good deal about the logos, sometimes with little sense of its history, which may be deliberately or just casually ignored. Yet historical tensions or lacunae within the interpretation of the logos are worth considering in these ante-Nicene days – ante-Nicene because of our sundry disputes over the logos and our sundry readings of ancient texts. My example raises a further question. The logos is now sometimes associated with masculine (i.e. rational) discourse, so that feminine discourse must choose between separatism and a renewed federalism (to speak in Canadian terms). The contraries of logos and melos may be conceived as masculine and feminine modes of discourse, if we observe how the language used of melos, as against the language used of logos, tends to be the language used of women, as against the language used of men. I am aware that this is a wide generalization, that the long history of the logos is exceedingly complex, and that I am arguing by analogy. Nonetheless the point stands, and the question becomes how far the analogy holds and what it can tell us.

I began to think about this matter because of a coincidence in the rhetorical strategies of Milton and Karl Barth. These two powerful representatives of a logocentric tradition, separated by some three hundred years, desire to find (and know the strategic importance of finding) a divine origin for music in Scripture. Both Milton in 1667 and Barth in 1947 take the Wisdom figure of Proverbs 8:22–31, who is said to rejoice or play during or before creation, and both extend the word for "rejoice" or "play" to musical playing. The passage from Proverbs is well known:

> The Lord possessed me in the beginning of his way,
> Before his works of old . . .
> Then I was by him, as one brought up with him:
> And I was daily his delight,
> Rejoicing always before him;
> Rejoicing in the habitable part of his earth;
> And my delights were with the sons of men.
>
> (King James version)

Here is Milton, in the invocation to Book VII of *Paradise Lost*, lines 1–12:

> Descend from Heav'n *Urania*, by that name
> If rightly thou art call'd, whose Voice divine

Following, above th'*Olympian* Hill I soar,
Above the flight of *Pegasean* wing.
The meaning, not the Name I call: for thou
Nor of the Muses nine, nor on the top
Of old *Olympus* dwell'st, but Heav'nly born,
Before the Hills appear'd, or Fountain flow'd,
Thou with Eternal Wisdom didst converse,
Wisdom thy Sister, and with her didst play
In presence of th'Almighty Father, pleas'd
With thy Celestial Song.[3]

Milton's grammar in lines 9–12 does not say that the rejoicing or playing of Wisdom includes musical playing or Celestial Song. But his unobtrusive phrase, "with her," merges Urania's song with Wisdom's rejoicing or playing. Whatever Wisdom may be – and it would be the height of folly to inquire into God's activities before Creation, as Milton says in the *Christian Doctrine* (I.vii) – this mysterious personification of the Godhead offers a way of associating music and poetry with the divine. ("Poetical personification" is Milton's term for the Wisdom of Proverbs 8.)[4] Here at least, song is not what it is elsewhere, almost without exception: a creaturely activity – sometimes, to be sure, an activity of the highest creatures, but nonetheless creaturely. For Wisdom, if made, is not made as angels or the universe are made.[5] She is an agent of creation and part of the Godhead. She is in Scripture. And she plays.

In 1947, in the first essay of *Die Protestantische Theologie im 19. Jahrhundert*, Karl Barth speaks of Proverbs 8:27–31 and goes on to talk about music:

There is as we know a passage in the Bible according to which something like a conversation of the eternal harmony with itself takes place, just before the Creation, with a similar reference to playing [*eines Spielens*], i.e. Prov. 8:27–31: ". . . then was I by him, as a master workman: and had delight continually, playing always before him; playing in the habitable parts of the earth; and my delights were with the sons of men" [*und spielte vor ihm allezeit und spielte auf seinem Erdboden*]. Would it not be the revelation of a supreme will for form, a will for form manifesting perhaps only in this sphere its utmost absolutism, if the music of the eighteenth century sought to culminate the wisdom born of the Creator in its results and in the abandonment and superiority which cause us to forget all the craftsmanship behind it? Be that as it may, all earlier music is still too much involved in the struggle to subdue the raw material of musical sound, and it must be said that the later music, from Beethoven onwards, desired and loved the world of sound too little for its own sake, to be capable of looking upon it in the same unequivocal way as a game [*als Spiel*]. The music of the eighteenth century, the music of absolutism, plays [*spielt*], and for this reason it is in a peculiar way beautiful and that not only in its great exponents but in its minor ones too.[6]

Barth's moving if ingenious argument uses a similar strategy to Milton's, though a more self-conscious one. Music may be thought of as a beautiful game or play (whether or not eighteenth-century European music is unique in the way that Barth claims). Wisdom is said to play before God. Such a notion of play ought also to include the play or game that is music. Of course, the pun on "play," in German as in English and Latin, helps greatly in this argument. What helps most of all is the Hebrew pun on "play," and both Milton and Barth could read the original text in Hebrew.[7] The King James version of Proverbs 8:30–1 uses the word "rejoicing" and the Junius-Tremellius Bible, which Milton generally follows, uses *laetificans*, as W. B. Hunter observes.[8] But Harris Fletcher tells us that Milton's word "play," like the Vulgate's *ludere*, "translate[s] the Hebrew with more care than had his English Version. The Hebrew reads מְשַׂחֶקֶת. This is a piel participle with feminine ending of the verb שׂחק, and clearly means *playing* or *sporting*." Fletcher's useful commentary does not mention that the Hebrew itself suggests the possibility of musical play, at least in a secondary or punning meaning. As Fletcher himself points out, "The same verb, in the same stem and with the same meaning, occurs in Prov. 26:19; I Chron. 15:29; I Sam. 18:7; II Sam. 6:5; and *passim*. The meaning *ludere* or to play is perfectly clear in these passages." He does not say that three of his four examples are associated with musical play.[9]

What marks the tradition of Milton and Barth is its strict adherence to the biblical text, and the strict line it draws between creator and creature. Someone less strict can simply expand the metaphoric possibilities of the Bible in order to merge Word and Wisdom and Song, as Clement of Alexandria does. (He is altogether a cheerful merger, as he also merges man and God, this no doubt being one of Milton's "thick-sown heresies.")

> The Lord fashioned man a beautiful, breathing instrument, after His own image; and assuredly He Himself is an all-harmonious instrument of God, melodious and holy, the wisdom that is above this world, the heavenly Word . . . we were before the foundation of the world. . . . We are the rational images formed by God's Word, or Reason, and we date from the beginning on account of our connexion with Him, because "the Word was in the beginning." Well, because the Word was from the first, He was and is the divine beginning of all things; but because He lately took a name – the name consecrated of old and worthy of power, the Christ – I have called Him a New Song.[10]

The seventeenth-century heir to Clement is Calderón, as E. R. Curtius has shown. Curtius is unsympathetic to Milton's "rigorism," and sees Calderón's syncretic "Logos as poet" as "a Christian solution to the problem of the

Muses." It is a solution also informed by the useful figure of Hebrew Wisdom in Proverbs 8:22–31.[11]

How strict Milton is about these matters, we may see by his diction for the activities of God in *Paradise Lost*. God speaks, beholds, calls, says, sees, names, makes, and so on – all biblical verbs for his activities. But some things God does not do. He does not "charm" in either the magical or musical sense, though creatures, fallen and unfallen, may do so. All the language of magic is kept away from his activities. When Northrop Frye speaks of "the charm that created order out of chaos" or "the Word of God itself, which pronounced the original spell to keep chaos away,"[12] it sounds a little strange until we recognize a romance strategy of charm versus counter-charm. So also Collins, when he makes Wisdom into a Fancy figure, breathing "her *magic* Notes aloud" ("Ode on the Poetical Character;" my italics). But this is not a strategy that Milton allows himself in his later poetry.[13]

Proverbs 8:22–31 is of great importance for Milton. It resounds through his work more often and more profoundly than we have realized. I want to consider briefly how it echoes through several lines of *Paradise Regained* before moving on to its extended use in *Paradise Lost*. For, as we shall see, the relation of Wisdom to Adam and Eve is as significant as her relation to Urania. In *Paradise Regained*, IV.331–4, Milton extends the implications of the invocation to Book VII of *Paradise Lost*. The words of Proverbs 8, verses 30 and 31, echo through Christ's reply to the last temptation:

> Or if I would delight my private hours
> With Music or with Poem, where so soon
> As in our native Language can I find
> That solace?

Christ in his "private hours" chooses the true "solace" of Hebrew rather than classical music and poem, which as solace would be a harlot's solace, at least in this context. For in Proverbs 7 may be found Wisdom's opposite, Madam Folly, in all her harlotry, including a harlot's "solace" (Prov. 7:18). The contrast would be even more pointed for readers of the popular Geneva Bible, where Eternal Wisdom "toke my solace in the compasse of his earth" (Prov. 8:31). *Paradise Regained* is intimately involved with Wisdom and wisdom literature, both thematically and formally, so that Milton has good reason for using a specific echo. If I am right about this, then Milton has here extended the "delight" that Wisdom gives in Proverbs 8:30 to the delight of music and poetry. An earthly delight it may be (this is the incarnate Word speaking) but the echo affirms the pleasure of the Godhead in these things, as in the invocation to Book VII of *Paradise Lost*. And indeed, that invocation anticipates Milton's later explicit argument that even the best of classical song and wisdom is illusion in comparison with biblical. It echoes but revises Horace's ode, "Descende caelo . . . Calliope"

(III.iv.1–2), which also invokes a Muse to give general (not just political) "wisdom and order" (to use the title in Loeb). Milton opens, "Descend from Heav'n *Urania*," and closes, "thou are Heav'nly, shee [Calliope] an empty dream." It is appropriate that he petition Wisdom's sister to "govern" his song.[14]

In Book IX of *Paradise Lost*, Milton plays throughout the temptation scene with a subtext of Proverbs 7 and Proverbs 8, or the harlot Folly against eternal Wisdom. We know in a general way how Eve and then Adam undo wisdom and harmony. But Milton is specific and forceful. Eve, having eaten the fruit, plays with thoughts of usurpation: "Nor was Godhead from her thought," as "to herself she pleasingly began" (IX.790, 794). Just as God was "pleas'd" with Wisdom and Urania, so Eve speaks "pleasingly" but "to herself" in a parody of the self-sufficiency of the Godhead (809–11):

> thou [the Tree] op'n'st Wisdom's way,
> And giv'st access, though secret she retire.
> And I perhaps am secret . . . .

Milton's conjunction "though" shows how grim this parody is. It is not that the sexual possibilities of the passage from Proverbs have been exploited, as if in a Kabbalistic or Gnostic reading.[15] It is that Wisdom will be opened no matter how secretly she retires, and retires from, not with, whoever would "possess" her, to use the biblical word. A sense of sexual violation is part of the general sense of violation in this passage, and it foreshadows in a paradoxical way the first fallen sex in Eden, when Eve will be only too open of access, with nothing of her old "sweet reluctant amorous delay" or "obsequious Majesty." The same dialectic of worldly wisdom against heavenly wisdom, of worldly secrets against heavenly mystery, continues through the temptation scene. We may map diction from Proverbs 8:27–31 all through Book IX: delight, play, solace, and of course, wisdom, wise, sapience. Milton places just before the fall the figure of the author of Proverbs, proverbially wise Solomon: "the Sapient King / Held dalliance with his fair *Egyptian* spouse" (IX.442–3). Sapience can hold such dalliance and still be wise, though, as with other figures in Book IX, a fall will come later. (Solomon is also remembered as someone seduced from his faith by heathen wives.)

As soon as Adam eats the forbidden fruit, he too is implicated in the violation of Wisdom and the move toward harlotry. His famous word-play on taste (*sapor*) involves "Sapience," Eve's first word for wisdom in her address to the Tree – all Wisdom now reduced to this merely clever play. "Now let us play," says Adam, and the language of fallen playing echoes through this passage (1027–48): toy, disport, amorous play, play'd. We are meant to hear a rhyming echo of Eve's "amorous delay" in the "amorous play" of this undelayed sex, with no sweetness (musical or other) in the play. It is not just the use of the words wisdom and sapience, or this rhyming echo, that suggests Milton's deliberate reversal here of Wisdom's heavenly play. His judgment is very clear (1042–4):

> There they thir fill of Love and Love's disport
> Took largely, of thir mutual guilt the Seal,
> The solace of thir sin.

"Come, let us take our fill of love until the morning; let us solace ourselves with loves." This is the harlot of Proverbs 7:18. Milton's readers would easily call up the entire context of Dame Folly in her harlotry and Eternal Wisdom in her rejoicing or play or solace in order to read the violation of Wisdom here. The context is strengthened in the next sentence, for, just as "they rose,"

> So rose the *Danite* strong
> *Herculean Samson* from the Harlot-lap
> Of *Philistean Dalilah* . . . .   (1059–61)

Samson, like Solomon famous for his wisdom with riddles, has like Solomon been seduced and betrayed by a woman, and so rises fallen, as we always rise from any "harlot-lap." (There is a pun on lap and *lapsus*, fallen.) Milton's grammar is very clear: both Adam and Eve are like Samson. Nonetheless readers have insisted on identifying Eve with Dalilah and Adam with Samson,[16] thus falling precisely into Adam's later sin. (Milton is so sensitive to lapses in our fallen wisdom that his figuration may be a deliberate testing of the accuser in all of us, and a foreshadowing of Adam's later blame of Eve before God.) For Adam only later turns on Eve; here he assumes a mutual guilt, unlike the careless reader of the harlot lines above. From Godhead to harlotry then: the fall has undone Wisdom just as Raphael forewarned.

For Adam is told that he must learn to govern, and by Wisdom, which is potentially in danger from Adam's "transport," "touch," "passion," and sole weakness: "here only weak / Against the charm of Beauty's powerful glance" (VIII.528–59). In Adam's own self, and between Adam and Eve, a hierarchy must be kept (549–56):

> what she wills to do or say,
> Seems wisest, virtuousest, discreetest, best;
> All higher knowledge in her presence falls
> Degraded, Wisdom in discourse with her
> Loses discount'nanc't, and like folly shows;
> Authority and Reason on her wait,
> As one intended first, not after made
> Occasionally

Raphael is appropriately admonitory (562–4, 589–91):

> be not diffident
> Of Wisdom, she deserts thee not, if thou
> Dismiss not her
>
> true Love . . . hath his seat
> In Reason, and is judicious.

Adam, in defence, moves away from the terms of his first perplexing to a reaffirmation of his "delight" (Wisdom's word) in "Union of Mind, or in us both one Soul; / Harmony . . . / More grateful than harmonious sound to the ear" (600–6). He gently rebukes the angel's high-minded pronouncement on carnal intercourse (598–9) so that Raphael has to rephrase it (622–3). Hierarchy includes mutual education, while harmonious order prevails. Potential discord is still only a passing shadow.

Here I want to depart from orthodox reading and raise a further question. Would Milton have said of his own art what Adam says of Eve? His celestial song also touches the senses and may transport and is itself a thing of beauty. Does his art keep "Adamic" wisdom superior over "the charm of Beauty"? Or is it in his art as in the Godhead, where Urania and Wisdom are sisters and play together – and are sometimes identified with the Logos. There are two harmonies here, the hierarchical harmony of unfallen Adam and Eve, and the sisterly harmony of Urania and Wisdom. The potential discord between Adam and Eve is the potential discord between the Word as Adamic wisdom (higher knowledge, Love with his seat in Reason)[17] and the Word as song and play, as Urania and Wisdom. Should the word as "Adamic" wisdom always govern the word in its melic and playful and charming and touching and beautiful – its "Eve-like" – functions? The same question arises every time the trope of marriage is used for the processes of Milton's art: what marriage?

When we turn back to Book IV and the first appearance of Adam and Eve, we may hear Milton preparing us for Eve's fall from wisdom. Yet his hierarchy sounds arbitrary. For Eve begins by sharing with Adam "the image of thir glorious Maker . . . / Truth, Wisdom, Sanctitude severe and pure" (IV.292–3). But within two hundred lines, this first image is altered, and wisdom undergoes what we now call gender-marking, as Eve acknowledges "How beauty is excell'd by manly grace / And wisdom, which alone is truly fair" (IV.490–1). The association of wisdom with what is masculine becomes even more marked after the fall:

> From Man's effeminate slackness it begins,
> Said th'Angel, who should better hold his place
> By wisdom, and superior gifts receiv'd.
>
> (XI.634–6)

And we are never given an example of what Adam means when he says that Eve "degrades" higher knowledge or makes wisdom look like folly – harsh words for prelapsarian female foolishness, and different from Raphael's passing and uncensorious remark that Adam himself will sometimes be "seen least wise" (VIII.578). Satan is astute as well as canonical in appealing so strongly to wisdom when he tempts Eve ("O Sacred, Wise, and Wisdom-giving Plant" (IX.679); cf. "a tree to be desired to make one wise" (Gen.3:6)). Given her inexperience of deception, Eve's logic is clear enough. "His words replete with guile / Into her heart too easy entrance won" (733–4). (Again, the language of entry as of opening Wisdom's way (809, above) and of "keeping strictest watch" (363) is language used of Wisdom in Proverbs 8 (2–3 and 34), and it echoes back sadly and ironically against Milton's words about his blindness: "And wisdom at one entrance quite shut out" (III.50).) And Satan's temptation of Eve is far from paltry: among Christ's three temptations, it is most like the third and greatest, as the third is the greatest for Milton himself – the desire for more wisdom, including the wisdom of words. (If snakes can speak, thinks Eve, what might not I do? Suppose a speaking snake arrived as Muse before a writer's desk. Suppose a Muse said: you need knowledge of good and evil in order to write. How intelligent Milton is about the temptation of Eve, and how unpatronizing.) Yet a twentieth-century reader may still reflect that Eve might have withstood temptation better if she had not been taught to defer to the wisdom of another. To put my question a little sharply: is Milton willing to give his Muse what he will not give Eve – a sisterly (which is to say, co-equal) relation with wisdom? The answer seems to be, alas, yes.

It is true that in a sentence from *Tetrachordon* in 1645 Milton sounds more generous: "the wiser should govern the less wise, whether male or female." Yet the relation of females to the Wisdom figure in the *Tetrachordon* commentary on Genesis 2:18 is curiously mixed. It is not that toiling on the hill of wisdom is assumed to be a masculine activity. It is Milton's different languages for the various "recreations" of marriage. He begins with the beautiful and powerful example of Proverbs 8: "God himself conceals us not his own recreations before the world was built: 'I was,' saith the Eternal Wisdom, 'daily his delight, playing always before him.'" But later language falls off sadly: "Whereof lest we should be too timorous . . . wisest Solomon among his gravest proverbs countenances a kind of ravishment and erring fondness in the entertainment of wedded leisures." Even if "erring" can also mean "right wandering" etymologically, there remains a coy naughtiness in Milton that sounds like a fumbling with Spenserian language. (Spenser knows what he is doing when he uses words like "erring fondness" – Milton's unhappy paraphrase for the "ravishment" of Proverbs 5:19–20.) It is very unlike Milton, and, though brief, makes one wish for the clarity and cleanliness of some good witty Shakespearean bawdiness. Something in Milton is uneasy in this passage, where we may hear his own wisdom from its best through to its worst.

The practical problem of governing fallen music and governing the melic powers of poetry is an old one. Logos as word and right reason usually takes precedence. There is classical authority for this: "words contribute an *ethos* to sounds, placing them in the relation of the rational soul to body."[18] In questions of practical morality, the effects of music are all-important. Ambrose "believed that psalm singing effected remission from sin,"[19] but fears of even holy music's distraction are much more common. "For centuries after Augustine the leaders of the Church, following his lead, attempted to suppress the expressive claims of melody and rhetoric."[20] Or at least to ensure that the expression was means, not end, and means to a true end. (Milton says: "May I express thee," not "May I express myself.") Augustine's beautiful meditation on his own susceptibility to music ("melos omnes cantilenarum suavium") is the *locus classicus* of this fear of music's distracting power (*Confessions*, X.33). Music may be a good teacher, as in Calvin,[21] but it needs governing. Thus also Cato's rebuke to the enraptured but dilatory listeners to Casella's lovely song (Dante, *Purg.*, ii.106–33). Thus also Browning's David, who moves out of the lyric mode into prophetic logos, leaving melos behind. "Then the truth came upon me. No harp more – no song more!" (*Saul*, 237). (Browning, like Dante, is of course writing poetry with powerful melic effects, even as he moves from "song" to "truth.") The translators of the Bay Psalm Book put the matter bluntly: "we have respected . . . conscience rather than elegance, fidelity rather than poetry."[22]

All this sounds oddly modern, if we follow recent forms of the temptation story – for example, the seduction of logos by melos and trope, in Paul de Man's witty and provocative account, where even mimesis "dodges," metaphor is "wily" and wreaks "mischief," paronomasia is "dangerously seductive," and "euphony is probably the most insidious of all sources of error."[23] Or we may follow Derrida's play about words, with words, in words. Or we may desire (unwisely, I think) a bifurcation of the word into logic and song or play, with logical processes left to male writing, as the heir to a patriarchal tradition.[24] The division I have been sketching is very old and not just post-Cartesian. It is well illustrated by interpretations of Wisdom in Proverbs 8:22–31, and especially by interpreters' frequent discomfort with a Wisdom who plays, in any sense of the word. (Neither Milton nor Barth is so unjoyous.) One sees why Derrida refuses to govern his unpredictable, Apocalyptic word, *Viens, viens*: "Le 'viens' décide, si on peut dire; pas de règle (juridique, morale ou politique) pour décider à qui il faut répondre et quel 'viens' préférer."[25]

We might leave the matter there and simply conclude that Milton finds one use for the Wisdom figure when he wants to ground his art in the Logos, and another use for the Wisdom figure when he wants to mediate the Logos through males to females.[26] But that seems simplistic, especially when Milton implicates Adam as fully as Eve in the fall from wisdom. We might more usefully reflect on how Milton himself went back to the doctrine of the

Logos and wrestled with it. For his "traditional, masculine poetic inspiration" is not always traditional, and his "subservient female muses" sometimes question subservience.[27] Milton's well-known anti-Trinitarianism – that is, his restlessness with the orthodox doctrine of the Logos – is connected with the question in my title. So also is his attraction to the ante-Nicene Fathers. It is there that one finds diverse meditations on wisdom literature, the figure of Wisdom, and the Logos.[28] It is there that one would start if one wished to reform the doctrine of the Logos, reform it so as to enlarge it, using scriptural hints of music and poetry. And this would be easier to do with a subordinationist or modal doctrine of the Trinity. Whether Milton was attracted to Origen or Eusebius, or to a wider range of theologians,[29] I think the attraction is related to his love for music and poetry at their best. Similarly, I think Coleridge's attraction to the Alexandrian Fathers, especially Origen,[30] is part of his love of poetry, as is also his interest in the doctrine of the Logos. For Coleridge's famous definition of imagination and fancy properly belongs in his fresh consideration of the Logos, that never-written "treatise on the Logos or communicative intellect in Man and Deity" (*Biographia Literaria*, ch. xiii).

As for my second question, whether in Milton's art there is a hierarchical or else a sisterly harmony, I think the Miltonic answer would be yes to both alternatives. Certainly, Milton indicates that, in certain contexts, song and trope and charm need governance by reasonable wisdom, whether wisdom is male or female. But some of Milton's words in *Tetrachordon*, like his invocation to Book VII, offer another vision. The "recreations of God" may seem at first a lesser activity than life's serious business, and, as allegory, may seem only to trivialize marriage. Yet, on reflection, the word "recreation" need not be "vacation" (as in Karsten Harries' "poetry . . . a vacation from reality").[31] For the implicit pun in the word "recreation" is hard to avoid, especially when Proverbs 8 is about creation. It is as if God and humans re-create themselves continually through true play – a beautiful notion of play, both unfallen and fallen. Coleridge uses the same notion, without the pun, in his famous definition of imagination: "a repetition in the finite mind of the eternal act of creation in the infinite I AM . . . in order to re-create." By "true" play, I intend neither concept nor precept, nor art in its "expressive claim" or as "consolation."[32] I intend art in its authority, for this is its challenge (as Adam knew of Eve: "Authority and Reason on her wait"). We can understand this only if we know what Geoffrey Hill means when he says that the poet's "truthtelling" *is* his craft, when it effects "the atonement of aesthetics with rectitude of judgment."[33] There is a "true" play and a "false" play, apart from (though perhaps related to) conceptual or doctrinal truth. Many of us now, especially the daughters of Eve, are enjoying the discomfiture of "Adamic" wisdom in language. But to opt for a simple reversal, in which language's "Eve-like" functions dominate, only reinscribes the old division. We might better reconsider the old division itself, and muse again on the ancient figure of a Wisdom who rejoices and plays.

Notes

1. This raises questions about the canon but such questions are not to my purpose here. Christ sings in the apocryphal *Acta Johannis* (cited in Leo Spitzer, *Classical and Christian Ideas of World Harmony* (Baltimore, Johns Hopkins University Press, 1963), 27–8). Wyclif reports that "thei seyn that angelis heryen god bi song in hevene" but he has a low view of such speculation (cited in John Hollander, *The Untuning of the Sky: Ideas of Music in English Poetry 1500–1700* (Princeton, Princeton University Press, 1961), 251). God sings in some other traditions, for example, Egyptian and Indian. In the classical pantheon, lesser gods like Amphion create by song; Zeus speaks.

2. C. A. Patrides, *Milton and Christian Tradition* (Oxford, Clarendon Press, 1966), 45.

3. *John Milton: Complete Poems and Major Prose*, ed. Merritt Y. Hughes (New York, Odyssey, 1957). All quotations from Milton's poetry are from this edition.

4. "As to the eighth chapter of Proverbs, it appears to me that it is not the Son of God who is there introduced as the speaker, but a poetical personification of Wisdom" (*De Doctrina Christiana*, tr. Sumner, I.vii, in *The Student's Milton*, ed. F. A. Patterson (New York, Appleton-Century-Crofts, 1933), 973).

5. This remains true no matter how Wisdom is related to the Logos (e.g. whether helping to create the Logos as in pre-Philonic Jewish Alexandrian philosophy, or identified with the Logos as in Philo, or separate because created as in Pico). Milton's interest in origins may be labelled patriarchal and simply dismissed, but the dismissal, if not the label, seems to me to do violence to the historical imagination.

6. Karl Barth, *Die Protestantische Theologie im 19. Jahrhundert* (Zurich, Evangelischer Verlag, 1947), 52; in the selections translated as *Protestant Thought: From Rousseau to Ritschl* (New York, Simon & Shuster, 1959), 50.

7. Milton argues on the ground of the Hebrew language in *De Doctrina Christiana*, I.vii.

8. W. B. Hunter, "Milton's Muse," in *Bright Essence*, ed. W. B. Hunter, C. A. Patrides, and J. H. Adamson (Salt Lake City, University of Utah Press, 1971), 154.

9. Harris Francis Fletcher, *Milton's Rabbinical Readings* (Urbana, University of Illinois Press, 1930), 113, 113–14n. In the major rabbinical commentaries of Rashi, Ibn Ezra, and Gersonides, there is no development of the notion of play as music. Hunter suggests a reading of "play" as music by conflating Proverbs 8 and Psalm 33 and also arguing from the word *pulsate* for "play." It seems simpler to work from the original Hebrew. Musical playing need not exclude playing as "some kind of physical activity" (Hunter, op. cit., 154) – the usual reading of this problematic text. One may agree with Hunter, and with Robins (below), that Milton's Muse is Christ as Logos, but that leaves the question of why Milton bothered with Urania at all.

10. "The exhortation to the Greeks," *Clement of Alexandria*, tr. G. W. Butterworth, Loeb Classical Library (London and New York, Heinemann and Putnam's, 1919), 13–15, 17. On "how it is possible for man to become a god," see 23. The

translator may have had Proverbs 8 in mind in "before the foundation of the world," but Clement does not use the Greek of the Septuagint for the word "foundation." Song is ᾀσμά as in Psalm 149:1 in the Septuagint. The "celestial Word" uses a form of Urania's name: οὐράνιος λόγος. I do not know how widespread this phrase is in Greek patristic literature; it would be one logical source for Milton's Urania. On the Uranian Aphrodite or Heavenly Beauty, see Hunter, op. cit., 151–3.

11. Ernst Robert Curtius, *European Literature and the Latin Middle Ages*, tr. Willard R. Trask (Princeton, Princeton University Press, 1953), 235–45. Wisdom figures in the Excursus on Calderón (xxiii), especially in the remarks on children's play as "willed by divine Wisdom itself" (562). Curtius does not mention the likely reason for this, which is the text in Proverbs.

12. Northrop Frye, "Charms and riddles," in *Spiritus Mundi: Essays on Literature, Myth and Society* (Bloomington, University of Indiana Press, 1976), 129.

13. William Oram remarks on Milton's "increased distrust of pagan myth and . . . intensified awareness of the spiritual danger, for fallen man, of attempting to locate the sacred in created things" ("Nature, poetry, and Milton's genii," in *Milton and the Art of Sacred Song*, ed. J. Max Patrick and Roger Sundell (Madison, University of Wisconsin Press, 1979), 63–4). Similarly, his austerity about magical things.

14. The echo was identified by Bishop Newton and has been used to infer a political allegory but the general appropriateness goes unnoticed.

15. See Gershom Scholem, *On the Kabbalah and its Symbolism* (New York, Schocken, 1965), 104–9, on the notion of a feminine element in God. On various Gnostic readings of Sophia, see Hans Jonas, *The Gnostic Religion*, 2nd edn (Boston, Beacon, 1963), *passim*.

16. This important argument is taken from Mary Nyquist. For a full treatment, see Mary Nyquist, "Textual overlapping and Dalilah's harlot-lap," in *Literary Theory/Renaissance Texts*, ed. P. Parker and D. Quint (Baltimore, MD, The Johns Hopkins University Press, 1986), 341–72.

17. Reason for Milton includes right moral choice as well as logic.

18. Hollander, op. cit., 397. But see also Augustine: "So men who sing like this – in the harvest, at the grape-picking, in any task that totally absorbs them – may begin by showing their contentment in songs with words; but they soon become filled with such a happiness that they can no longer express it in words, and leaving aside syllables, strike up a wordless chant of jubilation." (Enarr. ii in Ps. 32, 8, cited in Peter Brown, *Augustine of Hippo* (Berkeley and Los Angeles, University of California Press, 1967), 258).

19. Cited in James Kugel's authoritative study, *The Idea of Biblical Poetry: Parallelism and its History* (New Haven and London, Yale University Press, 1981), 149.

20. James Anderson Winn, *Unsuspected Eloquence: A History of the Relations between Poetry and Music* (New Haven and London, Yale University Press, 1984), 55. For an excellent account of how Christian thought altered prevailing attitudes toward *mousike*, see 30–73.

21. John Calvin, *Institutes of the Christian Religion*, III.xx.31–3, tr. Henry Beveridge (London, James Clark, 1957), 2nd vol., 180–3. But see the anti-pietistic and non-Platonic tribute to Mozart in Barth's *Church Dogmatics*, vol. III, *The Doctrine of Creation*, Part III (Edinburgh, Clark, 1960), 297–9. Barth hears Mozart's music as entirely creaturely, and profound because it embodies the "no" as well as the "yes" of creation.

22. Cited in Perry Miller (ed.), *The American Puritans: Their Prose and Poetry* (New York, Anchor, 1956), 322.

23. Paul de Man, *Blindness and Insight: Essays in the Rhetoric of Contemporary Criticism*, 2nd edn (Minneapolis, University of Minnesota Press, 1983), 285.

24. On this, see Christopher Norris, "Reading as a woman" (*LRB*, 4 April 1985, 8–11); more generally, see K. K. Ruthven, *Feminist Literary Studies*, ch. IV, "Gynocritics" (Cambridge, Cambridge University Press, 1984), 93–128.

25. *Les Fins de l'homme: à partir du travail de Jacques Derrida* (Paris, galilée, 1981), 483.

26. As in the notorious line, "Hee for God only, shee for God in him" (IV.299), a line I have always read as unProtestant and even unChristian. UnProtestant because Protestant thought so vehemently objects to any mediator other than Christ. UnChristian because Milton here outdoes St Paul's analogy in Ephesians 5, and ignores his once-famous text, "There is neither Jew nor Greek, there is neither bond nor free, there is neither male nor female: for ye are all one in Christ Jesus" (Gal. 3:28). My word "unChristian" is more polemical than historical. But I think it is important not to make St Paul into a straw man by ignoring such visionary texts as Gal. 3:28.

27. The phrases are from Maureen Quilligan, *Milton's Spenser: The Politics of Reading* (Ithaca and London, Cornell University Press, 1983), 225–6, and Sandra M. Gilbert and Susan Gubar, *The Madwoman in the Attic: The Woman Writer and the Nineteenth-Century Literary Imagination* (New Haven and London, Yale University Press, 1979), 210.

28. Clement, Origen, and Hippolytus, as well as Didymus and Chrysostom, wrote commentaries on Proverbs. Augustine and Jerome use Proverbs 8:22–31 only sparingly, in order to establish the doctrine of the Trinity.

29. For Origen, see Harry F. Robins, *If This Be Heresy* (Urbana, University of Illinois Press, 1963). For Eusebius, see A. S. P. Woodhouse, *The Heavenly Muse: A Preface to Milton*, ed. Hugh MacCallum (Toronto, University of Toronto Press, 1972), 165–75. Patrides observes that Milton was likely to have read widely in "the formidable array of theologians from the patristic age to the Reformation and the late Renaissance" (4).

30. Cf. Thomas McFarland, *Coleridge and the Pantheist Tradition* (Oxford, Clarendon Press, 1969): "Coleridge . . . works rather in the counter-tradition of Origen" (317); "Coleridge was very sympathetic toward Alexandrian thinkers" (360).

31. As part of an argument toward another conception of poetry, in "The many uses of metaphor," in *On Metaphor*, ed. Sheldon Sacks (Chicago and London, University of Chicago Press, 1979), 86.

32. For "expressive claim," see the quotation from Winn above, p. 206. For "consolation" cf. Iris Murdoch: "Plato feared the consolations of art. . . . To present the idea of God at all, even as a myth, is a consolation, since it is impossible to defend this image against the prettifying attentions of art. Art will mediate and adorn, and develop magical structures to conceal the absence of God or his distance" (*The Fire and the Sun: Why Plato Banished the Artists* (London, Oxford University Press, 1977), 83). But see her remark: "as if the artist could indeed penetrate the creative reverie of the Demiurge where truth and play mysteriously, inextricably mingle" (83). Even so, the division between truth and play makes me uneasy. Deconstructive play tries to break this division; we may say, paradoxically, that deconstruction recreates itself through play.

33. Geoffrey Hill, *The Lords of Limit: Essays on Literature and Ideas* (New York, Oxford University Press, 1984), 10. Cf. also Milan Kundera on the "wisdom of the novelist," "Man thinks, God laughs" (*NYRB*, 13 June 1985, 11–12).

10

HERBERT MARKS

The blotted book

Of what consequence is it whether Moses wrote
the Pentateuch or not? . . . If historical
facts can be written by inspiration, Milton's
Paradise Lost is as true as Genesis or Exodus.
(Blake)

When Milton introduces the fallen angels, early in the first book of *Paradise Lost*, he presents them, following an appeal to the Muse, under the names of the heathen deities: "Say, Muse, thir Names then known. . . ." The ornate catalogue, drawn from scriptural sources, formed on epic models, and amplified with exegetical and classical borrowings, epitomizes Milton's technique throughout the poem, inviting us to pause again at his curious insistence that these names about to be invoked are not the true names. The fallen angels, like adorned images or "Idols," may still retain their "Godlike shapes and forms," but

> of thir Names in heav'nly Records now
> Be no memorial, blotted out and ras'd
> By thir Rebellion, from the Books of Life.
> (I.361–3)

At first reading, the passage recalls Christ's promise in Revelation not to "blot" the names of the faithful "out of the book of life" (3:5). There, the righteous are to receive a "new name" in heaven (3:12). Milton's fallen angels, by contrast, will only get "new Names" on earth among the "Sons of *Eve*" whom they corrupt (I.364–9). The word *exaleipsō*, "blot out," occurs three times in the New Testament, and Milton alludes to the other two passages as well, this time at the conclusion of the poem in Book XII (Col. 2:14, *PL* XII.413–17; Acts 3:19, *PL* XII.539–40). In Acts and Colossians the thing blotted is not the offending "name," but sin and the condemnatory power of the law respectively, so that the sequence of allusions corresponds to the change in perspective between the beginning and the end of the epic. Book XII also contains, one might almost say comprises, a reasoned catalogue of biblical names. "Things by thir names I call, though yet unnam'd" (XII.140), Michael announces, echoing, though without the divorce of meaning from name, the poet's invocation in Book VII, and the subsequent narrative fulfills this commission in a suitably literal fashion:

> Whom *faithful Abraham* due time shall call (152)
> . . . to a Land hereafter call'd (156)
> But *Joshua* whom the Gentiles *Jesus* call (310)
> Of *David* (so I name this King) (326); etc.

Both catalogues are prognostic – they relate names and events "then known" – but there is an obvious contrast between the roll call of the devils, warranted by an overtly pagan muse, and this list of true names, revealed by an archangel following a long trial of purification.

As proponents of the didactic Milton would be quick to point out, this contrast might be read as a progression. The epic roll call could then be explained as a rhetorical temptation, with Michael's retold Bible its chastened corrective. Like most orthodox readings, the pedagogical approach assumes that succession is invariably teleological, or, more familiarly, that a confessional choice blots out the possibilities and doubts that precede it. Yet one might equally argue that the opening of the poem instructs us not to take its own final claims too literally, hinting that within the context of human language and memory the insinuations of Book I may be tempered – or even suppressed – but never rased. Even the Muse must have recourse to fictive names, substitutes invented "for the trial of man" to replace the cancelled etyma or nominal truths. It would seem that this history at least may be adopted by both parties.

From the first, editors and critics have noted Milton's tendency to play on the etymological meaning of words, whether they have written approvingly of a "proper and primary signification" (Newton), cautiously of a "learned and less obvious signification" (Landor), or (restricting ourselves to alliterative judgments) censoriously of a "perverse and pedantick principle" (Johnson). The naïve notion that he shared the essentialism so prominent in Renaissance homiletics and the commentary tradition is more recent, the legacy of a generation of scholars who have turned the name Cratylus into a critical shibboleth.[1] This is not to deny that Milton establishes an analogy between linguistic derivation (the "infection of words") and the fall of man, or that he uses words in their primary (unfallen) sense to suggest the innocence of Paradise. One might even argue that there is a deep structural parallel between the two states thus conjoined in a single word and the double-author model of inspiration, with which Milton mediates the

Puritan distrust of rhetoric and the classical pride in the powers of language. Such patterning, however, is strictly *ad hoc*, the rhetorical means to a specific effect, which is usually dramatic. "Notation," Milton writes in his Ramist treatise on logic, is a "locus of invention" – not a *clavis scientiae*.[2]

Looked at dramatically, the blotting of the book helps define the extent of the devils' "ignominy" – Milton's precise term, which occurs with its root meaning ("nameless") most resonantly in a passage opposing the elect angels, "contented with thir fame in Heav'n," to Satan's troops, eager for "Renown . . . , yet by doom / Cancell'd from Heav'n and sacred memory, / Nameless in dark oblivion . . . / And ignominy" (VI.378–83; cf. VI.395, I.115, II.207). Dissociated both from the heavenly presence and from the human medium of representation, the devils subsist in a state of annihilation, an inherently contradictory position. It is much easier to think of a lost name as repressed, which is precisely what Satan himself wishes to believe, since repression would imply at least the hope of recollection. Commentators sometimes make the same mistake, misreading Raphael's words to Adam, "*Satan*, so call him now, his former name / Is heard no more in Heav'n" (V.658f.; cf. I.82), as intending the name "Lucifer;" yet Milton explicitly tells us that that name too is only applicable "by allusion" (X.425), apt but "in the Dialect of men / Interpreted" (V.761f.). The fact is that neither Milton's reader nor his heavenly muse can ever know Satan's former or true name, this being one of the key points at which the "Books of Life" and the poem tentatively coalesce.

In so far as it arouses our sympathy, Satan's rebellion against God takes the defensive form of identification, and the pattern includes his false appropriation of the alias "Lucifer," which belongs by rights to the true "light bearer," Christ (cf. Rev. 22:16; 2 Pet. 1:19), no less than his claim to aseity or his appearance in a "Sun-bright" simulacrum of the divine chariot – an "Idol of Majesty Divine" (VI.101). Properly speaking, "resplendence," "lightning," and "serenity" (from *serenus*, "bright") are all attributes of the Son, whom the pretender's hatred only "illustrates" or brightens, as Raphael explains immediately following his ironic allusion to Satan's "great name" and the comparison of his countenance to "the Morning Star" (V.707f.). Satan's nominal pretensions are thus imaginary, vain boasts which bring a smile to the Father seated within his golden lamps, as his physical and verbal dilations had brought a half-smile to Gabriel in Paradise.

There is, however, a deeper irony here, which shows the quality of Milton's attention to his biblical source. "Lucifer" in Hebrew is *helel*, an appellative whose verbal stem *halal*, "to shine," is indistinguishable from the homograph "to be boastful." Buxtorf, though he ignores examples of the perfect stem, lists both meanings in the same entry of his *Lexicon Hebraicum et Chaldaicum* (1621), along with the factitive form *hillel*, "to praise," found in the exclamation "hallelujah."[3] *Helel* occurs only once in the Bible, in Isaiah 14:12, the same verse that warrants the patristic legend of Satan's fall: "How art thou fallen from heaven, O Lucifer, son of the morning!" Since the verses that follow seem themselves to play on the ambiguous appellation, displaying the boast rather than the splendor ("For thou hast said in thine heart, I will ascend into heaven, I will exalt my throne above the stars of God"), Milton need not have been an accomplished Hebraist to have noticed the etymological nuance. Of course, the glory to which Satan aspires "Vain-glorious" (VI.383f.) is already a syllepsis (*gloriari*, "to boast;" cf. *SA* 334), but the mention of "praise" and "dispraise" in the same context – the comparison of angelic "renown" with devilish "ignominy" – suggests that Milton's Latin pun is itself a cover for the missing Hebrew name.

Etymological speculation on Hebrew roots was a common pastime in the sixteenth and early seventeenth centuries, before it gave way, outside of Cambridge at least, to projects for an artificial language. In general it was allied to the belief, revived in Renaissance Europe by Pico, Annius de Viterbe, and other Christian kabbalists, that Hebrew was "*the most ancient and holy tongue*, . . . the tongue of Adam and God,"[4] and so, properly manipulated, the unique key to all wisdom. Yet Milton never shared the kabbalistic premises or the philological optimism of the adamic speculators. *Helel*, the Hebrew "original" of Lucifer, functions rhetorically as a cryptonym, a semantic ghost analogous to the phonic hypograms or key-words educed by Saussure in his studies of Roman vaticinia.[5] Since it crops up at moments of pressure throughout the poem, it might indeed appear to be an object of repression, its latent content displaced into various periphrastic forms (for instance, the arrested echo following Satan's "self-begot, self-rais'd" speech, where the applause "as the sound of waters deep" (V.872) refers us to the cry "Hallelujah" in Revelation 19:6 – and perhaps to the underlying description of the divine chariot in Ezekiel 1:24, another form of Satanic imposture). Yet the basic semantic nucleus, no less than its manifest traces, remains self-divided: on the one hand radiance, on the other vanity. It is thus closer to what Freud would have called a "verbal bridge," a nodal point of ambiguity exploited within the poem's figurative system for purposes of condensation and disguise.

Satan first discovers his "lustre visibly impair'd" (IV.850) boasting before the guardian angels, and much of the emphatically verbal action in the scene, from the blazing powder simile (814–18) through the running references to "glory" and its diminution, seems organized about this doubling of Satanic and angelic motives in the stem *halal*. Thus, when Satan boasts his superior social position, Zephon taunts him with his diminished brightness, while the "regal port" in his parade toward "more glory" is undercut by Gabriel's opening assessment of his "faded splendor wan" (870). By the same token, Gabriel's concluding rebuff, "But mark what I arede thee now, avaunt" (962), both signals the move from words to action and curtly defines the false inflation of the adversary by a punning antonomasia (a vaunt).[6] "Arede" is itself an equivocal word, carrying the common meaning "to conjecture," "to divine," so that Gabriel can be said to divine the truth about Satan, or to decipher the cryptonym. The heavenly balance that finally establishes the lightness or vanity of Satan's swagger against what might for a time have seemed the equally "dilated" affrontery of the angels, allowing Gabriel soberly to conclude, "what folly then / To boast what Arms can do" (1007f.), resolves the etymological issue as well: not splendor but bluster – a vainglory whose very root is hollow ("avaunt").

Recent students of poetic language have referred to the dispersed hypogram as a *figurant*, a theatrical "extra" or marginal presence, but also the form that generates the figures of the text.[7] The term fits the enigmatic name *helel*, which like the "name of blasphemy" inscribed on the head of the beast (Rev.13:1) can be recovered only through a process of cryptic decipherment, numerological in Revelation, etymological in Milton. This restored identity remains extraneous, and in Satan's case the added step of translation deepens the dialogic estrangements. Ideally, a proper name – like poetry or a sacred text – would defy or obviate translation. But the spectral name *helel* rather challenges the proper, haunting the vocatives upon which the poet, in acts of invocation, apostrophe, and hymnic celebration, founds his fiction of presence and hence his authority. The more resonant the affirmation, the more persistent the counterclaim.

Perhaps the most striking instance in *Paradise Lost* is the conclusion of the angelic hymn in Book III, where Milton, joining his own voice to that of the celestial choir, seems at last to have discovered the true name by which to "express unblamed" the Holy Light:

> Hail Son of God, Savior of Men, thy Name
> Shall be the copious matter of my Song
> Henceforth, and never shall my Harp thy praise
> Forget, nor from thy Father's praise disjoin.
>
> (III.412–15)

This is usually taken as a moment of prescient clarity in the epic, a confident affirmation of mission, sustained by the fiction of angelic concord. The turn from narrative to direct address and the eruption of the poetic "I" invite us to align the passage with the opening invocation, "Hail holy Light" (III.1), which it appears to fulfill, the choice of metonymic substitutions which perplexed the poet in the earlier passage giving way here to the jubilance of untrammeled nomination.

The correspondence between the two vocatives, holy light in the opening invocation and the divine name in its hymnic complement, is, if not prescribed, at least supported by a strong tradition, emanation and prolation being the two principal modes of representing the divine in various symbolic schemes influenced by neo-Platonism. As Gershom

Scholem writes with regard to the symbolism of the kabbalists: "They speak of attributes and of spheres of light; but in the same context they speak also of divine names and the letters of which they are composed. From the very beginnings . . . these two manners of speaking appear side by side."[8] In kabbalistic speculation, God's name with its manifold derivatives – the *kinnuyim* or appellatives – constitutes a self-manifestation in the order of revelation analogous to the emanation of the *sephiroth* in the order of creation. In Christian theology, manifestation in both orders is the function of the Logos, and accordingly it is the name of the Son that Milton promises to celebrate. But does the act of nomination ever take place? or are the titles used to designate the Son only rhetorical substitutions for a proper name which the poet, for all his apparent *élan*, never actually pronounces?

This question, rather than any simple answer to it, seems to be the ironic burden of Milton's strategy at the end of the hymn, where the double negatives and striking enjambments ("Henceforth," "Forget") encumber the freedom of vocation. If we pause at the first verse, for instance, "thy Name" might be an endorsement apposed to the preceding epithets, "Son of God, Savior of Men." But just as this momentary possibility dissolves with the enjambment, leaving the vocatives unconfirmed and "Name" as the object of a prospective dedication ("Shall be the copious matter"), so too the poet's apparent triumph of discovery dissolves under further interrogation, admitting in its place the shadowy cryptonym *helel*, first as a phonetic echo of the salutatory "Hail," then as a semantic image of the repeated word "praise," whose Hebrew prototype *hillel* (whence *Tehillim*, the Book of Psalms or Praises) is also derived from the root *halal*. The ambiguities are subtle, but the uncertainty about the status of Christ's proper name seems deliberate enough to sustain an insidious play on the appellative most appropriate to the holy light, and thus on its rival claimant who meanwhile "alighted walks" on the border of the new creation (422). The oblique rhyme facilitates the traffic between "Name" and "praise," while reinforcing the echo in the opening verse ("Hail . . . Savior . . . Name"). The identical sound pattern recurs amid more extensive orchestration in Book IV, this time with the name Satan itself (a lie "trac't" or interwoven) in initial position:

[Gabriel:] To say and straight unsay. . . ,
Argues no Leader, but a liar trac't,
Satan, and couldst thou *faith*ful add? O *name*,
O sacred name of faithfulness profan'd! [Hebrew *halal*,
another play on *helel*?]

(IV.947–51; my emphasis)

One could naturally oppose the two passages as well as align them; but it is the fact of paronomasia itself, of verbal reification and semantic indeterminacy, that is here potentially Satanic.

Phonetic duplications aside, the poet's enthusiasm in Book III is doubly hedged; for instead of Christ's name, we are given two balanced epithets, skillfully chosen to represent the two natures, divine and human, of the Christological union. Both of course have scriptural authority: "Son of God" is the name more excellent than the angels', which we are told God conferred on "the brightness of his glory" in Hebrews 1:3–5 (cf. 1 John 5:13); while "Savior" is the gloss explicitly pronounced at the naming of Jesus in Matthew 1:21. Yet the first is ultimately a patronymic, the second an etymological translation, which, in a setting as poetically charged as Milton's, amounts to an almost programmatic evasion of the proper.

When the Son is finally called by name in Book XII, it is in a figural context: "*Joshua* whom the Gentiles *Jesus* call" (XII.310). Typology (despite the sly literalization here) is a proleptic figure, and the difference from the ostensible naming in Book III, which was not figural but figurative, is radical. To understand what Milton's options were, we must recognize that even in isolation the name Jesus Christ is as overdetermined as the name *helel*. Where the latter is ambiguous however, the former is redundant. Thus, *Christos* is the Greek translation of *mashiah*, "messiah," homophonous with *moshi'a*, "savior;" while *Iēsous* renders a contraction of Hebrew "Joshua," likewise derived from the root "to save." A literal gloss would be "YHWH is savior," so that in this case even the would-be proper name turns out to be a patronymic: "Son of God, Savior of Men." To an orthodox philologian, these redundancies might illustrate the mystery of the homoousian, in accordance with the primitive confession, "Jesus is Lord." But they lend themselves equally well to alternative theologies. At one extreme, we could cite the docetist premises underlying the Valentinian *Gospel of Truth*, which extends the incommunicability of the Godhead to the name itself: "Now the name of the Father is the Son . . . invisible because it alone is the mystery of the invisible."[9] Here the subject to whom the name belongs is not the Son at all but the Father. In Milton's passage, on the contrary, the Father turns out to be the name of the Son. Adopting the technical language of Arianism, such a name is, like its bearer, neither *agennetos* nor *agenetos*, neither "ingenerate" nor "self-existent." It is a derivative presence, contingent on paternal generation, and thus more fully human. Perhaps it was devotion to the secondary that led Milton to slight the unity, respect for beginnings that impelled him to redivide the origin. Within the dualistic world of the poem, however, his generate Christ ennobles by collateral descent the antithetical figure of Satan. In the conclusion to the hymn, both have a place by right of derivation. If Satan is only a spectral presence, the phantom product of a linguistic projection, Christ too remains an elusive or ghostly figure, accessible, beyond his nominal translations, only to faith or desire.

One must add that the passage is haunted by literary as well as nominal shades, which beneath the clear surface seem at times to throng several deep. In the first place, "Hail Son of God" reproduces the final words of the

Aeneid's hymn to Hercules: "salve vera Iovis proles" (VIII.301). Since Hercules was a conventional type of Christ, and since Virgil's Typhoeus and the Lernean hydra, whose destruction is the subject of the preceding verses, were both types of Satan, the echo might seem to strengthen the apparent or clear reading. Moreover, the cave of the monster Cacus, whose defeat Evander has been reciting, anticipates the descriptions of Milton's Hell, likewise veiled in "blinding gloom" and "blackness mixed with flame" (*Aen.* VIII.241–58). Yet here again, as when Milton in his principium translates Ariosto's version of the "originality" topos, the mere fact of allusion qualifies the claim to inspired naming in the direction of literary history with its rivalries and mediations. How seriously appears as soon as we read two lines further in Virgil: "talia carminibus celebrant; . . . consonat omne nemus strepitu collesque resultant" ("Such are their hymns of praise. . . . All the woodland rings with the clamour, and the hills re-echo," 303–5, Fairclough translation). Beneath Virgil, the doubled or transumptive re-echo comes from Spenser's *Epithalamion*, whose themes are precisely the proper mode of praise and the relation of the solitary poet to the universal chorus: "Sing ye sweet Angels, Alleluya sing, / That all the woods may answere and your eccho ring" (240f.). It is the voice that much of Milton's hymn aspires to join, if not to prevent.

The poet's dedication to "thy Name" is thus a more "copious" matter than Protestant hymnody might normally espouse. Since the derivative is, potentially at least, also the duplicitous, the poet himself is always in a vulnerable position, exposed to Satanic deception. Not only his text, but the very words he uses are invariably "secondary." The "drop serene" or *gutta serena* that clouds (brightens?) his vision (III.25) epitomizes his subjection to the duplicities of rhetoric, and his appeals for illumination only emphasize the uncertainty of his situation, his vulnerability to imposture: Which "lightbearer" will answer his appeal? As often noted, the invocations in *Paradise Lost* suggest numerous parallels between the narrator and Satan, and our criteria for sorting out the inversions of parody are hardly more dependable than those the Bible offers for distinguishing true from false prophecy.

Satan is the type of the false prophet, and we see him executing this role to the letter at the head of the passage celebrating Christ's (true) "resplendence:"

> So spake the false Arch-Angel, and *infus'd*
> Bad *influence* into th'unwary breast
> Of his Associate; . . .
>   . . . and casts between
> Ambiguous words and jealousies, to sound
> Or taint integrity.
>   (V.694–704; my emphasis)

The "ambiguous words" include "taint" itself with a play on rhetorical color, and "sound" with a double play on "integrity" and scrutiny. The ambiguities of sound, not least of measured sound, can taint our specious integrity, frustrating our efforts to sound out the unwholesome – to cast between the various meanings of a name. This is most subtly the case with the word "jealousies," derived in our "fallen" language from the Greek *zēlos*, "zeal." Zeale, "the invincible warriour" driving his fiery chariot "over the heads of Scarlet Prelats," was Milton's own chosen persona in his prophetic struggle against religious corruption two decades before (*Complete Prose Works*, I.900), and in *Paradise Lost* the same virtue is personified by Abdiel, the poet-prophet's ideal ego "than whom none with more zeal ador'd / The Deity" (V.805; cf. 807, 849, 900). For the poet, however, this identification is desired, not actual. Though he may pray for the splendor of true illumination, he remains, as poet, one who "sounds" integrity in ambiguous words, with a "zeal" that, unlike his angelic Servant's, betrays the features of derivative "jealousies." Hell finally is the negative case that gives this predicament its poignancy. For the devils, fluent as they are, there are no etyma to be recovered, even in fancy. The "Dialect of men" may be estranged from its roots, a wandering stream or faltering measure; yet for all the divagations of language, the desire for a renewed adequation remains, congruent in many respects with its dramatic translations, love of the father and hope of salvation.

* * *

Milton's rhetorical use of etymology as a locus of invention is finally only one aspect of his larger concern with the relation of the original (or sacred) and its secondary interpretations. We have noted the source for the blotted book in the New Testament. There is however an Old Testament context as well, one that provides the basis for the passage in Revelation; for the apocalyptic book of life is, from a literary point of view, itself a derivative notion. In Exodus 32, Moses, on the point of descending the mountain with the tables of the law, is alerted by God to the corruption of the people, who have begun carousing about the golden calf. The events that follow have a somewhat confusing sequence, due perhaps to redactional juxtaposition or to the elaboration of haggadic variants. This much is clear, however: before God, Moses humbly intercedes for the people, who are threatened with destruction; before the people, he smashes in his wrath the graven tablets. The intercession is then repeated:

> Yet now, if thou wilt forgive their sin–; and if not, blot me, I pray thee, out of thy book which thou hast written.
> And the Lord said unto Moses, Whosoever hath sinned against me, him will I blot out of my book.
>
> (32:32–3)

It is essential to recognize that in introducing the fallen angels in Book I Milton alludes to Moses' intercession, not to God's response. One clue is the tautologic phrase "blotted out and ras'd" (I.362), the verb "rase" being borrowed from the Geneva Bible where it is used instead of "blot" to translate *maḥah* in the first verse (intercession) but not in the second (response), which has simply "put." If we are trying to define the figure of the poet before his poem, this more covert allusion is crucial. It suggests, to begin with, an emphasis not on the visionary or vatic aspects of the prophetic role, but on the humble act of supplication.

> Let not my words offend thee, Heav'nly Power,
> My Maker, be propitious while I speak.
>
> (VIII.379f.)

So Adam in Book VIII, ignorant "by what Name" to adore his maker, yet bold to pursue his imagined desire, the inchoate thought of Eve. For Milton, petition holds the central place in the transition from absence to imaginative projection, whether the desire be erotic or poetic. (He perhaps gives us a final version of this dialectic in God's own self-retraction before the creation *ex se* in Book VII.)

Our assessment of the epic catalogue depends even more heavily on the second strand of the Exodus subtext: the smashing of the tablets and their subsequent replacement. According to both Exodus and Deuteronomy, the original tablets were inscribed "with the finger of God" himself (Exod. 31:18, Deut. 9:10): "And the tablets were the work of God, and the writing was the writing of God, graven upon the tablets" (Exod. 32:16). It is less clear, at least in the Exodus account, who wrote the second tablets. At one point, God tells Moses to hew two new stones, which he (God) will then inscribe with the same words as before. In the sequel, however, he instructs Moses to write the words himself:

> And the Lord said unto Moses, Write thou these words: for after the tenor of these words I have made a covenant with thee and with Israel. And he was there with the Lord forty days and forty nights; he did neither eat bread, nor drink water. And he wrote upon the tablets the words of the covenant. . . .
>
> (Exod. 34:27–8)

The subject of the concluding half-verse is ambiguous. Since it echoes the head of the chapter almost word for word, most commentators identify the subject as God, but this is perhaps the less obvious reading. (Modern scholars tend to read both 34:1 and 28b as editorial additions.) Regardless of who held the pen, however, there is more than a casual resemblance between the secondary or substitute code that Moses presents to the people in Exodus and the factitious naming in Book I of *Paradise Lost*. Both replace a blotted or broken original. Both invite, and will yield to, copious elaboration. Revision and profusion both recall the figure of Satan, who has been waving his spear throughout the first part of the paragraph. His magical manipulations appear to raise up and to order the "innumerable" host of phantoms preliminary to their appellation:

> As when the potent Rod
> Of *Amram's* Son in *Egypt's* evil day
> Wav'd round the Coast, up call'd a pitchy cloud
> Of *Locusts* . . .

(I.338–41)

The *Pirqe deRabbi Eliezer* – which it now seems Milton had read, if only in the Latin translation of Vorstius – lists Moses' rod together with the art of writing among the eight things created by God on the second day, along with, interestingly enough, the garments of Adam and Eve, and the *meziqim*, the evil spirits or devils.[10] Here, however, the reference to Moses veils the more likely allusion to Lucifer's own "rodde" (Isa. 14:5, Geneva Bible), indelibly present via the same biblical passage that authorizes both the name "Lucifer" and the story of his fall. This composite allusion is further shadowed by the resemblance between Satan's spear and the wand of Comus, in which the ambiguous powers of rhetorical and sexual generation are likewise conjoined. The spear is explicitly compared to a wand at its first mention (I.294), and the association is subtly renewed, via an iconographic commonplace, in the covert allusion to Circe, whose potentially imbruting powers of transformation are evoked in the reference to images and idols that immediately precedes the catalogue. The principal correspondences had already been noted by Sandys, who in his commentary to the fourteenth book of the *Metamorphoses* imagines Circe "waving her rod" over her victims: "Wherein the devill perhaps aped that rod of *Moses* wherewith hee performed such wonders."[11]

Within the poem, Satan's spear is the necromantic counterpart of Ithuriel's. Where the latter functions in Book IV as a chaste index of univocal meaning, arresting the Satanic metamorphoses at the point of the literal, the former stands as the potent organ of enchantment and fecundation. The phallic innuendos, extended perhaps by a Shakespearean pun in "Cope of Hell" (I.345), spill over into the climactic simile of the series, again describing the "multitude:" "like which the populous North / Pour'd never from her frozen loins" (I.351–2), and beyond. At a second remove, the rod recalls the introduction to the *Theogony* in which the Heliconian muses present Hesiod with a rod of laurel to accompany the gift of prophetic song. The gift follows immediately on their enigmatic warning that the songs they inspire may be either true or specious. It is the threat implicit in such an alternative that informs the last syncretic simile in *Paradise Lost*, the description of the Janus-faced cherubim dispatched to Eden

> with eyes more numerous than those
> Of *Argus*, and more wakeful than to drowse,
> Charm'd with *Arcadian* Pipe, the Pastoral Reed
> Of *Hermes*, or his opiate Rod.
>
> (XI.130–3)

To isolate the figure of Moses in the midst of this network of allusion might tax the powers of even a less equivocal watch. To begin with, the careful reference to *"Amram's Son"* points up the troubling duplicity of the biblical record: the rod residing alternately with Moses or with his brother Aaron. In either case, it is itself both an agent and a symbol of transformation, like the serpent whose form it assumes. When in Exodus 7 the Egyptian sorcerers also turn their rods into serpents, the serpent-rod of Aaron-Moses devours theirs, suggesting clearly that it is not here a matter of combating the fantastic or tropological with a literal truth. On the contrary, a refusal to credit the rod's transformative power amounts to Pharaonic hardness of heart. If this were finally a poetry of choice, we should indeed be responsible for discriminating among the rods. But the allusive texture of the verse is so dense that Moses' rod is indistinguishable from the magicians', unless it be that in the end it somehow manages to outdo them on their own ground. Ultimately, as Milton puts it in the hermetic conclusion to the *Epitaphium Damonis*, "the festal orgies rave in Bacchic frenzy under the thyrsus of Zion."

Considered from a hermetic perspective, the word "Mosaic" itself, taken via *mouseios*, may mean "belonging to the Muses," and I suspect that Milton reflected on the pun as he worked the flower passage, with its rhetorical or self-referential shadings, into his description of the bower in Book IV:

> the roof
> Of thickest covert was inwoven shade
> Laurel and Myrtle, and what higher grew
> Of firm and fragrant leaf; on either side
> *Acanthus*, and each odorous bushy shrub
> Fenc'd up the verdant wall; each beauteous flow'r,
> *Iris* all hues, Roses, and Jessamin
> Rear'd high thir flourisht heads between, and wrought
> Mosaic
>
> (IV.692–700)[12]

The passage, by its allusions no less than by its architectural details, represents the theme of artful metamorphosis. The prominent Spenserian echoes remind us that the mystery of wedded love enacted here, as "in the thickest couert of that shade" (*Faerie Queene*, III.6.44), is fundamentally the mystery of generation or origin, a mystery with the gravest meaning for the poet, underlined by recursions to the invocation in Book III (the "shadiest Covert" of the wakeful – later "th'amorous" – bird) and to the laurel and myrtle of *Lycidas*. Once more, however, the doubling allusion is doubled in turn; for Milton, ever attentive to Spenser's subtleties, has compounded Venus' bower with that second "couert shade," the scene of Calidore's chance intrusion upon Serena and Calepine in the final book of *The Faerie Queene* (VI.3.20). The scene is a crucial one to any understanding of the earlier epic. Looking backward to the Garden of Adonis, it measures the tantalizing proximity of innocence and experience – a proximity that invites the poet's own fictive interventions; looking ahead, it anticipates the subsequent intrusion on Mount Acidale, before which the constructions of poetry will succumb, to be replaced, if at all, by a more desperate desire for longing itself and for the scene of loss – a compulsion to repeat, beyond the pleasure principle and its sublimations, which Milton in *Paradise Lost* must try to resist. He does so in part by projecting the fallen world back into the fullness of Paradise, so that the two orders are never temporally discrete. "Covert . . . shade" exemplifies this strategy; for Calidore's disruption of the happy lovers in Book VI leads directly to Serena's "wandring" ("as liking led / Her wauering lust after her wandring sight . . . / Without suspect of ill or daungers hidden dred" (23)), and hence to her capture by the Blatant Beast; and Milton, in thus recalling the model for Eve's own "wandring" in Book IX, weaves the impending catastrophe into his very description of the bower, even as he creates an image of the innocent world from which all intrusion is explicitly barred (703f.).

The intruders in Spenser's poem seem finally to personify the iconoclastic impulse that shadows every allegorical fiction, coming between the poet and his desire, as between the knight and his quest. In Milton's writing, intrusion conveys a more specific anxiety about poetic legitimacy, most prominent in the early poetry (consider the intrusion of "forc'd fingers rude" into the Trinity manuscript of *Lycidas*), but still apparent in the discussions of accommodation in *Paradise Lost*, as in the potentially transgressive argument itself – its balance, shocking to Marvell, of "old Song" and "sacred Truths." Accordingly, in the bower passage, Milton goes on immediately to contrast his creation with its classical analogues:

> In shadier Bower
> More sacred and sequester'd, though but feign'd,
> *Pan* or *Silvanus* never slept, nor Nymph,
> Nor *Faunus* haunted.

(IV.705–8)

The momentary ambiguity of the syntax here is perhaps a test for the reader, but the concern with the status of the fictive, reiterated so frequently throughout the poem, is more serious. The ambiguity of Faunus himself, on the one hand a symbol of concupiscence, on the other, the ancestor of the

Latin race, who as oracle of the wood truly prophesies the birth of a son before whom "the whole world will role obedient" (*Aen.* VII.100f.), is further amplified by another Spenserian mediation; for in the first Mutabilitie canto Faunus (another intruder) is a parodic type not only of Christ, but of Moses, sequestered "where he close might view / That neuer any saw, saue onely one" (*Faerie Queene*, VII. 6.45; cf. Exod. 33). Here the "feigned," or, as Milton elsewhere calls it, the "mystic," includes not only the fabled matter of chivalry and the stories of classical myth, but Scripture itself.

The issue bears on the one Empson took up so eloquently: Milton's "broad melancholy from the clash of paganism with Paradise," or, more crudely put, his sense that the "poetic or symbolical meaning" of *both* biblical and classical stories was "more important than their truth."[13] When, after the fall, Adam and Eve finally pray together, they are compared by Milton to Deucalion and Pyrrha, "th'ancient Pair / In Fables old, less ancient yet than these" (XI.10f.), which Empson, following Bentley, takes to mean that Genesis too was an old fable. The substitution of Deucalion's flood for Noah's in a subsequent scene from the prophetic theater raises similar problems (XI.738–53; cf. Ovid, *Met.* I.262–347). Even Fowler, generally no friend to Empson, is forced to admit that the relation, though commonplace, "could be used either to prove or to disprove the truth of pagan myth, either to prove or disprove the historicity of the Bible."[14] The opposition between the two sources has been greatly overdrawn by proponents of the prophetic Milton. The lyric fall of Mulciber, "Sheer o'er the Crystal Battlements," which seems to suspend time, is not negated with an editorial comment. On the contrary, as denial of vision seems to accentuate the visibility of "vernal bloom" and "Summer's Rose" in the invocation to Book III, so the sharp rebuke, "thus they relate, / Erring," sends us back across the enjambment to relive that fabled fall "from Morn / To Noon . . . from Noon to dewy Eve" (I.742f.). Time here is "the medium of human existence," in John Guillory's words, a gloss that attempts to do justice to "the human priority of fiction, the trope of allusion over the power of invocation."[15] To many readers, *Paradise Lost* is finally an elegiac poem, and the musical figure of extension and continuity that drops with the setting sun is too intimate a part of the poet's world not to rise again. As Stevens says of his own derivative version of the "sovran Planter:" "An unaffected man in a negative light / Could not have borne his labor" (*Notes toward a Supreme Fiction*).

The pagan architect Mulciber has his biblical counterpart in Tubal-Cain, whose work in Book XI might well be viewed as a "demythologized" version of the building of Pandemonium, which it clearly echoes. But the question of true versus fabled or figured, if it is susceptible to resolution at all, does not break down along scriptural or non-scriptural lines. Immediately after the treatment of Tubal-Cain, beginning in mid-verse, Milton takes up the story of the "Sons of God" from Genesis 6 and gives it an equally demythologized interpretation ("by thir guise / Just men they seem'd" (576–7)), in contrast to the treatment in Book III, where they appeared among the vanities of Limbo. The identity of the "Sons of God" (Christological complications aside) is one of the most notable cruces in biblical exegesis, and I would suggest that Milton introduces the matter here, euhemeristic pun and all, in order to emphasize the fabulous and equivocal nature of even the biblical history. Let me refer again to the *Pirqe deRabbi Eliezer* to give an idea of the exegetical quandaries involved:

Rabbi Joshua said: The Israelites are called "sons of God," as it is said, "Ye are the sons of the Lord your God" [Deut. 14:1 (and *PL* XI.621ff.)]. The angels are called "Sons of God," as it is said, "When the morning stars sang together, and all the sons of God shouted for joy" [Job 38:7 (and *PL* V.447f.)]; and whilst they were still in their holy place in heaven, these [fallen angels] were called "Sons of God," as it is said, "And also after that, when the sons of God came in unto the daughters of men, and they bare children to them; the same became the mighty men, which were of old, men of renown" [Gen.6:4 (and *PL* III.460ff.; cf. *PR* II.178f.)].

(*Pirque deRabbi Eliezer*, 22)

The issue for Milton is twofold: on the one hand, the logical definition of truth as unique, impassive, and abstract; on the other, the dogmatic divorce of revelation and invention, a reflex of the same rationalizing impulse, as Blake would argue. Its conventional source is the writings of Plato, whose attack on poetic fiction in the *Republic* also happens to contain a reference to "sons of gods" – Socrates' ironic epithet for those "poets and prophets" whose slanderous accounts of divine history threaten to undermine the ideal of true justice (2, 366b). Taken literally, Plato's familiar phrase would seem to discover the motive for mythopoesis in filial rebellion, a suggestion clearly relevant to the author of *Paradise Lost*. But Milton's defense against the presumptions of reason is more subtle than Satan's. By covering the classical commonplace with a notoriously equivocal figure from Scripture, he defies the philosophical assault on fable while simultaneously protesting the dogmatic premise that poetry and prophecy are discontinuous.

The Sons of God figure once more in what may be the most baroque of Milton's syncretic fictions, the fabulous account of the devils' dispersal in Book X following their transformation to serpents:

However some tradition they dispers'd
Among the Heathen of thir purchase got,
And Fabl'd how the Serpent, whom they call'd
Ophion with *Eurynome*, the wide-
Encroaching *Eve* perhaps, had first the rule
Of high *Olympus*, thence by *Saturn* driv'n
And *Ops*, ere yet *Dictaean Jove* was born.

(X.578–84)

"Purchase" has a primary meaning of irregular or conniving profit, but it also means concubinage, the sexual innuendo recalling the miscegenation of Genesis 6 as well as phallic interpretations of the seduction in the garden. "Got" would then have the sense of "begot," and the heathen would correspond to giants – the biblical nephilim or "fallen ones," "men of renown" (Gen. 6:4), but also the Greek Titans, mentioned by name. The promiscuity is verbal as well, allusive and linguistic indeterminacy figuring one another. Eve, the prolific "mother of all life," becomes Eurynome, whose name translated generates the iconic epithet "wide-encroaching," then used to qualify her own mythic gemination. Ophion, traditionally derived from Ophis, "serpent," likewise gives way to Saturn, from *satus*, "sowing," and to the "power" of Ops, goddess of abundance. *Satus*, one might add, can mean "begetting" and "origin" as well. Since his Greek prototype Kronos was sometimes confused with *chrōnos*, "time," we are at a loss to decide whether Ophion is displaced by temporal succession, or by its unific source. In any case, since Saturn leads the patricidal Titans, we have a myth that reverses the structure of the Christian theodicy, so epitomizing both the danger and the allure of fictional dissemination (*satus* again).

As such endless pullulations of mytheme and phoneme suggest, Milton's project has ultimately to meet at least three orders of resistance: the indeterminacy of the allusive network; the ironization that is a potential concomitant of all allegory; and the "derivation" (in the sense of deviation or semantic drift) that is the inevitable condition of "fallen language." This is true even of a sacred text like the Bible, which is why the idea of a prophetic poetry is so unstable. "Purchase" and wide encroachment are already implicit in the idea of the secondary, determining the strong cadence on "got" in the Ophion passage. In the context of dispersion, the word echoes unmistakably the striking enjambment that follows in Book I, as though by consequence, the blotting of the books of life:

> Nor had they yet among the Sons of *Eve*
> Got them new Names, till wand'ring o'er the Earth
> (I.364f.)

Conned with an evening ear, these lines contain a reference to Eve's naming of Cain in Genesis 4 – a reference that exemplifies Milton's license with Scripture, written "in the Dialect of men," while reflecting a critical self-awareness that transcends the categories of revisionary will. In the Hebrew Bible, the words Eve speaks at the birth of her son, "I have gotten a man from the Lord" (4:1), appear to motivate the proper name itself. *Qaniti* (I have gotten) is the presumptive root of *qayin* (Cain), a rhetorical fiction so transparent as to deter any belief in biblical etymology or in the special ontological status of biblical names.[16] Milton's metric inversion, "Got them new names," draws attention to this rhetorical sleight, which, like the language of Satan, "taints integrity" at its very root, while the conjoined phrase, "wand'ring o'er the Earth," confirms that the echo is not fortuitous (cf. Gen. 4:12).

Paradise Lost is rife with macaronic wordplay, including etymological puns on a variety of Hebrew names. The biblical etymology of Cain, however, stands out against these as particularly forced. It is as if Milton, on the point of inaugurating his own synecdochic fiction of naming, wished privately to stress the fictive quality of his sacred source. At the same time, Cain becomes, as elsewhere in the poem, a powerful counterfigure for the poet-prophet, balancing the inflated figure of Moses. From Cain, according to tradition, were descended all the generation of the fallen angels – but also the artificers and musicians of Book XI and Genesis 4. Critics have noted the conjunction of "first," "fruit," and "forbidden" in the opening lines of *Paradise Lost*. The predicament of the poet is potentially analogous to the predicament of Cain, whose offering of first fruits was not accepted because, to take the view of Augustine (*De Civ. Dei* 15.7), the motive that prompted it was impure. A poem that stages its own forfeiture of voice, that invents a simulacrum of inspiration, would risk rejection by the same criterion.

According to a well-known Targumic tradition, Cain (not mentioned in Genesis 5 in the list of offspring in Adam's likeness and image) was the son of Sammael or Satan, so that by the dangerous logic of filiation, it is the Satanic name that again haunts the text. We might even recognize a Satanic logic of filial presumption in the way the name of the son figures before the name of the father in the larger hypogrammatic sequence of the poem. In a sense, it is Hebrew itself, the language of Scripture, that returns to haunt the text of Milton's poem, but as a homeless *revenant*, not as the original logos or authorizing ground of meaning. Onomancy here yields only nominative ghosts, daemonic parodies of the holy spirit which the poet openly invokes. Milton's text is possessed by these blotted names, which, although in the "original" language, are not the true or proper names. Such etymological subterfuge is equivocal beyond human attempts to weigh or to compensate. On the one hand, it masks and mocks the original, yet at the same time it threatens the anarchic verve of the secondary, which for all its aggressive self-assurance is continually committing us to the tortuous reconstructions of allegory.

To reiterate, Scripture itself, in the almost Freudian reading of the drama that authorizes Milton's own potential profanation – the drama of catastrophe and restitution on Mt Sinai – originates as substitution. The shattering fall of the first tablets suggests that the sacred truths were "ruined" before we ever heard of them. Like the fall into sin, the linguistic fall and the shattering of the tablets are "fortunate," but only in so far as they eventuate in a text. This makes the poem itself potentially an idol, evoking the scandal of all prophetic poetry. Esteemed as good in itself, it becomes a false object of desire. But even conceived as offering or task, there is still the problem of prerogation. "All worship is prerogative," George Herbert writes, decrying in an act of voluntary devotion the impossibility of what he is in the process of achieving: "Therefore we dare not from his garland steal, / To make a posie for inferiour power" ("To all Angels and Saints"); or, since the Satanic is none other than the aspiring self, the stark question buried like an illicit sacrifice within the very foundations of *The Temple*: "Thy rod, my posie?" ("The Thanksgiving").

Milton is less inclined than Herbert to identify the Satanic with natural man; on the contrary, he seems at pains in his depiction of the fall to preserve the integrity of the human psyche, to demonstrate the power and subtlety, rather than the purity or impurity, of the human will. The issue of justification is worked out on the cosmic plane, and here Milton tropes most powerfully on his epic sources, for in *Paradise Lost*, far more than in Homer or Virgil, we are made to feel the gulf that separates the two orders. One might argue that the *Iliad* shows divine logic to be an imitation of human logic, which it thus ennobles, while the *Aeneid* shows the human developing in harmony with the divine will, however foreign or mysterious. In both, although the direction of participation changes, the human and the divine continue to coinhere. In *Paradise Lost*, however, the occasional descent of the angels with their imperious talk of accommodation only emphasizes the distance between the creature and the creator. Participation or continuity is compressed in the Christian scheme into a single historical moment, the advent of Christ – *and then withheld*, although the whole poem intends it and Michael in Book XII will, without venturing on an actual depiction, talk about it. Coinherence defines the nature of Christ, whose presence within the human narrative is a function of faith. If the drama of justification has a human theater, it is not Adam but the narrator, whose motivation for writing, in its final indeterminacy, is at once the structural reflex and the existential model of God's own inscrutability in Book III. Milton might well be accused of a kind of moral sophistry here, which allows him, on apparently orthodox grounds, to indulge his own poetic ambition, or what Romantic critics perceived as his sympathy with Satan.

Aspiration is not in itself necessarily Satanic, since the presence or absence of grace can never be anticipated. To chastize aspiration would involve a pride of judgment more pernicious than the poet's pride of creation. Although he can only characterize it negatively (*not* "Artifice or Office mean"), Milton approves the ambition for "that which justly gives Heroic name / To Person or to Poem" (IX.40f.). Apophatic definition and the evasion of the proper are again hedges against idolatry, which is here a transparent risk. When he speaks one line later of a "higher Argument, . . . sufficient of itself to raise / That name," the echoes of Satan's great assertion of autonomy in Book V compete quite openly with the raising of Christ's name, as "hailed" in Book III, where deferral seemed, however ambiguously, a sign of deference. Translated literally, the third commandment says, "Thou shalt not raise [lo' tissa'] the name of the Lord thy God in vain [or falsely?]," and the obscurity of Milton's phrase reflects his awareness of the potentially self-damning echo. Such balanced conjurations are themselves a form of power, countered in the invocations by Milton's professed diffidence about the ultimate source of his poem: Does the poet "implore" his muse (VII.38), or does she come "unimplor'd" (IX.22)? Does she visit him "Nightly, or when Morn / Purples the East" (VII.29f.)? or is it rather he who pays the visits (III.21)? The final invocation ends with an unresolved conditional: the risk of failure "if all be mine, / Not Hers. . . ."

It is one of the ironies of language – one Milton must have brooded over – that the archaic verb "aread," meaning "advise," but also "prophesy," came early to have a cognate form with the meaning "interpret, especially written symbols." The deeper relationship between prophecy and interpretation, or re-creation as inevitable gloss, resists definition. According to a famous saying found in the Talmud, "a sage is greater than a prophet."[17] In the earliest Hebrew treatise on poetics, the *Shirat Yisrael*, Moses ibn Ezra explains that the sage, unlike the prophet who merely transmits the divine word, takes what he has received from the prophet and elaborates it, adding, in accordance with the powers granted by his study of torah, his own rational reflections: "His therefore is the excellence of originality."[18] This reads almost like a vindication of revisionism: the secondary work is praised for being both more comprehensive and more strenuously personal – and hence "original" – than the text it interprets. Yet the deference here accorded to biblical interpretation was never extended to poetry, which was rather dismissed or feared. Dismissed, because of the accepted association of fiction and falsehood; feared, because of the similarities between its vatic conventions and the rhetoric of prophetic vision. Classical, and later Islamic, poets might lay claim to direct inspiration, but the rabbis, for whom "the word of the Lord" was no longer directly accessible except through Scripture, could only hope to be guided, as they waited for the Messiah, by *bat qol*, the "daughter of voice," formerly heard by those like Hagar or Manoah "not prepared for prophecy" and still active in the post-biblical age as the muse of inspired interpretation.[19]

Milton acknowledges this hermeneutic fiction at the critical juncture in *Paradise Lost* where Eve, waylaid by Satan, begins to interpret the divine prohibition:

> But of this Tree we may not taste nor touch;
> God so commanded, and left that Command
> Sole Daughter of his voice; the rest, we live
> Law to ourselves, our Reason is our Law.
>   (IX.651–4)

In mentioning touch, as commentators like to note, Eve was amplifying God's words; hence her sole daughter is of doubtful legitimacy to begin with. "Law to ourselves" and "Reason" extend the irony (not least by anticipating the rationalist hermeneutic that would convert the directive power of the law into a heuristic fiction). But Milton's use of the rabbinic tradition is provocative beyond such merely dramatic ironies. "And left that Command / Sole Daughter of his voice" could imply either that obedience to command is the essence of interpretation, or, more darkly, that command is inaccessible beyond its secondary voicing. Both emphases are valid: the first intends Eve, and with her the reader; the second, the poet-prophet, thus giving the hint of illegitimacy an amplitude of its own. *Bat qol* evolves with the closing of the canon; however, the idea of inspired interpretation tends intrinsically to challenge the limits of the secondary. Like her sister Sophia, the hypostatized figure of secondary voice eventually yearns to be at one with the father.

This brings us back to the Romantic Milton, the apostle of poetic will and the pride of the secondary, but I should prefer in ending to stress that the covert struggle with Moses was a struggle to preserve not only the integrity of imagination but the physical world in which it lives: more precisely the fullness of the epic. We have been too quick to set a Hebraic Milton, drawing on the revisionary radicalism of Protestant poetics, over against his classical precursors. From the perspective of the inmost bower, the view of the catalogue in Book I as transuming Homer is perhaps inverted; for the dramatic, the epic, and the elegiac all live in Milton's pages thanks to the blotted book. When Wordsworth proclaims his theme of Man, Nature, and human life in contradistinction to Milton, he is superbly misreading; for the spousal verse he would claim as his own had already been tenderly sounded at the heart of the earlier poem. *Paradise Lost*, for all its sublimity, remains a paradoxical *empire des lumières*, its private light repealing the daylight around it, yet making the common sky more lambent.

Between Milton and the Romantics the most powerful figure in the English prophetic line is surely Christopher Smart, and his evasions of Milton were, tragically, less adequate than Wordsworth's. This makes his work, however, more dependable as commentary, and I would conclude with a verse from the *Jubilate Agno* which represents with appropriate indirection my final impression of Milton's prophetic burden:

> For Eternity is a creature & is built upon Eternity
> *katabolē epi tē diabolē.*

> (B170)

The Greek phrase may be translated in a number of ways: *katabolē* means "fall," but it also means "foundation." *Diabolē*, "slander," or "falsehood," incorporates the root of "Devil," whose representation as the "father of lies" is etymologically sound. Smart makes no distinction between

Languages and Creatures – both have "the breath of Life" (A2) and all "work into one another by their bearings" (B624) – so that the predicament of "Eternity," faced with an endless regress in its pursuit of a foundation, depicts the snares of etymologizing itself. Yet, Smart seems to be saying, Eternity *is* a creature, which for all the obscurity of its origins, shall always be with us, perpetuating versions of itself. One thus returns to the final phrase with a braver resignation: our foundations are treacherous, and the lies of Satan are prelude to our own fall (*katabolē epi tē diabolē*); but eternity is a creature, and we erect it with fictions.

Notes

Quotations from Milton's poems follow the text of *John Milton: Complete Poems and Major Prose*, ed. Merritt Y. Hughes (New York, Odyssey, 1957).

1. According to Arnold Williams, who means us to refer the same attitudes to Milton, the commentators who built on the notion of Hebrew as the adamic language "were the inheritors of a tradition stemming from Plato's *Cratylus*, according to which the etymology of the word gives a glimpse into the true nature of the thing" (*The Common Expositor: An Account of the Commentaries on Genesis, 1527–1633* (Chapel Hill, University of North Carolina, 1948), 230). Christopher Ricks cites this idea verbatim in explanation of Milton's "etymological faith" (*Milton's Grand Style* (Oxford, Clarendon Press, 1963), 68), and Stanley Fish devotes a lengthy discussion of "language in Paradise" to the history of seventeenth-century Cratylism (*Surprised by Sin: The Reader in Paradise Lost* (New York, St Martin's Press, 1967), 107–30). William Kerrigan, who at least recognized the Heraclitian thrust of Plato's dialogue, epitomizes the will to mystification which underlies such studies when he writes (apropos of the beginning of Book III), "From start to finish, Milton is the poet of the *archē*. . . . Even the Miltonic style is marked by its exploitation of etymology. His very language perpetuates a linguistic past, giving new vigor to the genesis of words in a present whose corruption may be measured in part by its forgetful drift away from these earlier and revelatory definitions" (*The Sacred Complex: On the Psychogenesis of Paradise Lost* (Cambridge, Mass., Harvard University Press, 1983), 157–8; cf. *The Prophetic Milton* (Charlottesville, University Press of Virginia, 1974), 27–8).
2. *A Fuller Course in the Art of Logic* (1672), ed. and tr. Walter J. Ong and Charles J. Ermatinger, in *Complete Prose Works of John Milton*, vol. VIII, ed. Maurice Kelley (New Haven, Yale University Press, 1982), 296; cf. Aristotle, *Rhetoric*; 2.23; Cicero, *Topica*, 35.
3. It is perhaps worth noting that Buxtorf begins his article by rendering the perfect stem (*qal*) as *insanivit*, a word that could be used in Latin with reference to poetic inspiration (see Horace, *Carmina*, 3.4.6 for the *amabilis insania*, indebted ultimately to the Greek conjunction of *mantikē* and *mania*, as in *Phaedrus*, 244–5, *Ion*, 533–4, and the sources cited in E. R. Dodds, *The Greeks and the Irrational* (Berkeley, University of California Press, 1951), 64–101).
   For evidence of Milton's close, if occasional, dependence on Buxtorf's 1621 *Lexicon* in *De Doctrina Christiana*, see Maurice Kelley, "Two sources for Milton's Hebrew" (*Notes and Queries*, n.s. 13, 1966, 259). The debate about

Milton's knowledge of biblical (as distinct from rabbinic) Hebrew begins with E. C. Baldwin, "Milton and the Psalms" (*Modern Philology*, 17, 1919, 457–63), and continues with M. H. Studley, "Milton and his paraphrases of the Psalms" (*Philological Quarterly*, 4, 1925, 361–72); H. F. Fletcher, *Milton's Semitic Studies* (Chicago, University of Chicago Press, 1926), 97–110; H. S. Gehman, "Milton's use of Hebrew in the *Doctrina Christiana*" (*Jewish Quarterly Review*, n.s. 29, 1938, 37–44); and W. B. Hunter, Jr, "Milton translates the Psalms" (*Philological Quarterly*, 40, 1961, 485–94). The primitive reading knowledge presupposed here may be taken for granted.

4. Edward Leigh, *Critica Sacra* . . . (London, 1650), sig. A2 recto.
5. See Jean Starobinski, *Les Mots sous les Mots: Les Anagrammes de Ferdinand de Saussure* (Paris, Gallimard, 1971): "An asyndetic sequence of names and paradigms runs beneath poetic discourse, which it sustains as pillars do a bridge. Hence, the poetic message (which is a 'verbal act') is constituted not only *with* words borrowed from *language*, but also *upon* names or words taken individually" (123). Saussure, of course, was concerned principally with phonic paraphrase; it was the *form* of the name or key-word that was displaced across the poetic text, usually with the vocalic sequence intact. Milton's procedure might better be considered an example of the kind of intertextual punning studied by Michael Riffaterre, for whom "the *sememe* of the kernal word functions like an encyclopedia of representations related to the meaning of that word" (*Semiotics of Poetry* (Bloomington, Indiana University Press, 1978), 26; my emphasis). Nicholas Abraham and Maria Torok have elaborated a psychoanalytic theory of the cryptonym, based on the revisionary notion that words themselves may be objects of repression, in *Cryptomanie: Le verbier de l'Homme aux loups* (Paris, Aubier Flammarion, 1976).
6. The 1667 and 1674 editions both print "avant," although according to the *OED* the fuller spelling was also available, which might suggest that Milton intended only the interjection without any pun (cf. *PL* IV.84). However, both verbal and nominal forms of the homonym meaning "boast" (from OF *avanter* or *avaunter*, from late L. *vanitare*) could also be spelled "avant" (*OED* shows this spelling for the verb in an edition of Foxe's *Actes and Monuments* printed in 1684); not to mention the possible role of Milton's amanuensis.

    As a point of curiosity, one might note that Joyce exploits the same ambiguity in *Finnegans Wake*: "some Finn, some Finn avant!" (074.01) . . . "Sonne feine, somme feehn avaunt!" (593.09), where the verbal matrix seems to be the rebel slogan "Sinn Féin, Sinn Féin Amháin" (Ourselves, ourselves alone!). HCE might be said to manifest himself here (the setting in both passages is dawn) as Lucifer, the feigned or would-be sun and son, no less the fiend (cognate with German *Feind*, or "enemy," the literal meaning of Hebrew "Satan") – a boastful claim: avaunt! (forward? backward?)
7. See Geoffrey Hartman's discussion in *Saving the Text* (Baltimore, Johns Hopkins University Press, 1981), 83.
8. Gershom Scholem, *On the Kabbalah and its Symbolism*, tr. Ralph Manheim (New York, Schocken Books, 1965), 36.
9. *The Gospel of Truth*, 1.3, tr. George W. MacRae, in *The Nag Hammadi Library: In English*, ed. James M. Robinson (Leiden, E. J. Brill, 1977), 47.
10. *Pirqe deRabbi Eliezer*, 3 (text of the second printed edition, Venice, 1544, followed by Vorstius). There is an English translation by Gerald Friedlander, *Pirke de Rabbi Eliezer* (1916; rpt New York, Sepher-Hermon, 1981), 14n. On Milton's use of Vorstius (1644) see Golda Spiera Werman, "Midrash in *Paradise Lost: Capitula Rabbi Elieser*" (*Milton Studies*, 18, 1983, 145–71). The translation was previously noted by Don Cameron Allen, "Milton and

Rabbi Eliezer" (*MLN*, 63, 1948, 262–3) following Richard Laurence, *Ascensio Isaiae Vatis* (Oxford, Oxford University Press, 1819).

11. George Sandys, *Ovid's Metamorphosis. Englished, Mythologized, and Represented in Figures* (1632), ed. Karl K. Hulley and Stanley T. Vandersall (Lincoln, University of Nebraska Press, 1970), 652. In the translation itself *virga* is rendered as "wand" (14.278–30, pp. 627–8).

12. Compare "Upon Appleton House," 569–84, where Marvell evokes the "light mosaic" of the leaves in "Nature's mystic book" after praising the language of the birds and trees (rather than Hebrew) as the "learn'd original." Both poets are playing against the speculative tradition that sought a "loftier origin" for the word "muse" in the Hebrew name of Moses; see John Minsheu, *Ductor in Linguas* (London, 1617), s.v. "muse;" and Estienne Guichard, *L'Harmonie étymologique des langues* (Paris, 1606).

13. William Empson, *Some Versions of Pastoral* (1935; rpt. New York, New Directions, 1960), 177, 180.

14. Alastair Fowler (ed.), *Paradise Lost* (London, Longman, 1968), 601.

15. John Guillory, *Poetic Authority: Spenser, Milton, and Literary History* (New York, Columbia University Press, 1983), 145.

16. Although, as Arnold Williams notes, the commentators often came to the opposite conclusion (Williams, op. cit., 228). For an overview of onomastic speculation with particular attention to biblical names, see I. Opelt, "Etymologie," *Reallexikon für Antike und Christentum* (Stuttgart, Anton Hiersemann, 1966), VI.797–844; for early interpretations of Cain in particular, Franz Wutz, *Onomastica Sacra: Untersuchungen zum* Liber Interpretationis Nominum Hebraicorum *des Hl. Hieronymus* (Leipzig, J. C. Hinrichs, 1914), 397–8.

17. Baba Batra 12a; cf. Ber. 34d; y. Ber. 17:11.

18. *Shirat Yisrael* [*Kitab al-Muhadara wa al-Mudhakara*], Hebrew tr. Ben-Zion Halper (Leipzig, Styble, 1924), 51–2. See the discussion by Shalom Spiegel, "On medieval Hebrew poetry," in *The Jewish Experience*, ed. Judah Golden (New Haven, Yale University Press, 1976), 174–215.

19. Moses Maimonides, *The Guide of the Perplexed*, II.42 *sub fin* (Pines, 390).

11

STANLEY FISH

Driving from the letter: truth and indeterminacy in Milton's *Areopagitica*

I

It has been some time since John Illo pointed out that Milton's *Areopagitica* has almost always been read as a classic liberal plea for "complete liberty." "The preponderance of English scholarship," Illo writes, "has drawn Milton into its own liberal centre, which claims a Western and ultimately an Attic heritage of universal freedom."[1] This is especially true in the twentieth century when the *Areopagitica* (through an irony its author would have understood but not appreciated) becomes a basic text supporting the ethic of disinterested inquiry, and Milton the revolutionary becomes a man with the ability "to look at social issues without using the glasses of sectarian theology, which . . . is very rare in this passionate time."[2] The commentator here is Harold Laski who writes with a host of others in a volume commemorating the three hundredth anniversary of *Areopagitica* and titled, significantly, *Freedom of Expression*. In this volume, Milton is not only the apostle of unrestrained freedom (precisely the *accusation* levelled at him by his contemporaries), he is also and "above all, a Humanist – the greatest representative in England of that movement which had abandoned the dogmatism of the middle ages and was seeking for a natural or empirical basis for its beliefs" (125). The same encomiast declares of the *Areopagitica*, "there is no encroachment on 'the liberty to know, to utter and to argue freely' which it does not . . . oppose" (122), apparently forgetting the encroachments it itself urges. Only the Dean of St Paul's, W. R. Matthews, is apparently aware of the fact that "Milton's conception of the nature of tolerable books was limited." "It appears," he says gently, "that many who have not recently read his book have an exaggerated notion of what he urges as reasonable liberty" (78).

That many, as Illo reminds us, would seem to include almost the whole body of Milton scholars. There have of course been exceptions: Illo himself, writing from the left, and Willmore Kendall, writing from the right, have argued for a Milton less generous in his ecumenism, a Milton who is not above acts of exclusion and sharp judgment.[3] And Ernest Sirluck has given us a pragmatically political Milton who in the *Areopagitica* argues in several directions at once, hoping thereby to please the several constituencies whose support would be necessary for the revoking of the Act of 1643.[4] But by and large, in the writings and minds of most men and women, the *Areopagitica* remains what it was for those who celebrated it in 1944.

In what follows I would like to continue in the direction indicated by the work of Illo and Kendall and advance a series of theses even more radical (at least in terms of received opinion) than theirs. Specifically, I will argue that Milton is finally, and in a profound way, not against licensing, and that he has almost no interest at all in the "freedom of the press" as an abstract or absolute good (and, indeed, does not unambiguously value freedom at all); and that his attitude towards books is informed by none of the reverence that presumably led the builders of the New York Public Library to have this sentence from the tract preside over their catalogue room: "A goode Booke is the pretious life blood of a master spirit, imbalm'd and treasur'd up on purpose to a life beyond life."

Let us begin with that sentence and with the famous paragraph from which it comes:

> I deny not, but that it is of greatest concernment in the Church and Commonwealth, to have a vigilant eye how Bookes demeane themselves, as well as men; and thereafter to confine, imprison, and do sharpest justice on them as malefactors: For Books are not absolutely dead things, but doe contain a potencie of life in them to be as active as that soule was whose progeny they are . . . ; who kills a Man kills a reasonable creature, Gods Image; but hee who destroyes a good Booke, kills reason it selfe, kills the Image of God, as it were in the eye. Many a man lives a burden to the Earth; but a good Booke is the pretious life-blood of a master spirit, imbalm'd and treasur'd up on purpose to a life beyond life. 'Tis true, no age can restore a life, whereof perhaps there is no great losse; and revolutions of ages doe not oft recover the losse of a rejected truth, for the want of which whole Nations fare the worse. We should be wary therefore what persecution we raise against the living labours of public men, how we spill that season'd life of man preserv'd and stor'd up in Books; since we see a kinde of homicide may be thus committed, sometimes a martyrdome, and if it extend to the whole impression, a

kinde of massacre, whereof the execution ends not in the slaying of an elementall life, but strikes at that ethereall and fift essence, the breath of reason it selfe, slaies an immortality rather than a life.[5]

The first thing to say about this passage is that, detached from the literary idealism it apparently breathes, it is decidedly *un*Miltonic; first because it locates value and truth in a physical object, and second because the reverence it apparently recommends toward that object is dangerously close to, if not absolutely identical with, worship. The passage seems, in a word, to encourage idolatry, and that of course is exactly the purpose to which it has been often put when it has been cited as a central "scripture" in the "religion" of the book (the religion, that is, of humanism). This, however, is not Milton's religion. The center of *his* theology is the doctrine of the inner light and his entire career can be viewed as an exercise in vigilance in which he repeatedly detects in this or that political or social or ecclesiastical program one more attempt to substitute for the authority of the inner light the false authority of some external and imposed rule. It is in this spirit (a word precisely intended) that Milton makes a series of related arguments in the *Apology* (written only a year and a half earlier than the *Areopagitica*): he rejects set prayers in favor of "those free and unimpos'd expressions which from a sincere heart unbidden come into the outward gesture;" he rejects the rules of rhetoric and composition in favor of the "true eloquence" that inheres naturally in the speech of one who is "possest with a fervent desire to know good things, and with the dearest charity to infuse the knowledge of them into others;" he rejects any criticism of his own style that would measure it by some external decorum, and claims as a justification for his bitter, vituperative and even obscene words the spirit of zeal that moves him ("there may be a sanctified bitternesse against the enemies of truth") and he insists (in the most famous passage in the tract) that a true poem can only be written (and by implication read) by one who is himself "a composition and pattern of the best and honourablest things; not presuming to sing high praise of heroic men . . . unless he have in himselfe the experience and practice of all that is praise-worthy."[6] In this and every other sentence in the *Apology* Milton is continually alert to the danger of reifying some external form into the repository of truth and value.

In the first edition of the *Doctrine and Discipline of Divorce* (published in 1643) the form of the danger is no less than the Bible itself. Milton's scorn in this tract is directed at those who believe that the essence of the law is to be found in its letter, in the actual words of the text; these he calls "extreme literalists" and "letter bound men:" they display an "obstinate literality" and an "alphabetical servility:" and have made the text into "a transcendent command" that is "above the worship of God and the good of man."[7] This refusal to equate wisdom and truth with what is written in a book, even if the book is the Bible, will later lead him in the *Christian Doctrine* to reject the authority of the ten commandments because he follows the Pauline rule that "whatever is not in accordance with faith, is sin" which is something quite different, he points out, from holding that "whatever is not in accordance with the ten commandments, is sin."[8] And later still, this fierce anti-literalism turns into an even fiercer anti-literaryism as the Christ of *Paradise Regained* declares (in a passage that has given Milton's admirers fits) that the reading of books is "wearisome" (*PR* IV.322).

If we return from this brief excursion into Milton's other writings (and additional examples could have easily been adduced) to the *Areopagitica*, the paragraph that offers so extravagant a praise of books looks very curious indeed. It seems strange to hear Milton asserting that the spirit of a man can be abstracted from the conditions of its daily exercise and that the truth which finds an expression in varied and "unbidden" outward gestures can be so perfectly captured in one of those gestures that it can be "preserved" (in amber, as it were) between the covers of a book. And it is stranger still to find Milton displaying what he himself would describe as a papist idolatry of relics when he exalts the dead letter of a physical object ("imbalm'd" and "preserv'd" indeed) above the living labors of faithful men, and dismisses as "no great losse" the truth that perishes with a life, reserving for the loss of an "impression" or edition the vocabulary of homicide and massacre. It is almost as if he were writing an early draft of the sonnet on the Waldensians and had decided to begin that poem not with "Avenge O Lord thy slaughtered saints," but with "Avenge O Lord thy slaughtered books."

I do not, however, want to rest my case for the falseness of this passage on what Milton had previously written or on what he was later to write. My best evidence comes from those places in the *Areopagitica* itself where Milton gives voice to sentiments that undermine (if they do not flatly contradict) any argument for the sanctity of books. Consider, for example, a sentence, some thirteen pages forward in the tract, that begins, "Banish all objects of lust." The phrase "objects of lust" is ambiguous between two readings; it can mean "banish all lustful objects," that is all objects that have, as a special property, the capacity to provoke lust; or it can mean banish all objects to which an already existing lust can attach itself. The attraction of the first reading is that it specifies a course of action that can be followed – let's get rid of these lust-provoking objects – while in the second reading the recommended course of action is self-defeating because it would require the banishing of everything. As it turns out, however, the second reading is the correct one:

Banish all objects of lust, shut up all youth into the severest discipline that can be exercis'd in any heritage, ye cannot make them chaste that came not hither so.

(297)

That is to say, chastity is not a property of objects, but of persons; and one can neither protect it nor promote it by removing objects from the world. Indeed, even if one went to the impossible lengths of removing all objects, the flourishing of lust and other sins would continue unabated, for, "though ye take from a covetous man all his treasure, he has yet one jewel left, ye cannot bereave him of his covetousnesse:" and with that "covetousnesse" as the driving force of his very being, such a man will populate the world – even if it is only the inner world of his imagination – with the objects of his desire, with the objects of lust.

It is easy to see how this line of reasoning fits into the case against licensing: in so far as licensing is urged as a means of combating sin, it is, as Milton says, "far insufficient to the end which it intends" (297), because sin does not reside in the objects licensing would remove. But, curiously, if this is a strong argument against licensing (and it is so strong that Milton makes it at least six times) it is equally strong as an argument against the alternative to licensing, the free and unconstrained publishing of books; for it follows that if men and not books are the source of sin, then men and not books are the source of virtue; and if sin will not be diminished by removing its external occasion, then virtue will not be protected by preserving its external representation. In short, the argument against licensing, which has always been read as an argument *for* books, is really an argument that renders books beside the point; books are no more going to save you than they are going to corrupt you; by denying their potency in one direction, Milton necessarily denies their potency in the other and undercuts the extravagant claims he himself makes in the passage with which we began. Whatever books are, they cannot be what he says they are in those ringing sentences, the preservers of truth, the life-blood of a master spirit, the image of God.

II

Why then does he say it? It will be the business of this essay to answer that question and we can begin by noting that at least on the local level he says it *in order* to move away from it. As the prose reaches the rapturous height of calling books an "ethereall and fift essence" and "the breath of reason it selfe," Milton suddenly checks its flight: "But lest I should be condemn'd of introducing licence, while I oppose licencing." This rhetorical flourish looks forward to the historical digression of the succeeding paragraphs, but for a moment it also refers backward to the license Milton has himself committed in transforming books, which are, after all, *only* objects, into the means and vehicle of grace. The moment passes quickly, almost before it has registered, but it is enough, I think, to cast the shadow of a qualification on what has just been said, a qualification we carry with us as we move into the brief history of "what hath been done by ancient and famous Commonwealths, against this disorder" (272).

By "this disorder," Milton means license, the supposed harm that follows from allowing books to be "as freely admitted into the world as any other birth" (281). It is this liberal practice, Milton tells us, that characterized the societies he is about to survey; and one would expect the point of the ensuing history to be that in these "ancient and famous commonwealths" the absence of licensing would have as one of its effects the flourishing of virtue; but it is an expectation that is disappointed by a history that never achieves so sharp a focus. Milton begins with what one would think would be his strongest example, the city of Athens "where Books and wits were ever busier than in any other part of Greece" (273); but rather than celebrating the benefits of this "busyness" he turns immediately to the measures taken by the Athenians to curtail it, and finds "only two sorts of writings which the magistrate car'd to take notice of; those either blazphemous . . . or Libellous." The tonal instability of this section is established immediately by "car'd to take notice of" which hesitates between an expression of approval for the magistrate's restraint and the suggestion that if he had been properly vigilant, he would have taken notice of *more*. When the survey turns from Greece to Rome the double argument continues as Milton simultaneously reports on the restraint exercised by magistrates who decline to license and describes the fruits of that restraint (or, more precisely, absence of restraint) in terms that call into question its wisdom. Is it, after all, a good or a bad thing, that the "naked plainness" of Lucullus and Catullus and the "wanton" poems of Ovid are allowed to do their work unchecked? This question is never asked in so many words, but Milton's judgmental vocabulary is continually implying it; and, moreover, there is nothing to counter the question on the other side, no instancing of books whose publication is causally related to a virtuous result. The only books Milton ever mentions are those that were allowed to appear despite the fact that they were impious or impudent or scurrilous or loose; it is this fact (established ever so casually but with a cumulative force) that dominates the history, a history which therefore makes the rather narrow and negative point that in a number of societies – some good, some bad, some cultured, some brutish – the absence of pre-publication licensing doesn't seem to have made very much difference at all.

Significantly, the lack of a difference goes in both directions; not only is it the case that what Milton will later call "promiscuous reading" did no particular harm; neither, at least on the evidence offered here, did it do any particular good. It seems in fact a "thing indifferent" not correlated in any observable way with the moral status of a commonwealth; and if licensing is thus indifferently related to the production or protection of virtue, so also are books, and the entire history becomes discontinuous with the encomium that introduces it.

It is only after the history has been concluded that Milton takes up the question it might have been expected to answer: "what is to be thought in generall of reading Books, . . . and whether be more the benefit, or the harm that thence proceeds?" (283). Earlier, when it seemed that what was or was not *in* books was going to be the issue, this would have been just the right question. Now, however, in the wake of the inconclusive account of Greek and Roman practice, the question sounds oddly, as if it were posed by someone who hadn't yet realized that the agenda it assumes – the agenda of separating the bad from the good in books – has more or less been abandoned. In these early pages the *Areopagitica* displays a curious inability to settle down and to pursue unambiguously the line of argument that was so strongly promised when books were the object of an apparently unqualified praise.

But then, almost before we know it, the tract takes a decisive turn and apparently stabilizes (at least for the moment) when Milton invokes a vision reported by Eusebius as he was debating with himself whether or not it was lawful to "venture . . . among" the "defiling volumes" of "hereticks." Milton identifies this second vision as one "sent from God" who speaks to Eusebius in these words: "Read any books whatever come to thy hands, for thou art sufficient both to judge aright, and to examine each matter" (285). "This revelation," as Milton terms it, decides the issue by dissolving it, by transferring the question of value from books, of whatever kind, to Eusebius, who is "sufficient" in the strong sense of *self*-sufficient, capable by virtue (literally) of what is already in him of turning all that he reads into good. Lest we miss the point, Milton drives it home by supplementing the Eusebius citation from Thessalonians ("prove all things, hold fast to that which is good") with "another remarkable saying of the same Author: To the pure all things are pure," which is then immediately and powerfully glossed: "not only meats and drinks, but all kinde of knowledge whether of good or evil; the knowledge cannot defile, nor consequently the books, if the will and conscience be not defil'd." Indeed, books are even more "things indifferent" than meats, for while "bad meats will scarce breed good nourishment in the healthiest concoction," bad books "to a . . . judicious reader serve . . . to discover, to confute, to forwarn, and to illustrate." Of course, by the end of this sentence, there are no bad books, in the sense of books that can in and of themselves do harm; for all books, once they enter into the heart of the judicious reader, become the occasion and means by which that judicious-ness is exercised and extended; but by the same reasoning, neither are there any good books, in the sense of books that can in and of themselves produce wisdom; for as Milton says within a few pages, if "a wise man like a good refiner can gather gold out of the drossiest volume . . . a fool will be a fool with the best book, yea without book" (291–2). The logic of this is inescapable and certainly supports the conclusion that licensing will bring no benefits; but it also supports a corollary conclusion that whatever we make available to a wise man will not be essential to his wisdom, for he will be wise with any book, "yea without book."

At this point the argument of the *Areopagitica* seems simply to have reversed itself. Where at first the question to be answered was whether the power in books will work for good or evil (a question directly related to the case for and against pre-publication licensing), by the time Milton declares that all things are pure to the pure the issue is no longer what is or is not in books, but what is or is not in persons; and consequently it has become a matter of indifference as to whether or not books are licensed, since, at least by the arguments that have so far been marshalled, the flourishing of *either* good or evil does not depend on books. From here there is a straight line to the sentence that begins "banish all objects of lust" (a recommendation that only makes sense if books are the source either of lust or of virtue) and ends by asserting that "ye cannot make them chaste that came hither so."

But if the new point of the *Areopagitica* is that men and not books are the repository of purity, then it is a point that barely survives its own introduction; for within a page of saying that all things are pure to the pure, Milton also says that "we bring not innocence into the world, we bring impurity much rather" (288), and by saying that he immediately problematizes what had for a moment seemed to be a resolution (or a dissolution) of the dilemma initially posed, to license or not to license; after all it isn't much help to observe that purity is a condition of the heart if all of our hearts enter the world in a condition of impurity. This impurity is one of the reasons why licensing must be numbered among the "vain and impossible attempts" (291), but it is also a reason for something close to despair, since it leaves mysterious the process by which purity or even its near approximation can be achieved. If purity can be found neither in books, where it first seemed to reside, nor in naturally pure hearts, where the argument next seemed to place it, then it cannot be found anywhere.

That in fact turns out to be the right conclusion, but with a difference that redeems its negativity; for in the very same sentence that proclaims our congenital impurity Milton introduces us to its remedy: "Assuredly we bring not innocence into the world, we bring impurity much rather: that which purifies us is triall and triall is by what is contrary." If virtue is not to be found anywhere – either in a book or in an object, or even in a heart – it is because it must be *made*, and it can only be made by sharpening it against the many whetstones provided by the world, by "what is contrary." Not only does this give a positive direction to an argument that has for a while emphasized only what can*not* be done and what will *not* succeed; it also reanimates the question of licensing and makes it once again weighty; for if the emergence of virtue depends on the availability of materials against which it can be exercised, then it follows that the more materials the better, and that is why, after the tract has unfolded almost half its length, Milton can finally offer a coherent and non-contradictory argument against licensing; anyone who thinks that he can "remove sin by removing the matter of sin" is mistaken because sin is not a feature of the outer, but of the inner landscape and can only be removed (if that is the word) when that landscape is transformed; and since that transformation can only be accomplished by a continual exercise of the faculty of judgment, it is crucial that the judgment be supplied with occasions for its exercise; although it is offered as a way of promoting virtue, licensing will operate to eliminate the conditions of its growth by removing the materials on which growth can feed: "look how much . . . we thus expell of sin, so much we expell of virtue; for the matter of them is both the same" (297). Once again, then, books are declared to be absolutely essential to the maintenance of truth and virtue, not, however, because truth and virtue reside in books (as they were said to so many paragraphs ago), but because it is by (the indifferent) means of books that men and women can make themselves into the simulacrums of what no book could ever contain.

But this may seem a long way around the barn. If Milton had wanted to tell us (as he now tells us) that books are "necessary to the constituting of human vertue" (288) – as opposed to being the very essence of virtue – why didn't he just come right out and say so in the first place? The question is its own answer once one realizes that it amounts to asking why didn't he simply hand over the truth he wished us to have? To have done so, or, rather, to claim to have done so, would have been to claim for the *Areopagitica* the very capacity it denies to all other books, the capacity of being the repository of what no book can contain because it can only be written in the fleshly tables of the heart. In short, if the *Areopagitica* is to be faithful to the lesson it teaches, it cannot teach that lesson directly; rather it must offer itself as the occasion for the trial and exercise that are necessary to the constituting of human virtue; it must become an instrument in what Milton will later call "knowledge in the making" (321).

The tract performs this self-effacing office in two related ways. First it continually comments on its own inability to capture the truth that informs it. In the very first paragraph Milton reports that he is in the grip of a "power" within him that simply will not respect the decorums of the formal oration; and as a result he finds himself speaking with a "passion" (266) one does not usually find in a preface. A few pages later he makes a valiant attempt to monitor and control his discourse by "laying before" his readers the order of his arguments, but soon after he has concluded his inconclusive history he finds himself in danger of departing from that order and he catches himself up: "But I have first to finish, as was propounded" (283). He then gets himself back on track and is apparently proceeding according to plan, when suddenly he finds that he is already in the midst of making a point that was to have come later, finds, as he puts it, that the truth has prevented or anticipated him "by being clear already while thus much hath been explaining" (292). "See," he exclaims, "the ingenuity of Truth, who when she gets a free and willing hand, opens herself faster than the pace of method and discourse can overtake her" (292).

The image here is one that will loom larger and larger: it is of a truth that is always running ahead of any attempt to apprehend it, a truth that repeatedly slips away from one's grasp, spills out of one's formulations, and escapes the nets that for a moment promise to catch it. Here that net is the tract itself which is at this moment disqualifying itself as a vehicle of the truth it wants to convey; but at the same time and by the very same process, it is playing its part in the fashioning of another vehicle, the heart of the reader, who is the direct beneficiary of the *Areopagitica*'s failure, or, to be more precise, of Milton's strategy. That strategy is one we have been tracking from the beginning of this essay, and it involves encouraging the reader to a premature act of concluding or understanding which is then undone or upset by the introduction of a new and complicating perspective. As we have seen, this happens not once, but repeatedly. The result is, of course, disorienting, but it is also (or so Milton's claim would be) salutary, for in the process of being disoriented the reader is provoked to just the kind of labor and exercise that is necessary to the constitution of his or her own virtue. In this way, the tract becomes at once an emblem and a casualty of the lesson it teaches, the lesson that truth is not the property of any external form, even of a form that proclaims this very truth.

III

It is a strategy supremely pedagogical, and one that Milton both describes and names within the year in *Tetrachordon*, as he turns his attention to the manner of Christ's teaching. Milton is particularly struck by Christ's habit of breaking the external, written law in order to fulfill the law of charity; and he compares Christ's actions with the gnomic form of his precepts, and finds that both have the advantage of preventing his followers from too easily identifying the way of virtue with a portable and mechanical rule. "Therefore it is," says Milton "that the most evangelick precepts are given us in proverbiall formes, to drive us from the letter, though we love ever to be sticking there."[9]

In the *Areopagitica* we are continually being driven from the letter, first from the quite literal letter of books, then from the letter as represented by the history of Athens and Rome, and then from the letter of a comforting, but finally too comforting, scripture ("to the pure all things are pure"). Of course all of these letters, along with others that could be instanced, are provided by the *Areopagitica* itself, which also provides the arguments that make them momentarily attractive; so that one of the letters the tract is driving us from is itself, as we are not allowed the comfort and false security of sticking to and with any of the formulations it presents in

what is finally a self-cancelling sequence. By saying you won't find it there –
in books, in history, in verses of scripture – the *Areopagitica* is also saying
you won't find it here – in the pages of this tract – and finally saying that
you won't find it, because you can only become it, which is what the tract in
its small and self-sacrificing way is helping you to do.

It is a help the need for which is self-replenishing. That is, driving from
the letter is a strategy that can have no end; for each time it succeeds it
generates the conditions that once again make it necessary: the very act of
demonstrating that truth and virtue do not reside "here" will always have
the side-effect of suggesting that they will instead be found "there;" and at
that moment "there" becomes a new letter from which we must then be
driven. The only *positive* lesson that the *Areopagitica* teaches (a lesson it
also exemplifies), is the lesson that we can never stop, and it receives a
particularly powerful (although of course not definitive) formulation when
Milton declares that

> he who thinks we are to pitch our tents here and have attain'd the utmost
> prospect of reformation that the mortall glass wherein we contemplate,
> can shew us, till we come to *beatific* vision, that man, by this very
> opinion, declares that he is yet farre short of truth
>
> (316)

By "here" Milton means both the present state of human knowledge and
understanding and this particular moment in his own tract. Whatever place
or object or condition holds out the possibility of rest and attainment has at
that moment become a letter, the occasion for idolatry. Those who think of
the Reformation as a finite program or agenda, as a series of steps at the end
of which the job will have been done and the goal accomplished, make
exactly the same mistake that is made by the proponents of licensing. The
would-be licensers think that the moral life will be perfected when the
landscape has been cleared of all objects of lust; the reformers think that the
moral life will be perfected when, in accordance with the precepts of
Zwingli and Calvin, we have divested ourselves of some of the trappings of
popery. Licensing and the premature closure of a weak reformation are
alike forms of a single temptation, the temptation to substitute for the
innumerable and inconclusive acts that go to make up the process by which
the self is refined and purified some *external* form of purification that can be
mechanically applied. As I have argued elsewhere it is a temptation felt by
every one of Milton's heroes (even the young Jesus of *Paradise Regained*)[10]
and it is a temptation that Milton makes the readers of *Areopagitica* feel
again and again as he beckons us forward in the name of a truth that always
escapes his formulations and our straining apprehensions.

This pattern of seeking and *not* finding is most spectacularly displayed in
those passages in which the nature of truth is the overt subject. As we first
come upon it the assertion that a "man may be a heretic in the truth"

(310) seems available to a comfortable reading in which an independent truth can be held by a man in one of two ways, either with personal conviction or simply on the strength of what someone else – a pastor, a pope – had told him. Only the first kind of holding is authentic, and as for the other, "the very truth he holds becomes his heresie." But if the logic of this distinction is pursued the very notion of a truth that one can hold either rightly or wrongly is problematized; for on the one hand, a truth that has not been internalized is no longer the truth, and is merely an empty letter; while on the other, a truth sincerely held cannot be given a literal form such that it can be said that someone else is not really holding "it." There is no "it" that is detachable from the holding or being held, and therefore no real sense can be given to the phrase "a heretic in the truth." In so far as it seems for a moment to have a sense it is itself one more letter – one more invitation to premature closure – from which we must be driven.

We are driven from it again in a sequence that begins with a famous question: "Who ever knew truth put to the wors in a free and open encounter?" (327). Here truth and falsehood are imagined as opposing armies – clearly distinguishable – who meet on a battlefield. But as the military image is developed, its configurations change. Rather than being a participant in the battle, truth is suddenly the name of its outcome; the distinguishability of truth from falsehood is not something with which we begin, but something we must achieve by marching out "into the plain" and trying "the matter by dint of argument" (328). Truth in short has receded from our view, but the rhetoric of the passage still allows us to assume that she will once again come into focus if only we allow "the wars of truth" to continue without prior restraint. The point is made by a comparison of truth with Proteus, the notorious shape-shifter and emblem of deception. Proteus, Milton reminds us, would only appear in his own shape when he was bound; but in the case of truth it is exactly the reverse; if you bind or constrain her, "she turns herself into all shapes except her own" (328). The moral is clear: "give her but room," allow those who claim to know her to contend in the field, and she will soon be discernible. But that moral becomes unavailable with the very next sentence. "Yet, it is not impossible that she may have more shapes than one." But if she has more shapes than one, then she has no shape, and is exactly like Proteus, a figure who escapes every attempt to bind her, even when that attempt takes the form of a carefully staged battle at the end of which she is to emerge; and when Milton concludes this sequence by declaring that "Truth may be on this side, or on the other, without being unlike herself," the reflexive pronoun is an almost mocking reminder that the object of our quest has never more escaped us than when we think to have it in view, and is *always* unlike herself.[11]

That object is held out as a lure and a temptation in still another passage, perhaps the most famous of all. It begins with a sad tale. Once upon a time,

"Truth indeed came . . . into the world . . . and was a perfect shape, most glorious to look on;" but then "a wicked race of deceivers . . . hewed her lovely form into a thousand pieces" (316–17). One might say then that truth has receded from this story before it even begins; but all, it would seem, is not lost, for the dismemberment of truth has left us with a definite task, the task of "gathering up limb by limb" still as we can find them, the pieces of her body. "We have not found them all," says Milton, an observation that would seem preliminary to one more exhortation to continue in our search and not to pitch our tents here. But then he adds something much more devastating in its apparent finality: "nor ever shall doe, till her Master's second coming." This is at once the low point and the high point of the tract. It is a low point because it denies the possibility of *ever* achieving knowledge and thereby renders the search pointless, of no more efficacy than licensing; but it is the high point if we are able to apply the lesson the *Areopagitica* has repeatedly taught, the lesson that knowledge and truth are not measurable or containable entities, properties of this or that object, characteristics of this or that state, but *modes of being*, inward dispositions, conditions of a heart that is always yearning for new revelations. The search is only futile if we conceive of it as a search for something external to us, as a kind of giant jig-saw puzzle made up of pre-cut and prefabricated pieces; but if we think of the search as the vehicle by means of which our knowledge is "in the making" and our virtue is in the constituting, then it is always and already succeeding even when, as in this story, it is forever failing. We will indeed never find all the pieces of truth, but if we nevertheless persist in our efforts, when Christ finally does come "to bring together every joynt and member" each of us shall be one of them.

The moral, then, is not "seek and ye shall find," but "seek and ye shall become." And what we shall become in a curious Miltonic way is a licenser, someone who is continually exercising a censorious judgment of the kind that Milton displays when he casually stigmatizes much of Greek and Roman literature as loose or impious or scurrilous. This is the judgment, not of one who is free of constraints, but of one whose inner constraints are so powerful that they issue immediately and without reflection in acts of discrimination and censure.[12] Ironically it is only by permitting what licensing would banish – the continual flow of opinions, arguments, reasons, agendas – that the end of licensing – the fostering of truth – can be accomplished; accomplished not by the external means that licensing would provide, but by making ourselves into the repository of the very values that licensing misidentifies when it finds them in a world free of defiling books. Books are no more the subject of the *Areopagitica* than is free speech; both are subordinate to the process they make possible, the process of endless and proliferating interpretations whose goal is not the clarification of truth, but the making of us into members of her incorporate body so that we can be finally what the

Christ of *Paradise Regained* is said already to be, a living oracle (*PR* I.460).

To be a living oracle is to be a totally unified being, one whose "heart / Contains of good, wise, just, the perfect shape" (*PR* II.10–11). This, however, is the condition only of Christ; all other men exist at a distance from that which would make them whole, exist in that state of seeking and searching which for Milton marks at once the deficiency and the glory of this vale of tears. Like the moment of mortality, the moment of the *Areopagitica* is situated between two absent unities, one always and already lost, the other to be realized only in the absorption of those consciousnesses that now yearn for it. Although truth "indeed came once into her divine Master and was a perfect shape most glorious to look on," she has long since withdrawn, leaving us to the delusive attraction of those many shapes that would compel us in her name; and although she shall one day be reassembled "into an immortal feature of loveliness and perfection," that day is ever deferred and is only projected that much more into the future each time its dawning is prematurely proclaimed.

Meanwhile, man lives in the gap. Indeed, he *is* the gap, a being defined negatively by the union that perpetually escapes him, and which, once achieved, will mark the cessation of his separateness, his end, in two senses. The impurity we bring into the world is the impurity of difference, of not being one with God; yet it is because of that impurity that difference must not be denied or lamented but embraced. The temptation of idolatry, of surrendering ourselves to the totalizing claims of some ephemeral agenda, can only be resisted by the relentless multiplication of that which signifies our lack, the relentless multiplication of difference. We will be "wise in spirituall architecture" (322) only if we build with dissimilar – disunified – materials: "there must be many schisms and many dissections made in the quarry and in the timber, ere the house of God can be built." This allows us for a moment to assume that in time the house of God will in fact be built, but this is exactly like the assumption, so often encouraged, that the truth will finally emerge, and it is immediately disappointed: "And when every stone is laid artfully together, it cannot be united into a continuity, it can be but contiguous in this world." The first half of this sentence increases the expectation that the second half will report an eventual triumph ("when every stone is laid artfully together, the building will be complete"), but the triumph is, as it has been so many times before, deferred, and we are left with more of the same, that is, with more difference, with side by side (in space and time) efforts which do not cohere except in so far as they signify, in a variety of ways, their own insufficiency and incompleteness. It is an incompleteness that must be at once lamented and protected; lamented because it is the sign of our distance from bliss, protected because as such a sign it is a perpetual reminder that bliss awaits us in a union we can achieve (precisely the wrong word) only when we are absorbed by another into a structure not made by hands.

IV

I am aware that this reading of *Areopagitica* is open to the objection that it merely reinscribes the terms of Milton's ideology and is not properly oppositional. It does not go *behind* the manifest concerns of the argument, but accepts those concerns as its own limits, and extends them by what amounts to an elaborate paraphrase. What is required, one might say, is a reading that resists the lure of the text's surface coherence and lays bare its internal fissures and contradictions, the tensions that its discursive progress labors to occlude. I, in turn, might respond by pointing out that it is precisely my method to find tensions and discontinuities where others before me had found only the steady unfolding of a classic liberal vision; but that response no doubt would be met by someone (gleefully) pointing out that I acknowledge discontinuities only so that they could be gathered into a new or higher unity (of authorial strategy), and that in this way I recuperate both the unity of the text and the totalizing power of the author's intention.

It would be helpful to have before us an example of the kind of criticism this essay isn't, and fortunately there is now available Christopher Kendrick's *Milton: A Study in Ideology and Form*.[13] Kendrick offers a complex and nuanced reading of *Areopagitica*, and although I cannot do complete justice to it here, I can focus on a few salient points and compare them with my own. On one point we are in agreement, that *Areopagitica* displays a double structure of discursive argument and anti-discursive eruptions that "uncenter" the overt rhetorical movement of the oration. Kendrick generously notes that I long ago identified this characteristic of Milton's prose (in an essay on *The Reason of Church Government*), but, as he points out, our interpretations of this "anti-discursive bias" are "very different" (222). The chief difference is that whereas I see Milton continually undermining the forms within which he necessarily moves in order to make his tract a (self-consuming) emblem of its message, Kendrick sees contradictions that Milton does not control because they mark his implication in the ideological structure of emerging capitalism. Truth may be declared by Milton *not* to be a "ware" available to trading and monopolization, but the language of monopolization and trading everywhere saturates his prose: "the commodity places its shadowy imprint on much of the imagery of the tract; as a result, market ideology comes to be inscribed most intimately within Milton's argument, and to motivate its very figuration" (41). This "paradox" fissures the entire tract. "On the one hand, the commodity structure informs the monistic argument and affords it a basic ontological rationale. . .; on the other hand, the 'false concrete' of the commodity, its intrinsically reifying structure, is repeatedly attacked and exploded" (57), and if Milton is regarded as a "spokesman for a whole class," then to "expose the aporias contained in his ethical resolution will likewise be to disclose the contradictions forced upon and played out by the revolutionary bourgeois class" (47).

Now on first appearance this is certainly a thesis more capacious than mine (reaching out as it does to seventeenth-century politics, the history of capitalism, class struggle, and so on) but it would be no trick at all, just a standard move in the repertoire Kendrick and I share with other members of the profession, to outflank and assimilate his reading. What Kendrick sees as an aporia – a place of undecidability – in Milton's thought, I see as an extension of the strategy I describe him as pursuing throughout: Milton again and again employs forms (of argument, imagery, justification) that are then discarded or repudiated or denounced; and he does this because it is precisely his contention that *all* forms – except the ever-receding form of truth – hold out the temptation to idolatry, a temptation he combats by never allowing any structure to gain control of his argument, indeed, by not allowing his argument to gain control of itself. The fact that he simultaneously has recourse to the vocabulary of commodification and "explodes" that same vocabulary is nothing special, is not a key (Kendrick has one too, everyone does, that's what interpretation is all about) to the tract; the presentation of truth as a "ware" is no more serious (in the sense that we are supposed to *stay* with it) than the presentation of truth as a fountain or a journey or a beacon or an army or a body. In Milton's terms, they are all letters, partial and inadequate expressions of a reality they cannot contain, and Milton is always driving us from them.

You get the idea (you probably got it before I articulated it), but this is not really the most interesting kind of response to a piece like Kendrick's or to the brand of criticism it represents, if only because it doesn't touch the strongest claims of that criticism: (1) the claim to be political rather than merely literary; and (2) the claim that its politics is in the direction of liberation, of loosening the hold of entrenched and hegemonic ways of thought. The first of these claims is false. No criticism is more political than any other, at least not in the sense one normally means by "political," an intervention in the affairs of the greater – non-academic – world. Some criticism is more political than some others in another sense: its materials are the events and concerns of political life rather than the events and concerns of theology or anthropology or psychology. But all that means is that the act of literary thematizing can be performed on diverse materials; you can do a literary reading of *anything*, but no matter what you do it of, it will still be a *literary* reading, a reading that asks literary questions – about form, content, style, unity, dispersal, dissemination – and gets literary answers, answers that would be immediately recognizable and intelligible to those who had undergone a certain course of institutional training. I find it bizarre that so many people today think that by extending the techniques of literary analysis to government proclamations or diplomatic communiques or advertising copy you make criticism more political and more aware of its implication in extra-institutional matters; all you do (and it is nothing to sneer at) is expand the scope of the institution's activity, plant the flag of literary studies on more and more territory. The recent prominence of criticism that is militantly historicist and political is not a victory for politics and history, but for criticism which once again (and always in the nick of time) saves itself from being played out by invading and appropriating domains hitherto closed to it. The result (a happy one from the professional point of view) is that there are more ways to do the literary job, but all of the ways are equally literary. Kendrick thematizes politics and ideological class struggle; I thematize theology and theologically derived aesthetics. Neither of us is going to be answerable to Jim Merod's requirement that the critic's work "increase human agency, critical strength, and the possibility of justice within our economic and political system;"[14] the best we'll do is generate more readings, influence more readers, modify (but not break away from) the literary conversation, and by modifying it, keep it going.

Certainly neither of us is going to loosen the hold of entrenched and hegemonic ways of thought. This, you will recall, is the second claim of political or oppositional criticism and it is itself based on two assumptions, first the assumption that political criticism is *deeper* than criticism that stops short of political questions, and second the assumption that political criticism of the oppositional kind troubles and disrupts the conditions within which our work is routinely and mechanically done. The first assumption is false by the same reasoning that the first claim (that political criticism is political) is false: political criticism, whether of texts or of institutions themselves, is just one more variation in the literary game as it is currently played. You may study Jacobean tragedy under the rubrics and categories provided by Aristotle, or you may study Jacobean tragedy as a form complicit with (or subversive of) the policies of James I, or you may study Jacobean tragedy as an instance of criticism's recuperative and containing strategies, but whatever you do you will not have taken one step away from the confines of the literary institution, since the moment the institution *hears* you, it appropriates you by absorbing you into its structure of intelligibility. Just as political criticism is not political (except in the sense that it substitutes "politics talk" for, say, "genre talk" or "unity talk"), oppositional criticism is not oppositional; or rather it is oppositional only in an internal sense as younger critics look for arguments and methods by which they can be distinguished from the older practitioners they hope to replace. Here is a genuine (because institutional) politics in which both Kendrick and I are surely implicated, because it is a politics whose goal is to continually refurbish the profession by providing new materials and problems on which it can exercise itself. At a recent meeting of Milton scholars, James Turner spoke of himself as "hungry for a bit of the fresh meat of history." Turner's intentionally inelegant phrasing makes my point: it is the freshness of a performance not its status as "genuine" history or politics that is crucial. I am betting that readers will find my reading of *Areopagitica* as fresh as Kendrick's, as renewing of the energies that animate our enterprise; but whether I win or lose my bet, the attenuated and mediated relationship between literary activity and social and political change will not have been altered at all. What will have been altered is the social and political shape of the profession, or at least of one corner of it, and while that may strike many as being a consequence of little import, it is the only consequence any of us is ever likely to achieve.

This will be a distressing conclusion to those who, like Merod, complain that "the study of texts does not have an apparent or clearly delineated relation to anything other than further mastery of texts" (8). I confess that I can only hear that as a complaint that the business of literary studies continues to be literary. It is as if someone were to say that the trouble with the practice of medicine is that it continues to center on the diagnosis and treatment of sick people or that the trouble with engineers is that all they can think of is how to get things built. Let me emphasize that I am not suggesting that literary studies (or any other form of work) is an isolated, free-standing activity, without mutually constitutive affiliations with other activities. I know with everyone else these days that literature is socially constituted and that finally it cannot stand apart from the general conditions of intelligibility that underlie the various gestures – political, domestic, military, culinary – that find expression in a society. But once it has been acknowledged that the shape of literary studies is constituted and diacritical, that shape (that is, the present version of it) still remains, and someone who wants to do something literary will have to do it in accordance with (which is not to say in conformity with) the going notions of what literary activity is, even if it is his intention – destined never to be realized – to break away from those notions.

In making this argument I may have seemed to reinforce the notion of institutional life as enclosed, arid, and moribund. I may have been understood to be saying something like, "if you're looking for dynamism, innovation, and the opportunity to effect meaningful changes in our lives, you'd better get out of the academy and run for office, for all you are going to find here is more of the same." But in fact what I want to say is that "more of the same" includes everything that one might hope to find by going elsewhere or by turning literary studies into a "truly political" enterprise, includes, that is, connectedness, a field for social action and the opportunity to enrich the experience of others. The fact that Kendrick thematizes politics and I thematize theology indicates more than the ability of a conversation to sustain and extend itself; it indicates that for many the stakes in the conversation are high, that it matters to them whether Milton is seen as an antinomian (which is how I see him) or as an early agent-victim of the emerging corporate bureaucratic state (which is how Kendrick and Barker see him); it matters whether you tell a story that goes from Milton to

Derrida (my story) or from Milton to Terry Eagleton (their story). It matters in part because such issues are inseparable from others – the structure of the curriculum, the availability to modern students of older texts, the makeup of English departments, the question of whether there should continue to *be* English departments – and these issues, and others related to them, are central to the hopes, anxieties, and lifelong projects of a considerable number of men and women. One need only attend a fraction of the conferences and symposia mounted in any one year to realize how passionately committed the participants are to debating and exploring the questions that come before them. One need only attend a single session of the Milton Society of America's annual meeting to realize that for many Milton is living at this hour and that the manner of his living is a matter of deep concern indistinguishable from everything they hold dear and valuable, including not only their jobs (and who can be faulted for an investment in that?), but the nature of their workplace and the quality of the contribution they can make to their fellows and their students.

To all of this someone might reply, "that's just the trouble; these people you describe are all bound up in the petty world of the institution and never see beyond it to something larger." My answer to that is that there is nothing larger, that institutional life (of some kind or other) defines and exhausts the possibilities, but (and this is the crucial point) that those possibilities are rich and varied, and they are, in the only meaningful sense of the word, political. The distinction between institutional politics and "real" politics is a version of the tendency to transcendental thought that is so marked in intellectual life; in that thought the everyday routines of institutional practices are devalued and stigmatized as narrow, self-enclosed, hegemonic, self-serving, and contrasted to some other kind of practice in which parochial concerns are replaced by the concerns of the entire human community. What I am saying is that that other kind of practice does not exist, that the choice is not between institutional life and some other, but between different kinds of institutional life, and that in the strong sense it isn't even a choice, since we arrive at our institutional places through routes characterized by serendipity, luck (good and bad), the surprises and disappointments of education, etc. Once in those places we are implicated in a network of projects, problems, desiderata, goals, obstacles, rewards, punishments, in a world no less real than any other, a world in which there is scope enough for every action and aspiration that men and women can know. Despite what Coriolanus says, there is no world elsewhere, and the world we have, the world of the various institutional structures we inhabit (at least til our Master's second coming), is sufficient, is even brave and continually new.

Notes

1. John Illo, "The misreading of Milton," in *Radical Perspectives in the Arts*, ed. Lee Baxandall (Harmondsworth and Baltimore, 1972), 190, 189.
2. *Freedom of Expression: A Symposium Based on the Conference Called . . . To Commemorate the Tercentenary of the Publication of Milton's Areopagitica*, ed. Hermon Ould (1944; rpt Port Washington, 1970), 169.
3. Willmore Kendall, "How to read Milton's *Areopagitica*" (*Journal of Politics*, 22, 1960, 439–73).
4. Ernest Sirluck, "Introduction" to *Complete Prose Works of John Milton*, vol. II (New Haven, 1959).
5. John Milton, *The Tract for Liberty of Publication*, in *The Prose of John Milton*, ed. J. Max Patrick *et al.* (Garden City, 1967), 271–2. All references hereafter are to this text.
6. *Complete Prose Works of John Milton*, vol. I, ed. Don M. Wolfe (New Haven, 1953), 941, 949, 890.
7. *The Doctrine and Discipline of Divorce*, in *The Prose of John Milton*, ed. Patrick, 183, 184, 164, 162.
8. *Complete Prose Works of John Milton*, vol. VI, ed. Maurice Kelley (New Haven, 1973), 639.
9. *Complete Prose Works*, II.637.
10. See S. Fish, "The temptation to action in Milton's poetry" (*ELH*, 48, 3, Fall 1981, 516–31); and "Things and actions indifferent: the temptation of plot in *Paradise Regained*" (*Milton Studies*, 17, 1983, 163–85).
11. On its first appearance in the tract as a topic, truth is "compar'd in Scripture to a streaming fountain" (310). Even as it is introduced truth is twice removed, coming to us through the double mediation of writing (Scripture) and metaphor.
12. See on this point Henry Limouze, "'The surest suppressing': writer and censor in Milton's *Areopagitica*" (*The Centennial Review*, 24, 1 Winter 1980, *passim*. It is on the question of "inner constraints" that I part company with Francis Barker's powerful reading of the *Areopagitica* in his recent book, *The Tremulous Private Body: Essays in the Subjection* (London and New York, 1984). Barker takes issue, as I do, with the traditional characterization of Milton's tract as a major exhibit in the history of the achieving of "human freedom" (42); indeed he believes that Milton is an (unwitting) participant in the formation of an "emergent pattern of domination" (47) which "founds itself on a separation of realms between the public arena of the state apparatus and another domain of civil life" (46). Here, says Barker, "a new liberty is encoded, although it is but a negative one" since "the subject . . . may do as it pleases up to the point of transgression where its activity will be arrested by the agents of the apparatus who patrol the frontier between the two spaces." That is to say, the supposed freedom granted to the individual in this "modern settlement" is already compromised by a demarcation that excludes from his consideration (or meddling) the realm of public discourse. As a result the operations of the individual – the very shape of his thought and actions – are precisely circumscribed by the powers from whose interference he is supposedly free. "The state succeeds in penetrating to the very heart of the subject, or more accurately, in pre-constituting the subject as one which is already internally disciplined, censored, and thus an effective support of the emergent pattern of domination" (47). By psychologizing difference and conflict – making them the timeless attributes of a timeless self – the new order succeeds in quarantining the very energies that might subvert it. In a supremely political act, a realm of the

apolitical is created so that the agenda of the powers that be will be exempt from challenge by a domesticated and "free" self.

However accurate this may be as an account of a shift in the conceiving (and therefore the production) of the relationship between self and state – and I for one find it compelling – it will not do I think as an account of Milton or the *Areopagitica*. The separatist position with which Barker would saddle Milton belongs more properly to (for example) Roger Williams who in *The Bloudy Tenet of Persecution* (1652) and other texts does in fact argue for a strict distinction between the realms of nature and grace and for the restriction of the magistrate's power to matters of civil peace. Milton, however, finds such a distinction unacceptable because it would mean that whole areas of one's everyday life would be exempt from the obligation to be ever doing the will of God, as dictated by the light of conscience. It is just such a separatist accommodation that Milton satirizes in the figure of the man who gives over his religion to some "factor" so that he can sit comfortably in his shop "trading all day" (312) free from the pressures of spiritual duty. This for Milton is a travesty of the doctrine of Christian Liberty which while it releases believers from the external constraints of "human judgments" and "civil decrees" puts them under the even severer constraints imposed by the injunction to obey the law of Love: "So far from a less degree of perfection being exacted from Christians, it is expected of them that they should be more perfect than those who were under the law. . . . The only difference is that Moses imposed the letter or external law . . . whereas Christ writes the inward law of God by his spirit on the heart of believers, and leads them as willing followers" (*Christian Doctrine*, in *The Student's Milton*, 1027). Thus led, they follow not at this or that moment, but at *every* moment, with the result that their every action – in prayer, in the shop, at home, in public – is an expression of a perpetual and unrelenting commitment. Rather than being segregated from one another, the realms of the political and the private form an unbroken continuum united by the overriding obligation to be faithful to an unwritten but always-in-force law. The result, as Barker observes, is an extraordinary (because unrelenting) "inner discipline" (47), but far from being in the service of the state, it is a discipline that threatens to subvert the state (as it will in 1649) because in the event of a clash between what it demands and what the state would compel, the state will always be the loser. Moreover, since it is a discipline that is never relaxed, it extends to every aspect of daily life. When Milton points out that the logic of licensing would finally mean the extension of control to styles of dress, dance, music, he does not, as Barker would have it, contemplate this prospect with "horror" (48); what horrifies him is the mistake of thinking that such control can be exercised from the outside; what he himself envisions is the same control exercised from the inside by a censor whose strictness is an expression of the commitment that founds his being. Milton, in short, is much more revolutionary than Barker takes him to be: rather than encysting the self in a sanctuary of illusory privacy, he imagines the self as always open to the transforming actions to which its vision calls it, actions that will also transform the material reality in which it operates. If this seems unconvincing, just ask Charles I.

13. Christopher Kendrick, *Milton: A Study in Ideology and Form* (New York and London, 1986).
14. Jim Merod, *The Political Responsibility of the Critic* (Ithaca, 1987), 174.

IV
Re-memberings

12

DAVID RIEDE

Blake's *Milton*: on membership in the Church Paul

Perhaps no poet has responded to the works of another in fuller, more complex, and more radically revisionary ways than William Blake responded to the writings of John Milton. Throughout his career, Blake continually returned to Milton, from his critical attack in *The Marriage of Heaven and Hell* to his usurpation of the Miltonic sublime in *Milton* and the other prophetic writings. Blake's response to Milton's influence has been much discussed by theorists of literary tradition and poetic influence, but as Blake said of the Judeo-Christian tradition, "this history has been adopted by both parties."[1] For Harold Bloom it magnificently illustrates a theory about anxiety and discontinuity in the tradition of "strong poets," while for Joseph Anthony Wittreich it demonstrates confidence and continuity in the "Miltonic tradition," the "line of vision."[2] Such opposed positions might seem to be the very stuff of Blakean mental warfare, but they have not produced a very informative debate. Wittreich, dismissive of Bloom's position, has continued as the spokesman for a relatively unproblematic Miltonic and Blakean tradition of prophecy, and Bloom, disdainful of explanation, has declined to argue his position in any detail. In fact, Bloom's psychoanalytic model for the transmission of the tradition continues to romanticize the unconscious as a realm of imaginative inspiration. I would like to propose a reading that supports some of Bloom's views about combative reading, but without the Bloomian apparatus of strong fathers and strong sons. My reading will call into question the whole idea of a "line of vision" by rejecting such fundamental romantic mystifications as "inspiration" and "vision." Blake himself established the terms for his romantic critics by insisting on the authority of his inspiration, the truth of his vision, but I will argue that his own accounts of that inspiration in

Milton undermine themselves and subvert the very idea of authoritative inspiration. A close look at his oddly neglected account of precisely how Milton's spirit entered into him and at his parody of Milton's invocation of the muse in *Paradise Lost* will reveal that side by side with Blake's suggested "line of vision" are not quite compatible signs of a very different tradition descending from St Paul. Drawing out the neglected threads of Pauline allusion in *Milton* leads, I think, to a fresh perspective on Blake and on the idea of a Miltonic tradition. I will suggest in particular that the very idea of "visionary" poetry ought to be looked at more critically than it usually has been, and that we may need to reconsider the received doctrine concerning a "line of vision" descending from John of Patmos through Milton and Blake. It may be that Milton and Blake must be understood instead in a "line of reading" descending from St Paul.

Blake's analysis of Milton's accomplishment involves, most obviously, a radical critique of Milton's Puritan (and essentially Pauline) Christianity, and consequently of the idea of Christian inspiration that enabled Milton to write with dogmatic authority by transcribing the word of God. As Blake saw it, such a claim for inspiration made Milton akin to Moses, not as a prophet, but as the founder of an absolute and tyrannical moral law. To attack this monolithic authority, Blake associated it not only with Moses but with the equally authoritarian teachings of the "Church Paul," the morally repressive institution of Christianity. In Blake's subtle and complex analysis, however, the Church Paul is not to be confused with the St Paul who wrote the epistles. Rather it represents the hardening of Paul's discourse into dogmatic authority by passive, obedient readers who take the letter as law. Blake had earlier associated Milton with the doctrines of the Church Paul – in *The Four Zoas* his list of the fallen sons of prophecy ends with "Paul Constantine Charlemaine Luther Milton" (pl. 115, l.6). Milton's acceptance of a vast gulf between human and divine, which Blake associates with the Church Paul, is attacked already in *The Marriage of Heaven and Hell*; there, Blake criticizes *Paradise Lost* for accepting and promulgating the "Pauline" doctrine "That Man has two real existing principles Viz: a Body & a Soul" (pl. 4) and that the body, representing energy and inspiration, must be chastened to elevate the soul, a repressive moral governor.

Paul can become the "Church Paul" and Milton can become the "Church Milton" if their fierce writings are not encountered by fierce readers. Part of Blake's argument in *Milton* will be that too much deference to a writer's claimed inspiration, or authority, will result in reducing that author to a "church," a mere codifier of repressive moral laws. Blake associates Milton with Paul, however, not merely to attack the false authority of the Miltonic "vision," but also to redeem a new kind of Miltonic and Pauline sublime. Both Milton and Paul are to be admired not as prophets uttering the authoritative word of God, but as combative readers who shattered and usurped the authority of earlier prophets. Paul's transformative typological readings of the Old Testament and Milton's combative utterances in *Areopagitica* become models for a Blakean mode of mental warfare that replaces the divinely authoritative voice of *Paradise Lost* with a contentious heteroglossia in which Blake, Milton, and Paul contend with and against one another, with and against the myriad voices of the living Judeo-Christian tradition. Such a view, of course, supports Bloom's idea of Blake as a strong reader who wrestles with Milton's works in a radically revisionary way, and even supports Wittreich's sense of Blake's confidence in the continuity of a tradition, but it removes the notion that transcendent vision and authoritative prophecy necessarily privilege *the* tradition. In a sense, Blake attempts to replace the univocal Miltonic sublime with a kind of dialogic sublime of spiritual strife in which *vision* is always combative *revision*. As we shall see, however, Blake himself runs into difficulty when he attempts to transcend this sublime combat, to meld dissonance into visionary, inspired, and therefore authoritative univocity – as if the tumult of his Babel were actually an inspired speaking in tongues.

The famous lyric that introduces *Milton* significantly summons the combative, revolutionary Milton of *Areopagitica* rather than what Blake saw as the authoritarian author of *Paradise Lost*:

> And did those feet in ancient time,
> Walk upon Englands mountains green:
> And was the holy Lamb of God,
> On Englands pleasant pastures seen!
> . . . .
> I will not cease from Mental Fight,
> Nor shall my Sword sleep in my hand:
> Till we have built Jerusalem,
> In Englands green & pleasant Land.

Would to God that all the Lords people were Prophets.
Numbers XI. ch. 29 v.

The motto, as has often been noted, refers not only to the Bible but also to Milton's defense of "Mental Fight," of "sects and schisms" in *Areopagitica*: "For now the time seems come, wherein Moses, the great prophet, may sit in heaven rejoicing to see that memorable and glorious wish of his fulfilled, when not only our seventy elders, but all the Lord's people, are become prophets." But what has not generally been noted is how fully the surrounding discussion in *Areopagitica* anticipates the symbolism of Blake's major prophecies.[3] Working within the typological traditions of Puritanism, Milton precedes Blake in equating Sion, or Jerusalem, with England's green and pleasant land, and the symbolic rebuilding of the temple with the establishment of Truth. And most important, he anticipates Blake in his adoption of the Pauline body of Christ imagery. Milton's famous description of the body of Christ as the "perfect shape" of Truth, of its mutilation and gradual restoration by the "sad friends of Truth," is recapitulated in Blake's central epic symbol of the "Human Imagination/ Which is the Divine Body of the Lord Jesus" (*Milton*, pl.3). Further, Blake's dormant Albion, a figure whose awakening will symbolize the spiritual awakening of the nation, is prefigured in Milton's ostentatiously "visionary" prophecy: "Methinks I see in my mind a noble and puissant nation rousing herself like a strong man after sleep, and shaking her invincible locks."[4]

The presence of *Areopagitica* in the background of Blake's *Milton* is not surprising. *Areopagitica* was written in response to Parliament's licensing ordinance, which threatened to silence dissent from received opinion and put an end to mental combat, and Blake's *Milton* was written, in part, for similar reasons. Under the patronage of William Hayley, Blake was being strongly urged to make money, not war, with art. Hayley pressured him to paint fashionable miniatures instead of writing and illustrating revolutionary epics. Blake was to conform to conventions as an artist, to stifle his inspiration, and silence his imagination. Consequently *Milton*, the epic Blake wrote in response to this pressure, quite naturally draws on Milton's proclamations of mental warfare. Perhaps inevitably Blake's particular debt to *Areopagitica* led him to adopt the stance of a combative writer with whom he is rarely associated. Milton's Biblical authority in defence of free expression is, more than anyone else, the pugnacious St Paul – Milton repeatedly alludes to Pauline doctrines of charity and restraint from judging one another in his defence of "this Christian liberty which Paul so often boasts of."[5] It is with this combative Paul, and combative Milton, that Blake aligns himself in *Milton*.

Blake scorned the "Church Paul," but the embattled apostle was, with Milton, a major influence on his epics about influence and inspiration. His comments about the composition of *The Four Zoas* and *Milton* reflect his sense of a joint Pauline/Miltonic idea of inspiration, and passages from *Milton* demonstrate a curious conflation of Paul and Milton as the very sources of Blake's own inspiration. In an 1803 letter to Butts, Blake described his inspiration for the nearly completed *The Four Zoas* and *Milton* (evidently still meant to be integrated into one poem): "I have written this Poem from immediate Dictation twelve or sometimes twenty or thirty lines at a time without Premeditation & even against my Will."[6] The passage plainly echoes Milton's inspiration by his "Celestial Patroness" who "dictates to me slumb'ring, or inspires/Easy my unpremeditated Verse" (*PL* IX.21–4). Although Blake's comments to Butts cannot be taken at face value, the statement certainly seems to indicate that Blake was at this point disposed to accept a Miltonic notion of inspiration. Nevertheless, the phrase "even against my Will" may suggest some reservations about such a notion, since it indicates that the author lacks control over his own imagination, is unable to combat successfully the imposition of an authoritarian will beyond his own. The desire to avoid such passivity is apparent in the motto prefixed to *The Four Zoas*. The motto, from Paul's Epistle to the Ephesians, reveals Blake's identification with the apostle's commitment to spiritual combat:

> For we wrestle not against flesh and blood, but against principalities, against powers, against the rulers of the darkness of this world, against spiritual wickedness in high places. (Eph. 6.12)

In *Milton* the Pauline reference is subtler, but is of fundamental importance because it directly links Blake, Milton, and Paul. The crucial passage describes Milton's descent from Eternity back into time and space to be incorporated in Blake:

> Then first I saw him in the Zenith as a falling star,
> Descending perpendicular, swift as the swallow or swift;
> And on my left foot falling on the tarsus, enterd there;
> But from my left foot a black cloud redounding spread over Europe.
>
> (pl.15, ll.47–50)

The passage is, to say the least, peculiar, but it would seem to conflate the entrance of Milton into Blake with the dramatic conversion of Saul of Tarsus on the road to Damascus (Acts 9:1–18).[7] Indeed, though this has not been previously noted, the startling image was very likely influenced by a passage in Milton's *The Reason of Church-Government* in which Blake would have seen his struggle of contraries and the Miltonic warfare of "sects and schisms" conflated with the sudden conversion of St Paul:

> For if we look but on the nature of elementall and mixt things, we know they cannot suffer any change of one kind, or quality into another without the struggl of contrarieties. And in things artificiall, seldome any elegance is wrought without a superfluous wast and refuse in the transaction. No Marble statue can be politely carv'd, no fair edifice built without almost as much rubbish and sweeping. Insomuch that even in the spirituall conflict of S. *Pauls* conversion there fell scales from his eyes that were not perceav'd before.[8]

Blake's almost ludicrous pun on "tarsus" as the locus of conversion and of the convergence of visionary poets is so bizarre that it seems to open an ironic gap between Milton and Blake even as it brings the two poets together. The peculiar anatomical precision is sufficiently explained by the pun on "tarsus," but Blake may also be punning on yet another meaning of the word, for "tarsus" means not only sole, but also the "rim of the eyelid" (*OED*), perhaps here the corporeal scales that prevent spiritual vision. The conversion of Saul of Tarsus to St Paul, of the vehement defender of Jewish law to the Apostle of Jesus Christ, is the type for both Milton and Blake of the triumph of spiritual warfare, both emphasizing the rubbish and debris of false vision that must be swept away. Blake's extraordinarily complex pun may, however, imply that Milton himself failed to recognize the hardening of the Church Paul into scales, a hindrance to vision.

The rubbish in Milton's vision is evident in the "black cloud" that "redounding spread over Europe" when Milton entered into Blake. It is the same as the rubbish in Saul's (and Paul's) vision, a continued adherence to the old law that Jesus had come to sweep away. The "black cloud" is Milton's spectre, or selfhood, identified throughout the poem with Satan, who "is Urizen" (pl.10, l.1), the Miltonic God of "Moral laws and cruel punishments" (pl.9, l.22) who perverts the "Divine voice in its entrance to the earth" (pl.9, l.23). When the "black cloud" becomes "the Cherub on Sinai" (pl.20, l.23), moreover, it emphatically associates Milton with Paul, for the "Covering Cherub" is both "Miltons Shadow" (pl.37, l.44) and, in part, the "Church Paul." Both Paul and Milton are associated with the repressive moral law that blocks imaginative vision, for it is the Covering Cherub who prevents the return to Eden with a flaming sword (notably at the end of *Paradise Lost*) and who adorns the curtains of the ark to prevent vision of the divine presence.

Blake's criticism of his predecessor's inspiration in *Milton* is essentially a repudiation of his dualistic separation of human and divine, his denial of human energy and imagination as he attempted to find inspiration from a far removed, non-human, law-giving God. In fact, *Milton* significantly locates Milton's "Spectrous body" on Horeb and Sinai (pl.20, ll.20–3), thereby mocking the inadequacies of Milton's sources of inspiration in an ironic allusion to the invocation of *Paradise Lost*:

> Sing Heav'nly Muse, that on the secret top
> Of *Oreb*, or of *Sinai*, didst inspire
> That Shepherd.
>
> (I.6–8)

It is true that Milton goes on to seek the spiritual inspiration of the New Testament as well, but Blake is concerned to point out an excessive emphasis in *Paradise Lost* on a religion of secrecy ("the secret top"), a hidden God, and a repressive Mosaic law. Immediately after Milton's descent into Blake's tarsus, the real sources of Milton's inspiration are described from a Blakean perspective. Milton is another Moses in the desert, writing on the "iron tablets" that Blake always associates with the ten commandments and the restraints of religion. Further, taking dictation from God and dictating in turn to his "Wives & Daughters," Milton becomes so hardened in his repressive, patriarchal character that "his body was the Rock Sinai" (pl.17, ll.9–14). Blake says in "The Song of Los" that "Moses beheld upon Mount Sinai forms of dark delusion," and in "The Book of Ahania" he says that "Mount Sinai, in Arabia" is a poisoned rock used by

Urizen to slay a Christ-like figure and to become the source of a religion of mystery and a "book of iron."

The phrase "Mount Sinai, in Arabia," a reference not to the Old Testament but to the New, begins to suggest how in Blake's view a different way of reading the New Testament might have redeemed Milton from the bondage of the old law. The phrase occurs in Paul's Epistle to the Galatians, in a passage that became the basis of St Augustine's, and Blake's, typological vision of the eternal City:[9]

> Tell me, ye that desire to be under the law, do ye not hear the law? For it is written, that Abraham had two sons, the one by a bondmaid, the other by a freewoman. But he who was of the bondwoman was born after the flesh; but he of the freewoman was by promise. Which things are an allegory: for these are the two covenants; the one from the mount Sinai, which gendereth to bondage, which is Agar. For this Agar is mount Sinai in Arabia, and answereth to Jerusalem which now is, and is in bondage with her children. But Jerusalem which is above is free, which is the mother of us all. . . . Now we, brethren, as Isaac was, are the children of promise.
>
> (Gal. 4:21–6, 28)

Like Paul, Milton read the Old Testament typologically, and saw that it prefigures its fulfillment in the New, but for Blake Milton's reading was not radical enough. Milton did not free himself from the bondage of the law because, like Paul, he continued to see the human condition in terms of separation from a transcendent kingdom that is inaccessibly above ("Jerusalem which is above") and in terms of an indefinite period of waiting for the fulfillment of "promise," in which, at last, Jesus will

> bring back
> Through the world's wilderness long wander'd man
> Safe to eternal Paradise of rest.
>
> (*PL* XII.312–14)

But although Milton interpreted the Old Testament typologically, in Blake's view he read the New Testament "in the letter." Consequently he accepted as law the Pauline distinction between Flesh and Spirit, and therefore perpetuated the religion of fear (though "filial" now rather than "servile" (*PL* XII.305–6)). Blake, in contrast, read both books typologically, or "in the spirit," rather than passively submitting to their literal authority. As Blake read the passage from Paul, the new Jerusalem is here and now if we have the imaginative vision to see it, and it frees us from bondage to the vegetative natural world, from natural law. For him the basic failure in Milton's vision was his acceptance of a dualistic universe in which God is above and eternal and humanity is below, wandering in time under conditions of enforced obedience, humility, chastity and, especially, patience in order to await the eventual fulfillment of the promise. This dualism has everything to do with Milton's limitations as a visionary poet because his assumption that inspired poetry is dictated from a divine source outside of humanity separates inspiration from imagination, which is Jesus Christ – the Eternal Human Form Divine. For Blake, Milton's poetry is too much a wandering and a waiting for vision, rather than an imaginative re-visioning of earlier texts. The most important single lesson that Milton can learn is to "Seek not thy heavenly father then beyond the skies" (pl.20, ll.31–2), and the first step he must take to be redeemed in Blake's poem is to engage in spiritual warfare by breaking the covenant: "He took off the robe of the promise, & ungirded himself from the oath of God" (pl.14, l.13). Blake's revision of Milton, then, uses Pauline typology to attack Pauline and Puritan dualism, the separation of spirit and flesh, God and humanity, inspiration and imagination. In order to combat the Church Paul in Milton, Blake simply reads Milton as Paul read the Old Testament.

The full complexity of Blake's response to Milton's peculiarly Pauline inspiration is implicit in the densely cryptic invocation to *Milton*. Blake's invocation is in some ways a parodic revision of Milton's invocation in *Paradise Lost*, and is consequently a critique of Milton's inspiration. The most crucial, and most obvious difference between Blake's and Milton's invocations is that Blake fully internalizes the muses:

> Daughters of Beulah! Muses who inspire the Poets Song
> Record the journey of immortal Milton thro' your Realms
> Of terror & mild moony lustre, in soft sexual delusions
> Of varied beauty, to delight the wanderer and repose
> His burning thirst & freezing hunger! Come into my hand
> By your mild power; descending down the Nerves of my right arm
> From out the Portals of my Brain, where by your ministry
> The Eternal Great Humanity Divine. planted his Paradise,
> And in it caus'd the Spectres of the Dead to take sweet forms
> In likeness of himself.
>
> (pl.2, ll.1–10)

Unlike Milton, who seemed to Blake to seek inspiration from a God beyond the skies, Blake seeks it in his own imagination, which is the "Eternal Great Humanity Divine." The invocation, then, does not simply place Blake in a "line of vision" with Milton, but establishes a wholly new idea of the imagination to displace the earlier poet's profound – and significantly Pauline – distrust of the imagination.

The tendency of modern romantic criticism has been to gloss over this obvious distinction between a Blakean and a Miltonic sublime by obscuring Milton's very un-Blakean antagonism to imagination. Wittreich, for example, attempts to illustrate Milton's commitment to a Blakean mental warfare with a quotation from *The Reason of Church-Government* that describes a "warfare, not carnall, but mighty through God to the pulling down of strong holds, casting down imaginations, and every high thing that exalteth it selfe against the knowledge of God." Wittreich does not note, however, that the passage is a direct quotation from St Paul, and that it is plainly an attack on the unaided imagination, on spiritual pride.[10] For Milton (and Paul) divine inspiration made one "mighty through God," and was therefore radically different from idolatrous "imaginations." As we know from Eve's dream, imagination is the province of the toad-like Satan, who assays "his Devilish art to reach/The Organs of her Fancy" (*PL* IV.801–2). For Milton, inspiration and imagination are not only different from one another, but are opposed in mutual warfare. The one is of God, the other of Satan.

Blake regarded Milton's Pauline separation of the "carnall" and the spiritual as the root of his error. For Blake, body and soul must be one; imagination must be incarnate. Consequently he attempts to redeem his predecessor's inspiration by summoning female muses. In *Jerusalem* Blake directly invokes the Divine Humanity within himself, his own imagination, but in *Milton* he calls upon the sexual "Daughters of Beulah" because it is they who are missing from Milton's vision. Milton had utterly rejected his fallen sexual nature, but now he must be redeemed by passing through the sexually liberated, female land of Beulah. Though the female sexuality he will experience there will lead him into "soft sexual delusions," it will destroy his worse delusion that spiritual inspiration comes from subjugating the "carnall" imagination. The sexual nature, though not an end in itself, is a source of creative energy that Milton had repressed, but that ought to minister to the higher powers of the imagination. In other words, Blake's Milton must recognize that true inspiration comes not from subduing the flesh to the spirit and taking dictation from a distant God, but from accepting the creative energies of the senses as a part of the Eternal Great Humanity Divine.

Because Milton must be separated from the false inspiration that misled him, Blake's invocation asks the Daughters of Beulah to "Tell also of the False Tongue! vegetated/Beneath your land of shadows" (pl.2, ll.10–11). The False Tongue is Blake's Satan (pl.27, ll.45–6) but Milton's God, the source of a religion that sacrifices even Jesus, the Divine Imagination, to its fallen and corrupt moral laws. The "False Tongue" that Milton mistook for inspiration is the lying tempter who perverts and frustrates moral vision. As the poem proceeds, Blake's characterization of this vegetated tongue shows what is wrong with Milton's inspiration, and exposes much that is false in visionary language. It is the fleshly tongue of fallen nature that, perceived as separate from the realm of spirit, can speak only in the terms of the law that abases the flesh to exalt the spirit:

> The Tongue a little moisture fills, a little food it cloys

A little sound it utters & its cries are faintly heard
Then brings forth Moral Virtue.

(pl.5, ll.25–7)

The vegetable tongue can only speak of its incapacity to speak spiritual truths: "Can such a Tongue boast of the living waters?" (pl.5, l.34). Consequently the immediate effect on Blake as Milton enters into his foot and his "Spectrous body" redounds over his sources of inspiration on Horeb and Sinai is to make him doubt the ability of his tongue to speak:

O how can I with my gross tongue that cleaveth to the dust,
Tell of the Four-fold Man, in starry numbers fitly orderd
Or how can I with my cold hand of clay! But thou O Lord
Do with me as thou wilt! for I am nothing, and vanity.
If thou chuse to elect a worm, it shall remove the mountains.

(pl.20, ll.15–19)

The lines parody Milton's view, frequently reiterated in *Paradise Lost*, that human (or even angelic) speech cannot adequately describe the works of the Almighty. As even the angelic chorus sings: "what thought can measure thee or tongue/Relate thee?" (VII.603–4). The limitations of language reflect, in Raphael's words, the mortal limits of "Human imagination" separated by an infinite distance from the "highth/Of Godlike Power" (VI.300–1). To Blake the idea that human faculties are incapable of divine utterance only reflects the Pauline belief that humanity is merely natural or vegetative. And fallen humanity is just that; it is the slain "Human Imagination . . . the Divine Body of the Lord Jesus" deformed by jealousy and Urizenic "doubt & reasoning" until the imagination is confined to a "stony hard" skull, the eyes are rolled into "two little Orbs & closed in two little Caves," the ears are "petrified" in spiraling "close volutions," and the tongue is a mere organ of natural appetite, "a Tongue of hunger & thirst" (pl.3, ll.1–23). The fragmentation of the speaker's being into the various bodily parts re-enacts the dismemberment of Truth or Christ described in *Areopagitica*, but Blake's point is that the unified body of Truth, the "Four-fold Man," is only perceived as fragmented by those who see themselves as fragments, as assemblages of various members. The fragmented consciousness results in "Differences between Ideas, that Ideas themselves, (which are/The Divine Members) may be slain in offerings for sin" (pl.35, ll.5–6), as Christ was. The disjointed carnal senses are of course incapable of imaginative perception, of perceiving the Divine Body as whole. The vegetated body is, Florence Sandler points out, the "body of this death" that St Paul prays to be delivered from (Rom. 7:24),[11] but it is also the "fleshly tabernacle" with which the Church Paul obscures the divine vision. One of Milton's first utterances in *Milton* assimilates him to the Pauline sense of entrapment within this body:

When will the Resurrection come; to deliver the sleeping body
From corruptibility: O when Lord Jesus wilt thou come?

(pl.14, ll.17–18)

But Milton – like Paul – remains entrapped within the body of death because he believes himself helpless and utterly dependent upon God for his release. Because he passively accepts the vegetative, shrunken state of his senses, he is incapable of the imaginative vision that would be, in fact, the savior he awaits, Jesus Christ.

Blake saw that at the heart of Milton's concern about the limitations of language is his sense of the vast gulf between a God who is outside of time and a language that must move sequentially in time. The need for language to unfold itself in time is the basis of Raphael's comment on the inadequacy of human speech or comprehension to understand God's timelessness:

> Immediate are the Acts of God, more swift
> Than time or motion, but to human ears
> Cannot without process of speech be told,
> So told as earthly notion can receive.

(*PL* VII.176–9)

Blake, of course, denied that God is inexpressibly other than man, but more specifically he denied that human speech and comprehension are trapped in time. For Blake, after all, it is only the dualistic corporealization of the body that reduces the receptiveness of the spirit to the "petrified close volutions of the ears." Similarly, "process of speech," trapped in time, is the function of the "gross tongue." Indeed, the *disjecta membra* of the Pauline body of death are paradoxically incapable of following the Pauline injunction to understand the matter-moulded forms of speech in the spirit, not in the letter. Milton's – or Raphael's – idea that comprehension is necessarily confined to narrative "process of speech" must have struck him as one more consequence of the deluded belief constantly reiterated in *Paradise Lost* that mankind, fallen into materiality, is exiled from eternity and so must learn to wait meekly and patiently in time.

Blake's impatience with Milton's patience emerges fully, if cryptically, in the final part of his invocation, a direct parody of various passages in *Paradise Lost*:

> Say first! what mov'd Milton, who walkd about in Eternity
> One hundred years, pondring the intricate mazes of Providence
> Unhappy tho in heav'n, he obey'd, he murmur'd not. he was silent
> Viewing his Sixfold Emanation scatter'd thro' the deep
> In torment! To go into the deep her to redeem & himself perish?
> What cause at length mov'd Milton to this unexampled deed?
> A Bards prophetic Song!

(pl.2, ll.16–22)

The most obvious target of these lines is the second part of Milton's opening invocation:

> Say first, for Heav'n hides nothing from thy view
> Nor the deep Tract of Hell, say first what cause
> Mov'd our Grand Parents in that happy State,
> Favor'd of Heav'n so highly, to fall off
> From thir Creator, and transgress his Will
> For one restraint, Lords of the World besides?
> Who first seduc't them to that foul revolt?
> Th'infernal Serpent;
>
> (PL I.27–34)

Blake ironically parallels Milton with Adam and Eve to contrast their aboriginal "happy State" with his unhappiness in the false heaven of his religious vision. Adam and Eve, however, were happy as long as they obeyed God, while Milton is unhappy even though "he obey'd, he murmur'd not. he was silent." From the start Blake's theme is that passive, obedient acceptance of restraint by a mysterious Providence is inimical to imaginative vision and prophetic utterance. Appropriately, the parallel invocations also equate the tempter of Adam and Eve, "Th'infernal Serpent," with the tempter of Milton, "A Bards prophetic Song!" The point is not far different from that made in *The Marriage of Heaven and Hell* – the true bard in Milton is in Milton's sense "Satanic," but in Blake's he represents the "true Poet." Milton was tempted to his "unexampled deed," by a creative impulse antithetical to quiet obedience – and the "unexampled deed," of course, is his departure from the false heaven to rewrite the cosmic scheme of *Paradise Lost*: "Things [still] unattempted yet in Prose or Rhyme."

Blake's lines mock Miltonic patience not only in the invocation to *Paradise Lost* but in other passages as well. Milton asks "what cause/Mov'd our Grand Parents ... Who first seduc't them ...?" but Blake adds a note of impatience: "what mov'd Milton . . . What cause at length mov'd Milton. . .?" The addition of "at length" implies that Milton has been rather slow, but it also echoes a later passage from *Paradise Lost* to show the source of his hesitation in his belief that Providence decrees the role of humanity to be an indefinite waiting in a vegetative state until

> by degrees of merit rais'd
> They open to themselves at length the way
> Up hither, under long obedience tri'd,
> And Earth be chang'd to Heav'n, and Heav'n to Earth,
> One Kingdom, Joy and Union without end.
>
> (VII.157–61)

The apocalyptic union projected in these lines is admirable, but from Blake's perspective it should take place here and now, in the human imagination, not in the indefinite future and beyond the skies. Milton's patient "long obedience" merely forestalls imaginative apocalypse, rather than bringing it about. Like the devils in Hell, whose discussion of Providence finds "no end, in wand'ring mazes lost" (*PL* II.561), Milton in heaven can only endlessly ponder "the intricate mazes of Providence."

Milton's heaven is a hell because it retains the notion of a separation between the human and the divine. Milton, in heaven, is still separated from his essential humanity, his imagination. Blake's invocation strongly implies that Milton's vision failed because his imitation of a patriarchal sky-god destroyed his human integrity, separating a masculine soul from feminine senses. Milton is "Unhappy tho in heav'n" because he has destroyed his senses by casting out female sexuality. He is separated from his "Sixfold Emanation" which is "scatter'd thro' the deep/In torment." As Blake sees it, Milton's false heaven is an illusion that mires humanity more deeply in the corrupt senses simply by insisting on their corruption. The false heaven is created by a maiming of the integrated human imagination, a dismembering of the Divine Body that splits it into repressive male and thwarted female fragments. As Blake saw it, Milton's misogynistic, literally dictatorial, treatment of his wives and daughters reflected his own divided nature. The Sixfold Emanation, in fact, represents the three wives and three daughters who "wrote in thunder smoke and fire/His dictate" (pl.17, ll.13–14). It is this dictatorial Milton who "was the Rock Sinai" of the Church Paul, and who therefore also represents the Pauline body of death: "his body was the Rock Sinai; that body,/Which was on earth born to corruption" (pl.17, ll.14–15). Dictating law to a subjugated female will, Milton covers over the divine vision of Jesus, thus re-enacting the tyranny of the leprous Jehovah, whose stony law created the "Body of Death . . ./Around the Lamb, a Female Tabernacle" (pl.13, ll.25–6). Evidently Milton's unredeemed emanation is also a "Body of Death," a repressive church of Paul and other patriarchs, a "Female Tabernacle:"

A Male within a Female hid as in an Ark & Curtains,
Abraham, Moses, Solomon, Paul, Constantine, Charlemaine
Luther, these seven are the Male-Females, the Dragon Forms
Religion hid in War, a Dragon red & hidden Harlot
All these are seen in Miltons Shadow who is the Covering Cherub.
(pl.37, ll.40–4)

To put the matter simply, by dictating law to a subordinate female will, Milton becomes just another patriarch, and his writings just another church. The unredeemed Shadowy Female, indeed, declares that she

will have Writings written all over [her garments] in Human Words
That every Infant that is born upon the Earth shall read
And get by rote as a hard task of a life of sixty years.
(pl.18, ll.12–14)

As soon as he "took off the robe of the promise, & ungirded himself from the oath of God," Milton recognized that his unredeemed emanation was "the daughters of memory, & not . . . the daughters of inspiration" (pl.14, ll.28–9). As his Preface to *Milton* makes clear, Blake's intention is to bring about a "New Age" in which "the Daughters of Memory shall become the Daughters of Inspiration" (pl.1), so in the invocation he indicates that Milton's vision can only be salvaged if Milton goes "into the deep . . . to redeem" his emanation, to replace remembered law with imaginative inspiration.

The historical Milton, the revolutionary iconoclast, had claimed that his inspiration would not come from "Dame Memory and her Siren Daughters, but by devout prayer to that eternall Spirit who can enrich with all utterance and knowledge."[12] To Blake, however, Milton's devout prayer to a remote law-giver was quite insufficiently revolutionary. It left Milton still constrained by the traditional authority most closely associated with the Church Paul, able only to *remember* past utterances, not to *redeem* them in the present as living, contentious, perhaps fallible voices that could be engaged in the spiritual warfare of the revisionary imagination. Though Milton had read the Old Testament creatively, he had made a church of the New Testament, and of his own writings. In the prescribed Pauline manner, he read the Old Testament in the spirit, but he read the New in the letter, and so remained a slave to law – remembering, not creating.

But as Blakean commentators point out, Blake's objections are not to Milton, but to Milton's Shadow, the Covering Cherub described by Bloom: "that something that makes men victims and not poets, a demon of discursiveness and shady continuities, a pseudo-exegete who makes writings into Scriptures."[13] Blake's purpose, and the character Milton's purpose, is to cast off this shadow, to annihilate it and so redeem Milton's inspiration, his genuine poetic genius. To do this Milton must redeem his emanation, and at the end of the poem he succeeds in separating his true emanation from the "Six-fold Miltonic Female" who destroys

> Imagination;
> By imitation of Natures Images drawn from Remembrance
> These are the Sexual Garments, the Abomination of Desolation
> Hiding the Human Lineaments as with an Ark & Curtains.
>
> (pl.41, ll.23–6)

The Daughters of Memory are replaced by "Ololon," a Daughter of Beulah. Since the Daughters of Beulah are Blake's own muses in *Milton*, it would seem that Blake has made Milton's redeemed inspiration his own. The difficulty, however, is that in a sense one veil over the Divine Vision is only replaced with another as Ololon descends over the "One Man Jesus the Saviour:"

> round his limbs
> The Clouds of Ololon folded as a Garment dipped in blood
> Written within & without in woven letters: & the Writing
> Is the Divine Revelation in the Litteral expression:
> A Garment of War, I heard it namd the Woof of Six Thousand Years.
>
> (pl.42, ll.11–15)

The "Divine Revelation" appears, but not as vision. It appears only in writing, not in the spirit, but in the letter, the "Litteral expression." What is saved, in the end, is not a fully liberated visionary imagination, but the combative words that both conceal and somehow protect the imagination, words that are a "Garment of War." For Blake, as for Milton, inspiration must come from the six thousand years of human writing, and must therefore depend on the contentious *reading* of fallible writings, not the *vision* of immortal truths. To some extent, at least, the muses must be the Daughters of Memory.

Blake, however, resisted accepting these implications about the impossibility of authoritative inspiration and genuinely visionary poetry, and his resistance drew him into a dualism as disturbingly sexist as that he attempted to rectify in Milton. His feminine muses can supply him with the "Litteral expression," but that expression conceals more than it reveals of the purely masculine imagination that is, unfortunately, quite inexpressible, quite beyond the realm of a language bound in space and time. The "weak & weary/Like Women & Children" remain always in the "soft sexual delusions" of Beulah, but "every Man" goes forward into a realm without Error, in the patriarchal "Bosom of the Father in Eternity on Eternity" (pl.31, ll.1–5). Blake redeems sexual love in Beulah from the religion of chastity, but he retains a Pauline dualism that separates male intellect from female sensuality, soul from sense, and vision from language. In fact, Blake's continuation of Milton's phallocentrism is strangely, and presumably accidentally, suggested in his bizarre pun on "tarsus." Milton descends into Blake's lowest member in one more sense than we have considered, for yet another pun on "tarsus" plays on the plural of "tarse," an archaism for phallus (*OED*).

Nevertheless, as Blake saw it, and as his critics continue to see it, his mental warfare with Milton had annihilated Milton's Shadow, the Covering Cherub, and so redeemed the essential Milton. Milton's Poetic Genius can join Blake, apparently, in the "line of vision." After Milton enters into his foot, Blake binds his "sandals /On; to walk forward thro' Eternity" and the composite Blake-Milton, joined at the tarsus, is joined there also by Los, the spirit of prophecy: "he also stoop'd down/ And bound my sandals on" (pl.22, ll.4–9). With apparent justice, Wittreich sees this moment as evidence that Blake does not anxiously spurn his predecessor, but joins with him in the tradition of prophecy.[14] Blake is evidently more ambivalent than

Wittreich, however, since the source for his image is not any of the usual figures in the "line of vision," but is once again St Paul. The Pauline passage used as a motto for *The Four Zoas* continues with an exhortation to the peculiarly Miltonic heroism of *standing*:

> Wherefore take unto you the whole armour of God, that ye may be able to withstand in the evil day, and having done all, to stand. Stand therefore, having your loins girt about with truth, and having on the breastplate of righteousness; And your feet shod with the preparation of the gospel of peace.
>
> (Eph. 6:13–15)

But Blake may well have intended this ironically: Milton stood still with the gospel of peace, not advancing it beyond Paul. He needed Blake's aid to "walk forward thro' Eternity." In any case, the relation is surely not as benign as Wittreich repeatedly suggests – without Blake's aid, Milton is not only unshod, but "his feet bled sore/Upon the clay now changed to marble" as he journeyed on in a hellish fallen landscape, just as Milton's own Satan's "unblest feet" suffered on the "burning Marl" of Hell's floor (*PL* I.238, 296). Even at the end of the poem, as the redeemed Milton re-enacts Christ's annihilation of Satan in *Paradise Regained*, he does so by parodying central doctrines of *Paradise Lost* (pl.38, ll.28–33). Further, when Satan is defeated, it is in terms that once again echo the conversion of Saul to St Paul. Struck down on the road to Damascus, Saul, "trembling and astonished," heard the voice of the Lord. So Satan is described twice as trembling "with exceeding great trembling & astonishment" (pl.39, ll.17, 31). The passage reflects the ambivalence of Milton's earlier incarnation in Blake. Once again the preparation of Milton (and of Blake) for prophecy involves a violent conversion in which Milton must be delivered from the body of death as Paul is delivered from Saul.

Blake's characterization of Milton – at least as expressed in *Milton* – does coincide in some ways with both Bloom's and Wittreich's theory of poetic influence and literary history. Blake reads Milton with remarkable critical acuity, and he shows no particular anxiety in taking what he wants and rejecting the rest, though he does follow the Bloomian pattern to the extent that he deceives himself into believing that he is "tougher-minded" than his precursor.[15] And in his uses of Milton and other "prophets" he is of course, as Wittreich argues, working within a tradition of some kind. Nevertheless, his critique of Milton is more coolly reasoned than Bloom's idea of psychologically induced misprision would lead one to expect, and Blake's total rejection of Milton's inspiration, doctrines, and poetic style make it difficult to place him in a "Miltonic tradition," let alone to use him in establishing *the* Miltonic tradition, as both Wittreich and Bloom attempt to do. Blake cannot even establish a Blakean sublime as a mode of visionary poetry that would redeem a dualistic universe in a monistic vision. Indeed, by continuing to privilege such terms as "vision" and "inspiration," modern criticism establishes an authoritative institutionalized literature, a Church Milton and Church Blake. Academic criticism, of course, has an interest in sacralizing literature in this way, but a full understanding of the Blake–Milton relationship ought to teach us to question the authoritarian claims not only of Milton, but of any discourse, including Blake's.

The problem at the center of Blake's "visionary" epics is that Blake, like Milton, does emphatically claim authoritative inspiration even as he teaches us to suspect such claims. Blake and Milton are the most extreme examples in the English language of major poets claiming such authority – both present themselves as secretaries taking dictation from a source of eternal truth. Yet Blake repudiates Milton's source, and strongly suggests that Milton failed because he did not read the New Testament correctly. Milton must learn to read St Paul as St Paul read the Old Testament. And despite his often transcendent language, Blake's inspiration comes from the works of human imagination, from a creatively combative reading of those works, so that every new text becomes a scene of battle as well as of continuity. Blake's demystification of divine inspiration is made economically explicit in a definition of the "Eternal Great Humanity:"

> As the breath of the Almighty. such are the words of man to man
> In the great Wars of Eternity, in fury of Poetic Inspiration,
> To build the Universe stupendous: Mental forms Creating.
>
> (pl.30, ll.18–20)

Blake, then, humanizes the sacred, and sacralizes the human imagination – and from a high Romantic perspective, one could end the discussion there, with general commendations. Yet Blake's demystification of the language of transcendence does not go far enough, and his excision of God from the sacred language he continues to use raises vexing problems about poetic authority.[16] In the spiritual warfare of imagination, no one voice should, presumably, be privileged as authoritative, or the spiritual conflict would end, superseded by a "body" of dogma. Yet Blake clearly wants to establish an authoritative, prophetic voice, wants to describe a timeless vision. He wants to establish a voice that *is* the "breath of the Almighty," though he knows that the result would be yet another authoritative patriarchal church. The problem is evident in all of his prophetic works: cut off from a transcendent, authoritative God, his language wanders endlessly in labyrinthine mazes as it attempts to develop contexts in which to accrete sacred meanings. Indeed, his mythic language, particularly when he sacralizes the "divine" imagination as Jesus, creates only an illusion of permanent truth and authority, though it is an illusion that he needs to cling to. The prophecies, with their extraordinarily allusive language and symbolism, plainly depend for their meaning on the past "words of man to man," on the long history of religious and poetic language, but in so doing they inevitably demonstrate the fallen condition of language that Blake desperately wanted to overcome. Not surprisingly, then, the various claims of inspiration throughout the poem ring rather hollow. For example, when the Bard is asked for the origins of his song, he asserts his inspiration in a fully sacralized language:

> The Bard replied. I am Inspired! I know it is Truth! for I Sing
> According to the inspiration of the Poetic Genius
> Who is the eternal all-protecting Divine Humanity
> To whom be Glory & Power & Dominion Evermore Amen.
>
> (pl.13, l.51–pl.14, ll.1–3)

But bald assertion in a largely demythologized idiom is less than convincing. It is a wish for inspiration, not the thing itself.

The extraordinary stridency of much of Blake's writing – the constant howling, and weeping, and shrieking, and lamentation – is generated, I think, by a profound sense of uncertainty underlying his extreme claims of inspiration. Decentered, with no transcendent origin, his language and vision sometimes seem to spin wildly, out of control. William Kerrigan is right, I think, in saying that after the Word of God lost its authority, after Milton, poet-prophets began to spin their wheels off-center: "The new 'poet-prophet,' defining his prophetic tradition with increasing eccentricity, spoke his fiery words from the margins of culture."[17] Eccentric to be sure – in his lifetime and long after, many thought Blake mad. And in fact one of his motives in writing *Milton* was to prove to himself and others that he was not insane but inspired. At the conclusion of the poem, Milton, now inspired in a Blakean way, commands (of all things) obedience: "Obey thou the Words of the Inspired Man." The primary purpose of the "Inspired Man" is to annihilate conventional, non-inspired thought so

> That it no longer shall dare to mock with the aspersion of Madness
> Cast on the Inspired.
>
> (pl.41, ll.8–9)

In 1801, possibly during the writing of *Milton*, Blake wrote to a patron to apologize for his "want of steady perseverance" in terms that seem to equate his "vision" with insanity. He could not get his work done because

> my Abstract folly hurries me often away while I am at work, carrying me over Mountains & Valleys which are not Real in a Land of Abstraction where Spectres of the Dead wander. This I endeavour to prevent & with my whole might chain my feet to the world of Duty & Reality. but in vain! the faster I bind the better is the Ballast for I so far from being bound down take the world with me in my flights.[18]

Blake's whimsy is not without a degree of seriousness and the letter throws a peculiar light on the symbolism of the sandals in *Milton*:

And all this Vegetable World appeard on my left Foot,
As a bright sandal formd immortal of precious stones & gold:
I stooped down & bound it on to walk forward thro' Eternity.
                                            (pl.21, ll.12–14)

The sandal – the prophetic and literary tradition, including the work of
Milton – is evidently ballast. It does not raise Blake above humanity in
visionary song, but restrains him from the excesses of his own decentered,
unauthorized imagination. The image betrays a profound distrust of the
unfettered imagination, and suggests that the poet must remain encumbered
by his predecessors. He is restricted to the "Litteral expression," and his
"vision" is obscured by the soiled garment of language.

Some of the implications of Blake's confrontation with Milton can be
summed up briefly. In order to establish his own poetic authority, Blake
needed to subvert Milton's, to establish a difference between himself and
Milton. He attempted to overcome Milton's dualism, to repudiate what
Milton saw as the essential structure of differences that constituted his
cosmos and his text, the differences between God and man, soul and body,
reason and sensuality, inspiration and imagination, man and woman. But
Blake is the inheritor of Milton's language, the language of a western
tradition built on dualisms, and he has no other language to express, or even
imagine, a monistic "vision." Blake cannot transcend Milton's dualism if
only because language itself, based on a structure of differences, cannot
present "godmansoul . . ." as a seamless whole. Inevitably, Blake's poem
does not end with seamless vision, but with a woven garment of language
that prevents, or defers, revelation. Ultimately *all* Blake can do is establish
his difference from Milton, and so generate yet another duality: Blake/Milton.

But as we have seen, establishing this ultimate duality is no small matter.
It re-establishes the act of reading as a form of combat, and turns the
subservient reader into a revolutionary reader/writer. In fact, Blake's
insistence on destroying the Church Paul and the Church Milton, in
subverting their authority, has a peculiarly modern ring. It is akin to the
post-structuralist criticism most clearly represented in the writings of
Barthes, whose distinction between the authoritative, classic, "readerly"
text and the decentered "writerly" text is precisely analogous to Blake's
distinction between the Church Paul and Paul, the Church Milton and
Milton, the classic Milton and Blake himself. For Blake as for Barthes, the
classic text imposes itself on the passive, obedient reader, but the
contentious reader transforms the "readerly" to the "writerly," and so
creates his own text. Blake does indeed insist on his own visionary
authority, but at the same time his confrontation with Milton shows us how
to subvert that authority, by insisting not on a truer vision, but on a
different reading, a contrary reading that combats the author's authority,
and so preserves the difference between author and reader that makes

continual intellectual activity possible. Establishing this difference, the reader avoids passive receptivity, and engages in active "mental warfare."

Notes

1. *The Marriage of Heaven and Hell*, pl.5, in *The Poetry and Prose of William Blake*, ed. David Erdman, with a commentary by Harold Bloom (New York, Doubleday, 1965). All further citations from Blake's works will refer to plate and line numbers in this edition.
2. See Harold Bloom, *The Anxiety of Influence: A Theory of Poetry* (New York, Oxford University Press, 1973), 29–30. For Wittreich's extensive discussions of the "line of vision" see *Angel of Apocalypse: Blake's Idea of Milton* (Madison, University of Wisconsin Press, 1975), "Opening the seals: Blake's epics and the Milton tradition," in *Blake's Sublime Allegory: Essays on The Four Zoas, Milton, Jerusalem*, ed. Stuart Curran and Joseph Anthony Wittreich (Madison, University of Wisconsin Press, 1973), 23–58, and "'A poet amongst poets:' Milton and the tradition of prophecy," in *Milton and the Line of Vision*, ed. Joseph Anthony Wittreich (Madison, University of Wisconsin Press, 1975), 97–142.
3. Northrop Frye, however, long ago pointed out that "It is in *Areopagitica* that Milton is nearest to Blake." See *Fearful Symmetry: A Study of William Blake* (Princeton, Princeton University Press, 1947), 159. But subsequent critics have not followed up Frye's comment.
4. Quotations are from *John Milton: Complete Poems and Major Prose*, ed. Merritt Y. Hughes (New York, Odyssey, 1957), 744, 741–2, 745.
5. ibid., 747.
6. In *The Poetry and Prose of William Blake*, 728–9.
7. As David Erdman has noted, Blake's illustrations make the point still more emphatically by showing the poet thrown backwards with his face towards heaven as the star approaches his foot – the posture is a variant of that in Blake's watercolor drawing of Saul. *The Illuminated Blake* (New York, Anchor Press, 1974), 233, 248, 253.
8. *The Reason of Church-Government urg'd against Prelaty*, ed. Henry Morgan Ayres, in *The Works of John Milton* (New York, Columbia University Press, 1931), vol. III, pt 1, 223–4.
9. See Northrop Frye, op. cit., 341–2.
10. Wittreich, *Angel of Apocalypse*, 241. Wittreich quotes Milton from *The Reason of Church-Government*, but Milton is quoting 2 Cor. 10:4–5.
11. Florence Sandler, "The iconoclastic enterprise: Blake's critique of Milton's religion" (*Blake Studies*, 5, 1972, 15). See also Thomas W. Herzing, "Book I of Blake's *Milton*: Natural religion as an optical fallacy" (*Blake Studies*, 6, 1973, 19–34).
12. *The Reason of Church-Government*, 241.
13. Bloom, op. cit., 35.
14. Wittreich, *Angel of Apocalypse*, 250.
15. Bloom, op. cit., 69.
16. See John Guillory, *Poetic Authority: Spenser, Milton, and Literary History* (New York, Columbia University Press, 1983). Guillory argues that "The 'imagination' names for the post-Miltonic poet an 'internal vision,' a source of poetry, but it does not name the sacred text so much as a desire for such a text. As a name for poetic power, the word preserves both the visionary longing, and the failure of that longing. The authority of the poet is henceforth more

problematic, and requires an ever more complex defense" (22).
17. William Kerrigan, *The Prophetic Milton* (Charlottesville, University Press of Virginia, 1974), 14.
18. *The Poetry and Prose of William Blake*, 716.

13

CAROLIVIA HERRON

Milton and Afro-American literature

Afro-American writers from Phillis Wheatley to Ishmael Reed respond to the works and high cultural status of John Milton in texts that are a record of strong conflict and ambivalence regarding western literary and cultural traditions. Afro-American writers certainly are not unique in this. Every work of literature, regardless of its ethnic source, reflects and elaborates received literary traditions in ways that are often openly antagonistic to the culture at large. Marginalized writers in particular often assume the roles of national prophet and isolated moral conscience for their groups as well as for the greater society. The conflict with western literary and cultural traditions which Afro-American literature reflects is distinctive, however, in that its social context – slavery, unparalleled racism, prolonged legal oppression, and the high visibility of black skin – has made it impossible for Afro-Americans, regardless of status, to escape the specific form of self-awareness that a discrepancy between high cultural ideals and racist practices brings about. This discrepant awareness constitutes a fundamental ethnic source from which a distinctively Afro-American artistic and critical perspective derives. As Robert A. Bone writes in *The Negro Novel in America*:

> Just as in real life the Negro is forced to assume an ambivalent attitude toward the dominant culture, so in the world of letters the Negro writer may adopt an ambivalent attitude toward the dominant literary tradition.[1]

As a culturally acclaimed transmitter of this dominant literary tradition Milton has provoked responses ranging from Phillis Wheatley's self-depreciating admiration of his epic genius in the eighteenth century to the violent rejection of Milton and all he is taken to represent in Ishmael Reed's *Mumbo Jumbo* (1972).

The identification and analysis of tensions between Afro-American writings and western literary tradition should be one of the major projects of Afro-American literary criticism and theory. As Henry Louis Gates, Jr states in "Criticism in the jungle:"

> in the case of the writer of African descent, her or his texts occupy spaces in at least two traditions: a European or American literary tradition, and one of the several related but distinct black traditions. The "heritage" of each black text written in a Western language is, then, a double heritage, two-toned, as it were. Its visual tones are white and black, and its aural tones are standard and vernacular.[2]

The present study of four black writers' responses to Milton's texts – or in some instances, less to his texts than to the multiple cultural meanings of his status – pursues the goal of analyzing the two tones of Afro-American literary tradition. Moreover, by focusing on four writers from different epochs of American history – Phillis Wheatley (c.1754–84), John Boyd (dates unknown, published during 1830s), Charles W. Chesnutt (1858–1932), and Ishmael Reed (b. 1938), I hope to show that their varying responses to Milton illuminate the historical development of an Afro-American tradition of epic literature.

Historically, works by Afro-Americans have not been accorded the respect given to works by white authors in that studies of relationships between black writings and prior works in western tradition have been used almost exclusively to affirm that Afro-American literature lacks creativity. Black artistic talent and accomplishment have often been discussed in terms of the racist belief that Africans and Afro-Americans have a natural propensity for mindless copying. Vernon Loggins, for example, writing of Wheatley's facility in creating heroic couplets in *The Negro Author: His Development in America*, states that Wheatley's "power to attain this place of eminence must be pronounced as due to her instinct for hearing the music of words, an instinct which was possibly racial."[3]

This history of biased or condescending attitudes toward black artistic accomplishment raises serious questions for the contemporary critic who seeks, as I do here, to analyze a relationship between Afro-American literature and a canonical western author. Studies of the relationships between figures like Milton and Afro-American authors often have been converted into discussions of black intellectual dependency on white accomplishment. Many contemporary writers, critics, and theorists respond to this habitual misuse by condemning studies of Afro-American and European/white American intercultural connections as racist and regressive by definition. Without ignoring the difficulties they give rise to, I feel such inquiries are a necessary intellectual task: the connections do exist, and to ignore them in order to avoid having one's work misappropriated is to combat one mistake by committing another. It is to respond to bigotry with willful ignorance.

Furthermore, studies such as this one provide a forum for debate about theoretical questions that are of vital concern to intellectuals today: questions about canon formation; and about the ways in which writers have been constrained as well as inspired by the canonical figures of a dominant cultural tradition. As soon as a study of Afro-American writers and Milton goes beyond the initial task of showing that blacks did indeed read him (and in interesting ways), such a study necessarily addresses complex critical questions about cross-cultural influence. The political and ideological problems inherent in cross-cultural influence are central to the difficult cultural dialogue now taking place between artists and intellectuals in Third and First World countries. For this reason among others, it may be more than a merely academic task to study the case of Milton's influence – enabling and inhibiting – on Afro-American writers. By "influence" I do not mean only instances of direct textual borrowing but also the transmission and effect of a cultural image which, in the case of Milton, necessarily encompasses the prestige of the epic genre and the cultural importance of the book of Genesis.

Unfortunately, even the initial task of this study – that of identifying relevant Afro-American texts – is incomplete. The compilation and analysis of references to Milton in Afro-American writing have been restricted by the oppressive circumstances under which Afro-American literature developed. Rarely have critics had the luxury of analyzing the genres of Afro-American literature. The struggle has been to discover and preserve indiscriminately all the words that could be salvaged from the devastating silences of slavery, and it is little wonder that there have been few occasions to pick and choose among the relics for particular generic developments and adaptations. The epic genre – associated as it is with high intellectual distinction and with prolonged and intense self-discipline rarely attributed to black slaves and their descendants – has been particularly ignored in discussions of Afro-American literature. Afro-American literature has always had epic propensities, however, and these propensities often developed as responses to Milton. Not only in the work of Phillis Wheatley, John Boyd, Charles Chesnutt, and Ishmael Reed, but also in the writings of Jacob Rhodes, Frances Ellen Watkins Harper, Albery A. Whitman, George Hannibal Temple, James Madison Bell, Robert E. Ford, Fenton Johnson, George Marion McClellan, and George Reginald Margetson there is an intricate and explicit dialogue with the scope, style, and themes of Milton's epics.[4]

The earliest responses to Milton in Afro-American writings reflect the fusion between Christian doctrine, the Bible, and Milton's poetic and political works that occurred in early America. Critical works such as "John Quincy Adams on the opening lines of *Paradise Lost*," by Henry Wasser, "Cotton Mather against rhyme: Milton and the *Psalterium Americanum*," by Sacvan Bercovitch, and *Milton in Early America* by George Frank

Sensabaugh refer to the adulation of Milton in colonial and revolutionary America.[5] One of the effects of this adulation was that often the plot and imagery of *Paradise Lost* were assumed to be those of Genesis. In some instances readers and church congregations appeared unaware of the discrepancies between Milton's Biblical elaborations and the Bible itself, and could not tell when Biblical exegesis commented not so much upon the Bible, as upon Milton's extended and often radical Biblical plots.[6] In the political realm, tracts such as *Areopagitica* and *Pro Populo Anglicano Defensio* were used by American revolutionists to justify their repudiation of British rule and to reaffirm the belief that the colonists were a chosen people, ordained to be vessels of God's truth in the New World.[7] Thus Milton, Christian doctrine, political freedom, and revolution became fused in the minds of many early Americans. Milton was a source both of accepted "orthodox" Christian doctrine and of political revolution and subversion.

The fusion between Christian doctrine, the Bible, and Milton's works may have affected the development of Afro-American religion; it is conceivable that scenes from *Paradise Lost* were merged with Biblical scenes during the years when African slaves were converted to Christianity. Such a hypothesis helps explain the residue of Miltonic imagery in the sermons of contemporary black churches. As a teenager attending black Baptist churches in Washington, DC, I heard sermons that included Miltonic descriptions of the fall of Satan, the activities of Adam and Eve before the fall, the geography and activities in hell, the war of the angels, the misogynous interpretation of Adam's rib, Jesus in heaven at the beginning of time choosing to be born, and Lucifer's jealous interior monologues and dialogues while in heaven. In some of these sermons Miltonic echoes were particularly notable. For example, in the "Fall of Satan" sermon, Satan was described as flipping over nine times as he fell, a numerical specificity that echoes Milton's "Nine times the Space that measures Day and Night / To mortal men, hee with his horrid crew / Lay vanquisht" (*PL* I.50–2) and "Nine days they fell; confounded *Chaos* roar'd" (*PL* VI.871).[8] The preacher of the "Fall of Satan" displayed his creativity by presenting each of Satan's "flips" with a fully elaborated inner monologue, together with a commentary on the manner in which Satan's thoughts boded ill for mankind. In similar Miltonic elaborations, the "Adam and Eve in Eden" sermon described visits from angels, and included explicit conversations and prayers (cf. *PL* IV–VIII); the "Geography of Hell" sermon insisted upon the variety of locales and activities (cf. *PL* I–II); and the "Jesus choosing to be born" sermon included a long description of the silence in heaven when no angel would volunteer to be the saviour of mankind (cf. *PL* III.217–65).

In subsequent conversations with the preachers of these sermons, I have determined that these plots developed from black oral tradition rather than from individual contemporary readings of *Paradise Lost*. Perhaps it is the orality of the tradition that makes it so difficult to trace. The task has also been made more difficult by the suppression of a parallel tradition in the white Southern Baptist Church. Several years ago I heard a white Southern Baptist minister discouraging a small group of college students from reading or relying upon Milton's works. When I asked why, I was told that Milton had "ruined Christianity" by writing things which were not in the Bible but which many Christians believe. Through further investigation I discovered that this negative view of Milton was taught to him and other seminarians at the Southern Baptist Theological Seminary (Louisville, Kentucky), the major seminary of the major religious denomination of the South.

In any event, when we consider Milton's radical and heretical Christianity as expressed in *De Doctrina Christiana*, it is tempting to think that black theology adapted and created Miltonic plots and themes to express dissatisfaction with the oppressive status quo and to encourage rebellion, at least intellectually, against slavery and racism. The writings of Alexander Crummell, a black religio-political activist in the nineteenth century, certainly support this view. In his many sermons and essays defending the rights and intrinsic value of Africans and Afro-Americans – including a powerful plea that white men cease the sexual violation of black women – Crummell (1819–98) cites Milton as an ally in his fight against American racism and refers to Milton as a prototype of wisdom, morality, and political and intellectual freedom.[9]

These scant historical and contemporary facts cannot, however, be inflated to ascribe to Afro-Americans a pervasive appropriation of Milton and his work for rebellious socio-theological purposes.[10] For in contrast with the generally favorable view of Milton derived from early Afro-American religion and literature, twentieth-century Afro-American writers often respond to Milton as one whose work and cultural status are repressively ethnocentric and bigoted. In *The House Behind The Cedars*, for example, Charles Chesnutt presents Milton as one of a cluster of British writers whom the mulatto protagonist must possess intellectually if he is to gain entrance into white society and partake of its financial and cultural advantages. As we shall see, Chesnutt anticipates Ishmael Reed's view of Milton as the proponent of the established powers of racist white America and the western world in general.

The remainder of this essay, through more detailed discussion of Wheatley, Boyd, Chesnutt, and Reed, pursues the thesis that their varying modes of responding to Milton contribute to a developing tradition of Afro-American epic. The line of Afro-American epic from Phillis Wheatley to the present is a persistent accumulation of aspiration and protest that is issuing in its own recovered stories, realigned histories, and distinctive Afro-American epic. Works of such writers as Derek Walcott, Toni Cade Bambara, John Wideman, Gloria Naylor, and Edward Braithwaite are contemporary additions to this continuing epic tradition.

Phillis Wheatley

Although Pope exerted the most obvious influence on Wheatley's poetic style, her religious intensity, her longing to create an African epic, and certain elements of her style testify to Milton's equally powerful presence in her consciousness.[11] Wheatley's poetry, like that of her white contemporaries, employs Miltonic syntax, imagery, and even, at times, blank verse. Milton's influence is also evident in her taste for companion poems.

The most significant connection between Wheatley and Milton, however, is her admiration of his epic vision and her resultant sense of incapacity to create an African epic. The seeds of this conflict are evident in one of her earliest poems, "To the University of Cambridge in New England," which uses Miltonic blank verse to express her admiration of the union between cosmic knowledge and Christian truth.

> Students, to you 'tis giv'n to scan the heights
> Above, to traverse the ethereal space,
> And mark the systems of revolving worlds.
> Still more, ye sons of science ye receive
> The blissful news by messengers from heav'n,
> How *Jesus'* blood for your redemption flows.
>
> (Wheatley, 5)[12]

In an early version of this poem Wheatley contrasts the earthly advantages and divine inspiration given to the privileged students (who of course are white, male, and Christian), with the lack of inspiration available to Africans. She states that unlike the students, she has come from a land without muses.

> 'Twas but e'en now I left my native shore
> The sable Land of error's darkest night.
> There, sacred Nine! for you no place was found.
>
> (Wheatley, 63)

Throughout her brief career Wheatley continued to link admiration for cosmic/epic vision with statements about her inability to create an epic poem, as can be seen in "Phillis's Reply to the Answer in our last by the Gentleman in the Navy" (87), where she gives Milton the epithet, "British Homer."

"Phillis's Reply" is the last of a series of three poems, the first of which, "To a Gentleman of the Navy," also by Wheatley, praises the "gentleman" in Homeric terms, and then claims that the author's muse, Calliope, the muse of epic poetry, grants only half her prayer and "scatters half in air" (83). The second poem in the series, "The Answer," is written by the "gentleman," evidently a lieutenant who admired Milton and Newton and whose service off the coast of Africa made him feel qualified to write of the

Gold Coast. After calling on the celestial muse (presumably Milton's Urania), to praise Wheatley, the lieutenant states that Wheatley has received the gift of the muse and that Africa is blessed because the Gold Coast is, among other things, the source of "strains divine and true poetic fires" (84). Observing that Britannia, which formerly excelled other nations in art and wisdom through the genius of Newton and Milton, now can boast only of "the power to kill," the poet concludes that:

> For softer strains we quickly must repair
> To Wheatly's song, for Wheatly is the fair;
> That has the art, which art could ne'er acquire:
> To dress each sentence with seraphic fire.
>   Her wondrous virtues I could ne'er express!
> To paint her charms, would only make them less.
>   (Wheatley, 85)

In "Phillis's Reply," Wheatley follows the lieutenant and Milton by calling on the heavenly muse rather than Calliope. She states, however, that the heavenly muse can give her only "one bright moment," and laments that her pen can "never rival" that of the lieutenant.

> While I each golden sentiment admire
> In thee, the muse's bright celestial fire.
> The generous plaudit 'tis not mine to claim,
> A muse untutor'd, and unknown to fame.
>   The heavenly sisters pour thy notes along
> And crown their bard with every grace of song
> My pen, least favour'd by the tuneful nine,
> Can never rival, never equal thine;
> Then fix the humble Afric muse's seat
> At British Homer's and Sir Isaac's feet.
> Those bards whose fame in deathless strains arise
> Creation's boast, and fav'rites of the skies.
>   (Wheatley, 86)

Self-deprecatingly Wheatley portrays her African muse as sitting humbly at Homer's and Sir Isaac's feet, implying not only that her muse is less creative than the "tuneful nine" but also that whatever her muse knows has been learned from Milton and Newton.

It would be easy to blame Wheatley's extreme self-effacement – and perhaps self-hatred – entirely upon the negative effect of white racist society. Certainly racism provided the unfortunate terms in which she describes her incapacity, but in fact, as a poet of high critical intelligence, she accurately assessed that her work lacks the power, complexity, and effectiveness of Milton's *Paradise Lost*. Although it would be incorrect to deny the power of slavery to consume self-respect in many of the enslaved, it is nevertheless an insult to Wheatley's unique and creative achievement to assume that she was a mere victim of her society, and that she had no capacity to interpret and evaluate. Wheatley is one among many European and American poets who desired but failed to create great epics in the Miltonic tradition, but her failure is accentuated by her race and status, by negative racist perceptions of her by her audience, and by the racist terms in which she describes her incapacity.

Wheatley's use of these self-depreciating terms was probably aggravated by her distance from African and Afro-American traditions. "Phillis's Reply" reveals her desire for such an ethnic epic tradition when she states that the gentleman's description of Africa has carried her back in memory to her African homeland, which she compares to Eden. By equating Eden and Africa she implies that her homeland is a valid subject for great epic. She then apostrophizes Milton as "Europa's bard:"

> Europa's bard, who the great depth explor'd,
> Of nature, and thro' boundless systems soar'd,
> Thro' earth, thro' heaven, and hell's profound domain,
> Where night eternal holds her awful reign.
> But, lo! in him Britania's prophet dies,
> And whence, ah! whence, shall other *Newton*'s rise ?
>
> (Wheatley, 87)

The last two lines are particularly intriguing. By stating that Britain's epic prophecy and the best it can inspire ends with Milton and Newton, Wheatley seems to be proclaiming an end to Miltonic epic tradition – a break that must affect her as a writer of English in that tradition. Since Wheatley appears to accept that Africa is an appropriate subject of epic poetry (and the home of the epic poet according to the gentleman), she may, however, believe unconsciously that African poets writing in English may escape the break within European epic tradition.

The concept of an African or Afro-American epic that can develop and emerge in spite of the demise of the European epic tradition is never made explicit in Wheatley's writings. Several of her poems, however, particularly "To Maecenas," reveal her belief that the European muses are unacceptably partial in their giving, and that she herself should be permitted to "snatch a laurel" and create great African poetry. "To Maecenas" was written to honor John Wheatley, her owner, for having encouraged her writings. (The original Maecenas, in first century BC Rome, was a patron of the poets Virgil, Horace, Propertius and his own freed slave, C. Melissus.) Addressing Homer in "To Maecenas" Wheatley exclaims:

> O, could I rival thine and *Virgil*'s page
> Or claim the *Muses* with the *Mantuan* Sage;
> Soon the same beauties should my mind adorn,
> And the same ardors in my soul should burn . . . .

285

> The happier *Terence* all the choir inspir'd
> His soul replenish'd, and his bosom fir'd;
> But say, ye *Muses*, why this partial grace,
> To one alone of *Afric*'s sable race;
> From age to age transmitting thus his name
> With the first glory in the rolls of fame.
>
> (Wheatley, 3–4)

This passage not only reveals Wheatley's intense longing to create a significant long poem in Homeric tradition, but also shows her identifying with Terence and thereby imaginatively creating for herself an African racial/cultural predecessor. She places herself clearly within both European and African traditions.

Completely isolated from African culture, having no Afro-American traditions to speak of (even though she knew several black slaves and servants, she certainly knew none who were in a position comparable to her own), not even possessing the vernacular language of Afro-America, Wheatley would have had no particular impulse, it would seem, to seek antecedents different from those of her white counterparts. The fact, then, that she sought an African predecessor and defined a relationship between that predecessor and herself suggests that even without a direct black heritage Wheatley was quite aware of the "two-toned" nature of her writings. Although we have few poems from her later years it is evident that she maintained her interest in Milton and epic throughout her life. One of the poems lost after her death mentions the epic muse in its title ("Cloe to Calliope").[13] Also, although she died in severe poverty, she did not sell her valuable edition of *Paradise Lost*; it was sold in payment of her husband's debts after her death.[14]

John Boyd

There are few biographical facts known about John Boyd, whose two collections of poetry were published in London in 1829 and 1834.[15] From the introduction to the second volume, *The Vision and Other Poems: In Blank Verse*, we learn only that Boyd was a free black living in the Bahamas and that he was poor and self-educated. The title poem, *The Vision*, consists of 334 lines of blank verse describing the poet's vision of heaven and the Christian universe. Like Blake, Wordsworth, Shelley, and Keats, Boyd makes a revisionist reading of Milton and *Paradise Lost*, re-creating his universe for new artistic and political ends. Boyd's work is neither as skillful nor as complex as the mature works of the British Romantics. *The Vision*, however, appears to be the work of a highly gifted young poet and we can only regret the accidents of time and place that have denied him and us his later works.

Boyd's *The Vision* shows Miltonic influence not only through its use of blank verse, but also through such devices as the Miltonic "Argument," through replacing Milton's muse, Urania, with the muse Mercy, and through rearranging and transforming Miltonic images and scenes. In the opening lines of *The Vision*, for example, Boyd echoes Milton's invocation to light by introducing his comparable vision of heaven with his own images of light. Like Milton's, Boyd's light is "ethereal," and he too awakens to a vision of the "invisible." In general Boyd's echoes and rearrangements of Milton give a strong sense of change and possibility. Boyd is adept at convoking Miltonic elements into a fluid background upon which he develops more significant changes.

One such change occurs in Boyd's description of God's throne (*The Vision*, 31–43), which revises *PL* III.56–65. Boyd directly echoes Milton's positioning of Christ through the phrase "Far on the right . . . Sat" (in referring to Christ). Also, the passage immediately preceding these lines from *The Vision* has echoes of *PL* III.343–415, which describes and presents the angels' hymn of praise to the Father and Son. Boyd not only echoes Milton but also revises him by reversing the Father/Son hierarchy to give precedence to the Son — referring to the Son as "pre-eminent." Moreover, whereas Milton describes the Son here in less than two lines, using attributes devoid of explicit moral content ("radiant image of his Glory"), Boyd takes thirteen lines to describe Christ with attributes conveying the goodness of his choice to suffer and die for mankind — "meek," "all-righteous, immaculate,/Once bleeding, suffering," "memorial of his love!" Further, in the passage from *Paradise Lost*, "the Sanctities of Heaven/Stood thick as Stars" around the Father; in Boyd, however, it is Christ who is "Encircled with glory's resplendent beams" which "play'd around his crown . . . forming his grand tiara!"

Another of Boyd's significant changes in this scene is in the time frame; his vision occurs after the crucifixion whereas Milton's is before the fall. Boyd's vision is also static rather than progressive. Milton's God is moving, bending down his eye to look at his creation, but Boyd's God and Christ are still. Boyd's changes give his vision of heaven a greater stability, permanence, and contemporaneity. Boyd clearly participates in the early American tradition of admiration for Milton as described by Sensabaugh and others. Boyd's vision of heaven, however, is portrayed as occurring at a time greatly in the future of the moment in which Milton's archangel Michael stands upon the mountain with Adam and tells what is to come. Boyd portrays Christ in heaven after the crucifixion ("at his feet, the broken crimson'd cross/Of crucifixion lay, whereon he bled/For man," 41ff.), enthroned, yet prior to the end of the world (in the latter part of the poem the spirits of good are still intervening to improve the life of mankind). Boyd gives us, in fact, a visionary reading of his own present time.

The world that Boyd imagines differs most radically from Milton's in the ascendance Boyd gives to mercy over justice. Both *Paradise Lost* (III.406ff.) and *The Vision* discuss the conflict between justice and mercy when God is determining the fate of fallen humankind. *Paradise Lost* emphasizes the agency of Christ in resolving the conflict. Boyd, however, links Christ chiefly with suffering, and then later develops a personification of mercy distinct from both God and Christ. The personification of mercy (182–257) begins when the poet interrupts himself after a description of the birth of Christ.

> E'en here let us pause, and deeply ponder
> On the wondrous, mystic combination,
> That mitigates grim death's envenom'd sting,
> And redeems from the angry penal curse,
> On Adam past, by th' Eternal's decree.
> In the wide vista of life's chequer'd scene,
> Mercy preserves the component accordance
> Of this sphere.
>
> (Boyd, 9)

In moving abruptly from Christ's nativity to focus on the benevolent acts of mercy at the beginning of human history, Boyd implies that mercy is the progenitor of Christ, rather than that Christ is the dispenser of mercy. Boyd makes no references to the crucifixion as he discusses humankind's redemption here, but rather explains the "mystic combination" of salvation by describing the works of mercy in the universe and within human spirits. Mercy maintains the earthly sphere (188), gives moral excellence to humankind (189), "sheds balm" – hope, joy, life – on the devastations of pestilence and war (192ff.), prevents fratricide (200), eliminates materialistic oppression (203ff.), and, as Boyd's rare use of the first person seems to suggest, cures the poet's grief and care (207ff.). After this effusive description of the virtues of mercy, Boyd personifies it as his muse: "Oh mercy! ethereal maid! thee I invoke! Inspire my strain, and let me sing thy charms" (10). This muse who loves and grieves for humankind is categorically different from the elevated and selective muse of *Paradise Lost*, Urania, and the difference accentuates the differing purposes of the two works. *Paradise Lost* explicitly aims to "justify the ways of God to men" (*PL* I.26). The purpose of *The Vision* is not stated explicitly, but Boyd's insistence that Mercy is his muse, his description of the ongoing terrestrial acts of relief and release from oppressions (probably an oblique reference to racial injustice), and his focus on the effects of mercy within his own spirit and lifetime imply that he was seeking a contemporary and socially active Afro-American counterpart of Milton's Urania.

Charles Waddell Chesnutt

Evidence for Chesnutt's familiarity with Milton comes chiefly from his novel, *The House Behind the Cedars*, and his short story, "The Fall of Adam." In *Cedars* the mulatto John Walden leaves his home, becomes a lawyer, gains entrance to the white world, and establishes political rights with the ruling class by implementing knowledge gained from reading all the books left behind by his deceased white father.[16] These books include an edition of Milton's poetry. Upon revisiting his home town, Patesville, North Carolina, after several years of living as a successful "white" lawyer in another state, John reflects upon the books which still sit, rarely disturbed, in his mother's house.

> On these secluded shelves Roderick Random, Don Quixote, and Gil Blas for a long time ceased their wanderings, the *Pilgrim's Progress* was suspended, Milton's mighty harmonies were dumb, and Shakespeare reigned over a silent kingdom. An illustrated Bible, with a wonderful Apocrypha, was flanked on one side by Volney's *Ruins of Empire* and on the other by Paine's *Age of Reason*.
>
> (*Cedars*, 145–6)

Chesnutt's emphasis on the mute immobility of Milton's poetry and the loss of other masterworks of western literature points to the protagonist's loss of his sense of connection with these works. There was a time in John's childhood, prior to his encounter with the white world outside his mother's house, when Milton's epics sang powerfully for him, when Don Quixote wandered in his life and thought, when Shakespeare ruled with language rather than with silence. The later adult glance of John Warwick, a white lawyer (he has changed his name from Walden to Warwick to emphasize his British blood), has seemingly eliminated these works from his immediate life and marked them with powerless inactivity.

In other references to these books, however, Chesnutt reveals that far from being powerless, they form the initiating and effective outline of John's encounter with life, the framework from which he chooses his particular path toward advancement and success, and the subtle overarching context which is an aesthetic and descriptive record of the supernatural powers that predict and bring to pass the tragic failure that is the subject of the novel. Chesnutt describes John's reading of his father's books as the act of eating from the Tree of Knowledge and expands this concept thematically throughout the novel to such an extent that *Cedars* may be interpreted as a nineteenth-century rendition of the first chapters of Genesis; that is, as a modern counterpart of *Paradise Lost*:

> When he had read all the books – indeed, long before he had read them all – he too had tasted of the fruit of the Tree of Knowledge: contentment

took its flight, and happiness lay far beyond the sphere where he was born.

(*Cedars*, 147)

Although Chesnutt does not state explicitly that *Cedars* is a transformation of Genesis comparable to *Paradise Lost*, it is possible that Genesis and *Paradise Lost* are so fused for Chesnutt that he finds it unnecessary to make explicit references.[17] In *Cedars* Chesnutt develops numerous parallels between his plot and the fall of Adam and Eve. These references, along with passages which, as we shall see, identify *Cedars* as a cultural and temporal counterpart to the *Iliad*, imply that Chesnutt, like Milton, felt that an elaboration of the Genesis story was the most fitting subject for a cultural epic.

The mulatto family consists of the mother, Molly Walden, her daughter, Rena, and her son, John, who, after reading his father's books as a child, became "persuaded that he had certain rights" (72), and went to Judge Straight requesting to be trained as a lawyer. Judge Straight agreed after a brief hesitation, thereby helping John to acquire the education that lets him live as a white man in another state.

On John's return to Patesville several years later he decides to take Rena away with him so that she may be white as well. Rena has not read as much as John, only "some of the novels," we are told (69). She has not absorbed the full range of western thought contained in their white father's bookcase, which has treatises on freedom side by side with slavery statistics. But Rena's attempt to become white fails. She goes with her brother and becomes engaged to one of his white associates. She decides, however, to visit her mother who is ill in Patesville, and the plot complications of this visit reveal to Tyron, her fiance, that she is black. Tyron immediately rejects her. After several other rather melodramatic complications, Rena dies in her mother's house after having been rescued by her dark-skinned neighbor, Frank, from the pursuits of two undesirable lovers – an unscrupulous black educator, Jeff Wain, and the repentant Tyron.

Throughout the presentation of Rena's failure to become white there are tragic echoes of western epics, especially the *Iliad* and *Paradise Lost*. The most explicit of these echoes occurs in Chapter XI, "A letter and a journey," in which Chesnutt sets up the unfortunate incidents that will bring Tyron to Patesville where Rena is known to be black. The chapter begins with a prologue which is an extended metaphor linking warfare and lawsuits with the interracial tension about to bring unhappiness and death to the characters. This prologue sets the scene of epic conflict and ends by telling us that the Iliadic "apple of discord" has been thrown "into the narrow circle."

This prologue is similar in purpose and tone to the opening lines of the *Iliad*, which also delineate the source and the effects of the conflicts to come.

290

In addition, the structure recalls the invocation to *Paradise Lost* Book IX, where Milton tells us "I now must change / Those Notes to Tragic" (5–6). Through the metaphor of gathering war, Chesnutt relates the interracial tensions of *Cedars* with the intestine wars that are conventional in the *Iliad*, the *Aeneid*, *Paradise Lost*, and other epics in western tradition. That these associations were developed self-consciously can be seen from his journals, where we learn that in his earliest contact with the *Iliad* Chesnutt began to clarify his vocation as a writer by projecting a parallel between himself and Homer, and by choosing racism and prejudice as the "war" that would be his subject.[18] Thus we can say, adapting words from Phillis Wheatley, that Chesnutt aspired to be an "Afro-American Homer" and as such his goal was comparable to Milton's, whose "mighty harmonies" were among the works that initiated and framed John's quest for social equity.

For John the fruit of the tree of knowledge is that he can be white. For Rena, however, the knowledge is that she can never be white. Thus Chesnutt displays the ironic and somewhat treacherous relationship between the black reader and white western epics, particularly the *Iliad* and *Paradise Lost*. As intellectual objects to be known and possessed, *Paradise Lost* and the other books on the father's bookshelf permit the mulattoes to enter the white world successfully. Thematically, however, *Paradise Lost*, with its tragic foreshadowings, is used to take away what it pretends to give. For instance, Rena's brief entrance into the white world and her expulsion thence is presented in the imagery of a paradise that is first gained and then re-lost. And when John tries to persuade Rena to make a second attempt to live as a white person by returning to stay with him and his motherless child, Rena uses the imagery of temptation and knowledge to describe her utter defeat.

> Ah, do not tempt me, John! I love the child, and am grieved to leave him. I'm grateful, too, John, for what you have done for me. I am not sorry that I tried it. It opened my eyes, and I would rather die of knowledge than live in ignorance.
>
> (*Cedars*, 161)

The contradictory uses that Chesnutt makes of *Paradise Lost* – as empowering agent and debilitating idea – again show the "two tones" of Afro-American literature. And in its complex elaboration of the tension between the two tones, *The House Behind the Cedars* displays how distinctly Afro-American epic can be forged.

Chesnutt's short story, "The Fall of Adam," presents a humorous retelling of the Genesis story and echoes several elements of Miltonic tradition.[19] Since Chesnutt does not refer directly to *Paradise Lost* in his story, it is difficult to know to what extent he was responding specifically to Milton. It may be that "The Fall of Adam" is a satire on all the accumulated popular beliefs, myths, and interpretations of Genesis, especially since it comments upon Canaan (a son of Ham) as the accursed father of the black race, a story that occurs neither in the Bible nor in *Paradise Lost*.[20] In Chesnutt's story, Brother 'Lijah Gadson visits Brother Gabriel Gainey in order to ask two questions. The first question is about the fall of Adam. "I ain't never yit be'n able to find out whar Adam fell from, nuh how he come to fall?" (178). The second question has to do with the origin of the black race.

> Some says it's de cuss o' Caanyun but I never could'n' understan' bout dis here cuss o' Caanyun. I can see how de Lawd could turn anybody black jes' by cussin' 'im; 'case 'fo I j'ined de church – dat was 'fo de wah – I use' ter cuss de overseah on ole marse's plantation awful bad – when he was'n' da' – an' all de darkies on de plantation use'ter cus 'im, an' it didn' make de leas' changes in 'is complexion.
>
> ("Fall," 178–9)

Brother Gabriel, after "ras..n' in pra'r," has a vision in which he is shown the answers to these questions and discovers that they are the same question. He presents this answer the following Sunday in a sermon that includes many elements that appear to be derived from *Paradise Lost*, Book XI (in which the archangel Michael shows a vision to Adam), and the tradition of dream visions to which it belongs. Brother Gabriel begins:

> It seemed to me, when I fell into dat trance, I see a tall white angel comin' right down f'om hebben to wha'r I wus. He had a golden harp in his han', golden slippuhs on his feet, and a crown of gold upon his head. He flewed right down 'side o' me an' says: 'Rise up, Gab'l, an' go along wid me, an' all will be made cla'r to you.' I followed de angel th'ough de aiah, ovuh de mountains an' valleys an' oceans 'tel we come to a big gyahden where all kin's o' trees an' flowuhs was growin'! Den de angel says to me: 'Dis is de gyahden of Eden. Look! Den de angel lef' me an' I looked, an' see Adam an' Eve in de gyahden jes' as dey wus when de wuhld was made.
>
> ("Fall," 181)

Brother Gabriel watches as Adam and Eve eat of the fruit of the tree of knowledge. The Lord comes with a big hickory stick in order to punish Adam. Adam runs from the Lord, jumping over the tree of life, the world, the sea, Jupiter, the moon –

> When he got to de sun, he was so tired he couldn' jump high 'nuff, an' de bright light blind' 'im so he couldn' see whar' he was goin', an' he fell – fell right down into the rivuh Jordan; an' befo' he could pull hisse'f out'n de mud at de bottom, de Lawd cotch 'im – an' sich anuthuh whippin' de Lawd give Adam de worl' have nevuh hearn tell uv sence. An' dat 'splains, bro'rs an' sisters, de fall of Adam.

Brother Gabriel goes on to explain the origin of the black race.

When Adam jump' ovuh de sun, de fiah wus so hot, it scawched 'im black as a crips, an' curled up his ha'r so he nevuh couldn'n't git it straight agin. ... An' so Adam nevuh turn' white no mo', but stayed black all de rest of 'is life. All Adam an' Eve's chillun bawn fo' de Fall wus white, an' dey wus de fo'fathers ob de white race o' people – all Adam an' Eve's chillun bawn aftuh de Fall wus black, an' dey wus de fo'fathers ob de black race of people.

("Fall," 181–2)

Brother Gabriel's congregation is not particularly pleased with this explanation, and Brother Isham speaks out, "Well, it kindah 'peahs to me, elder, dat unduh all de sarcumstances ob de case dem chillun bawn aftuh de Fall oughtah be'n mullatahs." Brother Gabriel ends the discussion by telling Brother Isham to stop talking in church and by calling for a hymn.

This sermon, which begins with an evocation of the divine vision of *Paradise Lost*, Book XI, ends by humorously attacking all the religious and social mores of the larger society in which it is preached. Through the myth of Canaan as the father of the black race, Chesnutt lets us know that if being cursed could turn somebody black there would not be a white man left in all Christendom. In the sermon itself, the relationship between God and humankind is reduced to a ludicrous slave scene with "the Lord" as a cruel white slave-master and Adam as a frightened and unfortunate black slave whose supernatural and heroic powers are not enough to save him from punishment. We are made to understand that in the Judeo-Christian world only blacks are punished – the whites were born in paradise and partake of it still. But we also learn that the parents of all humankind lived in interracial cohabitation and were involved in miscegenation. Race itself is portrayed as both superficial and unalterable, and the black and white races are portrayed as utterly confounded since the beginning of time. Although Brother Gabriel may not understand what commentary he is making on *Paradise Lost* as the major Protestant epic of the western world, Chesnutt is clearly chipping at the foundations of the west by imposing a contrary history on the story we all know. In its concern with racial origins, and its description of a cult hero, "The Fall of Adam" expresses in abbreviated form the most prominent features of the epic genre wherever it occurs.

Ishmael Reed

In his novel *Mumbo Jumbo* Ishmael Reed attacks Milton and Christianity much more explicitly than does Chesnutt.[21] Reed sees Milton as the major apologist for "Atonism," the Osirian religion derived from the ancient Egyptian monotheist, Akenaten, who is portrayed as the eternal adversary of the polytheistic, life-celebrating, fundamentally black dance and religious movement "Jes Grew." Reed's portrayal of Milton begins with a discussion of Julian the Apostate who supposedly attempted to stop the spread of Atonism:

> He failed in his gallant attempt to reverse the Atonist challenge. He foresaw the Bad News it was going to bring to the world. John Milton, Atonist apologist extraordinary himself, saw the coming of the minor geek [magician] and sorcerer Jesus Christ as a way of ending the cult of Osiris and Isis forever.
>
> > The brutish gods of *Nile* as fast,
> > *Isis* and *Horus*, and the dog *Anubis* hast.
> >
> > Nor is *Osiris* seen
> > In *Memphian* grove, or Green
> >   Trampling th'unshower'd Grass with lowings loud:
> > Nor can he be at rest
> > Within his sacred chest,
> >   Naught but profoundest Hell can be his shroud;
> > In vain with Timbrel'd Anthems dark
> > The sable-stoled Sorcerers bear his worshipt ark.
>
> This from his Hymn "On the Morning of Christ's Nativity," which is nothing but a simple necktie party out to get Osiris' goat. And those "Timbrel'd Anthems dark" is the music that old Jethro played, the music of the worshipers of those festivals where they had a ball. Boogieing. Expressing they selves. John Milton couldn't stand that. Another Atonist; that's why English professors like him, he's like their amulet, keeping niggers out of their departments and stamping out Jes Grew before it invades their careers. It is interesting that he worked for Cromwell, a man who banned theater from England and was also a hero of Sigmund Freud.
>
> (*Mumbo Jumbo*, 195–6)

Reed here characterizes Milton as exclusionary, bigoted, repressed, unexpressive, and symbolic of American culture, literature (Reed follows with an insult to William Stryon), and Departments of Literature. Milton is credited with single-handedly keeping blacks out of English Departments. The poetry of Milton is a book of power, but power only for whites. If, for John Walden, the power of Milton's poetry is linked with the realization, "You are black, but you can be white;" and if for Rena this power says, "You are black, and you can never be white," in *Mumbo Jumbo* the power of Milton as Reed sees it says to black women and men, "You are black, and you can never approach the white holy of holies presided over by Milton." For Reed, Milton and his work represent an enormously oppressive and destructive white myth of western cultural superiority which is not only used to exclude blacks, but would be self-annihilating for blacks to believe in.

As the supreme literary emblem of the cultural power of whites, Milton has become for Reed the focus of anti-western sentiment so strong that the contemporary relationship between Milton and blacks seems to be not a dialogue of epic with epic, but a categorical refutation of Milton and Miltonic epic by blacks. The power and anger of Reed's rejection of Milton might point towards a literary version of black separatism. *Mumbo Jumbo* actually depends, however, on the reader's comprehensive knowledge of western literary traditions and history for its polemical effects. Indeed, Reed's work derives much of its power from its stark juxtapositions of scenes of contemporary history with descriptions of the founding moments of the western world. Readers must correlate photographs of Jacqueline Kennedy waving from a balcony with images of Moses learning "the truth" at the court of Jethro in the ancient Middle East. Nor are Reed's references to western history restricted to the very old and the very new. *Mumbo Jumbo*'s retelling of the history of the world from the Afro-American perspective is filled with detailed and intricate references to discrete moments throughout western history. Reed is indeed such a virtuoso in identifying and reassessing these moments that a thorough reading of his work is inevitably a valuable lesson in western cultural traditions.

To a great extent, then, Reed appropriates and wields elements of western culture for the ostensible purpose of attacking and rejecting the west. But is this a categorical rejection? Readers of Milton, and especially of *Paradise Regained*, are certainly familiar with this tactic. In his brief epic Milton used all of the arts of the classical world in getting his Christ to reject the best that the classical world has to offer. Scholars still debate the sincerity of Milton's rejection of classical knowledge, but that Milton's epics are extensions of classical epic and expansions of Homeric epic tradition cannot be questioned. *Paradise Lost* and *Paradise Regained* are within the line of Homeric tradition in spite of Milton's grumblings about the religion of Homer. In a similar manner, despite the verbal harshness of Reed's depreciation of the west, *Mumbo Jumbo*, through its facility in enlisting the very building blocks of the west to subvert and reinterpret its power, is itself a contemporary candidate for the line of western epic tradition. It is an unexplored work of the epic genre in the west and it will probably be our descendants rather than ourselves who decide whether to accept it or throw it out. My purpose here is to present it for consideration by placing it in the context of earlier patterns and changes in Homeric epic tradition.

Ishmael Reed himself, in the conclusion to his novel *Yellow Back Radio Broke-Down*, appears to be fully aware of the dialogic nature of his relationship with Milton and western epic traditions. In this hoo-doo/fantastic novel, the black hero, Loop Garoo, is miraculously saved from being executed (read crucified) and swims off to join Pope Innocent VIII as he sails away from America.[22] Speaking of this ending in an interview Reed states:

The ending of *Yellow Back Radio* was based on an introduction that Carl Jung wrote to *Paradise Lost* in which he traced the origin of Satan. What he claims is that the devil climbed out of art at a certain period along about the time of John Milton and that Milton was using an old gnostic idea of the devil as superman, "a man capable of all things." Jung contends that the devil became eminent in the world. In the ending of *Yellow Back*, which is kind of both a quasi-anarchistic and Tom Mix ending, the symbols of religion, the gods, return to art. They return to where they belong as something one contemplates but that doesn't participate in the world. That's one level of it. It's a trick ending. Some people interpreted it as Loop Garoo going back to Rome. But all the events that Pope Innocent VIII was talking about were taking place in art. And what happens is that people are on their own and Loop Garoo and the Pope return to art.[23]

The link between evil European power and Milton's Satan has also been perceived by such influential black thinkers as Malcolm X, who writes in his autobiography:

In either volume 43 or 44 of The Harvard Classics, I read Milton's *Paradise Lost*. The devil, kicked out of Paradise, was trying to regain possession. He was using the forces of Europe, personified by the Popes, Charlemagne, Richard the Lionhearted, and other knights. I interpreted this to show that the Europeans were motivated and led by the devil, or the personification of the devil. So Milton and Mr. Elijah Muhammad were actually saying the same thing.[24]

We see then that contemporary Afro-American responses to Milton, while flaunting protests against and rejections of the west, are rooted in detailed knowledge and analysis of western history and culture. Reed and Malcolm X have familial knowledge of European Popes, kings, and history.

The anger toward Milton expressed in *Mumbo Jumbo* appears to have increased through time for Afro-American writers, with origins in the cultural frustration and self-depreciation of Wheatley's encounters with Milton; in the transformation of Miltonic themes by Boyd; and in Chesnutt's ironic and mocking responses to Milton's epics. Read together, these texts comprise a history of increasingly overt protest-literature that converts and subverts the power of the English language and western literary traditions into distinctively Afro-American art that is the developing core of an Afro-American epic tradition.

Recent examples of this tradition include Gloria Naylor's *Linden Hills*, which explicitly refers to Milton as an epic poet, and which successfully re-envisions elements of Dante's *Inferno* in a masterful presentation of the black middle and upper classes who strive downward from the First to the Eighth Crescent of a black neighborhood. Naylor's novel is one of many Afro-American literary responses to Dante, and thus has a kinship not only with the *Divine Comedy*, but also with such works as *The System of Dante's Hell* by LeRoi Jones. Such multiple connections, the "two tones" as it were, nourish the complexity and cultural distinctiveness that is becoming characteristic of the "tale of the tribe" that is the Afro-American epic genre.

Derek Walcott's *Another Life* is another epic that proclaims its connections with multiple traditions. In an earlier poem, "A Far Cry From Africa," Walcott writes of the extreme tension caused by writing in the language and literary modes associated with those whose oppression of Africans has evoked so much violent hatred:

> I who am poisoned with the blood of both,
> Where shall I turn, divided to the vein?
> I who have cursed
> The drunken officer of British rule, how choose
> Between this Africa and the English tongue I love?
> Betray them both, or give back what they give?
> How can I face such slaughter and be cool?
> How can I turn from Africa and live?[25]

Notes

1. Robert A. Bone, *The Negro Novel in America*, rev. edn (New Haven, Yale University Press, 1970), 25.
2. Henry Louis Gates, Jr, "Criticism in the jungle," in *Black Literature and Literary Theory*, ed. H. L. Gates, Jr (New York, Methuen, 1984), 4.
3. Vernon Loggins, *The Negro Author: His Development in America* (New York, Columbia University Press, 1932), 27.
4. See especially: Jacob Rhodes, *A Nation's Loss: A Poem on the Life and Death of the Hon. Abraham Lincoln* (Newark, NJ, F. Starbuck, 1866); Frances Ellen Watkins Harper, *Moses. A Story of the Nile* (Philadelphia, Merrihew & Son, 1870); Albery A. Whitman, *Not a Man and Yet a Man* (Springfield, Ohio, Republic Printing Co., 1877) and *An Idyl of the South: an epic poem in two parts* (New York, Metaphysical Publishing Co., 1901); George Hannibal Temple, *The Epic of Columbus' Bell, and Other Poems* (Reading, Pa, Reading Eagle, 1900); James Madison Bell, *The Poetical Works of James Madison Bell* (Lansing, Wynkoop, Hallenbeck, Crawford, Co., 1901); Robert E. Ford, *Brown Chapel: A Story in Verse* (Baltimore, 1905); Fenton Johnson, "The Vision of Lazarus," in *A Little Dreaming* (Chicago, Peterson Linotyping Co., 1913); George Marion McClellan, "The Legend of Tannhauser," in *The Path of Dreams* (Louisville, J. P. Morgan, 1916); and George Reginald Margetson, *The Fledgeling Bard and the Poetry Society* (Boston, R. G. Badger, 1916).
5. Henry Wasser, "John Quincy Adams on the opening lines of Milton's *Paradise Lost*" (*American Literature*, 42, 1970, 373); Sacvan Bercovitch, "Cotton Mather against rhyme: Milton and the *Psalterium Americanum*" (*American Literature*, 39, 1967, 191); George Frank Sensabaugh, *Milton in Early America* (Princeton, Princeton University Press, 1964). Critics such as Gordon S. Wood (*The New England Quarterly*, 37, 1964, 543) have attacked Sensabaugh's generalizations regarding Milton's effect on early America, stating that Milton's influence was "broad but not profound" and that since he affected language and

syntax rather than meaning, Milton's writing "was never determinative of American thought." Wood particularly objects to Sensabaugh's "overdrawn conclusions" regarding Milton's effect upon Jefferson's ideas of religious liberty. While it is evident that Sensabaugh often ascribes too much consciousness of Milton's politics to the Americans who quoted him somewhat haphazardly, it is nevertheless true that Americans used Milton whether or not they understood or agreed with him. Milton's works may not have been read carefully, but in many early American writings he is revered along with Locke and Newton as a great genius of England. He received adulation even though his image may have been a false projection created by uninformed admirers.

6. Sensabaugh, op. cit., 66.
7. ibid., 122.
8. All quotations from Milton's poetry are taken from *John Milton: Complete Poems and Major Prose*, ed. Merritt Y. Hughes (New York, Odyssey, 1957). References are included in the text.
9. See especially Alexander Crummell, *The Man: the Hero: the Christian: A Eulogy of the Life and Character of Thomas Clarkson* (New York, Egbert, Hovey & King, 1847).
10. To be properly assessed, this subject of the interconnections between Milton and the black church requires much additional research, along the following lines:

(1) A historical description and analysis of the relationship between oral and written textual traditions in black sermons – including a full analysis of the manner in which blacks were Christianized in North America. In many areas it was illegal for blacks to read or to become Christian. We need to know exactly how such laws and attitudes affected the religious conversion and the acquisition of reading skills by blacks.

(2) A fully interrelated history of black and white southern churches, with detailed analysis of the religious texts developed especially for the conversion of black slaves during the Great Awakening and during other periods of religious intensity in the United States.

(3) A historical analysis of ideological changes in textbooks used in black and white theological schools and seminaries, along with a study of secondary materials – letters, journals, and memoirs of theology students and professors; course syllabi and reading lists; school newspapers, bulletins, official pronouncements.

(4) An analysis of contemporary black sermons to be recorded as necessary using current anthropological recording methods.
11. See especially Wheatley's poems: "To the University of Cambridge in New England" (Miltonic blank verse and themes); "An Hymn to the Morning" and "An Hymn to the Evening" (Miltonic companion poems); "On Virtue" (blank verse with echoes of Milton's "Il Penseroso"); "On the Capture of General Lee" (compare with Satan's speeches in *PL* I); "Thoughts On the Works of Providence" (Miltonic device of "vague exactness in measurement" – Mason, in Wheatley, op. cit., xxiii); "Isaiah LXIII: 1–8" and "Niobe in Distress for Her Children Slain by Apollo, from Ovid's Metamorphoses, Book VI, and from a View of the Painting of Mr. Richard Wilson" (brief epics that echo the *Iliad* and *Paradise Lost* – "Niobe" also links echoes of western epic with allusion to her African parents in their bereavement of her); in Wheatley, op. cit.
12. All quotations from Wheatley's poetry are taken from *The Poems of Phillis Wheatley*, ed. Julian D. Mason, Jr (Chapel Hill, University of North Carolina Press, 1966); page references are included in the text.

The three versions of Wheatley's "On the Death of the Rev. Mr. George Whitefield. 1770" illustrate how the cross-cultural and cross-disciplinary fusion discussed earlier was used to create subversive anti-slavery poetry. In the first (1770) version Wheatley associated freedom for Africans with their acceptance of Christianity; the word "free" was, however, eliminated in the two versions published primarily for colonial rather than British audiences. The Whitefield poem was Wheatley's earliest publication and was written to honor an evangelist who "while sympathetic with the plight of Negroes, . . . defended slavery on Biblical grounds" (Wheatley, 67). Since Wheatley was privy to the public and private conversation of white society, I assume that she was fully aware of Whitefield's stance, though there is no hard evidence to support this. Wheatley, perhaps in appreciation of being allowed to convert to Christianity, attempted to praise Whitefield unambiguously in accepted Christian terms when she spoke of the conversion of Africans; but her own almost unconscious interpretation of her religion, encouraged by the society's linking of freedom with Christianity, led her to express what she felt to be true: that Christianity and enslavement are incompatible. In the 1770 British version of the poem Wheatley wrote:

> Take him, ye Africans, he longs for you,
> Impartial Saviour is his Title due.
> If you will walk in Grace's heavenly Road,
> He'll make you free, and Kings, and Priests to God.
>
> (70)

In the 1773 version for the American audience, the last two lines are changed to read: "Wash'd in the fountain of redeeming blood,/You shall be sons, and Kings, and Priests to God" (Wheatley, 10), the substitution of the less politically charged "sons" for "free" revealing that the association of freedom for Africans with Christianity was a threat to the upholders of slavery in colonial society.

13. For titles of many of Wheatley's lost poems see Wheatley, op. cit., 112.
14. Wheatley was given a copy of the 1770 Glasgow folio edition of *Paradise Lost* by the Lord Mayor of London in 1773, when she visited England. The copy is now in the library of Harvard University. See Wheatley, op. cit., xv, for further details.
15. John Boyd, *Poems on Various Subjects* (London, Cowie & Strange, 1829); and *The Vision and Other Poems: In Blank Verse* (London, Longman, 1834).
16. Charles Waddell Chesnutt, *The House Behind the Cedars* (1900, rpt New York, Collier, 1969). References are included in the text.
17. There appears to be such a fusion between the Bible and *Paradise Lost* in the conclusion to another of his novels, *The Marrow of Tradition*, in which the character Janet, upon obtaining her heart's desire, "found it but apples of Sodom, filled with dust and ashes!" (Chesnutt, *The Marrow of Tradition* (1901, rpt Ann Arbor, University of Michigan Press, 1969), 328). Chesnutt gives no referent for these "apples of Sodom," but their prototype is not from the Bible but from *Paradise Lost*, X.547–72, in which Satan and the fallen angels eat apples of bitter ashes. An early source for Milton's "apples of Sodom" is Josephus, the first century AD Jewish historian who describes the fruit (not the apples) of Sodom as smoky and ashy, though they appear healthy and firm. See *The Wars of the Jews* in *Josephus: Complete Works*, tr. William Whiston (Grand Rapids, Kregel Publications, 1960), 540. There is also a verse in Deuteronomy which may have influenced Josephus and Milton: "For their vine is of the vine of Sodom, and of the fields of Gomorrah: their grapes are grapes of

gall, their clusters are bitter" (Deut. 32:32). Chesnutt may have had a more contemporary source for the term "apples of Sodom," since it is also used by Herman Melville in his *The Encantadas,* in *Selected Writings of Herman Melville* (New York, Random House, 1952), 53.

18. Frances R. Keller, *An American Crusade: The Life of Charles Waddell Chesnutt* (Provo, Utah, Brigham Young University Press, 1978), 58–63, *passim.*
19. Charles W. Chesnutt, "The Fall of Adam" in *The Short Fiction of Charles W. Chesnutt,* ed. Sylvia Lyons Render (Washington, DC, Howard University Press, 1974).
20. In the Biblical story, Canaan, the son of Ham, is cursed, although Ham is the wrongdoer (Gen. 9:22–7). Ham and the other sons of Ham are not cursed and neither Ham nor any of his sons is identified in the Bible with the black race. Canaan, of course, is the progenitor of the people whom the Hebrews are to conquer and displace.
21. Ishmael Reed, *Mumbo Jumbo* (New York, Bard/Avon, 1978). References are included in the text.
22. Ishmael Reed, *Yellow Back Radio Broke-Down* (Garden City, Doubleday, 1969), 147–74.
23. "Ishmael Reed" in *Interviews with Black Writers,* ed. John O'Brien (New York, Liveright, 1972), 180.
24. Malcolm X (with the assistance of Alex Haley), *The Autobiography of Malcolm X* (New York, Grove Press, 1965), 186.
25. Derek Walcott, *Collected Poems 1948–1984* (New York, Farrar, Straus & Giroux, 1986), 18.

14

ROBIN JARVIS

Love between Milton and Wordsworth

To try to write love is to confront the muck of language.
(Barthes, *A Lover's Discourse: Fragments*)

There is a durable critical tradition which regards the relation of one poet to another as being fundamentally benign and supportive, consisting in an attachment that is little short of love. How appropriate is such a perspective to the relation between Milton's poetry and that of his major descendants? It is over sixty years since R. D. Havens wrote about *The Influence of Milton on English Poetry* on the serene assumption that "one of the uses . . . of great poets is to furnish inspiration and guidance for those who come after them;" but one could read much recent criticism of Milton's Romantic heirs without being aware that anything had happened to challenge such complacency. Few have matched the afflatus of Abbie Potts's marriage of genealogy with literary rites of passage: "There is a kinship among poems; they have all one face *sub specie aeternitatis*. Recognizing this, the novice will acknowledge his poetic kindred gladly, and with their help he will gratefully accomplish his own identity, his unique imaginative life: a *nova progenies*." But J. A. Wittreich, for example, commenting specifically on Shelley but with implicit reference to the Romantics generally, has insisted on the "healthy, vital, and continual influence of Milton on the future course of English poetry" in terms reminiscent of Havens; and even Leslie Brisman, a critic not otherwise noted for inattention to trends in contemporary literary theory, has argued for a "choice submissiveness" to poetic fathers in which the self is not "obliterated" but "re-created."[1] It is only in the revisionist theory of Harold Bloom that the love of one poet for another has been construed as fundamentally ambivalent.

My concern in this essay is with Milton and Wordsworth. With what complexities and consequences, and with what economy of meaning, does the Miltonic engage with the Wordsworthian? Is Wordsworth's remembrance of Milton a loving one, or does this question already presuppose too much to give more than a self-serving answer? I propose to examine the issue, rather obliquely, by seeing what *Paradise Lost* and *The Prelude* have to say about "love" itself. Roland Barthes, whom I have quoted above, points to a predicament wherein language, asked to speak of love, seems to be permanently surrendered to either over- or under-statement (rank emotionalism or the poverty of existing codes).[2] I would suggest that in these two texts there is a similar irremediable contradiction; and if this is so – if the term "love" is itself suspect and indeterminable – then there are bound to be repercussions for the critical tradition that has adopted and exploited it in such an apparently innocent and uncontroversial way.

To be at once more specific and more dogmatic, Milton's poem, in invoking love, appeals to something invariable and essential, the "soul" of those qualities constituting the "sum of wisdom," but it cannot sustain (to another way of thinking it exceeds) that investment. *The Prelude*, like *Paradise Lost*, is a poem "centring all in love," yet one in which, variously and demonstrably, the centre cannot hold.[3] In hypostasizing love both poems summon a principle structuring a history, a life, a text; both reveal, through their deviations from the centre, the fallibility of such structures, suggesting, as Barthes says, that "the love story . . . is the tribute the lover must pay to the world in order to be reconciled with it."[4] But it is precisely these deviations that permit the reader – who, as we shall see, is by no means a dispassionate observer of the text and the tradition to which it belongs – to construct his own "love" stories, though these may be more intricately plotted, and have less definite endings, than the genre exacts.

To begin with, let us rough out a field of signification and suggest the main difficulties attaching to it. In *Paradise Lost* "love" encompasses a wide range of relationships: human love, narcissistic love, love of God, Divine love, angelic love, Satanic love, and so on. In *The Prelude*, so Wordsworth and his editors tell us, we are concerned with a love of nature which itself engenders, in time, a love of mankind. Yet in both poems we discern a contamination of love with other affects – something insinuating itself into what, as the soul or centre, should be clear of such intrusion. There is in both an untoward emphasis on discrepancy and choice – on economics – that calls into question love's unitive function and capacities. And in both a complex problematic of sexual difference embarrasses love's essentiality by pointing to occluded elements in its constitution. I shall take up these issues in turn, although there is room to deal with only the more remarkable or extreme symptoms of these forms of instability.

Firstly, the question of the contamination of love. The correspondence of a love of God *associated with*, but increasingly difficult to disentangle from, fear, with a love of nature that supports an alliance with fear, is one of the

more obvious indices of the reconstitution of Miltonic theocentrism as
"natural religion." The relation between these two versions of fearful love,
each of which produces themes of tutelage, obedience, misdemeanour and
punishment, and so on, is, however, an inverse one: Adam's resolution to
"love with fear the only God" – a love which forgoes all intent to repossess
its object, and will instead "Walk / *As in* his presence" (XII.562–3; my
italics) – is attendant on his transgression, and his fear is therefore a
postlapsarian burden; Wordsworth's education at the hands of loving but
punitive parental presences in nature ("unknown modes of being" that will
never have more than an allocutory existence) is, by contrast, a condition of
the development of his imagination and its virtual autonomy from nature
and is therefore preliminary to his fall (into self-consciousness). Adam's
fearful love is a consequence of his disseverance from the object of his love,
the "Presence divine" (VIII.314) that had at one time appeared to him
directly. Wordsworth attempts to reverse Adam's fall by repossessing his
first love more securely in maturity, but he does this only by misplacing and
then redefining the object: the tutelary "presences" give way to more subtle
notions of interaction between mind and nature. Indeed, *The Prelude* is,
among other things, the history of these revisions, culminating in a dualist
philosophy that stresses the "excellence, pure spirit, and best power, / Both
of the object seen, and eye that sees" (XII.378–9). Wordsworth falls out of
Adam's fall by falling out of fear, by decrying the constitutive relation of
love and fear, and this is formulated explicitly as a swerve *vis-à-vis Paradise
Lost*: "Even to the very going out of youth . . . I too exclusively esteem'd
that love, / And sought that beauty, which, as Milton sings, / Hath terror in
it" (XIII.215–19). It is intriguing that Wordsworth's allusion, a component
of lines praising his sister's female "tenderness" for gentling his (presumably
male) leaning towards love comprehending terror, directs us to the scene of
the Fall, in which Satan turns his attention to the terribly lovely Eve in order
to avoid a confrontation with Adam. This raises questions concerning the
sexual differences dividing and defining love which we shall take up later.
We have sketched, to begin with, a love (desiring presence) that is partially
constituted by that which contradicts it (fear of presence), and which in
Wordsworth's case can outgrow this contradiction only by further differing
from itself and from its configurations in an earlier text. For Wordsworth,
that is, fear of presence may disappear only to resurface as fear of sameness.
Or, as Barthes suggests, fear may be an inalienable component of the lover's
discourse concerning the "absent one," a function of the asymmetry
between speaking *to* the loved object (God or nature in our examples above)
and speaking *of* it:

> I am wedged between two tenses, that of the reference and that of the
> allocution: you have gone (which I lament), you are here (since I am
> addressing you). Whereupon I know what the present, that difficult tense,
> is: a pure portion of anxiety.

Barthes here describes an "insupportable present" in which the reassuring proximity implicit in the allocution is offset by the disabling loss implicit in the reference. The anxiety thus generated cannot easily be placated, for, as Barthes has already suggested, "isn't desire always the same, whether the object is present or absent? Isn't the object *always* absent?"[5] Since absence is a condition of desire, Barthes deploys language as a means of manipulating it or rendering it more manageable, converting predicament into practice ("there is a creation of a fiction which has many roles") and postponing the death which absence always prefigures. If fear and love, possession and non-possession, presence and absence, come together in a language that confounds the categories of tense, this may also have a bearing on Wordsworth's ambivalent relation to his precursor and, in turn, on the reader's relation to the texts in question. Reading, that is, may also inhabit an insupportable present in which allusions, sources, referents and so on are there and not there at the same time, and in which interpretation must constantly defer, through the idiosyncrasies of its own language, the discovery of its lack of a reliable ground. Critical discourse, like the lover's discourse, keeps in play an object which can never be possessed totally.

Let us turn now to the question of the economics of love, bearing in mind that an economic dimension must necessarily contradict the tenets of an unfallen.love. I want also to place this analysis in the context of a theme of observation or surveillance, which, denominating as it does both precise situations in the texts themselves and the role of a hypothetically detached and impartial critical mind, permits some useful reflections on the intertextuality of love – intertextuality, that is, conceived as a function that sets the reader, as well as the text and context (or pre-text), in productive motion. To begin at the beginning: before the Fall, from his perch in the "pure empyrean," God observes Adam and Eve "Reaping immortal fruits of joy and love, / Uninterrupted joy, *unrivalled love* / In blissful solitude" (III.67–9; my italics). "Unrivalled" may be taken, presumably, to mirror "solitude," to indicate the a priori lack of rivals; there is, one supposes, no competition for affection in Eden. This conception of the originary plenitude and perfect reciprocity of love is undermined, however, both by the mediation of Satan as voyeuristic observer and by the prescience of God, who makes plain that love, even in an unfallen world, must comprehend discrepancy and choice:

> Freely they stood who stood, and fell who fell.
> Not free, what proof could they have given sincere
> Of true allegiance, constant faith or love,
> Where only what they needs must do, appeared,
> Not what they would?
>
> (III.102–6)

From the beginning we know that Adam and Eve are not reaping "immortal fruits" of love: their love is seeded with the potential for change because it must be tested by conflicting claims. These claims, be they divine or underworldly, interfere with the conceptualization of a virginal love prior to all disparity and contestation: in testing the loyalties of Adam and Eve Satan probes the freedom which divides those loyalties *at the outset,* just as his own love, by virtue of its aboriginal burden of freedom – which here means essentially the freedom to differ – has itself been sublet to the struggles of volition. There is no love that is not already a question of economic imbalance, though Milton conjures with the idea of a monumental stasis of libido that would liberate the ego from such vicissitudes.

In the passage quoted, as at many points in these early Books, we witness Adam and Eve pinioned between the supervisory or supervisionary sight of God on "prospect high" and the subliminal attentions of Satan. Divine supervision has the effect of disordering the actual chronology of *Paradise Lost* and hence rendering suspect the semantic values that are dependent upon it. In Book III, for example, God "fore"-sees the moment, after the Fall, when "heavenly love," no longer a gratuitous emanation of a self-reflecting divine source, must become agonistic, must "outdo hellish hate;" but, through a modulation of tenses which orthodox criticism has not entirely recuperated, the Fall is presented as already having occurred:

> So heavenly love shall outdo hellish hate
> Giving to death, and dying to redeem,
> So dearly to redeem what hellish hate
> So easily destroyed, and *still destroys*
> In those who, when they may, accept not grace.
> (III.298–302; my italics)

If, on the other hand, it is argued that all time is eternally present, then the Fall has always already occurred, and "love" is always already fallen, subject to discrepancy and choice.

The same problematic appears when we turn to Satan. In echoing God's discourse on freedom the rebel angel collapses the opposition of love and hate:

> Hadst thou the same free will and power to stand?
> Thou hadst: whom hast thou then or what to accuse,
> But heaven's free love dealt equally to all?
> Be then his love accursed, since love or hate,
> To me alike, it deals eternal woe.
> (IV.66–70)

Satan, in recalling or conceding the possibility of a love "dealt equally to all," hypothesizes a transcendent passion self-identical in all its outgoings, undepleted throughout its massive expenditure, and gloriously prior to immersion in the human world of differences. But in that it *originates* in a differential freedom, and *consists in* the freedom to differ, this divine love *is* precisely the necessary condition of Satan's fall, and therefore permits a despairing nominalism ("love or hate, / To me alike") which is nonetheless more than a play on words. Or rather, no less than: by means of one of the mutual metaphors through which he unseats the ideological norms of the poem, Satan refutes the literality of love and hate and dispossesses them of their common-sense oppositional value. Again, when he remarks, later in this book, that he "could love" Adam and Eve, this love is excited by their proximity to God ("so lively shines / In them divine resemblance" (IV.363–4)) and must therefore be all the more a contaminated feeling, rather than the outcome of a momentary virtuous impulse. As voyeur, Satan ensures that the "unrivalled love" ascribed to Paradise is a "Sight hateful" in more ways than one. His mediation of our perception of the Garden guarantees, as Donald Bouchard points out, that we are always in the realm of a simulacrum, and underlines the fact that "the literature which attempts to represent Paradise is a sequel to the fall."[6] In this scene, in which Eve recounts to Adam the story of their first encounter and then embraces him in one of the poem's delicately erotic moments, Satan is present as a kind of unconscious: representing, contrary to the motions of a "pure" conjugal love, the residual undercurrent of "fierce desire," which "Still unfulfilled with pain of longing pines" (IV.509–11). This substratum is recognized after the Fall, when Eve foresees Adam "languishing" with "desire" (X.996–7) if they abstain from sex in order to contain the threat of death.

We have temporarily lost sight of Wordsworth. Or have we? Is it too far-fetched to suggest that the reader habitually finds her/himself in the position of Milton's God, who beholds simultaneously "past, present, future" (III.78)? If all poetry is eternally present (that is, equally accessible to, and open to reactivation by, the reader), we must explore the consequences of our readerly prescience. In particular, it would be interesting to know where to draw the line between the predestinating of our perceived allusions or poetic relationships and the freedom which we must nevertheless resign to language in order to avoid the obloquy of a critical tyranny. Certainly, we cannot help but "foresee" Wordsworth in reading *Paradise Lost*. On this issue of love as comprehending division and discrepancy, one envisages the entire thematics of love of nature *leading to* love of man, conceived in the economic metaphor of a gradually altering "scale of love" (*Prel.* VIII.867): love involving *distance*, as with Wordsworth's love for the "abject multitude" in France, modified only by his feeling for the symbolic individual (the hunger-bitten girl); and the doctrinal impasse of the social conditions of possibility of love: Wordsworth, that is, insists that love is a gift of "vulgar Nature" and does not require "Retirement, leisure, language purified / By manners" (XII.188–90), but then disallows its possibility under conditions of material oppression and in cities. Part of his problem here, as Gayatri Chakravorty Spivak indicates, is the attempt to sustain his fiction of a "universal heart" in the face of asymmetries whose politico-economic foundations he refuses to interrogate, but which prevent the successful resuscitation of that trope. As she says, "why should a man who does not want to reduce Man (*sic*) to a homogenizing abstraction be unable to entertain the question of heterogeneity?"[7] "Individual Man" in Wordsworth, as Spivak argues, is always on the verge of becoming an ideological generality; but the passions which this "composition of the thought" elicits are as variegated as one could imagine. Consider the passage in Book X in which Wordsworth describes his "second love" of love for man as an "after-worship" succeeding the "strong / And holy passion" (X.382–3) for nature. The "ritual" of this after-worship, nourished on the Terror and the Revolutionary wars in France, comprehends feelings of self-righteousness, sharp discriminations (though a "lamentable time for man" (mankind, one would assume), the "invaders," those "snakes about [the] cradle," "fared as they deserved"), furtive pleasure in man's suffering, and "sympathies with power" that are "prolonged" until the final version of the poem.[8]

This exceedingly inwrought conception of love returns us, far from perversely, to the divine foreknowledge, the "love accursed" that "deals eternal woe," of Milton's God. There is, in fact, a spiralling series of mediations, of scenes of surveillance, which, as I indicated earlier, not only brings Milton's poem into view but problematizes our own role as critical observers. This series begins with Wordsworth's self-association with the "ancient prophets:"

> But as the ancient Prophets were enflamed,
> Nor wanted consolations of their own
> And majesty of mind, when they denounced
> On Towns and Cities, wallowing in the abyss
> Of their offences, punishment to come;
> Or saw like other men with bodily eyes
> Before them in some desolated place
> The consummation of the wrath of Heaven,
> So did some portion of that spirit fall
> On me, to uphold me through those evil times.
>
> (X.401–10)

This recalls in the first instance Michael's previewing to Adam of Noah's self-righteous denunciation of antediluvian society:

> fearless of reproach or scorn,
> Or violence, he of their wicked ways
> Shall them admonish, and before them set
> The paths of righteousness, how much more safe,
> And full of peace, denouncing wrath to come

On their impenitence; and shall return
Of them derided, but of God observed
The one just man alive.

(*PL* XI.811–18)

The correspondence is more generously fleshed out: just as Adam weeps tears of "pious sorrow" at Michael's depiction of the Flood,[9] so Wordsworth refers the "heaviest sorrow earth can bring" to a "reservoir of guilt / And ignorance, fill'd up from age to age, / That could no longer hold its loathsome charge, / But burst and spread in deluge through the Land" (*Prel.* X.436–9). In this *mise en abîme* – the "abyss / Of their offences" – we observe Wordsworth apparently observing Michael observing Adam observing Noah – observed by God. In *Paradise Lost* God's exteriority is absolute ("for what can scape the eye / Of God all-seeing?"); but the reader interiorizes God's observations, remarking, for example, the similarities between this conjuncture at which heavenly love is disarmed almost fatally by a desire to "blot out mankind" (observation is here an *oversight* of cosmic significance) and all those other instances of ambivalent love in the divine observatory – not least the passage in Book III already quoted in which God makes, in Empson's phrase, "grisly jokes" about Satan's "escape" from hell. Wordsworth's conflicting feelings at the spectacle of Revolutionary France may seem of an altogether different order from the vicissitudes of divine love in Milton's epic, but we have Wordsworth's authority for the linkage and for the discordant images thus superimposed: "Great God . . . what a change is here!" (*Prel.* X.385–92).

If, however, we *foresee* Wordsworth while reading Milton and *recall* or *re-view* Milton while reading Wordsworth, the snugly elevated exteriority of our *readerly* observatory begins to seem a little suspect, since in these circumstances we shall never be able to escape the consciousness of being observed, if only by ourselves. To foresee oneself remembering one's foresight is disorientating to the extent that it makes it impossible to *situate* oneself, to the extent that one finds oneself *in transition*; as though all reading shared the nature of metalepsis or transumption as that trope is deviously redefined by Harold Bloom: a transferring or far-fetching which conceals "no presence or time in itself, for transumption can seem comic through its surrender of the living present."[10] There are limits to our readerly prescience because in reading we open onto a wordscape which refuses to stay still, and the prospect differs according to the position which we take up. The "observatory" is a mystification, and the simultaneous spectacle of past, present and future always over the horizon, because in reading we cannot but enter into the field of observation. We do not, for example, "observe" the migrations of love: *reading is a migratory movement.*[11] It is for this reason that intertextuality must be defined as a *function*, not simply a large and essentially polymorphous context (which risks reification). It is a function, above all, that exceeds or suspends the conscious control of the reader, who must be considered rather as a function of the intertext.

Another major issue we must consider is that of love in its relation to sexual difference. What is the sexual constitution of love in each poem? If love can be shown to divide along sexual lines, then it can scarcely lay claim to be an invariable and inviolable essence. And what is the structure of the two poems' sexual relations? In *Paradise Lost*, according to Dr Johnson, the love of Adam and Eve is "pure benevolence and mutual veneration;" but, he adds, "both before and after the Fall the superiority of Adam is diligently sustained." And nothing, of course, can obscure the fact that Milton's Garden embodies a historically finite politics of love, sometimes comic in the unwittingly banal discomfiture of would-be unfallen ideals. Johnson merely reproduces Milton's blind spots: "O when meet now / Such pairs, in love and mutual honour joined?" Milton asks, in the wake of Eve's withdrawal from the dining-table, leaving Raphael and Adam to the port and cigars; though capable of grasping "studious thoughts abstruse," she prefers to receive a digest of the argument later from Adam, who will deflect her impatience or boredom with the odd "digression" or "conjugal caress" (VIII.39–58). In the gendered hierarchy of *Paradise Lost*, love is "feminine" towards a superior and "masculine" towards an inferior, a structure reinforced by the implicating of love with obedience in certain relations. Such a division of the amorous relation organizes the embrace of Adam and Eve which excites Satan's envy, where it is overwritten with the spatial connotations of high and low in the classical simile of Sky Father and Earth Mother:

> he in delight
> Both of her beauty and submissive charms
> Smiled with *superior love*, as Jupiter
> On Juno smiles, when he impregns the clouds
> That shed May flowers.
> (IV.497–501; my italics)

Eve is constituted, paradoxically, as an *unequal half*: in this scene in which she moves rapidly from a hermetic narcissism, a self-halving into subject and reflection, to a love-relationship comprehending sexual difference, she finds herself as a half that *belongs* unilaterally to its "other half" ("of him thou art"), is "excelled" by that other half, and therefore "yields" to it. Eve is initially reluctant to sacrifice her own propriety of self-image ("back I turned"), but, "seized" by what is apparently a prior meaning ("he / Whose image thou art"), she consents to divide her integrity and *represent* Adam, who would signify only himself. Masculine love is thus primary, superior and literal; feminine love is secondary, submissive and figurative. Adam is in love with his own image and wishes to bring Eve to identity, to confine her capacity to signify, but, as Bouchard says, Eve is dangerously "the first literary creation" (originating in "dreams and desire" and then becoming an independent entity) and will eventually forget her pact with Adam in order to "maintain her difference" from him.[12]

The question of unfallen sexuality, which tested C. S. Lewis' apologetics and exercised his imagination, articulates with especial clarity the roles we have identified. The question hinges on the impossibility of defining such a state other than negatively. The passage which Lewis cites from St Augustine's *De Civitate Dei* confronts the difficulty squarely:

> I speak of a thing which they two who alone could have experienced it never did experience: how then when mention is made of it *now* can it be presented to human fantasy except *in the likeness* of the turbid lust we have tried and not of the tranquil volition we conjecture?[13]

The condition of speaking of unfallen sexuality is its a priori status as metaphor: circularly conjectured by comparison with what should be its fallen copy or imitation, it is enunciated only at the cost of a total foreclosure of literality ("they two who alone could have experienced it never did"). Milton's controversial innovation, of course, was to reposit the literality of the experience, but he is no less confined to a rhetoric of likeness or unlikeness – a limitation that sometimes becomes exaggeratedly apparent. The encomium on "wedded love" in Book IV is a case in point. It is not simply that this love, this "mysterious law," is mysterious partly in so far as it conceals its origins in a cultural institution of sexual inequality: reflected, for example, in such fadings into postlapsarian sexual behaviour as that of which Lewis complains, that "Eve exhibits modesty too exclusively in sexual contexts, and . . . Adam does not exhibit it at all."[14] Nor does it reduce to an accompanying vein of male mystification: Augustine's grounding of unfallen love in likeness would suggest, in view of the sexual/rhetorical homology adumbrated above, that it is in some sense *feminine*; but Milton, curiously celebrating prelapsarian wedded love in the fallen terms of a remedy for (Augustine's turbid) lust, is constrained to place it within a uniquely *male* economy:

> By thee adulterous lust was driven *from men*
> Among the bestial herds to range, by thee
> Founded in reason, loyal, just, and pure,
> Relations dear, and all the charities
> Of *father, son, and brother* first were known.
> (IV.753–7; my italics)

And yet, in denying that such love is a notion "unbefitting holiest place" (IV.759), in arguing for the appropriateness of one image to another, Milton, in effect, "feminizes" it (since it is feminine love that is held to be *answerable* to another) or renders its sexual status ambiguous.

More interesting than these foreseeable snares, however, is the strain of supererogatory projection or contrast into which Milton's tactic of negative definition seduces his writing:

> Here Love his golden shafts employs, here lights
> His constant lamp, and waves his purple wings,
> Reigns here and revels; not in the bought smile
> Of harlots, loveless, joyless, unendeared,
> Casual fruition, nor in court amours
> Mixed dance, or wanton mask, or midnight ball,
> Or serenade.

> (IV.763–9)

There is a definite element of overkill here in the immoderate and gratuitous conjuration of associations which cannot help but leave their trace on love, even as they are differentiated from it. The excess in the stipulation of *what love is not* merely engenders an ever slighter phantasm of *what love is*; *contra* Augustine, Milton multiplies *unlikeness* to the point where he risks stripping his concept to an insignificant bone.

The subordination or exclusion of Eve and femininity which we see in *Paradise Lost* is inseparable from a doomed subordination or exclusion of metaphor; and just as Eve eventually asserts her independence regardless and thus makes explicit the divisions within and between her and Adam (and henceforth all human beings), so metaphor or likeness appears within every attempt to found a literal image of human origins and therefore confirms a world of arbitrary signs. The exclusion of woman scales new heights in Adam's prophetic vision of the birth of Christ in the final Book: "virgin Mother, hail, / High in the love of heaven, yet *from my loins* / Thou shalt proceed" (XII.379–81; my italics). The theme of procreation or lineage is an appropriate one with which to insinuate Wordsworth into the argument. In a playful sense, the excluded mother in the terrestrial drama of *Paradise Lost* reappears in Hell, in the person of Sin, as the source of all monstrous creativity, the disowned offspring of what was initially, like Adam's, a narcissistic object-choice ("Thy self in me thy perfect image viewing" (II.764)). The conception, the birth of meaning, is here unnatural, perverted, catastrophic – tricks returning to plague the inventor or progenitor. The failure of meaning to coincide with itself consorts with the engendering of a grim and "growing burden:" it is all but a reversal of the Oedipal scenario of influence, and one which re-echoes suggestively the double-faced reading experience I have already outlined, in which Milton is viewed as much through a Wordsworthian lens as Wordsworth is regarded against the backdrop of Milton.

The relation of Sin and Satan is also, of course, an incestuous one, and this is one obvious ground of comparison between *The Prelude* and *Paradise Lost*. Richard Onorato's psychoanalytic reading of *The Prelude*

was only the most rigorous and single-minded attempt to demonstrate the
extent to which Wordsworth is "fixated to a trauma, obsessed by a vital
relationship with Nature which has come to stand unconsciously for the lost
mother."[15] To deviate only slightly from Onorato's inquisition into the
consequences of Wordsworth's "outcast, bewildered and depressed" state
at the death of his mother, I would advert to his insistent sense – repeating
Adam's predicament and, doubtless, elements of Milton's own relations
with his wives and daughters – of *betrayal* by women. Consider, for
example, the image of the "Parent Hen amid her Brood" (*Prel.* V.246)
which elides unnoticeably into "my honour'd Mother" (V.257), who in turn
merges with "old Grandame Earth" (V.346), whose love is "Unthought of"
by the Infant Prodigy whom Wordsworth opposes to the mother's belief in
natural development. The qualifications in this section – "She left us
destitute," "Nor would I praise her but in perfect love" (V.259, 263) – are
premonitory of the subsequent betrayal by nature. This repetition of the
sexual drama of *Paradise Lost* is resumed and displaced figurally in a
substitutive series of maternal entities (England, nature in various forms,
and so on): the compulsion to repeat the structure incites ever more
sophisticated rephrasings of the reproached object or term. But if
Wordsworth repeats Adam's sense of betrayal *by* women, he also repeats
Adam's reproduction or repetition of God's "superior" (masculine) love
towards women or creation generally, as in the passage of somewhat
condescending praise for the "maid" who was "Nature's inmate," in Book
XI:

> Her the birds
> And every flower she met with, could they but
> Have known her, would have lov'd . . .
> God delights
> In such a being; for her common thoughts
> Are piety, her life is blessedness.
>
> (XI.214–23)

As Spivak points out, "Wordsworth's delight in his sister makes him more
like God than like her,"[16] though he moves on to identify with her ("Even
like this Maid . . . I lov'd whate'er I saw; nor lightly loved").

However, though Wordsworth from one perspective aligns himself with a
"masculine" love cathected pseudo-incestuously on the mother or her
equally treacherous and untrustworthy substitutes and surrogates, repeating
in this way a certain structure of relations in *Paradise Lost*, from another he
appears to perform an *inversion* of the Miltonic scene. The relational model
for Adam's "heavenly love" is filial (and this, as we have seen, in a sense
"feminizes" him), but his human love for Eve is modelled on the Father: his
love, that is, divides between a mirror-image and a reflection of God's love
for man. Wordsworth's love for nature, by contrast, divides between a filial

responsiveness to maternal care and a self-imaged maternal tenderness for the dependent forms of the external world; in his final speculations on "intellectual love" the perfectly "fashioned" human heart is characterized by just such an identification:

> he whose soul hath risen
> Up to the height of feeling intellect
> Shall want no humbler tenderness, his heart
> Be tender as a nursing Mother's heart;
> Of female softness shall his life be full.
>
> (XIII.197–201)

Identification with the former model reverses priorities: whereas Adam reproduces God's "superior" love towards (female) creation, Wordsworth reproduces the devotion of Mother Nature in his caressing adult consciousness. Wordsworth thus transumes both Milton and his own earlier poetic stance. Transumption, according to Bloom, is organized psychically around introjection and projection, and the introjection here of "female softness," with the accompanying projection of a masculine "over-sternness," suggests the melancholic's defensive introjection of a lost object. The basic point is that by constituting himself as at once (God the) father, loving mother and betrayed son/lover, a singularly complex androgyne,[17] Wordsworth places himself in contradiction with himself as well as with Milton; and in the same way that the terms operate in *Paradise Lost*, his "femininity" bereaves his love of all literality, splitting it as meaning and affect between the poles of various asymmetrical relations. The superimposition of these relations on the androgynic complexities of Milton's text fails to produce a coherent historiography of the concept of love, but encourages rather a kaleidoscopic textual vision in which the pieces fail to compose themselves into a stable pattern. Nor does such superimposition uphold the patrilinear relation of one poet to another favoured by literary history and common sense. It leaves us instead with a fretful and indeterminate form of consanguinity in which the reader too is implicated, belying the apparent impartiality of his undertaking.

This is influence in the performative sense which it seems more fruitful to assign and develop. Influence, that is, not as a historical and biographical phenomenon, or as a factor in the genesis of the poem, but as the active construction and pursuit of relations, an influencing of the poem by the reader. Adopting the traditional view would oblige one to follow the trail, to decipher the signs, of a falsely hypostasized father who is assumed to be missing or concealed in Wordsworth's text. A psychoanalytic reading of the *poem* would hunt down its quarry in such figures as the Discharged Soldier of Book IV, who "evokes an unconscious sense of the father in Wordsworth," and the confrontation with whom is an example of the poet's unconscious desire to "free himself from his obsession with the mother and from the very bondage to Nature he was celebrating."[18] A psychoanalytic account of *literary history*, on the other hand, would unmask the culprit in Milton himself, whose "uncanny blend of cultural lateness and poetic earliness," the "self-presence" which he treats "as almost his birthright," makes him "a kind of Gnostic father-figure for subsequent poetry written in English."[19] But as we have seen, this self-presence, in so far as it applies to the univocality of Milton's principal terms of reference, is an illusion, as are the literality and masculinity of the father. The lesson for influence-theory of our study of *The Prelude* and *Paradise Lost* is that poetic fathers are always in a sense self-divided, androgynous, effeminate, in that their texts are themselves always self-divided, shored against an otherness which inscribes them in the irrecuperable ebb of meaning.

We have been tracing some of the wanderings to which the concept of love is prone, divagations which seem only to give greater impetus to the centripetal, reiterative movement around the term itself, which is credited not infrequently with a self-evidency which on closer analysis it cannot guarantee. On the other hand, there is in both texts an explicit attempt to define and categorize love: in Raphael's homily on the scale of love in Book VIII (579–92), and Wordsworth's allusive discourse on different forms of love in his final philosophical statement in Book XIII (146–58). Rather than pursue the ins and outs of these new problem areas, which have to some extent been foreshadowed in my earlier discussion, I shall offer a more compact showcase for the conclusions which, on inspection, they enforce. If we move, that is, to the endings of the two epics, we shall find in each case evidence of a strained realization of the vagaries of meaning in a fallen world.

Milton appears at times to look to the Apocalypse for the restoration of pure meaning, when "golden days" will see "joy and love triumphing, and fair truth" (III.337–8), but at the conclusion of his poem he admits in the present to the burden of unceasing interpretation. In the final two Books Adam is instructed by Michael through a vision of the future in how to decipher the evidences of God's love: withdrawing from revelation, the presence of God must henceforth be read in circumambient "signs," which, "compassing thee round / With goodness and paternal love, his face / Express, and of his steps the track divine" (XI.351–4). The extra-syntactic ambiguity of "divine," which couples the omnipresence of God with the notion of prognostication or representation, is relevant too at the end of *The Prelude*, where the theme of prophetic tuition resurfaces. Wordsworth looks down and back on his poem and sees it as "centring all in love, and in the end / All gratulant *if rightly understood*" (XIII.377–8; my italics). The point is taken up in the final paragraph, where love is to be *taught* to an audience "too weak to tread the ways of truth" (XIII.424): "what we have loved, / Others will love; and we may teach them how" (XIII.437–8). And yet, two hundred lines earlier, "intellectual love" is declared to be unteachable: "No secondary hand can intervene / To fashion this ability;" it is "far / From any reach of outward fellowship, / Else 'tis not thine at all" (XIII.185–90). Why does Wordsworth, while stipulating that love is a natural growth and a private responsibility, nevertheless arrogate to himself the role of its chief exegete and apostle? By becoming the master-interpreter of love he underlines the non-self-evident, non-literal *interpretability* of the term at the same time as he fastens the prophet's mantle more securely – exceeding Adam's brief by simple virtue of being poet and protagonist at the same time.

There are also more exact, if somewhat ghostly, intertextual connections here, which reinforce the privative or disorientating effect of intertextual activity. By figuring himself forth as a "lasting inspiration, sanctified / By reason and by truth" (XIII.436–7), does Wordsworth not ally himself with the Comforter sent from heaven to dwell within the faithful, and who, "Working through love, upon their hearts shall write, / To guide them in all truth" (*PL* XII.489–90); and does he not shade too into the "respiration" (XII.540) of the second coming of Christ? This large metalepsis gives Wordsworth priority over Milton by representing him (Wordsworth) as the "one greater man" of whom Milton sings: not only was he around before Milton, but he comes to fulfil Milton's prophecy. In this dizzying shift from the beginning to the end of history, which may be taken as paradigmatic of the migratory interpoetic movement we have traced, the present, both of time and of meaning, disappears.

We finish with a valediction: literally, the sadness at parting of the French youths who, inspired by "patriot love," go to fight in the Revolutionary wars. Their farewells excite a sympathetic sorrow in the poet:

> Yet at this very moment do tears start
> Into mine eyes; I do not say I weep,
> I wept not then, but tears have dimm'd my sight,
> In memory of the farewells of that time.
>
> (IX.273–6)

What moment, exactly, is Wordsworth talking about? The moment of composition? The moment when the text was revised and "authorised"? With the rapid shuffling from present to past to the intermediate past of "have dimm'd" it is difficult to determine precisely when the tears *start*. Why the awkward disclaimers in any case? Love is here conceived as surviving time, collapsing the difference between past and present, but is equally that which suffers a break in continuity, falls victim to time: to "farewells," "severings," "separation." If a valediction marks the boundary between a cherished past and a grudgingly accepted future, the tears which here accompany the valediction prove capable of dissolving that simple boundary. In the same way, the kind of reading I have practised in this essay disarms the conventional boundaries of literary history at the same time as, by continually reconstructing and re-imagining them, it silently respects them. *This* tearful text, with its simultaneous emphasis on recuperation and loss, cries out to form the coda of this study of Wordsworthian and Miltonic love.

Notes

1. R. D. Havens, *The Influence of Milton on English Poetry* (Cambridge, Mass., Harvard University Press, 1922), 200; Abbie Potts, *Wordsworth's "Prelude": A Study of its Literary Form* (Ithaca, Cornell University Press, 1953), 23–4; Joseph Anthony Wittreich, "The siege of hateful contraries," in *Milton and the Line of Vision*, ed. Joseph Anthony Wittreich (Madison, University of Wisconsin Press, 1975), 229; and Leslie Brisman, *Milton's Poetry of Choice and its Romantic Heirs* (Ithaca, Cornell University Press, 1973), 241.
2. Roland Barthes, *A Lover's Discourse: Fragments*, tr. Richard Howard (New York, Hill & Wang, 1978), 99.
3. References are to *Paradise Lost*, XII.574–85, and *The Prelude* (1805), XIII.377. The texts used are Alastair Fowler's corrected edition of *Paradise Lost* in the Longman Annotated English Poets series (London, Longman, 1971), and Stephen Gill's corrected edition of de Selincourt's text of the 1805 *Prelude* (London, Oxford University Press, 1970). All line references henceforth are included parenthetically in the text, together with abbreviated titles (*PL* and *Prel.*) in the few instances where it is not immediately obvious which poem is being cited.
4. Barthes, op. cit., 7.
5. ibid., 15.
6. Donald F. Bouchard, *Milton: A Structural Reading* (London, Edward Arnold, 1974), 78.
7. Gayatri Chakravorty Spivak, "Sex and history in *The Prelude* (1805): Books Nine to Thirteen" (*Texas Studies in Literature and Language*, 23, 1981, 355).
8. The 1850 text defends these "sympathies with power" as "Motions not treacherous or profane, else why / Within the folds of no ungentle breast / Their dread vibrations *to this hour* prolonged?"
9. For a subtle reading of this passage in *Paradise Lost*, considered in the aspect of schemes of repetition and in structural comparison to parts of Wordsworth's *The Ruined Cottage*, see Neil Hertz's "Wordsworth and the tears of Adam" (*Studies in Romanticism*, 7, 3, 1967, 15–33). Hertz argues that in both texts ordinary historical time is unseated in favour of a mode of narrative time in which "a chain of mediations is established that brings the reader into the continuum, into the repetitive process by which reality is turned into truth" (32).
10. Harold Bloom, *A Map of Misreading* (New York, Oxford University Press, 1975), 102.
11. In a very different context, Shoshana Felman writes that a habitual mistake is "to believe that one is on the *outside*, that one *can* be outside," to talk "as though the reader could indeed know *where* he is, what his place is and what his position is with respect to the literary language which itself, as such, does not know what it knows" ("Turning the screw of interpretation," in *Literature and Psychoanalysis: The Question of Reading: Otherwise*, ed. Shoshana Felman (Baltimore and London, Johns Hopkins University Press, 1980), 199, 201).

12. Bouchard, op. cit., 87.
13. Quoted in C. S. Lewis, *A Preface to Paradise Lost* (London, Oxford University Press, 1942), 122; second italics mine.
14. ibid., 124.
15. Richard Onorato, *The Character of the Poet: Wordsworth in "The Prelude"* (Princeton, Princeton University Press, 1971), 64.
16. Spivak, op. cit., 333.
17. The entire first section of Spivak's article (see note 7) is of central interest in this connection. She traces a movement of self-separation, and of growing "indeterminacy of inside and outside," in the final Book of the poem, and contends that the resulting semblance of androgyny is that of Imagination as the union of man and nature.
18. Onorato, op. cit., 253, 274.
19. Bloom, op. cit., 78.

15

KENNETH GROSS

Satan and the Romantic Satan:
a notebook

Our moods do not believe in each other.
(Emerson)

§ What kind of claims might I make on behalf of Milton's devil? It has become far too easy, or too easy to attack, to call him a hero, even if we see in him aspects of Milton in his roles of poet, visionary quester, rebel against tyranny, conspirator for liberty, propagandist, worshiper in a church of one. And yet he remains an inescapable object of attention, and of troubled admiration – whether we admire the character or the force that calls him into being. I might call him a modernist hero, a hero of the fallen imagination, though I am then not sure where or when I would place, or how describe, the Fall. Perhaps I could demonstrate his claims to a kind of heroism that one cannot identify as fully or as adequately in any other character of *Paradise Lost*. Of course, most of us presume that the battle has been fought already, that the heroic Satan (the Romantic Satan) is primarily an error of neophytes, a figure whose claims on the mind are admitted only to be cast out by a sophisticated appeal to Milton's way of testing and tempting the reader (and perhaps himself). But still I would want to account for so persistent a fascination, one that repeated readings in Milton criticism have, in my own case, clarified rather than dispelled. I would want to speak about Satan not as *advocatus diaboli* – almost always a tool of orthodoxy, a ventriloquist's dummy – nor as heretic – though real heresy, were it possible here, might sharpen debate more than any pluralism. I would rather speak as someone willing to take seriously his own naïveté, to examine its stakes.

"Don't *for heaven's sake*, be afraid of talking nonsense!" warns Wittgenstein. "But you must pay attention to your nonsense."[1]

§ One must say that Milton could scarcely have believed in anything like a heroic devil, indeed that the whole structure of his religious thinking committed him to an ultimate deprecation of the devil as absurd or ungrounded. (And why else are there devils and demons, if not to focus our will to deprecate?) Yet any appeal to Milton's beliefs (his categorical distinctions, his constitutive habits of representation, his usable or intractable authorities, his investments in possibility) is hardly unproblematic. And it is not only that the poet may seem to have had hidden or conflicting beliefs, divided loyalties, secret identifications, or that the burdens of poetry and belief are not always compatible – all recurrent and much studied issues. It is also that, even if I am convinced that Milton shared basic stances or habits of mind with, say, Luther or Calvin, and that these are powerfully incarnated in the poetry, I am not perfectly sure of what it means for us to try and ground our reading of the poetry on a hypothetical commitment to the polarized terms of the poet's belief. Such a commitment is often seen as a necessary, even a sufficient condition for reading Milton's epic. Yet this asks a kind of critical fideism, a *sacrificio intellectus*, that in this particular context can breed its own sort of pride and bad faith. Must one simply give up the game, then? A philosopher might say that our skepticism lies not simply in our not knowing what to believe, but in not knowing quite what belief itself looks like, how it speaks, though we may think we have a sense of how it *has* spoken. Even many of our sympathetic ways of talking about religious beliefs – assuming that we do not blandly deplore religion as divisive ideology, mystified politics, or spilt poetry – tend to mark an abysmal separation from the things they seek to name, the forms of life they seek to describe. And if I am uncertain of what belief looks like, what its grammar is, what its scope and stakes are, how can I calmly suspend disbelief, or speak coherently of the beliefs of another?

§ It is a matter of keeping faith with one's skepticism. And yet if one is not to become merely a version of Blake's "idiot Questioner" ("who sits with a sly grin . . . Who publishes doubt & calls it knowledge; whose Science is Despair") one must find a way to justify, or at least take responsibility for, the impulse so to read Milton against the grain of his beliefs.[2] A clarifying mirror for the project lies to hand in a text published a quarter century before Milton's. Descartes' *Meditations on First Philosophy* is likewise a strenuous reconsideration of the problem of origins, though in this case epistemological and metaphysical origins rather than mythic and moral ones. Of most immediate interest here is not the philosopher's final proof of God's existence, but rather that moment in the first meditation when he holds up the hypothesis that there is an evil demon or genius who creates and controls the sensible world, who deceives our credulity with the illusion that we have bodies, that we perceive objects.[3] That demon is no residue of archaically dualistic or buried gnostic sentiments. It is not a response to metaphysical paranoia nor a devious expression of heresy. It is not, in any common sense, a metaphor. Rather, the demon in Descartes is a pragmatic, dialectical tool, an ironic limiting case or hyperbolic fiction which frames the difficult opening stance of his skeptical program. The idea of the evil demon is, at the least, a piece of serious nonsense, a prop to his "laborious wakefulness." It is a consciously, tentatively sustained illusion that helps hold at bay other, more habitual illusions, stories, authorities, gods – hence a means to press forward the philosopher's quest through opinion to certainty, though the ghost of that hypothesis may haunt even subsequent, and more pious reconstructions of the idea of God. Would it make sense to ask for a version of Satan which could do something of the same work?

§ I should remember that, in considering Satan's status as possible hero (or one of several versions of the Miltonic hero) I am not really talking about that opposition figure who is commonly called the *Romantic* Satan. For that Satan exists mainly as a straw-man, something of a slander of Milton's stark and foolish angel, as well as a slander of the sophisticated work of many nineteenth-century readers. Stuart Curran writes: "Romantic Satanism, the pervasive heresy supposedly celebrated by the younger Romantics, does not exist, but, like the chimeras of Eve's dream, continues to distemper the mind."[4] For this vaguely defined, brittle, childish, and falsely Promethean Satan tends to emerge as a polemical, accusatory myth, an object of the critic's easy exorcism, a hollow idol created to be the victim of the orthodox iconoclast or an image conjured up to terrorize and embarrass us with the spectre of our failed, abandoned romanticisms. Strangely enough, I sometimes think that Satan's declared enemies are the ones that do most to keep the Romantic Satan alive, partly because it ultimately conceals the more subtly problematic character which Milton has given his devil, partly because an anxious, litigious attention to the "problem" of Satan may distract one from considering what may seem both grimly and nobly "satanic" aspects of the poet and his other creatures and gods. Romantic readers like Shelley and Blake, for all of their skewed emphasis on the place of the devil, rather use Milton's picture of Satan as a way of exposing something crucial about the complex, dynamic system of religious values and images which are taken over and re-imagined in *Paradise Lost* as a whole.

§ Percy Shelley has a clear eye for Satan's complex of moral failings, and he is indeed quite ready to condemn the habits of "pernicious casuistry" which lead sympathetic readers to rationalize or excuse the "taints of ambition, envy, revenge, or a desire for personal aggrandisement" in Milton's devil on the grounds that his sufferings outweigh his crimes.[5] But he also refuses to allow that Milton's deity can yield us any purer, contrastive perspective by which to frame a critique of Satan, or that any isolable theological convictions have the power to limit what might seem purely humanistic or aesthetic responses to the imaginative shape of the poet's fable. Shelley's comments on Satan in his *Defence of Poetry* are keyed to his central argument that the "truths" of inherited theologies must be seen as, at best, the remnants of calcified *effects* of prior poetic intuitions rather than the proper causes or grounds of new creation. Given this situation, the attempt to expose the ways that Milton's figurings of the devil wrench apart the doctrinal or ideological frame of the poem becomes for Shelley a way of extending his defense of the moral imagination against mere morality or religious moralism. (Shelley's refusal to grant the constitutive authority of theology would hold, I suspect, even were he shown that Milton was dependent on a theological *poetics* that traced God's presence and doctrinal values not only abstractly, but also through the turns and tropes of the scriptural Word, a Word which could be, as required, metaphorical or veridical, humblingly opaque or apparently transparent.)[6] Just because his argument has elicited more protest than reflection, however, one needs to examine its implications rather carefully.

Shelley begins by claiming that "Milton's poem contains within itself a *philosophical* refutation of that system of which, by a strange and natural antithesis, it has been a chief popular support" (my emphasis).[7] The writer's "philosophical" may jar us somewhat. The usage has a distinctly eighteenth-century flavor, as if it referred to some sort of rational discourse opposed by nature to superstition or scholastic system. And yet the word clearly points not to overt argument but to something implicit in the poetic narrative, to a conceptual drama or parable, an iconoclastic counterplot or pattern of images such as resist the "strange and natural" ways that culture can turn poetry into propaganda. He continues immediately, as if to explain this, that "nothing can exceed the energy and magnificence of the character of Satan as expressed in *Paradise Lost*." Here one again hesitates, for this seems so naïve, so *un*philosophical a reaction, since it neglects the evidence that the devil's energy tends to be dumbly antithetical, that it feeds on willfulness, hate, self-loathing, and betrayal, and is ultimately self-destructive; that his magnificence borders on the cheaply theatrical, that it is materialistic rather than spiritual, grotesquely compensatory and competitive, as well as self-blinding. We needn't suppose, however, that Shelley himself does not see this, given his obvious recognition of Satan's "taints." The real issue is whether the fateful history of Satan's energy allows of any simple moralization, whether its causes and hidden poisons can be traced back to the devil alone. (For to the degree that Satan reflects the "energy" and "magnificence" of Milton's imagination, our appreciation or criticism of the fictive character will be inescapably involved – *pace* C. S. Lewis – with our appreciation or criticism of his creator.) Shelley goes on to insist that "it is a mistake to suppose that [Milton's devil] could ever have been intended for the popular personification of evil." The fact that Satan *is* metamorphosed at the close of Book X into a mythic or folkloric dragon, as if such were his authentic shape or *telos*, will not really weigh against an argument like Shelley's that ardently refuses to accept any such teleological simplifications, even as it refuses to locate any singular idea of evil informing the complex, dramatic picture of the devil. For what concerns Shelley most crucially is to disentangle the ideas of "Satan" and "evil," to show that one does not own the other, and to point instead to the sharing out of a deeper sense of evil among the supernatural characters of the poem:

> Implacable hate, patient cunning, and a sleepless refinement of device to inflict the extremest anguish on an enemy, these things are evil; and although venial in a slave are not to be forgiven in a tyrant; although redeemed by much that ennobles his defeat in one subdued, are marked by all that dishonours his conquest in the victor.[8]

Shelley here covertly echoes one of Satan's own self-descriptions (as he does so shrewdly in parts of *Prometheus Unbound*), such that we may at first think that the hate, cunning, and refinement of device belong to the devil alone. But the list is carefully poised so as to further suggest the specularity or mutual contamination of devil and deity. It is God in his foreknowledge, working through the intricate and conscious turns of Milton's plot, who inflicts the extremest anguish on Satan through a sleepless refinement of ironic control. The poem, of course, asks us to interpret such anguish as merely the redounding back upon Satan of his own evil – something which Satan himself seems willing to confess. But Shelley's case proceeds according to a more human, as well as a dramatically acute wisdom, one that argues, moreover, not from hidden or subversive authorial intentions (which would only rationalize the conflict) but from the plain shape of Milton's fable. And for Shelley it is quite sufficient evidence of tyranny that a God, full of laughter and accusation, should watch his creature bringing himself to pain and despair by following through a course of action made possible only through that God's unacknowledged allowance:

> Milton's Devil as a moral being is as far superior to his God as one who perseveres in some purpose which he has conceived to be excellent in spite of adversity and torture, is to one who in the cold security of undoubted triumph inflicts the most horrible revenge upon his enemy, not from any mistaken notion of inducing him to repent of a perseverance in enmity, but with the alleged design of exasperating him to deserve new torments.[9]

Again, one may protest that the "purpose conceived to be excellent" decays into actions that seem petty, spiteful, victimizing, that possess at best an illusory nobility. Certainly the idea that God himself may be a tyrant, a moral agent, rather than a being untouched by the liabilities of human ethical choice, seems to fall in with Satan's politic and self-gratifying picture of God as an oppressive king. But for Shelley, I suppose, to insist in orthodox fashion that God as an agent is inevitably above moral choice and human tyranny, and yet to be counted on and obeyed as the author of moral law, is a dangerous and dehumanizing abstraction, nor can saying so make it so without the aid of human work and human persuasion (however much this turns thought and imagination blindly against the more liberating exercise of their powers). Skeptic that he is, Shelley can acknowledge the strength of such a sublimation, but he must deny its ultimate authority as well as deplore its common acceptance. His reading of God's "tyranny" will tend to look literalistic, if not satanic, from the point of view of a theological poetics in which the Christian God is the master of all love and metaphor, but Shelley's more radical poetics refuses to credit what he would see as no more than a tyrannical and idealized trope. The dramatized relation of a triumphant power to a punished subject will inescapably be the projection of a human relation (moral, psychological, or political), a relation whose image will, moreover, tend to "tempt and slay" both master and slave, and it may be a questionable measure of our success in religious purification to try and reason ourselves out of the moral unease or horror that such a projection can generate. Still, it is not a question of blaming God or exculpating Satan, which would only further literalize the conceptual drama Shelley is describing. The point is that Shelley calls into question the larger array of moral, religious, and aesthetic motives which made it possible for Milton to commit himself to such a picture within his dramatic epic in the first place.

§ From Shelley's preface to *Prometheus Unbound*:

> Prometheus is, in my judgement, a more poetical character than Satan because, in addition to courage and majesty and firm and patient opposition to omnipotent force, he is susceptible of being described as exempt from the taints of ambition, envy, revenge, and a desire for personal aggrandisement, which in the Hero of *Paradise Lost*, interfere with the interest. The character Satan engenders in the mind a pernicious casuistry which leads us to weigh his faults with his wrongs and to excuse the former because the latter exceed all measure. In the minds of those who consider that magnificent fiction with a religious feeling, it engenders something worse.[10]

The philosophical balancing act is similar to that of the *Defence*, but what sets this passage apart is its closing, the oblique (and little commented upon) reference towards "something worse," something more pernicious than false sympathy, which is engendered in the minds of pious as opposed to heretical readers. One clue to what we might make of the phrase can be found in the preface to another of Shelley's dramas, *The Cenci*, where he speaks of the "restless and anatomizing casuistry" which might move readers of his tragedy wholly to justify the murderous revenges of Beatrice Cenci on the father who raped her.[11] For if we can take this "restless" sympathy as clearly parallel to the "pernicious casuistry" of those who labor to excuse Satan's faults, it might be plausible to see the opposing fault, the "something worse," as somehow relating to the corrupt authorities of Church and State that took the part of the insidious, sadistic Count Cenci. Indeed, we might see the "something worse" as that self-perpetuating system of tyranny, revolution, and revenge which Shelley saw as built into the morality of both tyrant *and* rebel, both punitive father and violent, devouring child. Such a dynamic (which finds perhaps its starkest expression in what Frye called the "Orc Cycle" of Blake), Shelley understood as conditioning even the "merciful" Christian theology of sin, grace, and atonement (though in the preface to *Prometheus* such criticism of traditional religion is closely veiled). From the perspective of an account of the ways we understand Satan, we might also read that "something worse" as whatever can lead us so happily to slander certain sympathies or do violence to the serious ambivalence of our moral judgments by forcing a text to take on completely the cast of orthodoxy, and that on the basis of what for us may be purely intellectual assumptions. The worst such "something" might come through in the shrewd, nasty finesse with which a critic like C. S. Lewis reads Satan; it emerges in Lewis' loving attention to the details of Satan's self-degradation and absurdity, an attention which occludes any concern with what it means for the poet or critic to isolate so perfect an object of victimage; it is visible in an intensified spirit of accusation such as blinds Lewis to the unconscious and less impersonal disgust which his arguments can release – as when he speaks (authoritatively) of Satan's systematic degradation from heroic rebel, to party politician, to intruding thief, to toad-like seducer-spy, and finally to nothing more than "a thing that peers in at bedroom or bathroom windows."[12] It is Lewis' eye, and not Satan's, which has here converted the sacred Bower of Adam and Eve into a bourgeois bedroom or bathroom. We are left wondering which of those two possible similitudes is more subtly degrading, and also who is being most degraded in the adducing of them.

§ Milton himself in his account of Satan labors to elicit subtle dimensions of moral and spiritual disgust, working as he does from a sense that it is proper to turn a kind of liberated, satirical, and prophetic derogation on an evil enemy. If the voice of honest indignation and mockery speaks most plainly in Milton's prose, it also emerges more impersonally in the way that Milton associates Satan and his family with images of miscegenation, abortion, sexual violence, and degenerate creation (as exemplified by the history of Sin and Death, or the descriptions of Chaos and the Paradise of Fools). Milton shows behind Satan and Satan's world, even in their apparent rationality and magnificence, not only moral and theological error but the kind of scatological eschatology such as will later animate Pope's picture of the reign of Dullness. Such a strategy, as critics have argued, is one aspect of what the poet meant in *Areopagitica* by the need to know good by means of evil, the necessity, given our human confusion, of purifying ourselves and our moral visions by contrast and conflict, by carefully limning the scope of spiritual monstrosity underlying the human face of evil.[13] One might cite Northrop Frye here, for whom the agonistic, dialectical imagery of apocalyptic myth inevitably reveals our deep impulse to compose ever starker and more horrifying pictures of the nightmare world that human desire must face and reject, our need to give radical form to error in order to cast it out. But Frye himself rarely touches on the darker, more divisive aspects of such an apocalyptic rhetoric. One at least needs to supplement him by turning to Kenneth Burke, a more sophisticated dialectician. For Burke would push us to examine those cultural or poetic places where such apocalyptic polarizations collapse, or where such dualities calcify, where the evil that is to be "cast out" reveals itself as an illusory, defensive "projection" of something that may not be so easily evaded. Burke is our shrewdest analyst of what is satanic in the will to purify by contrast, to divide out the satanic victim or enemy; he is a student – like Freud – of the way that the divine *ecclesia* tends to found itself on, even as it is mocked by, the suppressed or pushed-away *cloaca*.[14] That Milton himself so carefully defends the affective violence of his combative rhetoric in *Of Reformation* suggests that he did not, after all, take its powers for granted; given the complex burdens of religious controversy, it is all too easy for a mythic rhetoric of contrast to turn divisive, to sustain what Blake called "cloven fictions." Hence it is, perhaps, that *Paradise Lost* always tests as much as it indulges our will to partisanship and oppositional definition, a process which the Romantics continue with the utmost seriousness, though in directions where Milton himself would scarcely have ventured.

I may admit that the discovery and defilement of an absolute enemy is part of what the poet is about in his work. Still, there are times when I am at least unsure as to what it is many *critics* are accusing in the person of Satan (who is himself the great accuser). Or rather, I am unsure as to what the stakes of such accusations are, what authorities they call upon or defend. Can I discover a determined conceptual or metaphysical enemy in Satan and yet be sure that that figure or trope contains everything I would accuse, that it does not blind me to what's been omitted? Can I be certain that neither

Milton nor Milton's God is implicated in the evil thus revealed? And must I take as the final measure of how accurately I have read Satan the degree to which I have accepted the completeness of Milton's orthodox, satirical persuasions? And if I do this, have I perhaps only proved something about the power of such persuasions, rather than exposing or teaching myself about the substance of evil? Could not the aesthetic and moral dilemmas raised by both the idea of an evil enemy and the volatile rhetoric of accusation be among the reasons why Satan himself disappears at the end of the poem, reduced to a grotesque, fairy-tale dragon feeding on Sodom apples, even as his deeper infection is humanized and demythologized in the troubled vision of post-lapsarian history that Michael shows to Adam in Books XI and XII?

§ One says: Milton cannot want us to think he is representing the substance of evil, nor should we assume that he did not see that there had to be a troubling, equivocal relation between the dramatic character of Satan and any theological notion of evil he might want to align with that character – especially if we see him as giving a face to what is fundamentally a privative quality. It is not enough to answer that talk of "evil" only confuses things, locks us into vacant labels or archaic idealizations. But even assuming we can still use that noun or predication, not rejecting the word as simply ideological "persuasion," the proper placing of it becomes crucial. Milton is not, after all, trying to tell us *who* is evil, or what evil *is* (as if Satan were a "who" or a "he"). Even in reworking the *vere istorie* of Scripture, Milton's major claims on us are those of a creator of fictive mirrors. So that Satan – who is in any case so little a Biblical character – offers primarily a dramatic, and often ironic *picture* of evil. The formula might go as follows: Satan is not evil; rather, evil looks like Satan. Evil talks like and reasons like Satan. That will work for a while at least, will help cut through a number of false questions. Certainly I can suspend any doubts as to whether evil looks rather more like, say, Shakespeare's Iago (whose own relation to the inherited figurations of the Devil need be no more problematic than Satan's). But can I give up asking, given the picture that Milton does draw, whether any other figure in *Paradise Lost* has a similar look about it? Milton makes me think about evil, about the shapes it takes, such that I may not be wholly satisfied with Milton's own more explicit thoughts about it.

§ Part of the fallen cherub's fascination lies in the way that his labors of mind, heart, and body seem to break down or degrade him, in the way his acts poison himself and others. The unstable evidences of an immense but flawed intellect, the lapses in logic, the hypocritical appeals to public reason or political good faith, the instances of "bad theology" which critics like

Alastair Fowler so carefully gloss – how are we to construe these things? Such flaws or lapses, however obvious or hidden, we may assume Milton himself to have set in place – unless we are to think that, having planted a few hints, he leaves it up to ingenious critics to find error in Satan wherever they will. (It is William Empson's perverse glory that, exasperated with the critical game of "finding out Satan," he instead argues for the devil's weird sincerity, even as he opens his ear to signs of trickery or illogic in the words of Milton's God.) In any case, whether we see in them satire or pathos, Milton offers us the convincing dramatic illusion that such errors are *proper* to the situation and character of Satan. And yet there is another sense in which Satan could be said to be *dispossessed* by his errors. As Arnold Stein, among others, has pointed out, there is at work in the poem a kind of ironic perspectivizing which suggests that even Satan's canniest and most controlled attempts at rhetorical deceit or mockery can be seen from a higher level as jokes on him, instances of self-exposure as well as self-entrapment.[15] In so far as we perceive this, we will tend to shift between feelings of superiority (entailing our implicit identification with divinity? or an implicit divination of dramatic irony and hermeneutic distance?) and feelings of guilty complicity with the flawed, fallen speaker. Given such a play of perspectives, however, it may be hard to say who it is that truly *owns* Satan's absurdity, that is, who is in a position most fully to measure its trajectory, its scope and its sources.

Even if I do not, like Empson, place major blame for Satan's career in error on that omniscient deity who apparently allows the fallen angel to misinterpret his own relative freedom, I find that the poem often puts at risk my clear sense of what it means to accuse or mock Satan himself. For example, I find my ability to locate a proper ironic distance compromised, my moral perspective confused, and my potential laughter at the devil stopped, when I find that Milton (at the opening of Book III) suddenly dramatizes or localizes this unstable sense of Satan's absurdity in the person of a Father God who amuses his Son by putting on the mask of a nervous, threatened tyrant, even while that (equally amused?) Son seems ready to accuse the devil for criminally having broken out of a jail whose door God himself had left unlocked. Granted that God is mocking Satan with Satan's own false and propagandistic picture of him; granted that the facts of the fictive situation do indeed make Satan look feckless, mock-heroic, and self-dramatizing. The question is whether I can confidently laugh at Satan when I find myself much more chilled at having to share the laughter of such a God. (Lewis says that when Satan butts his head against the real, laughter is inevitable; but why must it be God's laughter?) Is it sufficient to say, as some critics have, that the text's picture of God here projects or responds to an early imbalance in the fallen *reader*'s perspective (due to his or her just having emerged from the Hell of Books I and II), a perspective which later, less troubling images of divinity will correct? Or can I dismiss the problem as merely a local flaw in the dramatic texture of the epic, when it is exactly Milton's decision to commit theologically complex issues to dramatic discourse that is at the heart of his project of justifying "the ways of God to men"?

§ It is a commonplace to suggest that, in Satan, Milton is exploring his own pride, his own impulses toward rebellion, pre-emption, tyranny, magnificent display, isolate heroism and faith, his own desire for self-origination, and yet at the same time trying to exorcize or purge such impulses of their degraded, destructive aspects. What is "purer" in them, perhaps, is preserved in the proud, isolate, humble, threatened, and exploratory voice of the invocations, and even more in the image of elevated humility such as Milton shows us in the Son Christ's relation to the will and presence of the Father. (This latter relation is one type of what William Kerrigan wants to term "the sacred complex," a structure of debt and influence that overcomes the binds of wounded narcissism and Oedipal guilt and vengefulness that entrap Satan.)[16] Still, if one does not want to over-idealize Milton's dialectical labor, it might be fair to wonder whether the exorcism of Satan, or what goes by the name of Satan, really works. That is to say, would it be possible to think of Milton's attempt at purgation and purification as a deep "trick" played on the self in order to allow it to hold onto its ambivalent impulses on a different, more sublimated level, one that only *seems* purer or higher because those impulses have been more aggressively displaced and projected, their origins more aggressively hidden from both reader and author?

Kerrigan, in his first book, argues that the invocations are indeed haunted by Milton's sense of his own transgressiveness and hypocrisy, by a fear that, should he be writing without inspired authority, his devil will reveal itself to be only "a self-portrait drawn in perfect likeness to the hidden image of himself," the "destructive poet of pride, malice, and revenge" concealed by an "empty dream" of prophetic voice. "The last words of the last invocation [to Book VII] refuse to disallow this possibility."[17] That his own likeness to Satan should threaten the poet is comprehensible. But that the shadow of Satan, or the satanic, might fall across the picture of Christ is more troubling. The possibility of this, however, needs to be brought out. Two passages among others seem crucial here, in part because they offer the Son as something of a model for Milton's own iconoclastic and creative labor.

The first passage is the description of Christ riding out to do battle *against* the demonic rebels who challenge his place (VI.749ff.). The echoes of the visionary chariots in Ezekiel and Revelation, and of Milton's own picture of himself as the "invincible warrior Zeale" driving "over the heads of Scarlet Prelats," have long been noted. But alongside these, in the poet's curious, in some ways anomalous reference to Christ's divine vehicle as "the Chariot of

Paternal Deitie" (VI.750), we may recall a classical rather than the scriptural image, that of the proud son Phaeton riding in the misappropriated sun-chariot of his father Helios. No doubt one can take the allusion as an ironic mis-taking or sublime correction of the more satanic image from pagan history. But there are some other facets of the description which suggest a more radical, ambivalent strategy of displacement or substitution. The most important thing to note is that Milton's account of Christ's sublime entry into the eschatological battle, that act of transit or "coming" which itself seems to shine from "farr off" (VI.768), offers us a vision of the Son's advent that retrospectively pre-empts or comes before both the history of the Son's first coming and the dream of his second coming as they are set down in prior Scripture. W. B. Hunter has tried to cope with the strange placing of this narrative by arguing that, as a whole, the three-day war in heaven is indeed intended to mirror both the last battle of Revelation and key features of the passion narrative, and that the sudden emergence of the hitherto concealed Messiah and his defeat of Satan prefigures Christ's triumph over Sin, Death, and the Devil on the cross, even as it anticipates the casting out of ultimate evil that will mark the Last Judgment.[18] Hunter succeeds in demonstrating the typological and theological fitness of his theory, and yet there are some key issues that it evades. Not only does it neglect to comment on the strong, implicit identification of the poet with Christ, it fails to grapple with the poet's willful reinvention or skewing of the sequences of scriptural history, especially significant given the centrality of the episode in Milton's apocalyptic drama.

An issue of the same sort arises in the second passage I have in mind. One should recall here that the poet makes Satan appear to us as a parodic creator, one who, if only briefly, dreams of transforming Hell into the competitive mirror of Heaven. Christ, in his manifestation as "the Word," is presented as the true creator. And yet one may wonder whether in representing this creator at work Milton doesn't manage to outdo even Satan in his apparent will to reverse his own belated, fallen, or secondary status as maker. For Milton, recreating the book of Creation in the image of his own poetic project, goes so far as to pre-empt the magical optative of scriptural origins ("Let there be light") with an earlier first word of his own, one that begins the work of Creation not by voicing the visible but by suppressing all competing voices and sounds: "Silence, ye troubl'd waves, and thou Deep, peace,/Said then th' Omnific Word, your discord end" (VII.216–17). Though the picture of the creator subduing discord or chaos is itself scarcely new, much less its application to the magical power of the artist, what is remarkable here is that the poet has so bluntly, so literally and unallegorically projected the fantasy of omnific voice back into the sacred history – and in a way which suggests we read that picture of voice as itself a trope for the poet's own act of retrospective, allusive presumption, his way of finding a place in that history for a voice that had no place there before.

The two texts I've cited, in their strangely virtual visions of emergence, origination, or triumph ("farr off his coming shon," "Silence, ye troubl'd waves"), may suggest Milton's radical means of keeping faith with an idea of visionary speech or prophetic authority such as transcends any notion of humble fidelity to the sacred text. Their way of restaging or reappropriating that text goes far beyond the limits of what we usually see in typological allegory (though one might say that Milton's "presumption" is quite restricted, in so far as his twistings of the text here are not put to use in confirming the authority of any ecclesiastical doctrine). The second passage in particular suggests an attempt to recapture, though in a mediated fashion, both the antithetical and the positing power of the prophetic word. It is not easy to say what is at stake in these passages, elusively inventive as they are, but to compare the poet's efforts here to any ordinary picture of "ambition," satanic or otherwise, might on the surface seem unbearably reductive, even cynical. If one does, none the less, try to see in Satan's complex struggles with the elusive authority of God the uncanny mirror (and not just parody) of both the battles of Christ and the belated poet's attempts to answer or master the equally elusive authority of God's Scripture, it is because this effort may help us to de-idealize and de-sacralize the motives of Milton's text, even as it suggests something crucial about the sources of his power as a Biblical poet.

§ Satan's most intriguing lie concerns his claims to literal self-origination. In answer to Abdiel's insistence that Satan, though an angel, owes absolute allegiance to the deity who created him, Satan taunts,

> That we were formd then saist thou? and the work
> Of secondarie hands, by task transferrd
> From Father to his Son? strange point and new!
> Doctrin which we would know whence learnt: who saw
> When this creation was? rememberst thou
> Thy making, while the Maker gave thee being?
> We know no time when we were not as now;
> Know none before us, self-begot, self-rais'd
> By our own quick'ning power.
>
> (V.853–61)

What may strike us about the argument is that no sooner is it set forth than it begins to break down or obviate itself. For one thing, in order to challenge Abdiel's warning, Satan springs on a perhaps self-evident truth (we can't remember our creation), even as he draws from that truth illegitimate conclusions of his own (nobody else made us). Also, at the same time that he is vaunting his own originality, he mocks Abdiel for the heretical newness and strangeness of his "Doctrin" (though one cannot tell whether Satan is consciously making fun of the jargon of religious controversy or is himself mocked for his momentary and opportunistic lapse into what may sound like "Popish" questions about doctrinal authority). Furthermore, no sooner does Satan assert that he and the other angels are self-raised than he slides into imagining them as having been spontaneously generated by the ripe substance of heaven itself (V.861–3) – thus not owning their own origins but having "'just grew' like Topsy or a turnip" (as Lewis quips).[19] Since Satan himself, in his soliloquy on Mount Niphates, is willing enough to confess his createdness and debt, we might imagine that he is here displaying his brave false wit as a way of impressing and cheering up his troops, or else acting somewhat like the speaker of one of Donne's lyrics, who tries to keep his ground in an impossible or decaying situation by successively wilder flights of sophistry, speculation, and simile. But for all of the apparent absurdity it generates, the crucial fantasy of self-begetting remains nevertheless quite pregnant, and one should try to place the idea carefully. It is perhaps significant that Satan, in constructing so typically materialistic a history for himself, finds himself literalizing the kind of moral or tropical autonomy that God *does* grant to both angels and men, "Authors to themselves in all / Both what they judge and what they choose" (III.122–3). Satan, in contrast to Adam and Eve, is himself "self-tempted, self-deprav'd" (III.130), so that his story of self-begetting could as well interpret the mysterious, arbitrary origins of his own pride, that which, after all, does beget Satan as Satan (at least according to the "official story," to whose terms Satan would thus ironically be committing himself).[20] In such a speech as this, the figure of Satan may also (as one critic has argued) focus a specific distrust of the self-originating claims, the illusory autonomy, and ultimate negativity of the human imagination, even as he offers a kind of ironic limiting case for the tendencies of a Miltonic Protestantism, with its emphasis on the authority of the isolate, inspired self.[21] The point of bringing in such suggestions here is mainly to show that, whatever kind of logical or metaphysical double-bind Satan's argument gets him into, we cannot dismiss the speech as merely absurd, unless we also note that it turns our attention to problems and paradoxes which the poem as a whole continues to trouble over.

I wonder if the real error in the speech lies not in the ungraspable, paradoxical substance or trajectory of the fantasy of self-origination itself, but in Satan's way of appropriating that fantasy, his attempt to use it in a story which could explain or justify or refute. Satan's mistake may lie in his having tried to speak about it at all, something which only moves him from a deep absurdity into an obvious one. Perhaps one could say that Satan's failure here is that he is *insufficiently* a solipsist, both in Heaven (where he is moved by jealousy) and in Hell (where his claims are palpably defensive). He does not, or cannot, maintain the final silence that might be required of a solipsist. Or else, Satan loses himself because he is incapable of the sublime trick of a Miltonic solipsism, or what could be called the Miltonic sufficiency. Satan cannot give himself over so as to give himself back to himself. Satan loves the Other as himself, and so falls into envy and competition; he cannot love himself as the Other. He cannot, as Milton seeks to do, divide himself against, isolate himself from, and empty himself out before an image of authority so as to receive himself and his power back from that authority – an authority that was itself partly situated by the poet, or recreated by the poet's complex situating of himself (whether through a deep, pre-emptive identification of his poetry with the narrative authority of Scripture, or through open and covert appeals to an urgent, abstracted *idea* of authority that might be attractive and overdetermined enough to let him continually displace or render obscure and secondary all other myths and structures of authority). Satan's failure lies in his not being absolute enough a liar.

§ Anxiously contemplating a poet of sublime violence and sublime control, Andrew Marvell asks of Milton, "Where couldst thou words of such a compass find?/Whence furnish such a vast expence of mind?" ("On *Paradise Lost*," ll.41–2).[22] Those questions must remain for us both pertinent and troubling. They ask after the personal, historical, or metaphysical sources of the poet's words, about the power of those words to measure, map, or inhabit a world; they construe the poem as an "expence" of mind – that is to say, both a spending out or overflowing of energy from a mental source and a containing space or "expanse" of being, thought, and power. Even given their ambiguities, Marvell's questions define a crucial burden for the critic of Milton's poem: that of measuring the distance between any answers which he or she might make to such questions and Marvell's own "Miltonic" answer to them, an answer which asserts more bluntly than Milton himself ever did that the poet's words are words of prophecy, a divine gift, rather than merely the vengeful utterances of a blind, alienated singer: "Just Heav'n thee like *Tiresias* to requite/Rewards with Prophesie thy loss of sight" (43–4). If Marvell's sudden, hyperbolic insistence on Milton's higher sources of authority seems to protest too much, or attempts too perfectly to fill the conceptual gap which his own dark questions had opened, it may be because he needed to push away what would be a tempting but clearly satanic answer to the problem of mind, one which would see the poem as the work of a mind which sought at whatever cost to be its own place and source.

§ Milton "was a true Poet and of the Devils party without knowing it" – that is to say of the party of energy rather than that of reason, conceiving of energy as something neither simply from body nor from mind, but in any case as something of which reason could only be the outward bound or circumference – energy understood as the product of desire gratified rather than the bounded or bound energy which loathes its possessor.[23] Blake's famous aphorism, as Joseph Wittreich has suggested, may be itself subtly misleading, at least in so far as it tempts us to frame a Blakean account of *Paradise Lost* according to the divisive categories of partisan politics.[24] For *The Marriage of Heaven and Hell*, as many critics have realized, does more than merely reverse Milton's theological and political affiliations for ironic effect. Although such reversals are one of Blake's local, rhetorical strategies, his larger project is to help us reconceive, and even to find a new internal history for, the philosophical and eschatological polarities on which *Paradise Lost* seems to be based (which at times means seeing those polarities as themselves aspects of a cloven fiction like that of Body and Soul, or seeing them as having resulted from some prior but now concealed or forgotten reversal of terms).[25] One of Blake's crucial strategies in *The Marriage* is to expose the strange way that the fall of Satan, and his raising up of a counter-kingdom in Hell, somehow constitutes the narrative system and moral cosmology of Milton's poem. From this perspective, Milton's having made the fall or falling of Satan the first major vision of his poem must be understood as more than the epic narrator's trick of starting *in medias res*. Rather, that fall becomes the inescapable, overdetermined beginning of our readings, the real origin of the poet's story of Genesis and Creation, an event which is situated so as to mock any retrospective attempts at apology or justification, or at least guaranteeing that Heaven will always be defined in opposition to Hell, will first and always be the place from which Satan was cast out. (This may provide a gloss on Burke's notion that the creation of Hells tends to function as a tool for solidifying the rule of Heavens.) Blake's sense of the ironic, conceptual inter-involvement of the two realms – each giving birth to the other, both married and divorced – is unfolded in an obscure, if much annotated passage of his satirical apocalypse:

> Those who restrain desire, do so because theirs is weak enough to be restrained; and the restrainer or reason usurps its place & governs the unwilling.
>
> And being restraind it by degrees becomes passive till it is only the shadow of desire.
>
> The history of this is written in Paradise Lost. & the Governor or Reason is call'd Messiah.
>
> And the original Archangel or possessor of the command of the heavenly host, is calld the Devil or Satan and his children are call'd Sin & Death
>
> But in the Book of Job Miltons Messiah is call'd Satan.
>
> For this history has been adopted by both parties

It indeed appear'd to Reason as if Desire was cast out. But the Devils account is, that the Messiah fell. & formed a heaven of what he stole from the Abyss

(*The Marriage of Heaven and Hell*, plates 5 & 6)[26]

In appropriating Milton and the Bible for the sake of his own brief history of the career of desire, Blake allusively restructures *Paradise Lost* itself. The last lines of the passage point back most immediately to Satan's building of Pandemonium, that mimic Heaven which Satan builds out of what he steals from the bowels of the underworld. But Blake also seems to link that failed double of Heaven to the secondary creation of earth and paradise, the new world which Chaos complains God had stolen space for from *his* abysmal kingdom. Blake furthermore suggests that both of these stories of creation might be seen as secret histories of how Milton's heaven itself came to be established (something of which there is no explicit account in *Paradise Lost*). The stories partly feed a counter-history propounded by Blake's devils in which Satan's fall was, it appears, illusory, whereas the real fall, from which followed the belated creation of "a" heaven, was that of Milton's Messiah (later Jehovah), the god whom Blake identifies with the adversary/accuser and Idiot Questioner of the Book of Job. One must remember that the forming of heavens is never, after all, what Blake is about. His strange, muddled doubling of places and reversal of roles suggests that the Messiah must be as much of a usurping tyrant as Satan was; or rather, Blake's text ends up by implicitly identifying Messiah or Satan whether in the roles of rebel or tyrant, allowing no absolute priority to one hell or heaven over another. Indeed, if we read carefully, it will become evident that when Blake says Milton wrote *at* liberty when he wrote *of* the hell in which Satan was fettered (*The Marriage*, plate 6), he means not only that Milton identified with the fallen cherub but also that the poet felt freer in Hell to show the lineaments of Satan merging with or breaking through those of the divine tyrant, freer, that is, to show Satan and Jehovah as doubles.

Blake's ironic reassessment of Christian dualism is further elaborated in the closing "Song of Liberty," where a jealous, Urizenic father-god finds himself falling into a gloomy abyss at the very moment that he casts out a fiery, rebellious son — the fallen patriarch being subsequently identified with both Pharaoh drowned in the Red Sea and Moses founding the rule of the Ten Commandments, even as the son himself suddenly reappears as a resurrected Christ, his form seen rising "in his eastern cloud, while the morning plumes her golden breast, Spurning the clouds written with curses, stamps the stony law to dust, loosing the eternal horses from the dens of night, crying Empire is no more! and now the lion & wolf shall cease" (*The Marriage*, plate 27).[27] Blake's apocalyptic rhetoric is shrill here, lacking the subtlety and the solemn, purgatorial comedy that characterize his later re-imagining of the shape and stakes of *Paradise Lost* in *Milton*. One might also observe that Blake, or at least the "Voice of the Devil," misses the stern clarity of Milton's insistence that true liberty and self-rule come only from the acceding of unshaped, selfish energy to reason and authority. Yet one should nevertheless recognize the crucial twist that underlies Blake's revision of what Arthur Barker called "the Puritan dilemma:" "Milton wrote in fetters when he wrote of Angels & God, and at liberty when of Devils & Hell." This defines "liberty" – identified with the central liberty of prophetic writing – not in relation to a myth of inspiration or an ideal of fidelity to textual authority, but in relation to the phenomenal or figurative "place" which the imaginer at different moments inhabits, the diverse subjects whose story he tells. (The question of "liberty" is thus as much a literary or even aesthetic matter as it is ethical or metaphysical.) It is here that one may see the radical force of Blake's project in *The Marriage*. He doesn't simply make up new characters or authorities, nor does he seek to replace the old map of mind and cosmos with one that is entirely different. Rather, his dialectical satire and maddening dramatic ironies inflict a precise confusion of old and new perspectives on our reading of *Paradise Lost*, doubling over on one another previously discrete stories of origin, disallowing earlier oppositional measures of authority and authenticity, and re-envisioning our inherited mythic places as sites or states of imagination that may be haunted or poisoned by others we may have thought we had left behind or lost.

§ William Blake and Percy Shelley could be called monstrous, demonic readers – in their restructuring of Milton's figures and motives, in their ardent refusal of historical distance, in their lack of respect for an author's deeply meditated faith. But they have a more literally monstrous rival in that creature of Mary Shelley's who – finding *Paradise Lost* in an abandoned knapsack, together with a classical history and a romantic novel – not only reads Milton's poem with shifting sympathies for Satan and the fallen Adam, but takes it as one of three equally "true" histories of human life.[28] The episode is, of course, a parable about where *Frankenstein* itself came from (the monster being Mary Shelley as Romantic reader), but that episode must be read in the light of the subsequent part of the story in which the monster reads a more radically invented text, i.e. the disenchanting account of his own grim, unfathered origins unfolded in Victor Frankenstein's laboratory journal, with all of its "loathsome detail" and air of necrophilia.[29] These two scenes of reading a genesis story – moving from a dramatized translation of Biblical myth to the tale of what took place in "a workshop of filthy creation" – together gloss the larger trajectory of Mary Shelley's re-reading of *Paradise Lost*, a reading which is all the more uncanny because it is so fiercely unspiritual, skeptical, materialistic, even literalistic in its guiding motives.

To understand the claims of her "myth of the secular," we must see it as more than simply the reordering of Milton's already consistent story from the perspective of a later, though not necessarily more evolved, frame of ideology and experience.[30] As a Romantic revision, Mary Shelley's story must be read as a fable which has been recovered or projected from within Milton's own; it is a sort of Gnostic or Nietzschean genealogy, an attempt to articulate a plot or picture more primitive than that of *Paradise Lost*, a history which that book might be seen as concealing or sublating. As a radical, nightmarish "naturalization" of the dynamics of creation, authority, love, and rebellion as they are presented in Milton, *Frankenstein* urges us to call the bluff of any theological or piously humanistic reading of *Paradise Lost*. For given a world in which creation can only be an earthly activity; where all origins are secular, arbitrary, transgressive, their results ambivalent and unmasterable; where the creation of a man, or the idea of a man, inevitably troubles the idea of a God – given such a world, Mary Shelley's fantasy tries to show us what it would then really look like for a man or god to seek to father a race of men, for a son who is also a creator to create his own image out of himself, for that creator to betray or abandon his creature to its own ambivalent freedom, and for a creature to revolt against a creator who in the end has scarcely any rights to being called master. She shows us a creature who terrifies his creator with the spectacle of his decay and isolation, a creator whose own progress towards destruction is assured by the career of his creature, a creature who himself becomes a demonic master. Cutting through the more orthodox matrices of *Paradise Lost*, the novel's creation myth emerges into a brilliantly reductive dialectic – starker even than Blake's play of alternative positions – in which creator and creature become isolate, but mutually entangled doubles, both spectral versions of the tempted, fallen, and self-destroying angel, each pursuing the other, each dying for the other. If the monster at other moments mirrors the rationalistic Adam, the recalcitrant Eve, or even the purgatorial suicide Samson, perhaps the main point is that any absolute or unsullied father, any justifying or justifiable deity, wholly drops out of any equations we might propose. God ceases to be part of the system, though human and devil seem likely to remain.

§   The genius of misfortune
            Is not a sentimentalist. He is
            That evil, that evil in the self, from which
            In desperate hallow, rugged gesture, fault
            Falls out on everything: the genius of
            The mind, which is our being, wrong and wrong,
            The genius of the body, which is our world,
            Spent in the false engagements of the mind.
            (Wallace Stevens, "Esthétique du Mal")[31]

The lure of Satan, or the idea of Satan, lies partly in the dialectical leverage which he offers us in our attempts to construe the larger stakes of Milton's poem. But Satan possesses a less impersonal appeal as well, one that depends not so much on our sense of his relative heroism as on Satan's place as a dramatic myth of the self, or as a peculiar and persuasive illusion of what a self or a character might be. The sophisticated ironies of Romantic readers help one describe this appeal, but for the moment some flatter, more awkward impressions may do just as well.

The claims of Satan might be articulated as follows: it is not that I like Satan's voice, mind, or attitude better than those of other characters in the poem, but rather that Satan, at times, seems to be the only character *with* a voice, mind, or attitude of his own, or the one who places the stresses of voice, mind, and attitude most clearly. I am fascinated with Satan's character because he seems to be the only character. The lure of Satan is the lure of the dramatized mind; he is the vessel for what Milton learned from reading *Hamlet, King Lear,* or *Macbeth* (as well as a radical interpretation or translation of the spirit which haunts Shakespeare's voices of solitude, reason, suspicion, protest, and madness). To put it more strongly: I like to think about Satan because Satan is the only character in the poem who thinks, or in whom I best recognize what it feels like to think (though this may only mean, of course, to think like Satan). Satan is Milton's picture of what thinking looks like, an image of the mind, of subjectivity, of self-consciousness, a representation of the awkward pressures we put on ourselves to interpret our own situation within the mind's shifting circle of freedom and compulsion. Satan is the poet's most palpable image of what human thought is like as it is moved, wounded, or disowned by its memories, desires, intentions, sensations, as it confronts body and environ-ment, inertia and pain, as it engages the words and stories which shape and misshape it. Satan is an image of the mind in its dividedness from both itself and others, in its illusions of inwardness and power. (It is fitting that Adam's discourse to Eve about her dream (V.95–121), about the conflicts of reason and fantasy and the dangerous vagaries of imagination, is occasioned by the intrusion of a Satanic presence, and hence a witness to Satan's problematic place in the realms of mind. (The beautifully ambiguous association of Satan and Eve in such a scene is another matter. Adam's accusatory identification, "thou serpent" (X.867) is merely the most obvious example of the links between the two, these being more subtly apparent in the fact that Eve is the only mortal in the poem with whom the devil has any sort of "conversation.")) What is crucial to the focus on mind, however, is not any specific evidence in Satan of unconscious mental processes (e.g. Oedipal conflicts or sado-masochistic instincts), though we may discover these as well. For the moment, what counts more is the diverse attention to the mind working itself in any way, to the phenomenology or figurations of subjectivity in general. This Satan is not necessarily Romantic, though he may foreshadow the burdens of Romantic subjectivity and self-centering, the self's anxious quests for what Byron called "concentered recompense."

Satan, despite his unresting intellect, gets a lot wrong, perhaps gets everything wrong. But it is less than obvious what we are to make of this. Milton lets us know that, as opposed to Satan, the innocent and reasonable Adam gets things right, as when he knows on awakening that he has come to be not of himself, but of some "great Maker . . . in goodness and in power præeminent" (VIII.278–9); and yet the picture of thought here is unsatisfying. Adam's first speech sounds oddly like something learned by rote, or like a bit of preacherly ventriloquism (despite even the subtle pathos of his later words, which surmise that it is because of his creator that he can "feel that I am happier then I know" (282)). It may in fact be the compulsiveness, the unbending error of Satan's words which makes them feel like so proper an emblem of the mind's life, of the work of mind. The steady awareness of Satan's conscious and unconscious falsehoods – his lies against himself, his cohorts, his God – the feeling of things lost or evaded, the evidence in his speeches of a mind crossed by longing and pain, the awareness of contexts and unacknowledged truths which press in, threaten, and block: there is good reason why these also have carried more dramatic weight with readers than the accurate theology of a reasonable God who must have no inside, no underside, no shifts in motivation (indeed, no motivation at all), must in a sense have no mind. This is a God whose difficult, spare, authoritative, and often beautiful utterances may yet appear to us as more unabashedly "political," just because they come to us, as Satan's never do, with so little dramatic framing to remind us of the historical and rhetorical conditions of utterance (a framing which Empson, with novelistic fervor, tried nevertheless to sketch out for us).

It might be argued that we can study the unfolding of a more strictly poetic and prophetic subjectivity in the intricate movements of Milton's invocations, or that we witness the work of mind externalized, allegorized, and idealized in the dynamic account of the Son/Logos creating the world (one image of the poet's work as an "expence of mind"). Still, neither of these offers us the kind of dramatic center for our interest in the career of mind that Satan does. To understand Satan's affective power in this context, however, depends on our being careful not to condescend, on our resisting the temptation to literalize or divinize any apparent superiority to Satan which we may feel in reading his speeches; it depends on our allowing that there are occasions when we ourselves (for better or worse) may echo or be implicated in Satan's mode of self-description:

> Hail, horrours, hail
> Infernal World, and thou profoundest Hell
> Receive thy new Possessor: One who brings
> A mind not to be chang'd by Place or Time.

> The mind is its own place, and in it self
> Can make a Heav'n of Hell, a Hell of Heav'n.
> What matter where, if I be still the same,
> And what I should be. . .
>
> (I.250–7)

Satan's conditional gets him into trouble: he is, of course, neither the same as he was nor what he thinks he should be ("all but less then hee/Whom Thunder hath made greater"). The text does not quite allow us to know whether *he* sees this clearly. In any case, even if Satan were the same, we might rightly doubt his claims to a property or power of mind, to an enabled privacy, which could continually stand free of the pressures of place and history. We may sense that, by means of an elegant but desperately protesting chiasmus, he has only succeeded in converting the words "Heaven" and "Hell" into empty, interchangeable ciphers, and that he does so without the sort of dialectical energy we may feel in similar reversals of Blake's. (Hence he fails to know what it means to inhabit either place.) The deep solipsism that the mind discovers in its fall decays quickly into self-aggrandisement, tyranny, gaudy display; it acquires a dependence on others which only thrusts the mind into situations of greater moral and experiential solitude. That solipsism becomes a deadening and divisive egotism, it flourishes and sickens in Satan's desire for revenge, for reducing God's best creatures to his own level of suffering. Finally, Satan's will that the mind be its own place returns upon him with a vengeance: viewing the created world from the top of Mount Niphates, he finds that the "Hell within him" is indeed independent of place, not to be avoided or abandoned by mere change of site, that he cannot escape from the Hell which now *is* his self, nor from the deeper, even shadowier Hell of his speculative fears (cf. IV.18–23, 75–8).

And yet we need not assume that this later, ironic evolution of Satan's "error" wholly proves his desire an inevitable disaster, or inescapably confirms the emptiness of the claims articulated in the lines I have quoted from Book I. The questioning of teleology is crucial here. Satan's initial vision of mental place, of the metamorphosis of place within mind, does suggest something willful or delusive, and yet it seems to me that his vision feeds on the same fantasy which legitimates, or is legitimated by, Michael's last promise to Adam and Eve: that they can through piety and struggle come eventually to possess "a paradise within" themselves, "happier farr" than the one they had lost (XII.587). This is not just a divine, retrospective correction of Satan's mistaken claims, the true measure of an idea of which his is but a demonic parody. If Michael's words point to a state of mind not owned by one person alone, but rather to a state which is the gift of God to man and of men and women to each other – a product of the career of love as well as the career of mind – that state may nevertheless be part of Satan's gift to the human future, no blessing or temptation but a "desperate hallow."

Notes

All quotations from *Paradise Lost* are taken from *The Poetical Works of John Milton*, ed. Helen Darbishire (London, Oxford University Press, 1958).

1. Ludwig Wittgenstein, *Culture and Value*, ed. G. H. von Wright, tr. Peter Winch (Chicago, University of Chicago Press, 1984), 56e.
2. See *The Complete Poetry and Prose of William Blake*, ed. David Erdman (Berkeley and Los Angeles, University of California Press, 1982), 142.
3. See *The Philosophical Works of Descartes*, tr. Elizabeth Haldane and G. R. T. Ross, 2 vols (Cambridge, Cambridge University Press, 1931), I.148–9.
4. Stuart Curran, "The siege of hateful contraries: Shelley, Mary Shelley, Byron, and *Paradise Lost*," in *Milton and the Line of Vision*, ed. Joseph Anthony Wittreich, Jr (Madison, University of Wisconsin Press, 1975), 209.
5. *Shelley's Poetry and Prose*, ed. Donald H. Reiman and Sharon B. Powers (New York, W. W. Norton, 1977), 133.
6. See the discussion of "Milton's 'literary' theology," in Georgia M. Christopher, *Milton and the Science of the Saints* (Princeton, Princeton University Press, 1982), 3–29, and *passim*.
7. *Shelley's Poetry and Prose*, 498.
8. ibid.
9. ibid.
10. *Shelley's Poetry and Prose*, 133.
11. *Shelley's Poetry and Prose*, 240. I am indebted here to the late James Rieger, who first pointed out to me the parallel wording in Shelley's two prefaces.
12. See C. S. Lewis, *A Preface to "Paradise Lost"* (London, Oxford University Press, 1942), 99.
13. On this issue, see the account of the "dark world" in Michael Lieb, *The Dialectics of Creation: Patterns of Birth and Regeneration in "Paradise Lost"* (Amherst, Mass., University of Massachusetts Press, 1970), 16–34.
14. See Kenneth Burke, *The Philosophy of Literary Form: Studies in Symbolic Action*, 3rd edn (Berkeley and Los Angeles, University of California Press, 1973), 259.
15. Arnold Stein, *Answerable Style: Essays on "Paradise Lost"* (Minneapolis, University of Minnesota Press, 1953), 8–9.
16. See William Kerrigan, *The Sacred Complex: On the Psychogenesis of "Paradise Lost"* (Cambridge, Mass., Harvard University Press, 1983), 73–82, and *passim*.
17. Kerrigan, *The Prophetic Milton* (Charlottesville, University Press of Virginia, 1974), 187.
18. See W. B. Hunter, "The war in Heaven: the exaltation of the Son," in *Bright Essence: Studies in Milton's Theology*, ed. W. B. Hunter, C. A. Patrides and J. H. Adamson (Salt Lake City, University of Utah Press, 1971), 115–30.
19. Lewis, *Preface to "Paradise Lost*," 98.
20. John Guillory discusses this point in *Poetic Authority: Spenser, Milton, and Literary History* (New York, Columbia University Press, 1983), 119. See also Stein, *Answerable Style*, 29.

21. See Guillory, *Poetic Authority*, 112, 117–18.
22. Marvell's poem appeared as a prefatory verse to the second edition of *Paradise Lost* (1674). I quote from the text included in Darbishire, *Poetical Works of Milton*, 2–3.
23. Blake, *Complete Poetry and Prose*, 34.
24. See Wittreich, *Angel of Apocalypse: Blake's Idea of Milton* (Madison, University of Wisconsin Press, 1975), 214–15.
25. On the doctrine of contraries as it is explicated in *The Marriage of Heaven and Hell*, see Harold Bloom, *Blake's Apocalypse: A Study in Poetic Argument* (Ithaca, Cornell University Press, 1970), 72–96.
26. Blake, *Complete Poetry and Prose*, 34–5.
27. Blake, *Complete Poetry and Prose*, 45.
28. See *Frankenstein, or The Modern Prometheus*, ed. James Rieger (Chicago, University of Chicago Press, 1974), 123–5.
29. *Frankenstein*, 125–6.
30. I borrow the notion of a "myth of the secular" from George Levine who discusses its implications in his introductory essay to *The Endurance of "Frankenstein:" Essays on Mary Shelley's Novel*, ed. George Levine and U. C. Knoepflmacher (Berkeley and Los Angeles, University of California Press, 1979), 3–30.
31. See Wallace Stevens, *The Palm at the End of the Mind: Selected Poems and A Play*, ed. Holly Stevens (New York, Vintage Books, 1972), 254. Reprinted by permission of Alfred A. Knopf, Inc.

16

TERRY EAGLETON

The god that failed

All revolutions give birth to their own mythologers, men and women whose self-appointed task, as Yeats says with grim-lipped simplicity in "Easter 1916," is "to write it out in a verse." Yeats gathered the republican martyrs of the Dublin Post Office into the artifice of eternity, though not without an uneasy eye on the event's ambiguous implications for his own foolish Ascendency fictions; and one year later a rather different European revolution was to produce Blok, Eisenstein and Mayakovsky as its prophetic bards. Preparing himself for the vatic role of cultural spokesman of the nationalist movement, Yeats looked back to the greatest of British revolutionary artists, William Blake, whose poetry he edited in the 1890s, and into whom he had, by some frenzied Nietzschean self-willing, to "remake" himself. Blake himself is the most astonishing instance we have of a revolutionary myth-maker, a man who inserted the bric-à-brac of passing political events into a flamboyant cosmic drama of primordial unity, subsequent alienation and eventual recuperation in the New Jerusalem. To do this, Blake needed to come to post-Oedipal terms with his own mighty revolutionary precursor, John Milton, redeeming him from the Spectre of his residual false consciousness so that his energies might fertilize once more (though not quite in the way Wordsworth intended) an England which again had need of him.

The task of the revolutionary mythologer is to furnish the political process with a set of efficacious symbols, universalize its meanings by inscribing them within a global drama, unify its disparate forces by the power of the image, and summon the past into metaphorical compact with the present. At stake in such revolutionary mythologizing is a struggle over the signifier, a fight for the hegemonic symbol, which is appropriated now this way, now that, depending on the balance of discursive forces. If revolutions lend themselves to these ends it is because there is something theatrical about them in the first place, traced as they are by the play of fantasy, rhetoric and fiction, masking, posturing and unmasking, a costumed or uniformed *staging* which is always already symbolic and so easily translatable into poetic idiom. It did not take a Yeats to mythologize the Easter uprising: when James Connolly, setting out for the Post Office on that morning in 1916, whispered to a fellow republican that of course they didn't have the faintest chance of success, he was declaring the insurrection fiction and symbol from the outset, drawing upon the ancient Irish tradition (still alive in the Northern Irish hunger strikers of today) that failure and blood sacrifice are always finally more life-yielding than the odd military victory. As far as Connolly was concerned, the only good body was a dead one. But revolutions are symbolic to their core in another sense too: what the mythologer makes appear within the parochial content of a particular struggle is the glimmering substance of a broader, deeper political history, of which the particular event is microcosmic. Such indeed was the bold wager of Lenin and Trotsky in 1917 – that their own strike for power would prove *metonymic* of wider anti-capitalist insurrection in Europe, without which they knew very well that their own revolution was doomed to isolation, invasion and eventual loss. The mythologer must insist that what is in train here, for all its sordid contingent content, is of world-historical import; and it is for this reason that he will invoke Gabriel or Cuchulain, Lucifer or Los, Deirdre or the Druids, pressing these mythological figures into what Walter Benjamin would call a shocking "constellation" with the forces of the present, creating a revolutionary "monad" in which linear time (always on the side of Caesar) is abruptly arrested and the shades of the dead congregate around the empty pit of the present to brim it with their life-giving blood.

If mythologies tend to magnify the revolution, however, they also serve to mystify it. Writing it *out* in a verse has more than one meaning. What cannot yet be rendered intelligible in historical materialist terms is displaced instead into an idealist discourse of the authentic Albion, sin and redemption, ancient Ireland, good and evil. Bourgeois revolutions have a particular need to grace their activities with such imagery since, as Marx comments in the opening pages of the *Eighteenth Brumaire of Louis Bonaparte*, they are constantly embarrassed by the grotesque discrepancy between the paucity of their social content and the visionary heroism of their rhetorical forms. "Hegel remarks somwhere," Marx writes with strange insouciance (he had in fact just been reading the *Philosophy of History*), "that all facts and personages of great importance in world history occur, as it were, twice. He forgot to add: the first time as tragedy, the second as farce." As if shamed by the squalor of their social content – freedom is freedom to exploit, equality the equality of the marketplace – the great bourgeois revolutions live a hiatus between signifier and signified, tricking out their meagre ends in the flashy insignia of previous epochs:

In the classically austere traditions of the Roman Republic [the French revolutionary] gladiators found the ideals and the art forms, the self-deceptions that they needed in order to conceal from themselves the bourgeois limitations of the content of their struggles and to keep their enthusiasm on the high plane of great historical tragedy. Similarly, at another stage of development, a century earlier, Cromwell and the English people had borrowed speech, passions and illusions from the Old Testament for their bourgeois revolution. When the real aim had been achieved, when the bourgeois transformation of English society had been accomplished, Locke supplanted Habakkuk.[1]

Or, we might add, Milton gave way to Defoe.

The past is that which we seem doomed compulsively to repeat; the revolution is a neurotic symptom which at once conceals and reveals its true content in displaced rhetorical form. The repetition, Marx insists, happens just when we think that we are creating something new; Milton's revolutionaries, in seeking to repair the Fall, end up by rehearsing it. This is what is known as original sin – or, as Marx puts it in his own idiom, the way that "the tradition of all the dead generations weighs like a nightmare on the brains of the living." History is the nightmare from which we are trying to wake up, but which in doing so we merely dream again. Perhaps this is because the sin is original, there at the beginning: the origin itself is flawed, the first parents marred, and so history becomes a parodic repetition of a crime which was there from the outset. If the serpent lurks within the garden, the origin is already defaced. This is why, as Wittgenstein comments, it is hard to think of an origin without wanting to go back beyond it. Yet at the same time it is only by dreaming the past that we can wake from it: since the past is what we are made of, we can redeem the present only by converting images of nightmare into dreams of emancipation. The revolutionary repetitions, Marx reminds us, are not *merely* parodic, caricatures of what was no doubt already a caricature: they also make the spirit of revolution walk again:

> Thus the awakening of the dead in those revolutions served the purpose of glorifying the new struggles, not of parodying the old; of magnifying the given task in imagination, not of fleeing from its solution in reality; of finding once more the spirit of revolution, not of making its ghost walk about again.[2]

Only by turning back can we move forward; only if Milton turns round to face Eden with the horror-struck face of Benjamin's *Angelus Novus* can he be blown by its winds towards the kingdom of the future. The past must be pressed violently into the service of the present, classical traditions heretically appropriated and miswritten to redeem the time. If one can be a heretic in the truth, one can also be a truthteller in heresy.

All of this, as Marx suggests, has its farcical incongruity. Is all that high-falutin talk in heaven really about Cromwell & Co? If you "take your poetry from the past," Marx warns, you will magnify the present struggle only at the price of mystifying it. It is only the socialist revolution which, Marx comments enigmatically, will draw its poetry from the future, imagine from a place yet to be born. Yet by drawing their poetry from the past, the bourgeois revolutions do more than furnish imaginary solutions ("it was all because of original sin") to real political problems. The left wing of such revolutions, which will of course be constantly betrayed, is thereby also able to dream a future beyond such ephemeral matters as Bonaparte or Charles, nurturing in their mythological dramas the energies which the revolution quelled. Throwing history into reverse, the left wing retreats to an origin in order to keep alive a future beyond the shabby sell-outs of the bourgeoisie. Their mythologies glean the trace of the revolution within the revolution, a submerged subtext within the dispiriting narratives of official bourgeois history, whether this subtext is, as with Milton, the salvific history of the godly remnant or, as with Walter Benjamin, the tradition of the oppressed that haunts ruling-class history as its silenced underside. Blake knew that only a revolution which penetrated to the body itself could finally be victorious; Milton, as Christopher Hill remarks, believed that "the desire for reformation did not sink deeply enough into the consciences of supporters of the Revolution, did not transform their lives." Thus Hill reads *Paradise Lost* not as the expression of political defeatism but as the urging of a new political phase: "the foundations must be dug deeper, into the hearts of individual believers, in order to build more securely."[3]

Today, perhaps, after Gramsci, we would say such a project involves the question of hegemony. Writing after the débâcle of the European socialist revolutions, Gramsci in his *Prison Notebooks* is constrained to consider not only the structures of military and political power, but those less palpable, pervasive devices whereby a ruling order secures the internal assent of its subordinates, inscribing its imperatives in the very texture of their experience. Those who are heretics in the truth will tend to suppress that whole region – Gramsci names it "culture" – in their fervid pursuit of political goals, and will thus short-cut the struggle for hearts as peremptorily as did the puritan radicals. The heart of stone, modelled on the graven tablets of the Law, must yield to the heart of flesh, the interior space of subjectivity and the unconscious, if any transformative project is to succeed. The Name-of-the-Father must, however, give way to the Other of human flesh, discourse and desire, as Milton anticipates that the Father will finally abdicate power to his human son. Part of the task of what Gramsci terms the "organic" intellectuals is to spur on this process by challenging political hegemony in its spiritual-ideological forms. The organic intellectual is the product of a politically emergent class; and in seeking to organize its inchoate demands into the coherence of a unified "world view," he or she must strive at once to undermine the culture of the "traditional" intelligentsia, and to assimilate individual members of that key group to the revolutionary cause. John Milton, son of a prosperous bourgeois, emerged by a laborious process of self-production to become *the* organic intellectual of the English revolution, so placed within the traditional intellectual culture as to revise, reject, assimilate and appropriate its contents in the cause of his own people. His stout Baconian contempt for aspects of traditionalist Cambridge was not, of course, some infantile ultra-leftism: as a "centrist" ideologue, occupying a mediatory position, he could make that culture *work* for him, dislocate it from the inside, "refunction" it, as Brecht would have said, to alternative ideological ends. The organic intellectual reinflects tradition, as the revolutionary present parodies and reinscribes the past.

The contentions within the very form of *Paradise Lost*, between classical device, religious transcendentalism, and the discourses of representation and rationality, are surely a sign of this dialectical situation. Pierre Macherey has written of the ways in which literary texts, by dint of their formal or figural devices, tend to press into contradiction their own ideology, throwing its covert incoherence into embarrassing relief.[4] There is surely something very much like this at work in Milton's masterpiece, which struggles constantly with the problem of pressing into narrational and representational form a body of myth inherently resistant to such figuration. And it is precisely against the consequent slippages, aporias and inconsistencies that the poem's realist or Leavisian readers have most sternly protested. The work is not really very realistic: at one moment Satan is chained to the burning lake, and before you can look again he is making his way to the shore. George Eliot would have handled the whole thing incomparably better. What is fascinating about *Paradise Lost*, however, is precisely its necessary lack of self-identity — the persistent mutual interferences of what is stated and what is shown, the contradictory entanglements of epic immediacy and hermeneutical discourse, the fixing of significations at one level only to produce a sliding of them at another. The epic form of traditional intellectual culture at once magnifies and mystifies the prosaic realism of bourgeois revolution; and conversely, that discursive bourgeois realism is exposed in all its paucity by the epical splendour even as the realism appropriates and undercuts it.

What is at work in the poem's tortuous form, then, is an historically determined clash of semiotic codes. On the one hand, we could claim that the text's classical and sacred *mise-en-scène* is embarrassingly at odds with its discourses of sense and reason, in the manner of Marx's semiotically disrupted bourgeois revolutions. But at the same time we might see this embarrassment as working both ways. If the bourgeois ideological need to narrate, explain, apologize threatens in its discursive realism to undo the very rhetorical frames in which it is staged, this is at once to its detriment — for such magnifying, universalizing forms are as Marx points out a bourgeois revolutionary requirement – and the sign of a certain deconstruction of traditionalist culture at the hands of a progressive bourgeois rationality. Milton's Protestant commitment to sense and discourse, his refusal of the idolatry of the apodictic image, his secularizing faith in rational causality: all of these impulses subtly assert themselves over the very symbolic forms of which they stand in need. Traditional culture, reverently summoned to illuminate the present, finds itself in that very act appropriated, swerved from, rewritten in heretical terms.

The clash of semiotic codes in *Paradise Lost* highlights with peculiar visibility what we might call the "materiality" of the poem's forms; and nowhere is this materiality more evident than in its language. The remorselessly logocentric Leavis, for whom the signifier, emptied of any action or substance of its own, must be no more than the obedient bearer of a signified, can see little in the "Miltonic music" but an external embellishment, clumsily at odds with the springs of sense. When T. S. Eliot remarked that you needed to read the poem twice, once for the sound and once for the meaning, he too had been struck by its contrived dislocation of the unified sign, the sonorous excess of language over meaning, the way in which the poem's language works athwart the "natural" texture of the senses and so fails to repress its own artifice. Nothing could be further from the swift fusion of the Metaphysical conceit than the calculated self-conscious unfurling of the epic simile, with all its whirring machinery of production on show. As Habakkuk gives way to Locke, the materiality of the signifier in English discourse is on the point of yielding to the naturalized representational sign of bourgeois empiricism, which will serve the ideological ends of middle-class rule extremely well. Milton's rhetoric puts up a last-ditch resistance to this shackling of the sign, irreducible as that rhetoric is to the "natural" rhythms of a speaking voice. If a strain of Edenic sensuousness lives on, it can be found among other places in the carnality of the word, and the materialist in Milton takes delight in it.

It is not, of course, that Milton is anything other than profoundly logocentric as an ideologue; but aspects of his poetic practice run counter to the theory. One might argue, indeed, that logocentrism has been rendered in any full sense untenable by the fall from Eden, where thing and word were at one. Milton's God is purely, unmediately present as spirit in his "material" deeds; but he is so only from the standpoint of eternity. Viewed from the fallen realm of a revolutionary history gone awry, those acts must be painfully, laboriously decoded and elaborated, in a hermeneutical discourse ineluctably subjected to temporality, dispersion and ambiguity. Such indeed is the traditional nature of allegory, which as Fredric Jameson comments is "the privileged mode of our own life in time, a clumsy deciphering of meaning from moment to moment, the painful attempt to restore a continuity to heterogeneous, disconnected instants."[5] In short, to justify the ways of God to men; for the transcendental signifier has apparently

347

withdrawn aloofly from his own handiwork, leaving behind him a tormentedly ambiguous historical text which must be laboriously scanned for signs of his presence and purpose. Milton's own poem, then, is not only about the Fall but a consequence of it: if our first parents had not introduced difference, lack, deformity and desire into the world, nothing of this groping, besieged apologia would be necessary.

Milton's Arian heresy is perhaps relevant to this point, qualifying as it does any full-bloodedly logocentric view of Christ. The Son is not the full co-substantial presence of the Father; he is not Emmanuel, or "God with us." Yet this swerve from Christian orthodoxy is also, as Blake saw, part of Milton's patriarchal unregeneracy. For the teaching of orthodox Christianity is precisely that what we have in the coming of the Son is the coming of the Father. It is God himself, not some delegate or sub-committee, who is hung on a cross, to manifest the political truth that those who love sufficiently well will be killed by the state. The Father for traditional Christianity becomes through the Incarnation loving friend and fellow sufferer, which is to say that he is not the Father at all, for the Father is decentred in Christ to become brother and sister. It is this doctrine which the Pharisees of all ages find hard to take, with their stiff-necked assurance that respectability and self-righteousness will allow them to bargain their way to heaven, their idolatrous confidence that they can impress the living God by flexing their ethical muscles, showing him how very moral and right-living they are. It is the Pharisees who cannot accept the scandal that God has always already forgiven them, that they can forget about trying to impress him because he is part of their flesh and blood. It is they who define God as Satan ("The Accuser", in Hebrew), fear him as a punitive patriarch and so try to get even with him. They cannot swallow the sordid truth that the Name-of-the-Father has in the person of Christ become a broken human body, no longer the judge on the bench but co-criminal and counsel for the defence. Milton continues in part to define the Father as Satan, as a logical consequence of his Arian heresy.

If there is a twentieth-century candidate for Milton's Satan, it is surely Stalin. Both are overdetermined images of pompous princeling and perverted revolutionary, undecidable amalgams of traditional monarch and power-thirsty popular representative. The image of Satan is the point where the one blends inseparably into the other, as in the Eastern European bureaucracies. Stalinism has its own kind of satanic "fate" – the laws of development of the productive forces – but combines this economism with an equally satanic voluntarism: the mighty power of the people, and the rest. What after all was the forced industrialization and collectivization but the desperate flailing of a revolution which could not succeed in isolation, and so like Satan's strike against heaven was in a certain sense predetermined to devour its own children? Any society which seeks to use the theory and practice of Marxism to catapult itself from chronic backwardness into the twentieth century stands in grave danger of Stalinism, if more advanced forces do not come to its aid. For Marxism is a theory and practice of the transformation of developed capitalist societies into socialist ones; and that practice is dependent upon developed productive forces, accumulated capital and a skilled, advanced and organized proletariat. Without all this, along with international solidarity, a Third World revolution will be forced steadily towards state bureaucratic centralization, in its drive for the primitive accumulation of industrial capital, its need to protect itself against imperialist invasion, its tackling of material scarcity, and in its structural autonomy, as a state, from a dispersed revolutionary peasantry for which it will come to "stand in." These are the classic conditions of Stalinism, of which Lenin and Trotsky were well aware.

To blame Marxism for these conditions is then somewhat akin to blaming God for the failure of seventeenth-century revolutionary hopes. To blame God in this way, Milton sees, can mean only one thing: that the Puritan bureaucrats, opportunists and careerists are then let comfortably off the moral and political hook. It was destiny after all; nothing to feel guilty about. But the failure of revolutionary hopes was not of course predestined, and neither was Stalinism. To believe so is to exculpate a later set of bureaucrats, opportunists and careerists; the European social democratic parties who in betraying their own working classes helped to isolate the newly founded Soviet Union; and the imperialist invading armies who decimated the class which had made the revolution in Russia, thus leaving a bureaucratic workers' state suspended over a dwindled, exhausted popular base. There are always those who, like the Koestlers and the Orwells, find it convenient and persuasive to blame the God that failed; but if we wanted a more accurate analogue of *Paradise Lost* in the twentieth century, we might do worse than take a look at Trotsky's *The Revolution Betrayed*.

Notes

1. Lewis S. Feuer (ed.), *Marx and Engels: Basic Writings on Politics and Philosophy* (London, 1969), 361–2. For a semiotic analysis of Marx's *Eighteenth Brumaire*, see Jeffrey Mehlman, *Revolution and Repetition* (Berkeley, 1977), and my own *Walter Benjamin, or Towards a Revolutionary Criticism* (London, 1981), 162–70.
2. Feuer, op. cit., 362.
3. Christopher Hill, *Milton and the English Revolution* (Harmondsworth, 1977), 350.
4. Pierre Macherey, *A Theory of Literary Production* (London, 1978).
5. Fredric Jameson, *Marxism and Form* (Princeton, 1971), 72.

Index

Vulgate Bible 154, 200

Walcott, Derek 282, 297
Waldensians 237
Walker, Clement 87, 91
Walwyn, William 80
Wasser, Henry 280
Webber, Joan M. xvn, 124 n
Weber, Max 149–52, 154–5, 157, 159, 167–8, 175 n
Webster, Charles 147 n
Werman, Golda Spiera 232 n
Westminster Assembly 77–9, 82, 94 n, 109
Wheatley, Phillis 278–80, 282–6, 291, 296
Whitefield, George 299 n
Whitman, Albery A. 280
Wideman, John 282
Wilding, Michael xiii
Williams, Arnold 231 n, 233 n
Williams, Charles 72 n
Williams, Roger 254 n

Williams, W. C. 188–90, 192
Wilson, A. N. xiii
Winn, James Anderson 209 n–10 n
Wisdom figure, in Proverbs 198–208, 230
Wither, George 137
Wittgenstein, Ludwig 344
Wittreich, Joseph Anthony 93 n, 95 n, 257, 259, 264–5, 271–2, 301, 333
Wood, Gordon S. 297 n–8 n
Woodbridge, Linda 125 n
Woodford, Samuel 179
Woodhouse, A. S. P. 73 n, 210 n
Woolf, Virginia xii
Wordsworth, William 183, 230, 286, 301–4, 306–8, 311–16, 342
Wutz, Franz 233 n
Wyclif, John 208 n

Yeats, W. B. 342–3

Zwingli, Ulrich 244